STUDIES IN IMPERIALISM

General editor: Andrew S. Thompson
Founding editor: John M. MacKenzie

When the 'Studies in Imperialism' series was founded more than twenty-five years ago, emphasis was laid upon the conviction that 'imperialism as a cultural phenomenon had as significant an effect on the dominant as on the subordinate societies'. With well over a hundred titles now published, this remains the prime concern of the series. Cross-disciplinary work has indeed appeared covering the full spectrum of cultural phenomena, as well as examining aspects of gender and sex, frontiers and law, science and the environment, language and literature, migration and patriotic societies, and much else. Moreover, the series has always wished to present comparative work on European and American imperialism, and particularly welcomes the submission of books in these areas. The fascination with imperialism, in all its aspects, shows no sign of abating, and this series will continue to lead the way in encouraging the widest possible range of studies in the field. 'Studies in Imperialism' is fully organic in its development, always seeking to be at the cutting edge, responding to the latest interests of scholars and the needs of this ever-expanding area of scholarship.

Serving the empire in the Great War

Manchester University Press

SELECTED TITLES AVAILABLE IN THE SERIES

IMPERIAL EXPECTATIONS AND REALITIES
El Dorados, utopias and dystopias
ed. Andrekos Varnava

BRITISH IMPERIALISM IN CYPRUS, 1878–1915
The inconsequential possession
Andrekos Varnava

BEASTLY ENCOUNTERS OF THE RAJ
Livelihoods, livestock and veterinary health in North India, 1790–1920
Saurabh Mishra

ENGINES FOR EMPIRE
The Victorian army and its use of railways
Edward Spiers

THE CULTURAL CONSTRUCTION OF THE BRITISH WORLD
ed. Barry Crosbie and Mark Hampton

Serving the empire in the Great War

THE CYPRIOT MULE CORPS, IMPERIAL LOYALTY AND SILENCED MEMORY

Andrekos Varnava

MANCHESTER
UNIVERSITY PRESS

Copyright © Andrekos Varnava 2017

The right of Andrekos Varnava to be identified as the author of this work has been asserted by him in accordance with the Copyright, Designs and Patents Act 1988.

Published by MANCHESTER UNIVERSITY PRESS
ALTRINCHAM STREET, MANCHESTER M1 7JA

www.manchesteruniversitypress.co.uk

British Library Cataloguing-in-Publication Data
A catalogue record for this book is available from the British Library

ISBN 978 1 5261 0367 3 hardback
ISBN 978 1 5261 0369 7 paperback

First published by Manchester University Press in hardback 2017
This edition first published 2019

The publisher has no responsibility for the persistence or accuracy of URLs for any external or third-party internet websites referred to in this book, and does not guarantee that any content on such websites is, or will remain, accurate or appropriate.

Typeset by
Servis Filmsetting Ltd, Stockport, Cheshire

I dedicate this book to all those Cypriots who served in the Cypriot Mule Corps in the British army during and after the Great War, but especially to family members: my great grandfather on my father's side, Varnavas Michael Varnava, from Frenaros, Famagusta, who enlisted on 28 September 1916 and served until 24 September 1917 with the number 5048; my wife Helen's grandfather on her father's side, Nicholas Zacharias Komodromou, who enlisted on 3 November 1917 and served until 20 January 1919 with the number 8938 and his brother Leondis Zacharias Komodromou, who, with the numbers 3622 and 12287, served twice, first from 14 August 1916 to 24 September 1917, and then from 15 July 1918 to 28 May 1919, from Rizokarpaso, Famagusta. This book attempts to put forward their story within the wider social, economic, imperial, colonial and military contexts without fear and without prejudice. It also attempts to understand the political and cultural circumstances that have caused their story to be silenced from Cypriot national consciousness. I hope that I have done justice to their story.

CONTENTS

List of illustrations—page viii
*List of tables—*ix
*Acknowledgements—*xi
*Abbreviations—*xiii

	Introduction	1
1	Historiography and theories	9
2	British Cyprus, 1878–1918: from backwater to bustling war base	31
3	The formation of the Cypriot Mule Corps	58
4	Mule and muleteer recruitment: pushed or pulled?	77
5	Contracts, challenges, hardships and the 'liminal space'	107
6	Conditions for mules and muleteers	130
7	Muleteer behaviour during service	161
8	Veterans and their families after service	180
9	Remembering and forgetting the Cypriot Mule Corps	210
	Conclusion	227

*Select bibliography—*231
*Index—*246

The appendices referred to in the book can be accessed at
www.manchesteruniversitypress.co.uk/serving-the-empire-in-the-great-war-appendix/

LIST OF ILLUSTRATIONS

0.1	'Travoys Arriving with Wounded at a Dressing Station at Smol, Macedonia, September 1916', Sir Stanley Spencer	*page* xvi
1.1	Map of the Eastern Mediterranean.	22
1.2	Map of Cyprus.	23
3.1	'Fed No Complaints'. Courtesy of the Office of the Secretary of the Board of Governors, Nicosia English School.	59
3.2	Cypriot muleteers 1917, Photo I. Courtesy of the Office of the Secretary of the Board of Governors, Nicosia English School.	72
3.3	Cypriot muleteers 1917, Photo II. Courtesy of the Office of the Secretary of the Board of Governors, Nicosia English School.	73
4.1	Muleteers enlisting, with Canon Newman and *Zaptiehs*. Courtesy of the Office of the Secretary of the Board of Governors, Nicosia English School.	77
5.1	'Mule-Panniers for the Transport of Wounded: Two Wounded Serbians Brought Down from the Mountains', *Illustrated London News*, 1916.	108
5.2	'Light Railways Used for Bringing In Wounded: Two Stretcher-Cases on a Horse-Drawn Truck', *Illustrated London News*, 1916.	110
5.3	'Light Railways Built for Supply Transport: Truck-Loads of Provision Drawn by Mules Going Up to the Front', *Illustrated London News*, 1917.	111
5.4	'The Sleigh as a Transport Vehicle for Crossing Deep Mud: An Improvised Method of Carrying Timber', *Illustrated London News*, 1917.	113
5.5	'The Mule as Locomotive on a Light Railway: Giving the Animals a Push-Off with Their Ten-Ton Load', *Illustrated London News*, 1917.	114
5.6	'With the Greek Soldiers in Macedonia: Muleteers', *Illustrated London News*, 1917.	116
7.1	Photograph of British War Medal I, Macedonian Mule Corps, Eraklis Theodorou.	162
7.2	Photograph of British War Medal II, Macedonian Mule Corps.	163

LIST OF TABLES

2.1	Cypriot revenue, 1909–25	page 48
3.1	Distribution of Macedonian and Cypriot muleteers, 7 August 1916	63
3.2	Cypriot muleteers across various British units, 4 May 1918	64
3.3	Exports of mules and donkeys, 1905 to 1916	69
3.4	Number of muleteers across districts in Cyprus in 1901 and 1911 censuses	69
4.1	Mules purchased by 31 August 1916	81
4.2	Transport animal exports	82
4.3	Enlistment numbers until March 1919	84
4.4	Religious/ethnic distribution of the Cypriot Mule Corps	86
4.5	Religious/ethnic distribution of population, 1911	87
4.6	Enlistment numbers and percentages across Cyprus	88
4.7	Distribution of population in urban centres, 1911	88
4.8	Urban–rural spread in Cypriot Mule Corps	88
4.9	Ethno-religious composition of foremen	90
4.10	Urban–rural composition of Cypriot foremen	90
4.11	Ethno-religious composition of interpreters	91
4.12	Urban–rural composition of Cypriot interpreters	91
4.13	Next of kin results for Cypriot Mule Corps members	93
4.14	Next of kin breakdown of married men	94
4.15	Civil status of men, 1911 Census	94
4.16	Literacy in Cyprus, 1911 Census	100
6.1	Reason for discharging muleteers on HMS *Verbera*, 11 March 1917	141
6.2	Ethno-religious composition of discharged muleteers	141
6.3	Urban–rural composition of those discharged	142
6.4	Next of kin results for repatriated muleteers suffering venereal disease	142
6.5	Reasons for discharge of muleteers on HMS *Umballa*, 13 July 1917	143
6.6	Numbers with venereal disease from 31 October 1917 to 1 March 1918	149
6.7	Religious breakdown of those who died	154
6.8	Urban–rural spread of Cypriots who died	154
6.9	Next of kin spread of dead	155
7.1	Demographic distribution of desertion	165
7.2	Urban–rural composition of Cypriot deserters	165

LIST OF TABLES

7.3	Next of kin spread of deserters	166
7.4	Religious breakdown of those dismissed for misconduct	168
7.5	Urban–rural composition of Cypriots dismissed for misconduct	168
7.6	Next of kin spread for Cypriot muleteers dismissed	169

ACKNOWLEDGEMENTS

Researching and writing this book has been an amazing experience for so many reasons. It pushed me as a researcher and it has changed me as a person. There are therefore many people, institutions and organisations that I must thank.

First I must thank all those who funded and provided services to facilitate my research. Thank you to the Faculty of Social and Behavioural Sciences and the School of History and International Relations at Flinders University, and the Australian Academy of the Humanities for various grants to make research trips to the UK, Cyprus and Turkey, for an (albeit short-lived) research assistant (thanks Iliya Marovich-Old), and to present my work at various conferences. I am also thankful to the late Dr Vangelis Kechriotis who invited me to be a Visiting Professor at Bogazici University in Istanbul in the European Summer of 2012. Not only was this a memorable experience for my family and me, it allowed me to access the Başbakanlık Osmanlı Arşivleri (Office of the Prime Minister Ottoman Archives). I must thank the staff of the numerous archives, museums and libraries I visited for assisting me with my research: the National Archives of the UK, Kew, London; The British Library, London; the Imperial War Museum, London; the State Archives, Nicosia; the Başbakanlık Osmanlı Arşivleri in Istanbul; and last but not least the Flinders University Library, especially document delivery staff.

I am also thankful to the many historians and scholars from other disciplines for listening patiently whenever I explained my project, for their encouragement and their thoughts and comments. The following names are listed in no particular order: Tim Reardon, Ann Matters, Evan Smith, Rolandos Katsiaounis, Panikos Panayi, Michael J. K. Walsh, Joy Damousi, Nicholas Doumanis, John M. MacKenzie, Mete Hatay, Tabitha Morgan, Mehmet Polatel, Nicholas Coureas, Hubert Faustmann, Christopher Schabel, Costas M. Constantinou, Vangelis Kehriotis, Selim Deringil, Christalla Yakinthou, Michalis N. Michael, Eric S. Richards, Matt Fitzpatrick, Peter Monteath, David Lockwood, Melanie Oppenheimer, Catherine Kevin, Brian Dickey, Lance Brennan, David Close, Ian Copland, Giuseppe Finaldi, Trevor Harris, Klearchos Kyriakides, Yiannis Papadakis, Gareth Knapman, Erdem Erginel, Mehmet Erginel, Richard Scully, Alexis Rappas, John Connor, Marios Shammas, Roger Christofides, Jay Winter, Hew Strachan, Alison Fletcher, Peter Stanley, Malcolm Cook and Martin

ACKNOWLEDGEMENTS

Griffiths. I also thank the anonymous reviewers for their helpful suggestions.

I must also thank the conferences who accepted my papers on the Cypriot Mule Corps and the people who attended my various presentations at (1) 'And this island: who knows it?' Cypriot Identities across Millennia, University of Nicosia, Cyprus, 7–9 September 2012; (2) public talk at Kochinohorka Lyceum, 26 September 2012; (3) Flinders History Seminar Series, 2 November 2012; (4) Imperial Faultlines, 23rd meeting of the Australasian Association for European History (AAEH), Victoria University of Wellington, 2–5 July 2013; and (5) Perspectives on the 'Great' War, Queen Mary, University of London, 1–4 August 2014. Thanks to Michael J.K. Walsh for our collaboration and friendship which allowed us to organise The British Empire during the Great War: Colonial Societies / Cultural Responses conference at Nanyang Technological University, 19–22 February 2014, which also allowed me to present on the Cypriot muleteers.

Working with Manchester University Press on this, my third book with them, has been, once again, amazing. Thank you to all the staff and especially to Emma Brennan and the series editors for their support.

Researching and writing a book of this nature means sacrifices and help from family. First I thank my extended family for their help in Cyprus and the UK, which facilitated my research in those places, especially to my brother-in-law Michael Komodromou for his help in both the UK and Cyprus with matters of accommodation. I want to thank my father, Varnavas Michael Varnava, father-in-law, Christos Nicholas Komodromou, and his brother-in-law, Antoni Pitrakkou, for answering various questions about what they knew of the Cypriot Mule Corps. Finally, but by no means least, I want to especially thank my wife Helen Komodromou-Varnava and our son Barnabas and baby daughter Maria. Although I have juggled many projects, small and large, during the last five years, the Cypriot Mule Corps has dominated my focus. It was certainly not easy for either Helen to listen to the stories of the Corps or for Barnabas, Maria and Helen to share their spare time with it. I thank them for their patience, understanding and love.

Lastly, I must thank the men who served in the Cypriot Mule Corps. I hope this book will lead to the recognition that you deserve and your rightful place in the memory of all Cypriots.

ABBREVIATIONS

The entries are mainly to assist in deciphering acronyms in the footnotes. Sometimes for 'Assistant' or 'Acting' an 'A' has been added, for example Acting Chief Secretary (ACS) or Deputy Assistant Quartermaster General, Salonica (DAQGS), and these are not listed below. The full names of individuals are usually provided in the text.

ABS	Army of the Black Sea
AHQ	Army Headquarters
AKEL	Ανορθωτικό Κόμμα Εργαζόμενου Λαού (Anorthotikó Kómma Ergazómenou Laoú – Progressive Party of the Working People)
ASC	Army Supply Company
ANZAC	Australian and New Zealand Army Corps
AVSS	Army Veterinary Service, Salonica
CAB	Cabinet Papers
CCABS	Commander-in-Chief of the Army of the Black Sea
CCPC	Chief Commandant of Police, Cyprus (Cypriot Military Police – *Zaptieh*)
CFC	Conservator of Forests, Cyprus
CICAOA	Commander-in-Chief of the Allied Occupation Army
CICBSA	Commander-in-Chief of the British Salonica Army
CICEEF	Commander-in-Chief of the Egyptian Expeditionary Force
CICMF	Commander-in-Chief of the Mediterranean Fleet
CMC	Cypriot Mule Corps (also Macedonian Mule Corps)
CMOC	Chief Medical Officer, Cyprus
CO	Colonial Office
CPC	Communist Party of Cyprus
CSC	Chief Secretary / Colonial Secretary (from 1926), Cyprus
CWGC	Commonwealth War Graves Commission
DAG	Deputy Adjutant-General
DAS	Deputy Adjunct, Salonica
DCFa	District Commissioner of Famagusta
DCKy	District Commissioner of Kyrenia
DCLa	District Commissioner of Larnaca
DCLi	District Commissioner of Limassol
DCNi	District Commissioner of Nicosia
DCPa	District Commissioner of Paphos
DMO	District Medical Officer

ABBREVIATIONS

DMSS	Director of Medical Services, Salonica
DOSS	Director of Ordnance Services, Salonica
DPC	District Paymaster, Cyprus
DPE	District Paymaster, Egypt
DPS	District Paymaster, Salonica
DQMGC	Deputy Quartermaster General, Cyprus
DQMGE	Deputy Quartermaster General, Egypt
DQMGS	Deputy Quartermaster General, Salonica
DRS	Director of Remounts, Salonica
DSTBS	Director of Supplies and Transport, Black Sea
DSTS	Director of Supplies and Transport, Salonica
DVSS	Director of Veterinary Services, Salonica
EEF	Egyptian Expeditionary Force
EMSIB	East Mediterranean Special Intelligence Bureau
EOKA	Ethniki Organosis Kyprion Agoniston (National Organisation of Cypriot Fighters)
FO	Foreign Office
GHQC	General Headquarters, Constantinople
GHQS	General Headquarters, Salonica
GRD	Greek drachma
GRO	General Routine Orders
HCC	High Commissioner of Cyprus
HMSO	His/Her Majesty's Stationary Office
HMT	His/Her Majesty's Transport
HTC	Horse Transport Company
IO	India Office
IOR	India Office Records
IWM	Imperial War Museum (UK)
LCCMP	Local Commandant of Cypriot Military Police
NAUK	National Archives of the United Kingdom (Kew Gardens, London)
OCMPC	Officer Commanding Mule/Muleteer Purchasing Commission (Famagusta)
OCTC	Officer Commanding the Troops, Cyprus
PIO	Public Information Office (Republic of Cyprus)
QMGS	Quartermaster General, Salonica
RA	Royal Army
RAMC	Royal Army Medical Corps
RASC	Royal Army Service Corps
RE	Royal Engineers
RFA	Royal Field Artillery
SA1	Secretariat Archives (State Archives, Nicosia)
SMO	Senior Medical Officer

ABBREVIATIONS

SSC	Secretary of State for the Colonies
SSW	Secretary of State for War
WC	War Cabinet
WDSA	War Diary Salonica Army
WO	War Office

0.1 'Travoys Arriving with Wounded at a Dressing Station at Smol, Macedonia, September 1916', Sir Stanley Spencer, Imperial War Museum, IWM ART 2268, 1919, 1828 mm × 2184 mm.

INTRODUCTION

'Travoys Arriving with Wounded at a Dressing Station at Smol, Macedonia, September 1916' by Sir Stanley Spencer is one of the most recognisable and striking paintings of the Great War. Based on what he witnessed while serving in the 68th Field Ambulance, Spencer painted it in 1919 after the British War Memorials Committee of the Ministry of Information commissioned him to paint something for a proposed, but never built, 'Hall of Remembrance'. The painting shows mule-drawn stretchers carrying wounded men to a dressing station, an old Eastern Orthodox Church, while animals and humans watch the life-saving efforts of the surgeons. The image recalls the depictions of the birth of Jesus Christ. For Spencer the wounded men on the stretchers represented a wounded Christ on the Cross and the work of the surgeons represented the Resurrection. He wrote, 'I meant it not a scene of horror but a scene of redemption.'[1]

> One would have thought that the scene was a sordid one ... but I felt there was grandeur ... all those wounded men were calm and at peace with everything, so the pain seemed a small thing with them. I felt there was a spiritual ascendancy over everything.[2]

Now it may or may not depict Cypriot muleteers, but the painting represents the service of all muleteers (as does his Sandham Memorial Chapel), irrespective of their ethnic/religious backgrounds, during the Great War, and not merely those in the image, or those who served in Macedonia. It also includes the animals that were worked to exhaustion during the war. Paintings have the ability to be inclusive. Yet most Cypriots and British today do not know that Cypriots even served in the Great War. They have been excluded from the story of the Great War in the broader context of the Allied victory and commemorations, and their service silenced from the Cypriot national consciousness. At the most basic level this book reconstructs the story of their contribution, transporting wounded men and various supplies to the front, across steep mountains, with dangerous ravines and in a climate that changed from one extreme to another. Simultaneously, this book also endeavours to include the role of mules in Salonica into the Great War. But this book seeks to do much more than merely 'fill the gap'.

The reader may ask, Who cares about a group of Cypriot mule drivers and a handful of interpreters in the British army serving in Macedonia and Constantinople during and immediately following the

Great War? The importance is not merely in that nobody has written about them. This should be important to Cypriots, who have a highly nationalistic view of their past that excludes 'the other' and condemns the 'occupier', and for the British in order to understand the contributions of their Empire in the Great War. The reader interested in military and/or imperial history should be interested in why the corps was created and what value it offered, as well as in the role of the mules. Those interested in military history should, however, also be aware of the social implications of war. Thus, given the strong enlistment rates, it is important to understand what this means for imperial identity and loyalty. It was a mixed Christian–Muslim corps largely made up of peasants and unskilled labourers. How could such a successful corps have existed as a mixed Christian–Muslim force given the violent post-Second World War history of the war-torn island? For that matter, how did the British, the targets of that violence, at least from 1955 to 1959, manage to recruit so many Cypriot men? This necessitates a focus on the socio-economic conditions of the men and the urban and rural divide in the island. The experience of the men while serving and as veterans, as well as that of their families, also necessitates a socio-economic awareness. Finally, the reader is returned to the beginning and why nobody has written about this before, to show how culturally this case has been silenced from the memory of Cypriots. After war, forgetting is just as important as remembering. In this case, political considerations are at the fore of this silence, as they will be if this story ever enters Cypriot national consciousness.

This book argues that Cypriot mules and mule drivers played a pivotal role in British logistics in Salonica and Constantinople, especially the former. The Cypriot colonial government passed laws to facilitate the procuring of mules and the enlistment of men, offering incentives to breeders and to the men. The law prohibiting the emigration of men of military age was a major facilitator of enlistment, since Cypriot men were looking to emigrate, while excellent wages, 12-month contracts, bonuses for re-signing, and an allotment scheme for their dependents, amongst other incentives, attracted an incredible 25% of the male population aged 18–35 to enlist (not including the many rejected). Although men enlisted from all parts of Cyprus and from all communities, most came from rural areas, and from peasant or labouring families. Ethnic distinctions played little role in enlisting. The few men who had any nationalist affiliations, to the broader Pan-Hellenic or Pan-Islamic identities, were not prevented from enlisting. Loyalty to the British Empire was strong, even if it must be understood alongside the primary motive – the significant financial and material rewards. Had all Cypriots wanted the British

INTRODUCTION

out of Cyprus would there have been such enthusiasm to enlist? The experiences of the men were on the whole positive; most made money and supported their families. Some, however, did not go so well. Many contracted venereal disease during their training in Famagusta, while others became ill during their service and died, and others became invalids. Still others misbehaved in a criminal way. Although clearly a subaltern group, they did speak up when they thought that the British had failed to implement any of their responsibilities, such as early on with the allotment scheme or when they insisted on their understanding of the 12-month contract to force them to serve longer. The British listened when it suited them, namely when recruitment was at risk. But they also reduced their own responsibilities to the muleteers and their families, such as in case of invalidity and death, which had devastating consequences for veterans and their families. The failure to care for veterans coupled with various social and political developments during the interwar years saw the story of the Cypriot Mule Corps silenced from Cypriot national memory.

A brief service history of the Cypriot mules and muleteers

Officially, the Cypriot Mule Corps was operational from summer 1916 until April 1920, when it was disbanded. First the vast majority of the men served in Macedonia and, indeed, the corps was officially known as the Macedonian Mule Corps. The base camp of the mules and muleteers was at Lembet Road.[3] The personnel served in various units of the British army in Salonica. The reports on the strength of the forces and the letters of veterans to the Cypriot colonial government show which divisions and units they belonged to. In the XII Corps they were the 22nd and 26th Divisions and in the XVI Corps they were the 10th (Irish), 27th and 28th Divisions.

During the Great War a small number of muleteers and interpreters served in British units outside of Salonica. For example, Cypriots in British army units that left Salonica for Egypt went with them, such as Haris Panaou, from Rizokarpaso, who lost a leg in Alexandria.[4]

The Armistice at Mudros, signed on 30 October, resulted in the Allied (British, French and Italian) occupation of Constantinople. French troops entered the city on 12 November 1918, followed by British troops, including the Cypriot Mule Corps on the next day.[5] The Mule Corps was based at Bostancı in Kadıköy, on the Asian side of the city.[6]

It is important to understand the nature of the work done by the muleteers and mules. Muleteers drove mules that carried arms, ammunition and medical and food supplies to the front and wounded and dead soldiers back to camp, across the treacherous mountain terrain. Injuries, disease, death and misconduct, although not endemic, occurred. There is little information on the role of foremen, although they had 20 muleteers under their supervision, and even less on the 100 interpreters, who were based in each unit and at base camp.

Generally the Cypriot Mule Corps was a success for both those who formed it and those who served in it. Yet the focus of this book is not merely to explore positives. It is to provide a holistic portrait of the Corps, focusing on all the issues surrounding it, as well as broader imperial, colonial, military, social, economic, political and cultural lenses.

Sources and methodology

In 2010 I was in London undertaking research on the Legion d'Orient / Armenian Legion in the National Archives when I discovered the honour roll of the 'Macedonian' Mule Corps. Opening the file was a 'jaw-dropping' moment. Stunned by the number of names and the information, such as addresses and enlistment and discharge dates, I decided to write an article. But after realising that the Corps impacted upon almost the entire population of the island and that it was hardly 'Macedonian', but really Cypriot, leading to my renaming it 'Cypriot Mule Corps' (by which it was sometimes referred to in official documents), I decided to write a book. In Adelaide I began the slow, five-year process to reconstruct the story of the Cypriot Mule Corps and to understand its broader importance. This was no easy task since none of the men were alive nor, being mostly peasants and labourers, had they left any account, written or oral, like the diaries, scrapbooks and private letters left by many who served in the two Liverpool battalions (men who belonged to the middle class) studied by Helen McCartney.[7] Meanwhile the existence of the Cypriot Mule Corps had been erased from the Cypriot national consciousness.

The first step was to consolidate the main source, the honour roll. I acquired an electronic excel copy and began the long process of correcting the names and the place names, and adding the missing names and dates of enlistment and discharge, since the original honour roll was incomplete. This took years. This process was helped when I discovered local files on the subject in the State Archives in Nicosia in 2012.[8]

This archive, rich for its (and the region's) Cypriot history, contains the correspondence and memoranda to and from the Cypriot colonial government as they were catalogued by the Chief (later Colonial) Secretary.[9] I discovered several files on the Cypriot Mule Corps, which completed the story as regards its formation and administration (with

INTRODUCTION

Colonial and War Office files from the National Archives, UK) and opened a new line of enquiry on the experiences of the men during and after their service. These documents, usually complaints about outstanding pay, requests for welfare from those disabled, widows or destitute veterans, or applications from veterans for their medals, are the main primary sources containing the voices of the men who served and that of their families, even if in many cases others wrote for them.

A subsequent trip to the National Archives in the UK in 2014 to research the London Cypriot community during the interwar years afforded me the opportunity to access the War Office files. Although there was no official history produced, there were numerous diaries and memoranda that provided the day-to-day about the corps and policy debates that led to various decisions. This gave me something about the experiences of the men, but I wanted more.

The voices of the men from their graves being impossible, the next best thing was the project 'Europeana 1914–1918', a component of Europeana's broader programme to digitise European cultural heritage. Publicly announced in 2011 as 'Europeana Collections 1914–1918: Remembering the First World War', its goal was to digitise over 400,000 source items. Public online submissions were opened and roadshows were held inviting the public to bring physical artefacts or documents to be digitised, and to record stories connected to them. Fifty-one sessions were run across Europe until December 2013, with the Cypriot roadshow on 1–2 December 2012. The team in Cyprus also visited people's homes to scan and photograph items, and interview descendants.[10] The benefits of this collection outweighed the problems, since these sources offered some voice for those who served, even if it is relayed by others. The main problem was that there was not one entry on a Turkish Cypriot muleteer; clearly, whether intended or not, this was the result of the division of the island and their continued exclusion from Cypriot history. This is a major concern, especially since the project is pan-European. Another problem was that the interviews were conducted by people who knew little about the history of Cyprus, especially on the Great War and the Cypriot Mule Corps. This resulted in errors and the material gathered not being as useful as it may have been, especially if the right questions had been asked.

A trip to Istanbul in 2012 was surprisingly fruitful. I found a memorial to fallen Cypriot muleteers who served in the Black Sea at the British cemetery at Hader Pasha, but it was the Ottoman archives, namely the Başbakanlık Osmanlı Arşivleri (Office of the Grand Vizier's Ottoman Archives) in Istanbul, which proved most useful. That I found anything here on the Cypriot muleteers was a complete surprise. The material, discussed mostly in Chapter 7, was from the Ottoman

Interior Ministry and was mainly police reports on the behaviour of Cypriot and other muleteers in Constantinople. It was illuminating to have the Ottoman perspective on the Cypriot muleteers, especially since there were no corresponding Greek sources from their service in Macedonia. Indeed the reader may wonder why no Greek archives were accessed. This was not for want of trying. Although no personal visit was made, many archives were contacted in writing and colleagues searched high and low, all to no avail. Perhaps no material exists because the muleteers were, unlike in Constantinople, not easily able to obtain leave to visit Salonica.

The book is built around nine chapters. The first two provide valuable and necessary historiographical, theoretical and historical context, and the rest discuss, in a chronological and thematic framework, the Cypriot Mule Corps from its formation through to the issues that veterans had even into the 1940s, and finally ending with how and why it has been forgotten from Cypriot and British memory. Chapter 2 provides the necessary historical context. It first explores Cypriot society from late Ottoman through to early British rule, until the Great War. This is necessary to understand why so many men enlisted in the Mule Corps. The next part covers the role of Cyprus during the Great War beyond the Mule Corps to show that the Cypriot contribution was much greater. It also explores the impact of the war on Cypriot socio-economic conditions, particularly of so many men serving abroad on the local economy and society. The next chapter delves into the formation of the Mule Corps. It explores questions such as why and how it was formed, why Cypriot mules and men were selected, and its administration and organisation. This leads into a discussion in Chapter 4 on why and how so many mules were procured and so many men enlisted. Were the men pushed or pulled? If pushed, what pushed them? If pulled, what pulled them? What were the recruiting strategies? To begin to answer these questions, it is important to know how many enlisted, from which parts of the island, from which religious groups and from what civil status. This analysis helps to prove that the Cypriot Mule Corps primarily attracted peasants and labourers, especially rural labourers.[11] The following chapter explores what threatened recruitment and how these threats were overcome. It looks at how Cypriots, as subalterns and within the 'liminal space', had a limited voice. Only when their voice threatened enlistment did the British listen, while the Cypriot government served as a tempering force between the men and the military. The sixth chapter reconstructs the treatment of the mules and the experiences of the men while on service and upon their immediate repatriation. What were conditions like for man and beast in Salonica and Constantinople?

INTRODUCTION

How well did the muleteers treat their mules? What were the experiences of the men close to the front? The chapter focuses on the health of the muleteers, especially venereal disease, which jeopardised the mule corps, and provides statistics on casualties, which were high given the British promises of safety. The next chapter explores the behaviour of the men, namely the incidence of desertion and crime, and how these were punished. Although the vast majority of the muleteers were valued and got along well, there were some who did not. Their stories provide valuable insights into the overall experience and British reactions. Chapter 8 continues with the experiences of the men, now as veterans seeking welfare or their papers and medals, and how families, especially widows, struggled. These 'orphaned widows' were left unprotected and vulnerable, yet received little, if any, compensation from the military authorities, and none from the colonial government. Disabled men were not treated any better, while many veterans fell on hard times and some were supported by the branch of the British Legion in Cyprus. Still others emigrated and found it necessary to seek proof of their service for employment and social inclusion. Nevertheless, most veterans were proud of their service, despite the rise of anti-colonialism. One of the more extraordinary aspects of this story is its absence from Cypriot national memory. The final chapter explores how the service of the muleteers never entered national consciousness, buried, first, under the hardships of the interwar years and then underneath opposed 'Greek' and 'Turkish' nationalist narratives of the island's history. This necessitates an understanding of Cypriot political history and the eventual splitting of the integrated peasant and labouring classes and their reintegration into the 'Greek-Christian' and 'Turkish-Muslim' ethnic groups. This and the British neglect to support and commemorate the veterans of the Cypriot Mule Corps combined to see its story never entering Cypriot national memory. The existence of the Cypriot Mule Corps was incompatible with the programme and desire for *enosis* of Greek Cypriot political elites of both the right and left, who eventually won the hearts and minds of the peasant and labouring classes after the Second World War. The erasure of the Cypriot Mule Corps from Cypriot national consciousness and memory shows how epic events in a country's history can be excluded from that consciousness and memory.

The archive-driven account is given a human face through individual stories of Cypriot muleteers and their families, and their mixed fortunes as part of the British Empire and its war efforts, in what Jay Winter would refer to as 'the braiding together of family history and national history'.[12] One can see the lives of the muleteers unfolding alongside the wider, more powerful, forces at play: the different experiences of war service; life for families and veterans during the rise and suppression of nationalism and communism and the hardships of the Great Depression; and finally the Second World War. Ultimately this is the story of military service from a loyal mixed Christian-Muslim, primarily peasant and rural labouring, colonial society, which was controlled by the powerful British Empire and yet neglected by it after their service. Such a story opens the door for other studies of similar colonial groups that contributed to the British war effort during the Great War, even with few first-hand personal accounts.

Notes

1. Accessed from the website of the Imperial War Museum, http://archive.iwm.org.uk/upload/package/95/collections/art/stanley-spencer.html on 16 February 2015.
2. John B. Allcock, 'Stanley Spencer: An English Artist in Macedonia', *Macedonian Review*, 18(3), 233–42, 238; Also, *Art from the First World War*, Imperial War Museum, London, 2008.
3. Cypriot State Archives (SA1), SA1/722/1916/1, Sisman to Stevenson, 11 February 1918.
4. See the documents on Haris Panaou in SA1/978/1916 and SA1/607/1917. His story features in Chapter 8.
5. Nur Bilge Criss, *Istanbul under Allied Occupation, 1918–1923*, Brill, Leiden, 1999.
6. See DH.EUM.AYS/36/17/1338.B.4.
7. Helen McCartney, *Citizen Soldiers: The Liverpool Territorials in the First World War*, Cambridge University Press, 2005.
8. The original hand-written list is in WO/405/1. After the war, typed lists were produced, see WO329/2357 and WO329/2358. Along with the various files in the State Archives (SA1) in Nicosia, I produced a consolidated list. It is from this list that the service numbers, next of kin and addresses of the muleteers have been sourced.
9. When Cyprus became a Crown Colony in 1925 the post of Chief Secretary was renamed Colonial Secretary, while the High Commissioner became a Governor.
10. Jamie Andrews, 'Digitisation and the First World War: Europeana Collections, 1914–1918', *The British Empire and the Great War: Colonial Societies / Cultural Responses*, Nanyang Technological University, Singapore, 19–22 February 2014.
11. Two articles were developed from Chapter 4. One appeared in *Itinerario* (2014) and the other is under review.
12. Jay Winter, *Remembering War: The Great War between Memory and History in the Twentieth Century*, Yale University Press, New Haven, 2006, 2.

CHAPTER ONE

Historiography and theories

Two things I am interested in are my own family history and the life of Steven Georgiou/Cat Stevens/Yusuf Islam. How are these connected to this book let alone this chapter? As the dedication to this book reveals, my great-grandfather and my wife's grandfather served in the Cypriot Mule Corps and so did Yusuf's father. Stavros Georgiou, born in Tala, Paphos, in May 1900, to Georgios Adamou (his next of kin on the honour roll), enlisted on 9 May 1918, the month he turned 18, and served until 28 May 1919 in both Salonica and Constantinople.[1] Family history is important. It helps us understand who we are and where we and our ancestors came from, yet it can only go so far in providing meaning to our lives, unless it is understood alongside the experiences of others and wider historical forces.

This is of course not the only reason why this chapter is important. It places the history of the Cypriot Mule Corps and the experiences of the men who served in it and their families in the appropriate historiographical and theoretical contexts. It shows that the history of the Cypriot Mule Corps contributes to various historical debates and can only properly be understood by viewing it through various theoretical lenses.

Historiographical context

This book speaks to a number of interlocking historiographies. Obviously, it speaks to the historiography of British Cyprus during the Great War, on which there is no study. More importantly, it speaks to the historiography of British non-settler colonial enlistment and experiences, for which there is a small yet significant literature, especially around the involvement of Indians, east Africans and Jamaicans in the British West Indies Regiment. Including the Cypriot case within this historiography will contribute to various debates, especially around enlistment/volunteerism, imperial loyalty and veterans issues. Additionally, this study explores the agency and 'voices' of the Cypriots, situating these within the subaltern school, shifting the focus away from its Asian roots and onto a 'European' space. It also contributes to the historiography of war memory, again shifting the focus, this time away from the settler/former settler colonies and from remembrance to forgetting. Fourthly, this study contributes to the historiographies of the Macedonian Campaign and the Allied Occupation of Constantinople, areas little studied by historians. Finally, but by no means less important, is the contribution to understanding the role of mules in particular and equines more generally during the Great War.

Secondary sources on wartime Cyprus and the Cypriot Mule Corps

There has been little research carried out on British Cyprus during the immediate years before, during and after the Great War. My 2009 monograph remains the most comprehensive on British imperial aims and policy in Cyprus prior to 1915, while a recent effort, published six years later, fails to acknowledge or engage with this and other works.[2] Aside from a number of works on the British offer to cede the island to Greece in October 1915,[3] a study on the immediate post-war colonial policies and local politics,[4] and two recent articles on aspects of the Great War,[5] the historiography consists of generalist accounts,[6] studies that chronicle the minor (dwarfed alongside the service in the British army during the Great War) Greek Cypriot contributions in the Greek army,[7] or brief notes[8]. There has been some more focus on the Cypriot Regiment from the Second World War,[9] yet if the figures George Kazamias provided are accurate, and by the end of the Second World War 11,749 Cypriots had enlisted in it,[10] proportionally more served in the Cypriot Mule Corps.

It is not so astonishing that the Cypriot Mule Corps is rarely mentioned in secondary sources. It is surprising that it is not mentioned in the classic *A History of Cyprus*, volume 4, on the Ottoman and British periods, written by George Hill and Sir Harry Luke, because this (and Hill's other volumes) were meticulously researched, and Luke had served in the island during the Great War and mentions it in the *Handbook of Cyprus* he co-authored in 1920.[11] It was mentioned in *A Chronology of Cyprus* in 1930, which Sir Ronald Storrs prepared during his governorship for the other colonies and Whitehall.[12] This reflects the lack of information and interest in the Cypriot Mule Corps. This study aims to rectify this historical omission and show why its inclusion has significance for various historical debates for and beyond Cyprus.

HISTORIOGRAPHY AND THEORIES

Contemporary accounts and primary sources on the Cypriot Mule Corps

Numerous primary accounts on the Salonica front also fail to mention much about the Cypriot Mule Corps.[13] Some sources mention muleteers, but not specifically Cypriots, resulting in false assumptions and confusion about who these muleteers were. Such accounts tended to be about the men fighting rather than those in support services, who were sometimes written about as a burden. For example, in his 1919 *The Salonica-Side-Show*, his second book on the Salonica Front, V.J. Seligman wrote that the Brigade Supply Officer had the added complication of 'having to feed "foreign" troops attached to his Brigade: Indians, Greeks, Muleteers, Civil Labourers, Prisoners of War, Maltese, etc., who are all entitled to a different ration'.[14] The ethnic origin of the muleteers is unspecified, but since the majority were Cypriots and Indians, Seligman's muleteers must include the Cypriots. Labelled as 'foreigners', Indians, Maltese and Cypriots serving were denied their British colonial status. In his 1920 'history' of the Salonica front, A.J. Mann stated that a 'Greek Muleteers Corps had been formed on the civilian contract basis', but 'on the formation of the new army, most were absorbed in other Greek units'.[15] Mann failed to mention that Cypriots were added to the mule corps. Again this reflects a denial of both ethno-religious and imperial identity, since Greeks were not a part of the British Empire. It also hides the role of Cypriot Muslims. H. Ward Price, the official correspondent with the Allied forces in the Balkans, also mentioned only 'Greek muleteers':

> The Greek Muleteer Corps that we enlisted was at first dressed in khaki uniform, with only a tin badge on the arm as a distinguishing mark, and one used to have the shock of meeting what seemed to be the most rapscallion, untidy mob of English drivers you had ever set eyes on. Later on, however, the Muleteer Corps' dress was changed to black tunics and slouch hats. They get three drachmas (2s. 6d.) a day. They are not so good as English drivers, of course, but transport is such an immense problem in the Balkans that we had to have more drivers from somewhere, and Greek labour was the only solution. It is always undesirable, or course, to use aliens in the zone of any army in the field, and on a few occasions some of these people have been found carrying letters with spy-reports for the enemy, which they were to hide in pre-arranged places to be fetched by other agents, but we have never had enough men in the Balkans to do anything big as it is, and we should have had fewer combatants still if we had had to find drivers for all the horse and mule transport that we use.[16]

Price was referring to Cypriot muleteers, but he too had turned them into Greeks and 'aliens'.

On the other hand, Colonel R.H. Beadon, the official historian of the Army Services Corps, mentioned the Cypriot Mule Corps. He established that the Salonica Front had to help itself because of the commitment of resources to other fronts and so, despite the neutrality of the Greeks, in March 1916 100 Greek muleteers at a pay of GRD (Greek drachma) 3 a day were recruited into the Army Services Corps. They were subsequently increased to 250 and sent to field ambulances, proving so satisfactory that by August 1916 there were 1,250 Macedonian muleteers serving in field units and a further 850 being trained in the Base Horse Transport Depot.[17] Beadon explained that more were needed when in May 1916 the Allies advanced towards the Struma River and the 10 miles to the original front now became 50, necessitating increasing

> divisional trains up to the establishment sanctioned for mountain warfare, involving eight companies in each train, four being wheeled with limbered wagons or army transport carts and four consisting of pack mules – one company of each nature working in echelon for each brigade.[18]

For this reason Cyprus was asked to provide 3,000 muleteers through Major Sisman.

> By the 22nd of July over 1,100 [Cypriots] had been enlisted and the first detachment left at once with four hundred mules. A month later, of some 6,700 drivers required to complete the special Salonica establishments, there were slightly over that number in sight including 2,000 British promised from Egypt and the United Kingdom, and 2,000 Cypriots to complete the demand from Cyprus.[19]

Then in 1935, in his *Slouch Hat*, a British officer in Salonica, Captain Malcolm Burr, also mentioned the Cypriot muleteers. Visiting the Balkans in 1926, Burr found many friends from his time in Macedonia, including Major Saunders, who was living in Salonica, and who 'had commanded a unit much like my own, the Macedonian Muleteers, mostly Cypriots'.[20] Indeed Burr, an expert on orthoptera, was the officer commanding the No. 1 Civil Labour Battalion, a mixture of Serbian exiles and local Greek peasants tasked with improving the poor roads. Unfortunately, Burr provided little information on the muleteers and Saunders is not mentioned in the archival record.

Beyond British reminiscences, Luigi Villari, of the Italian contingent in Macedonia, mentioned in his 1922 book that because the strength of the divisions became dangerously low, the British sent to the front all able-bodied British men from the auxiliary services, and substituted them with 'Indians, Cypriots and Macedonian natives'. He revealed that 'a school for these new transport drivers was instituted at Lembet near Salonica and gave good results'.[21]

The information from those with first-hand experience of the Cypriot muleteers is thus scanty. This book aims to provide a comprehensive history of the Cypriot Mule Corps and the men who served in it.

Colonial enlistment, experiences and behaviour
Janet Watson has convincingly argued that 'service could lead to fulfilment as well as disillusionment' and many variables determined the experiences of those serving.[22] There have been few studies on the colonial experiences of military service, yet Watson's statement holds true for the periphery as it does for the metropolis, though not necessarily for the same reasons. An excellent example is Helen McCartney's book on two Territorial battalions from Liverpool. She breached, as this study aims to do, the blinkered approach of many war histories that focus on military organisation and policy often separate from social, cultural and economic factors by combining military knowledge with the impact of the war on society and identity. Class played an important role in her cases since her two Territorial battalions were from the middle class, unlike most Territorial battalions which were working-class men.[23] The same applies for this study, since the Cypriot Mule Corps mainly consisted of peasant and labouring men. This allows for a deeper understanding of society and identity beyond the traditional nationalist approach to colonial histories.

The historiography on British colonial enlistment and experiences distinguishes between those enlisting as combatants, auxiliaries and labour, yet no study mentions the Cypriot Mule Corps. In their study on military labour during the Great War, Starling and Lee disclose the various military labour corps. Under 'British and Dominion Units' they listed the Royal Marine Labours Corps, Middlesex Aliens, Maltese Labour Corps, Bermuda Royal Garrison Artillery, Cape Coloured Labour Battalion, South African Native Labour Corps, Seychelles Labour Battalion, British West Indies Regiment, ANZACs, Canadians, Indian Labour Corps, Fijian Labour Corps and Mauritius Labour Battalion. The Cypriot Mule Corps was not listed, not even under 'Foreign Labour Units', which lists the Egyptian Labour Corps, Jewish Labour (including the Zion Mule Corps), Greek, Macedonian and Serbian Labour, Chinese Labour Corps, Portuguese Labour, Italian Labour and German Prisoners of War.[24]

Research on the recruitment of non-settler colonial populations varies in both quality and quantity. There is more published on India, the West Indies and the informal empire in China, compared to Africa and the Pacific, with nothing on Malta and little on Cyprus[25]. There were, of course, several official and personal accounts published during and immediately after the war, most celebrating the Indian contribution.[26] More recently, numerous publications, mostly articles, have appeared on the fighting and labouring contributions of the non-settler colonies to the British war effort, especially on Indians,[27] West Indians[28] and Chinese,[29] but also on a smaller scale on Africans[30] and Fijians,[31] and the smaller informal empire in Latin America.[32] General accounts have attempted a trans-imperial and trans-colonial comparison across European empires and the colonial periphery.[33] Most of these studies focus on numbers rather than recruiting strategies, motivations to enlist and experiences, mostly during the war, and are often celebratory. One fine exception is the article on the service of the Sudanese, who interestingly were one of the few parts of the Empire to have suffered compulsory enlistment soon after the outbreak of the Great War because certain tribes were recalcitrant to volunteer and the British believed that by exposing certain tribes to military life they would instil them with a discipline and respect for authority, which would end their involvement in unrest against the British.[34] This was the opposite of the Cypriot case, since the British rejected conscription for the mule corps and enlistment for a legion of Cypriots, proposed by a Venizelist Greek Cypriot nationalist, for fear it would nationalise the Cypriot peasant and labouring classes and bring unrest against the British after the war.[35] No study explored any mule corps, which is interesting given that the Indian army had their own. The failure to thoroughly study the role played by colonial personnel, whether combatants or skilled/unskilled labourers, must be understood within the developing historical focus to include marginalised groups.

Smith's book on Jamaican war service is the most relevant to this study, but this is not a comparison of 'like with like'. A major difference was that Jamaicans enlisted to fight, but most were asked to labour, which they did not want, causing tensions. Yet as with the Cypriots, Jamaicans were used as indentured labour.[36] The Cypriot contracts were reminiscent, although not identical, to the Indian indenture system, having in common a set period of service, nature of labour, days of work per month, overtime without pay, and free repatriation.[37] Obviously the Cypriot example saw them serving in the British army and subject to military law. The experiences of Jamaicans compared to Cypriots is impacted by the fact that the Jamaicans wanted to fight while the Cypriots were not meant to and promised that they would not be in harm's way. So Jamaican grievances were greater and reflected in their mutinous behaviour and political activism after the war. Yet that they were meant to fight and the involvement of their elites in recruitment, as well as the political activism of veterans and their advocates, meant that veterans got a better deal than

Cypriots.[38] Cypriots had complaints too, mostly as regards the British failing to implement the financial scheme to benefit their dependents, or because they believed they were in harm's way on the Salonica front or for being forced to undergo treatment for venereal disease at their own expense once repatriated. Cypriot veterans, unlike Jamaicans, were largely ignored by both the British, whom they had served so loyally, and their own politicians, who wanted to forget such loyalty to the establishment of anti-colonialism.

Another area little explored in the literature is the behaviour of the armed forces. Work on the Great War has been limited to studies on British deserters and those who faced the firing squad,[39] or to more general accounts on the differences between military and civilian crimes during war.[40] In the dominions there have been studies on New Zealand[41] and Australia.[42] All of these have focused on the fighting man, not auxiliaries, male or female. This book seeks to rectify this, yet there are still comparisons to be made with Peter Stanley's *Bad Characters* on the Australians in the Australian Imperial Force. Australians and Cypriots were similarly engaged in offences ranging from malingering, disobedience, contracting venereal disease (Cypriots while training at Famagusta) and criminal behaviour such as theft, assault and murder. Stanley ultimately argues that these Australians were not really 'bad characters' and that the totality of the First World War can explain their misbehaviour, yet regardless of criminal intent or not, the application of military law usually meant that it ended very badly for them.

Veterans, grief and the Great War

The aftermath has not been a neglected aspect of the war experience, although it has been neglected in a colonial context. Little has been written about post-war consequences for veterans and families in the colonial world beyond Australia, Canada, New Zealand and a little on Jamaica, making the Cypriot case (a rare example of a non-settler colonial study) important for changing understandings of post-war experiences.

Bereavement for wives and parents and physical and emotional trauma for the disabled have preoccupied scholars over the last two decades. *Disabled Veterans in History* by David Gerber in 2000 challenged historians to explore the relationship between veterans and the state, private welfare groups and broader society.[43] This was explored in two special issues: *European Review of History* in 2007 and *First World War Studies* in 2015. The disabilities discussed in the 2007 articles crossed a more diverse historical period, yet two were on the Great War and Britain, one on the King's National Roll Scheme, an employment programme (something lacking in Cyprus), and the other on one experience of amputation, which challenged the assumption that disability was emasculating (contradicted by Cypriot cases in Chapter 8).[44] The 2015 articles discussed the emotional and physical problems arising from disability, the role of technology, such as prosthetics, and community care.[45] In a British context, there is much on the Great War and shell shock, death and disability from the lens of masculinity and its treatment and representation.[46] In a British colonial context there is little beyond the white dominions, where three studies standout: Serge Durflinger's study on Canadians blinded during the war;[47] and those on Australia by Joy Damousi and Marina Larsson.[48] Damousi shows that Australian widows grieved the loss of their husbands, as did Cypriot women, but Australian women did so publicly as well as privately, while Cypriot women only could in private, except momentarily if and when they went to accept the medal awarded to their husbands. Thus, unlike Australian women, their emotions were seldom on full show. Like Australian widows, they also sought welfare, but they received nothing from the government, and only some were 'compensated' by the military. Another difference was that although Australian women were left devastated, destitute and distraught, Cypriot women were additionally left 'unprotected', calling themselves 'orphaned widows', a reflection on their 'ownership' by their husbands.

The differences continued with those disabled. Australians were lauded as heroes, aided by government welfare, and associations were formed to protect their interests. This did not happen in the Cypriot case beyond the branch of the British Legion. Australian limbless veterans were also given preferential treatment for employment in the civil service, which occurred only for one Cypriot muleteer, who was eventually dismissed (see Chapter 8). More importantly, Australian disabled war veterans had a public presence, whereas disabled muleteers kept to their villages, living as peasants and rural labourers. Yet suffering and feelings of having lost their masculinity were common. Agathocles Haji Christodoulou's sentiment that he 'was tormented, felt useless to society because he could not work, and that he would have been better off dead' is one example. This suggests that although the role of government and civil society might differ between 'core' and 'periphery', personal feelings of helplessness are common.

Macedonian Campaign

Despite the recent thorough account by Wakefield and Moody,[49] the men who served in the Macedonian Campaign have never lived down the tag of 'the gardeners of Salonica'.[50] This is a shame. The front, established in October 1915, may not have had the carnage of the Western Front, or the catastrophic landings of the Eastern (i.e.

Gallipoli), but it had its own trials and tribulations for those serving. This book will bring these to light as they were experienced by the Cypriots who served and by the British who worked to make the front and the Cypriot Mule Corps a success. It will also show how linked (especially as regards supplies) the fronts in France, Macedonia and Egypt were, a fact neglected in the historiography. By showing that the Cypriots, a small colonial group, made such a significant impact on this front, the history of the Macedonian Campaign can be seen in a more inclusive and broader light.

Allied occupation of Constantinople

Historians have neglected to study Constantinople/Istanbul under allied occupation, with one solitary study on the subject.[51] The occupation of the Ottoman capital by British, French and Italian forces transpired in accordance with the Armistice of Mudros, which ended Ottoman participation in the Great War. French troops entered the city on 12 November 1918, followed the next day by British troops. The occupation had two stages: initially the occupation took place in accordance with the Armistice (from 12 November 1918); from 16 March 1920 it was sanctioned by the Treaty of Sèvres, which was then overridden by the Treaty of Lausanne on 24 July 1923, with the last Allied troops leaving on 23 September 1923. This study contributes to the understanding of allied-occupied Constantinople, where the Cypriot Mule Corps was based after Salonica. It compares the nature of the service given the differing situations between the Macedonian Campaign and the occupation of Constantinople, which allowed for greater freedoms and more scope for criminality at the latter location.

Mules and the Great War

This study also contributes to the historiography of equines in war. Several historians, perhaps inspired by Michael Morpurgo's 1982 novel *War Horse* (and probably more so by the subsequent award-winning Nick Stafford play in 2007 and Steven Spielberg's 2011 Oscar-nominated film adaptation), have explored equine history, especially in war. As Alan Mikhail has recently argued,

> For the vast majority of human history, until at least the early nineteenth century, the chief concern of human communities was their multiple relationships with animals – how to use them, eat them, avoid them, and wear them. Animals are indeed so ubiquitous in human history that they have remained largely invisible to historians.[52]

Mikhail explored the historical relationship between humans and animals in Ottoman Egypt. He argued that animals were central to the transformative socio-economic and energy changes occurring in Egypt between 1780 and 1810, so when their numbers were reduced during this period Egypt changed from an early modern agrarian subsistence economy to one based on commercial agriculture, large landholdings and human labour.[53] This book follows Mikhail's approach and discloses a great deal about the human–mule relationship. It explores the issues of breeding, selling, procuring, shipping, working and caring for mules in war. Chapter 3 explores the nascent mule-breeding industry that had a trans-imperial reach, since Cypriot mules were in demand across the British Empire and during various imperial wars in the later nineteenth and early twentieth centuries. This explains the choice of mules and muleteers from Cyprus in 1916.

Historians have written little on the army transport mule during the Great War, in keeping with a greater focus on horses in warfare more generally.[54] The other focus of the historiography has not been on equines as subjects, but rather as objects alongside the labour, usually colonial labour, recruited to handle them. Significant research has been published on the role of horses in warfare. Aside from general accounts,[55] there have been important works on their role in the English Civil Wars,[56] the American Civil War[57] and even in the highly mechanised Second World War.[58] For the Great War the focus has been on the role of horses and their fate.[59] Mules have been treated as an afterthought, with an obvious cultural bias against mules in favour of the more glamorous horse. Mules are 'half-breeds', with no real identity. Various colloquial expressions such as 'stubborn as a mule' and 'silly ass' make them less attractive to scholars and the general public, evident in the historiography and contemporary sources.[60] Singleton's article provides some information on the use of mules during the Great War, yet the title of his article mentions only horses.[61] Focusing on the functioning of the British Remount Department on the Western Front, he found that 'the success of the British war effort was heavily dependent on the horse'.[62] This may be true for the Western Front but on the Salonica Front mules were in greater numbers, as shown by Captain Sidney Galtrey.[63] Singleton also concluded that 'horses and mules were treated with greater care by the British army in the war than earlier wars because veterinary services and fodder rations were better'.[64]

Mules are also mentioned, although more as objects rather than as subjects, in the historiography of labour recruitment during the Great War. Three articles are worthy here for the British context in the Great War: one is on African labour in the East Africa Protectorate;[65] another on Chinese labour;[66] and a third on Indian.[67] They deal with the experiences of the men, but not the treatment of the mules, which are there, but little is said about them.

HISTORIOGRAPHY AND THEORIES

Theoretical context

This book engages with several interlocking theoretical concepts. Debates on wartime enlistment and volunteerism and experiences of service feed into theoretical discussions on imperial identity, local identity formation, peasant and subaltern studies, veterans issues, grief, and memory and forgetting, which must be understood for a nuanced picture.

Enlistment, volunteerism and migration

Historians have studied the motivations behind the enlistment of men (and women) during the Great War and the tensions between enlistment and volunteerism (i.e. was it voluntary?) and this book speaks to this. It attempts to fully explore and contextualise the push-and-pull factors behind the extraordinary scale of Cypriot enlistment.

The historiography of enlistment and/or volunteerism focuses on the metropole of the main belligerent powers, and not the colonial periphery. In the British case, this is well tackled by John Morton Osborne, Nicholas Mansfield and Catriona Pennell for 1914–16 and McCartney in the case of Territorials from Liverpool. Pennell's book explores the myriad of responses from the British and Irish publics and elites and shows that they depend on one's background and ideology, especially class.[68] The Territorial Army was a volunteer force mostly consisting of working-class men, yet traditionally their experiences and responses to their service have not been the focus of historical accounts,[69] until McCartney explored two Liverpool battalions which consisted of middle/lower- and middle-class men.[70] The experience of working-class Territorial battalions would certainly compare well in terms of motivation to enlist with that of the Cypriot Mule Corps, as does that of the 'Pals battalions', since, as Michael Durey showed in the case of the 11th (Lewisham) Battalion Royal West Kent Regiment, working-class men volunteered based on various push-and-pull factors.[71] Osborne showed that although the voluntary recruiting scheme was considered a failure, into 1915 it was still a success, built upon a national excitement, which was exploited around the themes of duty, honour and sacrifice.[72] Yet Osborne showed that the Labour movement believed that poverty played a major role in rural men enlisting:

> The 'calling up' of men has brought vividly to light the depth of the poverty in which many families of our brave troops have lived; for no sooner has the breadwinner gone than the poor penniless wife has had to fly to the Poor Law or the charity-organisers.[73]

Mansfield explored the 'contradiction in the actions of workers, trade unionists and even socialists, who, at odds with the established order, still volunteered to fight for their country'. Yet he showed that the men who enlisted did not do so to defend the established order, but for other reasons: poverty, adventure, duty, peer pressure and later fear of conscription. Recruiters used a mixture of persuasion, tangible benefits and emotional blackmail. Fundamentally, as was the case for most of the Cypriot muleteers, poverty was a key push factor for rural British men, and recruiters did, as in the Cypriot case, play to this.[74] Yet ultimately, unlike in the Cypriot case (and indeed in all the British Empire), conscription was introduced in Britain, whereas in Cyprus it was considered but rejected because more than enough men were volunteering.

Part of the reason was that the Cypriot government approached enlistment from the perspective of temporary migration. As already established above, the Cypriots were enlisted into a form of overseas indentured labour. Their service was a form of temporary overseas work, which some would have been used to, namely in Egypt. As Eric Richards has argued, 'one of the great themes of modern history is the movement of poor people across the face of the earth'.[75] In order to facilitate enlistment the Cypriot government banned emigration of men of military age, thus targeting those men most likely to want to emigrate, and offered them a 12-month well-paying job. The Cypriot government also defended the men when controversy arose over the duration of the contract, arguing that this was a pivotal component of enlistment strategies. Clearly these men fit the term 'temporary overseas worker'. The disproportionate contribution of Scottish Highlanders to military recruitment in the United Kingdom has been viewed, in part, as a form of out-migration driven by economic hardship, a useful parallel with Cyprus.[76]

Imperial and local identity

The enlistment of about 25% of Cypriot men aged 18–35 says something important about imperial and local identity, especially alongside the traditional nationalist Cypriot historiographies that have focused on elites and outlined a past that belongs to either a 'Greek' or a 'Turkish' nation[77] and the reflexive scholarly accounts that suggest that colonial subjects must always have yearned to resist their colonisers. There can be no doubting that such a rate of enlistment was a massive success for the British Empire. To be sure, most of the men enlisted for financial and material gain, yet many identified with the British Empire and its cause. Daniel Gorman wrote about imperial citizenship as regards the dominions and the complex nature of belonging,[78] while Sukanya Banerjee's *Becoming Imperial Citizens* showed how elite Indians formed an imperial citizenship before the anti-colonial nationalist movement and the idea of a free independent postcolonial nation state.[79] Such an imperial identity exists at the elite level in Cyprus before, and later alongside, nationalist ambitions, but has not been fully studied.[80] This study shifts the focus from the educated elites onto the peasant and labouring classes, showing that any ethno-nationalist loyalties to 'Greek' and 'Ottoman' motherlands did not exist or did not preclude loyalty to the British Empire and service in the British armed forces. McCartney's findings that her middle/lower- and middle-class Liverpudlian Territorials remained invested in thoughts of home and saw their war service as an interval that would protect their civilian identities and lives applies well to the Cypriots since many were the only financial support for their families.

Increasingly, nationalist discourses and approaches to Cypriot history are shown as exclusivist and not holistic.[81] Efforts to redress this, starting in the 1970s with theories such as 'peaceful co-existence', failed because these too were mired in political rather than scholarly aims.[82] This book adds to the new way of seeing Cyprus as a diverse place with a diverse past[83] and not merely from an ethno-religious perspective, because it focuses on showing that social diversity was as important as ethno-religious differences during the period when Cyprus was experiencing British modernisation.[84] Eugen Weber showed in his classic book on French modernisation that it was only in the late nineteenth and early twentieth centuries that the majority of the French people, the peasant and rural labouring classes, became Frenchmen.[85] In the Cypriot case, before (or with some rarer cases while) the peasants and labouring classes became 'Greeks' and 'Turks' (or with some rare exceptions 'Cypriots'), they first became imperial citizens because a quarter of the male population aged 18–35 served at one point in the Cypriot Mule Corps. If the French did not become a nation until the Great War, how could the Cypriots have become 'Greeks' and 'Turks' well before it as the traditional historiography claims?

Peasant and subaltern studies

Peasant studies, as a distinct focus of historians and anthropologists, promote critical thinking about social structures, institutions, actors and processes of change in and in relation to rural societies. It asks how agrarian power relations between classes and other social groups form, and are contested and transformed.[86] Agency is a key question in understanding these marginalised rural societies, particularly their autonomy and capacity to interpret and change their conditions.

1.1 Map of the Eastern Mediterranean.

This anti-essentialist approach is one of 'history from below', focused more on what happens among the masses, in this case rural masses, rather than among the elite. Linked with imperialism and colonial power dynamics, such an approach spawned 'subaltern studies'.[87] The term 'subaltern' derived from the Italian Marxist Antonio Gramsci's work on cultural hegemony, which identified the voices of social groups who were excluded from a society's established political structures. Focused around scholars interested in the postcolonial and post-imperial societies of the subcontinent, the geographical reach has expanded more recently to cover the developing world more generally, especially Latin America. This analytical re-essentialisation of the peasant rejected inauthentic European discourses as colonial impositions, thereby recovering an unheard grassroots voice that was authentically nationalist.

Can the Cypriot muleteers be considered 'subaltern'? The British colonised the Cypriots, and although they considered them 'European',

HISTORIOGRAPHY AND THEORIES

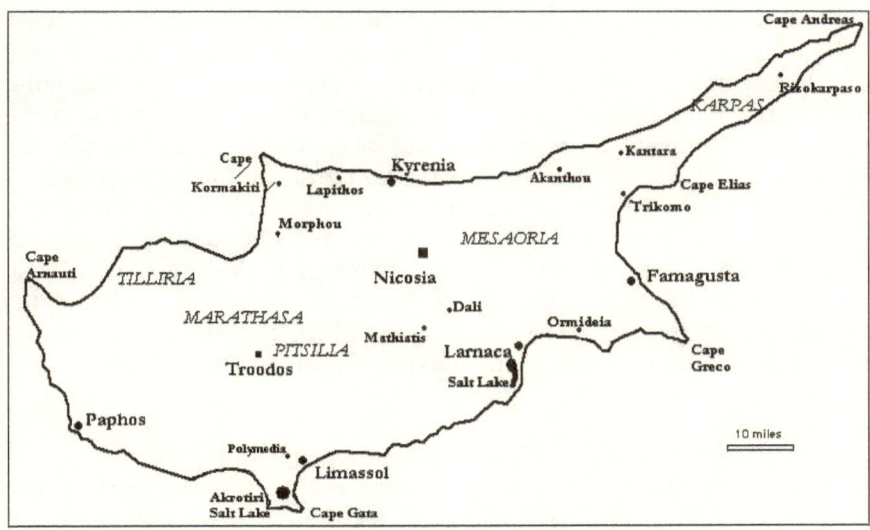

1.2 Map of Cyprus.

within the British imperial project they occupied a space on the fringes of Orientalism. The British, especially those back in London, considered the Cypriot Orthodox Christians as Greeks, partly based upon their misunderstanding of ancient Greece as a unitary state. This discourse dominated early British Cyprus, yet existed alongside an orientalist discourse of Cypriots as exotic others, not Greeks, nor Turks, but a mixture of various racial/ethnic settlers from its varied history. This complicates the categorisation of Cypriots, who do not easily fit into the 'east' and 'west' Saidian dichotomy, making them 'in-betweens'.[88] Like Said's dichotomy, Todorova's 'Balkanisation' theory does not precisely capture how Cypriots were categorised, represented and depicted, nor how they saw themselves. Contrary to what Milica Bakic-Hayden has interpreted,[89] Todorova does not claim that her Balkanisation theory is another form of Orientalism. She outlines various reasons for this, such as that the Balkans are concrete, whereas the notion of 'the Orient' is vague; the self-perception of Balkan peoples is not colonial; Orientalism posits Islam as the other, whereas Balkanisation deals with Christians and is fixed alongside an 'other', usually Islam; and Orientalism categorises non-white people, whereas Balkanisation deals with whites.[90] From the outside Cypriots were seen as occidental, oriental or a mixture. In trying to define a group along ethnic lines, other forms of identity are ignored.

Using Spivak's definition of the 'subaltern', the muleteers who enlisted and their families were indeed the 'men and women among the illiterate peasantry, the tribals, the lowest strata of the urban sub-proletariat'[91] and lacked agency in the relationship between the coloniser and colonised. Thus they fit the historical profile of subaltern. But to what extent did the Cypriot peasant and rural labouring classes 'volunteer'? Where they pushed, pulled or both? Did they control their service conditions and experiences? As Spivak asks, 'can the subaltern speak?'[92] They were sought after but were they able, in what Homi Bhabha called the 'liminal space', to negotiate with their colonisers?[93] British imperialism largely met the needs of the peasant and labouring classes, allowing the colonised to express their imperial identity and loyalty.

Silenced memory

A compelling conceptual contrast can be made between the Cypriot case of 'forgetting' versus the typical focus of so many scholars on remembering and memorialising. There are significant studies of memory and the Great War, from Winter[94] to other accounts on individual nations and regions,[95] with again Australia featuring prominently.[96] These studies focus on how the war has been remembered, commemorated and in some cases forgotten. With the case of the Cypriots it is only about forgetting, both consciously and unconsciously, and the exclusion of this extraordinary contribution to the Great War from national consciousness.

The erasure of the Cypriot Mule corps from Cypriot national narratives is striking for the stark contrast it presents to the more well-known cases of the impact of the Great War on other former colonial territories. In particular, scholarship has argued for the centrality of the experience of the Anzacs to national narratives of Australia and New Zealand and of the *tirailleurs senegalais* to the anti-colonial nationalist narratives of the successors to colonial French West Africa. In the West Indies and in West Africa, anti-colonial nationalists harnessed the memory of the unrecognised heroism and sacrifices of those men who served, precisely to argue for their worthiness of political independence.[97] Why did Cyprus follow the opposite pattern, even though on the surface it would seem to have emerged from similar structural conditions?

Conclusion

This chapter shows that the history of the Cypriot Mule Corps contributes to various rich historical and theoretical debates. There is a growing literature on volunteerism and enlistment in the Great War and this chapter shows how this book will contribute to it. How does it compare to British enlistment and other colonial cases? Were the Cypriots motivated by the same factors to enlist as British men from Liverpool or Jamaicans? The chapter also highlights the theoretical lenses through which this study is conducted, showing that in a colonial context volunteering and war and post-war service experiences were more complex than previously understood, given the imperial power imbalance between colonial societies and their imperial overlords. By understanding the broader historiographical debates and theories, the significance of the Cypriot Mule Corps and its silenced memory can be better understood beyond the significance for Cypriots.

Notes

1 See service no. 12152 in WO405/1; biographical information on Stavros Georgiou (excluding his service in the CMC) was obtained from http://web.archive.org/web/20120321144015/http://www.yusufislam.org.uk/lifeline/0/bdf531e09252cc-4c73fc5d84c4138cb3/. The one 'biography' of Cat Stevens/Yusuf incorrectly stated that Stavros Georgiou emigrated to New York at the age of 17. It is not possible that he could have done so because of the Cypriot government's ban on emigration from late 1916. Chris Charlesworth, *Cat Stevens: The Definitive Career Biography*, Proteus Books, New York, 1984, 8. In an interview, 'Islam and My Life', in 1980, Cat Stevens/Yusuf stated that his father had grown up in Egypt. It is likely that Stavros went back and forth from Cyprus and Egypt before the war.
2 Andrekos Varnava, *British Imperialism in Cyprus, 1878–1915: The Inconsequential Possession*, Manchester University Press, 2009; Gail Ruth Hook, *Protectorate Cyprus: British Imperial Power Before WWI*, I.B. Tauris, London, 2015.
3 George Georghallides, *A Political and Administrative History of Cyprus*, Nicosia, 1979, 88–102; Stavros Terry Stavridis, 'Greek-Cypriot Enosis of October 1915: "A Lost Opportunity"', *Balkan Studies*, 1996, 282–307; Loukis Theocharides, *The British Offer of Cyprus to Greece (1915)*, Nicosia, 2000; Varnava, *British Imperialism in Cyprus*, 246–71.
4 See Georghallides, *A Political and Administrative History of Cyprus*.
5 Andrekos Varnava, 'British Military Intelligence in Cyprus during the Great War', *War in History*, 19(3), 2012, 353–78; Andrekos Varnava, 'Recruitment and Volunteerism for the Cypriot Mule Corps, 1916–1919', *Itinerario*, 38(3), 79–101.
6 The best is Tabitha Morgan, *Sweet and Bitter Island: A History of the British in Cyprus*, London, 2010, 67–94. See my review, *The Cyprus Review*, 23(2), 2011, 149–54.
7 These are works (not peer-reviewed) by the Greek-Cypriot nationalist, Petros Papapolyviou, including: (ed.), Εμμανουήλ Μ. Εμμανουήλ, Ημερολόγιον ή Πολεμικαί Σελίδες: Το ημερολόγιο ενός Κύπριου εθελοντή του ελληνοβουλγαρικού πολέμου του 1913 (Emmanuel M. Emmanuel, diary or war pages: The diary of a Cypriot volunteer in the Greek–Bulgarian War of 1913), Germanos, Salonica, 1996; Η Κύπρος και οι Βαλκανικοί πόλεμοι: Συμβολή στην ιστορία του κυπριακού εθελοντισμού (Cyprus and the Balkan Wars: contribution to the history of Cypriot volunteerism), Nicosia, 1997; (ed.), Πολεμικά Ημερολόγια, επιστολές και ανταποκρίσεις Κυπρίων εθελοντών από την Ήπειρο και τη Μακεδονία του 1912–1913 (War diaries, letters and responses of Cypriot volunteers from Epirus and Macedonia 1912–1913), Nicosia, 1999; 'Ο κυπριακός εθελοντισμός στους πολέμους της Ελλάδας, 1866–1945' ('Cypriot volunteerism in the wars of Greece, 1866–1945'), in Andreas I. Voskos (ed.), Κύπρος: Αγώνες ελευθερίας

στην ελληνική ιστορία (Cyprus: struggles for freedom in Greek history), Athens, 2010, 204–29.
8   Antigone Heraclidou, 'Cyprus's Non-military Contribution to the Allied War Effort during World War I', *The Round Table*, 103(2), 2014, 193–200.
9   Jan Asmussen, '"Dark skinned Cypriots will not be accepted!" Cypriots in the British Army, 1939–1945', in Hubert Faustmann and Nicos Peristianis (eds), *Britain in Cyprus: Colonialism and Post-Colonialism 1878–2006*, Bibliopolis, Mannheim, 2006, 167–85; Anastasia Yiangou, *Cyprus in World War II*, I.B. Tauris, London, 2010.
10 Georgios Kazamias, 'Military recruitment and selection in a British colony: the Cyprus regiment 1939–1944', in E. Close, M. Tsianikas and G. Couvalis (eds), *Greek Research in Australia: Proceedings of the Sixth International Conference of Greek Studies*, June 2005, Flinders University Department of Languages, Adelaide, 333–42, 335.
11 George Hill, *A History of Cyprus*, IV, ed. Sir Harry Luke, Cambridge University Press, 1952 and see my review, *Reviews in History*, 1051, March 2011; H.C. Luke and D.J. Jardine, *The Handbook of Cyprus*, Eighth Issue, Macmillan, London, 1920, 293–4.
12 Sir Ronald Storrs, *A Chronology of Cyprus*, Government Printing Office, Nicosia, 1930, 35.
13 Harold Lake, *In Salonica with Our Army*, Andrew Melrose, London, 1917; G. Ward Price, *The Story of the Salonica Army*, Hodder and Stoughton, London, 1918; V.J. Seligman, *Macedonian Musings*, George Allen & Unwin, London, 1918; H. Collinson Owen, *Salonica and After: The Sideshow that Ended the War*, Hodder and Stoughton, London, 1919.
14 V.J. Seligman, *The Salonica Side-Show*, George Allen & Unwin, London, 1919, 93.
15 A.J. Mann, *The Salonica Front*, A. & C. Black, London, 1920.
16 Price, *The Story of the Salonica Army*, 101. There is no evidence of Cypriot muleteers spying for the enemy.
17 Colonel R.H. Beadon, *The Royal Army Service Corps: A History of Transport and Supply in the British Army*, II, Cambridge University Press, 1931, 196–7.
18 Ibid., 197–8.
19 Ibid., 198.
20 Malcolm Burr, *Slouch Hat*, George Allen & Unwin, London, 1935, 323.
21 Luigi Villari, *The Macedonian Campaign*, T. Fisher Unwin, London, 1922, 68–9.
22 J.S.K. Watson, *Fighting Different Wars: Experience, Memory, and the First World War in Britain*, Cambridge University Press, 2004, 51.
23 McCartney, *Citizen Soldiers*.
24 John Stirling and Ivor Lee, *No Labour, No Battle: Military Labour during the First World War*, Spellmount, Gloucestershire, 2009, 196–320; For the Zion Mule Corps see Matityahu Mintz, 'Pinhas Rutenberg and the Establishment of the Jewish Legion of 1914', *Studies in Zionism*, 6(1), 1985, 15–26; Yanky Fachler, 'The Zion Mule Corps and its Irish Commander', *History Ireland*, 11(4), 2003, 34–8; Martin Watts, *The Jewish Legion and the First World War*, Palgrave Macmillan, New York, 2004.
25 That is until my article, Varnava, 'Recruitment and Volunteerism for the Cypriot Mule Corps, 1916–1919'.
26 J.W.B. Merewether, and Frederick Smith, *The Indian Corps in France*, William Clowes & Sons, London, 1917; Sir Archibald Murray, 'Egyptian Labour Corps, January 1916–June 1917', Appendix F in Sir Archibald Murrays Despatches, 206–16; J.M. Dent, London, 1920; Government of India, *India's Contribution to the Great War*, Calcutta, 1923; Frank Cundall, *Jamaica's Part in the Great War, 1915–1918*, West Indian Commission, London, 1925.
27 Including: David Omissi, *Indian Voices of the Great War*, Macmillan, London, 1999; Omar Khalidi, 'Ethnic Group Recruitment in the Indian Army: The Contrasting Cases of Sikhs, Muslims, Gurkhas and Others', *Pacific Affairs*, 74(4), 2001–2, 529–52; Gordon Corrigan, *Sepoys in the Trenches*, Spellmont, Stroud, 2006; George Morton-Jack, 'The Indian Army on the Western Front, 1914–1915: A Portrait of

HISTORIOGRAPHY AND THEORIES

Collaboration', *War in History*, 13(3), 2006, 329–62; Radhika Singha, 'Finding Labor from India for the War in Iraq: The Jail Porter and Labor Corps, 1916–1920', *Comparative Studies in Society and History*, 39(2), 2007, 412–45; Roy Kaushik (ed.), *The Indian Army in the Two World Wars*, Brill, Leiden 2012; George Morton-Jack, *The Indian Army on the Western Front*, Cambridge University Press, 2014.

28 W.F. Elkins, 'A Source of Black Nationalism in the Caribbean: The Revolt of the British West Indies Regiment at Taranto, Italy', *Science and Society*, 33(2), 1970, 99–103; C.L. Joseph, 'The British West Indies Regiment, 1914–18', *Journal of Caribbean History*, 2, 1971, 94–124; Richard Smith, *Jamaican Volunteers in the First World War*, Manchester University Press, 2004.

29 Nicholas Griffin, 'Britain's Chinese Labor Corps in World War I', *Military Affairs*, 40(3), 1976, 102–8; Michael Summerskill, *China on the Western Front*, M. Summerskill, London, 1982; Paul J. Bailey, 'From Shandong to Somme: Chinese indentured labour in France during World War I', in A.J. Kershen (ed.), *Language, Labour, and Migration*, Ashgate, Farnham, 2000, 179–96; Gwynnie Hagen, 'The Chinese Labour Corps', in Dominiek Dendooven and Piet Chielens (eds), *World War I*, Lanoo, Tielt, 2008, 136–44; Paul J. Bailey, '"An army of workers": Chinese indentured labour in First World War France', in Santanu Das (ed.), *Race, Empire and First World War Writing*, Cambridge University Press, 2011, 35–52.

30 Donald C. Savage and J. Forbes Munro, 'Carrier Corps Recruitment in the British East Africa Protectorate, 1914–1918', *Journal of African History*, 7(2), 1966, 313–42.

31 Margaret Pointer, *Tagi tote e loto haaku* (My heart is crying a little), University of the South Pacific, Suva, 2000; Christine Liava'a, *Qaravi na'i tavi* (They did their duty), Polygraphia, Auckland, 2009.

32 Trevor Harris, 'British Informal Empire during the Great War: Welsh Identity and Loyalty in Argentina', *Itinerario*, 38(3), 2014, 103–17.

33 Christian Koller, 'The Recruitment of Colonial Troops in Africa and Asia and Their Deployment in Europe during the First World War', *Immigrants and Minorities*, 26(1/2), 2008, 111–33.

34 Karmal O. Salih, 'British Colonial Military Recruitment Police in the Southern Kordofan Region of Sudan, 1900–1945', *Middle Eastern Studies*, 41(2), 2005, 169–92.

35 Andrekos Varnava, 'The Politics and Imperialism of Colonial and Foreign Volunteer Legions during the Great War: Comparing Proposals for Cypriot, Armenian and Jewish Legions', *War in History*, 22(3), 2015, 344–63.

36 Smith, *Jamaican Volunteers in the First World War*.

37 Hugh Tinker, *A New System of Slavery: The Export of Indian Labour Overseas 1820–1920*, London, 1974.

38 Smith, *Jamaican Volunteers in the First World War*.

39 Anthony Babington, *For the Sake of Example: Capital Courts-Martial, 1914–1920*, St Martin's Press, New York, 1983; Cathryn Corns and John Hughes-Wilson, *Blindfold and Alone: British Military Executions in the Great War*, Cassell Military, London, 2001; David Johnson, *Executed at Dawn: British Firing Squads on the Western Front 1914–1918*, Gloucestershire Spellmount, Stroud, 2015.

40 Clive Emsley, *Soldier, Sailor, Beggarman, Thief: Crime and the British Armed Services since 1914*, Oxford University Press, 2013.

41 Christopher Pugsley, *On the Fringe of Hell: New Zealanders and Military Discipline in the First World War*, Hodder & Stoughton, Auckland, 1991.

42 Peter Stanley, *Bad Characters: Sex, Crime, Mutiny, Murder and the Australian Imperial Force*, Pier 9, Sydney, 2010.

43 David Gerber (ed.), *Disabled Veterans in History*, University of Michigan Press, Ann Arbor, 2012.

44 Meaghan Kowalsky, '"This Honourable Obligation": The King's National Roll Scheme for Disabled Ex-Servicemen 1915–1944', *European Review of History*, 14(4), 2007, 567–84; Wendy Jane Gagen, 'Remastering the Body, Renegotiating Gender: Physical Disability and Masculinity during the First World War, the Case of J.B. Middlebrook', *European Review of History*, 14(4), 2007, 525–41.

45 Julie Anderson, '"Jumpy Stump": Amputation and Trauma in the First World War', *First World War Studies*, 6(1), 2015, 9-19; Alice Brumby, '"A painful and disagreeable position": Rediscovering Patient Narratives and Evaluating the difference between Policy and Experience for Institutionalised Veterans with Mental Disabilities, 1924-1931', *First World War Studies*, 6(1), 2015, 37-55; Monika Barr, 'Prosthesis for the Body and for the Soul: The Origins of Guide Dog Provision for Blind Veterans in Interwar Germany', *First World War Studies*, 6(1), 2015, 81-98; Martina Salvante, '"Thanks to the Great War the blind gets the recognition of his ability to act": The Rehabilitation of Blinded Servicemen in Florence', *First World War Studies*, 6(1), 2015, 21-35.

46 Joanna Bourke, *Dismembering the Male: Men's Bodies, Britain, and the Great War*, University of Chicago Press, 1996; Peter Leese, *Shell Shock: Traumatic Neurosis and the British Soldiers of the First World War*, Palgrave, New York, 2002; Jeffery S. Reznick, *John Galsworthy and Disabled Soldiers of the Great War: With an Illustrated Selection of his Writings*, Manchester University Press, 2009; Fiona Reid, *Broken Men: Shell Shock, Treatment and Recovery in Britain, 1914-1930*, Continuum, London, 2010; Jessica Meyer, *Men of War: Masculinity and the First World War in Britain*, Palgrave Macmillan, Basingstoke, 2009; Emily Mayhew, *Wounded: From Battlefield to Blighty, 1914-1918*, Thorpe, Leicester, 2014.

47 Serge Durflinger, *Veterans with a Vision: Canada's War Blinded in Peace and War*, University of British Columbia Press, Vancouver, 2010.

48 Joy Damousi, *The Labour of Loss*, Cambridge University Press, 1999, 65-102; Marina Larsson, *Shattered ANZACS: Living with the Scars of War*, University of New South Wales Press, Sydney, 2009.

49 Alan Wakefield and Simon Moody, *Under the Devil's Eye: The British Military Experience in Macedonia 1915-18*, Pen & Sword Military, Barnsley, 2011 (orig. 2004).

50 Alan Palmer, *The Gardeners of Salonika*, Andre Deutshe, London, 1965.

51 Nur Bilge Criss, *Istanbul under Allied Occupation, 1918-1923*, Brill, London, 1999.

52 Alan Mikhail, 'Unleashing the Beast: Animals, Energy, and the Economy of Labour in Ottoman Egypt', *The American Historical Review*, 2013, 118(2), 317-48.

53 Mikhail, 'Unleashing the Beast'. I agree with Mikhail that the terms 'human' and 'animal' are inadequate, simply because 'human' refers to one species and 'animal' to many, yet I too use these words in their general meaning.

54 This conference title reflects this: 'War Horses of the World', School of Oriental and African Studies, University of London, 3-4 May 2014.

55 Richard St Barbe Baker, *Horse Sense: Horses in War and Peace*, St Paul, London, 1962; J. Edward Chamberlin, *Horse: How the Horse Has Shaped Civilizations*, A.A. Knopf, Toronto, 2006; see Chapter 4.

56 Gavin Robinson, *Horses, People and Parliament in the English Civil War*, Ashgate, Farnham, 2012.

57 Gervase Phillips, 'Writing Horses into American Civil War History', *War in History*, 20(2), 2013, 160-81.

58 Paul Louis Johnson, *Horses of the German Army in World War II*, Schiffer Military History, Atglen, PA, 2006.

59 John Singleton, 'Britain's Military Use of Horses, 1914-1918', *Past & Present*, 139, May 1993, 178-203; Simon Butler, *The War Horses: The Tragic Fate of a Million Horses Sacrificed in the First World War*, Halsgrove, Wellington, 2011; Jill Mather, *War Horses: Hoof Prints in Time: Amazing True Stories of Heroic Australian Walers and New Zealand Horses 1914-1918*, Jill Mather, 2012.

60 For a discussion on the perception and representation of the army transport mule during the Great War see Andrekos Varnava, 'The Vagaries and Value of the Army Transport Mule in the British Army during the Great War', *Historical Research*, forthcoming 2017.

61 Singleton, 'Britain's Military Use of Horses, 1914-1918', 178-203.

62 Ibid, 202.

63 Captain Sidney Galtrey, *The Horse and the War*, Country Life, London, 1918, 16.
64 Singleton, 'Britain's Military Use of Horses, 1914–1918', 203.
65 Savage and Munro, 'Carrier Corps Recruitment in the British East Africa Protectorate 1914–1918', 313–42.
66 Brian C. Fawcett, 'The Chinese Labour Corps in France, 1917–1921', *Journal of the Hong Kong Branch of the Royal Asiatic Society*, 40, 2000, 33–111.
67 Singha, 'Finding Labor from India for the War in Iraq', 412–45.
68 Catriona Pennell, *A Kingdom United: Popular Responses to the Outbreak of the First World War in Britain and Ireland*, Oxford University Press, 2012.
69 The focus has been on their contribution rather than their experiences. See Geoffrey R. Codrington, *The Territorial Army*, Sifton Praed, London, 1938; Peter Dennis, *The Territorial Army, 1906–1940*, Royal Historical Society, Woodbridge, Suffolk, 1987.
70 McCartney, *Citizen Soldiers*.
71 Michael Durey, 'South London's "Age-Fudgers": Kitchener's Under-Age Volunteers', *The London Journal*, 40(2), 2015, 147–70.
72 John Moreton Osborne, *The Voluntary Recruiting Movement in Britain, 1914–1916*, Garland, New York, 1982.
73 Ibid., quoting from *Labour Leader*, 29 October 1914, 83.
74 Nicholas Mansfield, *English Farmworkers and Local Patriotism, 1900–1930*, Ashgate, Aldershot, 2001, 79–96.
75 Eric Richards, 'How Did Poor People Emigrate from the British Isles to Australia in the Nineteenth Century?' *Journal of British Studies*, 32, July 1993, 250–79 (250).
76 Diana M. Henderson, *Highland Soldier: A Social Study of the Highland Regiments, 1820–1920*, J. Donald, Edinburgh, 1989; Andrew MacKillop, 'For king and country? The Highland soldiers' motivation and identity', in S. Murdoch and A. MacKillop (eds), *Fighting for Identity: Scottish Military Experiences, 1550–1900*, Brill, Leiden, 2002, 185–212.
77 See Costas Kyrris, *Peaceful Co-existence in Cyprus under British Rule (1878–1959) and after Independence*, PIO, Nicosia, 1977; Yiannis Papadakis, 'The Politics of Memory and of Forgetting in Cyprus', *Journal of Mediterranean Studies*, 1993, 139–54; Yiannis Papadakis, 'Greek Cypriot Narratives of History and Collective Identity: Nationalism as a Contested Process', *American Ethnologist*, 25(3), 1998, 149–65; Yiannis Papadakis, 'Nation, Narrative and Commemoration: Political Ritual in Divided Cyprus', *History and Anthropology*, 14(3), 2003, 253–70; Rebecca Bryant, *Imagining the Modern: The Cultures of Nationalism in Cyprus*, I.B. Taurus, London, 2004; Yiannis Papadakis, *Echoes From the Dead Zone: Across the Cyprus Divide*, I.B. Taurus, London, 2005; Michalis N. Michael, 'The Unchanging "Turkish Rule", the "Fair Ottoman Administration" and the Ottoman Period in the History of Cyprus', in Michalis Michael, Matthias Kappler and Eftihios Gavriel (eds), *Ottoman Cyprus: A Collection of Studies on History and Culture*, Harrassowitz Verlag, Wiesbaden, 2009, 9–24; Varnava and Michael, 'Archbishop-*Ethnarchs* since 1767'.
78 Daniel Gorman, *Imperial Citizenship: Empire and the Question of Belonging*, Manchester University Press, 2006.
79 Sukanya Banerjee, *Becoming Imperial Citizens: Indians in the Late-Victorian Empire*, Duke University Press, Durham, NC, 2010.
80 See Varnava, *British Imperialism in Cyprus, 1878–1915*, 152–201; Alexis Rappas, *Cyprus in the Thirties: British Colonial Rule and the Roots of the Cyprus Conflict*, I.B. Tauris, London, 2014, 88–122.
81 See Andrekos Varnava, 'The State of Cypriot Minorities: Cultural Diversity, Internal-Exclusion and the Cyprus "Problem"', *The Cyprus Review*, 22(2), 2010, 205–18.
82 Kyrris, *Peaceful Co-existence in Cyprus under British Rule*.
83 See Yiannis Papadakis, Nicos Peristianis and Gisela Welz (eds), *Divided Cyprus: Modernity, History, and an Island in Conflict*, University of Indiana Press, Bloomington, 2006; see my review, *The Cyprus Review*, 18(2), 2006, 167–72; Varnava, 'The State of Cypriot Minorities'.

84 Andrekos Varnava and Christalla Yakinthou, 'Cyprus: Political Modernity and Structures of Democracy in a Divided Island', in John Loughlin, Frank Hendriks and Anders Lidström (eds), *The Oxford Handbook of Local and Regional Democracy in Europe*, Oxford University Press, 2011, 455–77.
85 Eugen Weber, *Peasants into Frenchman: The Mobilization of Rural France, 1879–1914*, Stanford University Press, 1976.
86 See the *Journal of Peasant Studies* and the work of Tom Brass and Henry Bernstein.
87 See G.C. Spivak, 'Can the Subaltern Speak?' in C. Nelson and L. Grossberg (eds), *Marxism and the Interpretation of Culture*, Macmillan, Basingstoke, 1988; V. Lal, 'Review: Subaltern Studies and its Critics: Debates Over Indian History', *History and Theory*, 40(1), 2001, 135–48; D. Chakrabarty, *Habitations of Modernity: Essays in the Wake of Subaltern Studies*, University of Chicago Press, 2002; H. Singh, 'Caste, Class and Peasant Agency in Subaltern Studies Discourse: Revisionist Historiography, Elite Ideology', *Journal of Peasant Studies*, 30(1), 2002, 91–134.
88 Varnava, *British Imperialism in Cyprus, 1878–1915*, 22–4, 152–201; Andrekos Varnava, 'Sophronios III, 1865–1900: The Last of the "Old" and the First of the "New" Archbishop-Ethnarchs?' in Varnava and Michael (eds), *The Archbishop's of Cyprus in the Modern Age*, 106–47.
89 Milica Bakic-Hayden, 'Nesting Orientalisms: The Case of Former Yugoslavia', *Slavic Review*, 54(4), 1995, 917–31.
90 Maria Todorova, *Imagining the Balkans*, Oxford University Press, 1997.
91 Spivak, 'Can the Subaltern Speak?' 283.
92 Ibid., 271–313.
93 Homi Bhabha, *The Location of Culture*, Routledge, London, 2008, 5.
94 Jay Winter, *Sites of Memory, Sites of Mourning: The Great War in European Cultural History*, Cambridge University Press, 1995; Winter, *Remembering War*.
95 Paul Fussell, *The Great War and Modern Memory*, Oxford University Press, 1975; Angela Gaffney, *Aftermath: Remembering the Great War in Wales*, University of Wales Press, Cardiff, 2000; George Robb, *British Culture and the First World War*, Palgrave, Basingstoke, 2002; Ray Westlake, *Remembering the Great War in Gloucestershire & Hertfordshire*, Brewin Books, Studley, Warwickshire, 2002.
96 Alistair Thomson, *Anzac Memories: Living with the Legend*, Oxford University Press, 1994 (rev. 2013); Simon Miles, *Anzac Memorial, Adelaide, South Australia*, Workskil Inc., Adelaide, 1995.
97 Michael J.K. Walsh and Andrekos Varnava, 'The Great War and the British Empire: Culture and Memory', in Walsh and Varnava (eds), *Australia and the Great War: Identity, Memory and Mythology*, Melbourne University Press, 2016, 1–22; Myron J. Echenberg, *Colonial Conscripts: The Tirailleurs Sénégalais in French West Africa, 1857–1960*, J. Curry, London, 1991; Smith, *Jamaican Volunteers in the First World War*.

CHAPTER TWO

British Cyprus, 1878–1918: from backwater to bustling war base

A few days before the outbreak of the Great War, the officers of the German battlecruiser *Goeben* had lunched at the English club at Famagusta.[1] But by the time the war had started the *Goeben* had left Cypriot waters and there were 'no German submarines in the [eastern] Mediterranean in those early days' of the war.[2] The war impacted Cyprus in other ways, but it was not until mid-1916 that the island started to play a strategic role. This was the first time it had done so after the British occupation in 1878, even though the island had been occupied for strategic reasons.[3] This chapter has two aims: first to explore the development of Cypriot society from its late Ottoman period and the first decades of British rule in order to understand the conditions that pushed and pulled so many Cypriot men to enlist in the Cypriot Mule Corps; and second to provide an overview of the impact of the war and the role of Cyprus in it beyond the Cypriot Mule Corps.

By the end of Ottoman rule there were deep class/social cleavages in Cypriot society across the urban and rural divide and among religious communities. These divisions continued during British rule, yet were less pronounced by 1914.[4] They impacted on the political and socio-economic conditions, on local relations with the British colonialists and between the two main religious groups. British rule 'modernised' Cyprus, facilitating significant population growth, yet its inconsequence to British imperialism and strategy in the region meant little economic development, with the corresponding lack of employment for the growing population. When emigration for men of military age was banned in 1916 to expedite enlistment into the Cypriot Mule Corps, such men had little alternative. The Cypriot Mule Corps was a mammoth undertaking for the Cypriot government and a significant event for Cypriots given the numbers that served, yet Cyprus contributed to the war in other ways. Cyprus attained some strategic significance from mid-1916 as a bustling military, humanitarian and provisions base connected to the 'Eastern Campaigns', which impacted on the island.

Cyprus, 1800s to 1914

Society in Ottoman Cyprus

During Ottoman rule Cypriot society had greater socio-economic and sociopolitical cleavages than religious or ethnic. Collective identities were based upon religion, which is not the same as upon ethnicity. Some secular elites developed an ethnic identity, but they did not unite behind this with the clergy until the eve of the Great War. Religious differences between Muslims and Eastern Orthodox Christians did not preclude integration within classes, cutting across religion. During Ottoman rule there was little ethnic division and disturbances were mostly driven by economic inequalities. Thus, class, geography (urban–rural divide), and religion determined identities.[5]

The elites in Ottoman Cyprus were composed of both Muslims and Christians. Cyprus was incorporated into the Ottoman imperial system in 1571 (after centuries of Frankish and Venetian rule), meaning the implantation of the Ottoman civil and military bureaucracy. The leading clergy of the Eastern Orthodox Church gained much power because the Orthodox Church replaced the Catholic Church as the only recognised Christian authority.[6] The Cypriot Orthodox Church was autonomous of the Ecumenical Patriarchate in Constantinople and the three Apostolic Patriarchates in Jerusalem, Antioch, and Alexandria, giving it religious and political independence and authority. The Ottoman *millet* system, which allowed for religious autonomy so long as *millet* leaders ensured the loyalty of their people (*dhimmi*) to the government, allowed the Cypriot archbishop and the higher clergy to become secular as well as spiritual leaders, with the archbishop becoming the *ethnarch*. So the Eastern Orthodox Church elite were willingly co-opted into the ruling class and their power derived from the Ottoman imperial system. Within the context of this 'contract' they received power in exchange for guaranteeing the loyalty of their people, the lower-class Christians. They guaranteed this loyalty by either suppressing revolts led by the lower class or representing them to the imperial government during droughts, locust plagues and famine. Thus, Christian and Muslim elites relied on each other for power and control over the Cypriot masses.[7]

The Christian and Muslim lower classes also relied on each other and were integrated. They shared economic and social hardships, brought on by droughts, bad harvests, locust plagues, and a lack of technological advancement and government and private investment in industries and infrastructure. Together they opposed high taxes in memorials and revolts. They also shared a folklore, a commonly spoken language (i.e. Cypriot Greek), cultural events (even religious), and even intermarried.[8] The increase in mixed villages exemplifies integration: the 1832 Ottoman Census recorded 172 mixed villages;[9] in 1858 the British consul estimated 239;[10] in 1891, in the second British census, there were 346 out of 702 villages.[11]

Ottoman Cypriot society was divided along class/social lines as follows: (1) the Ottoman Muslim elites; (2) the Eastern Orthodox Christian elites, mostly the higher clergy and government employees; (3) the Muslim peasant and labouring classes; and (4) the Christian labouring and peasant classes. The problem with this typology is that the Christian elites sometimes exercised more power than the Muslim elites, who were not a consistent staple and often relied on the local knowledge of the Christians. Although when the Christian elites were considered to have broken 'the contract' and to be fermenting revolt, as they were falsely accused of doing in 1821 in support of the 'Greek' revolt, the imperial government agreed to the execution of leading Cypriot Orthodox Christian elites.[12] Ultimately the relations between the two classes (upper and lower) were far more fraught than what they were between the different religions.

The Cypriot Orthodox *millet* was not a Greek or Greek Orthodox Christian *millet*. The Cypriot Eastern Orthodox millet was indigenous to the island and independent of the patriarchs and the ecumenical patriarch. Cypriot Eastern Orthodox Christians continued to refer to themselves as *Romiee* (Romans), a term used by all Eastern Orthodox Christians after the spread of Christianity to the Roman Empire (because to call oneself a Greek denoted paganism),[13] yet there was also a regional differentiation from other *Romiee*. In 1868, ten years before British rule started, the Archbishop of Cyprus, Sophronios III, sent an autobiographical note to the Jerusalem Theological School, stating that 'my homeland is Cyprus and my parents are Orthodox Christians of the Eastern dogma'.[14] Sophronios characterised his identity according to his geographic space (Cyprus) and his religion (his Eastern Orthodox Christianity). His identity reflected his political and social position as an Ottoman subject of the high Eastern Orthodox clergy in an independent church, the geographical isolation of the island and his religion. Thus he was an Ottoman subject of some prominence (i.e. ruling classes) and the leader of his 'flock'. Neither Greece nor being Greek was mentioned, although he was aware of the rise of ethno-nationalism and the 'Great Idea' from his years in Smyrna and Athens. Sophronios remained devoted to the identity that reflected his understanding of Christianity (Eastern) and his homeland (Cyprus), rather than an imagined and imposed one from Greece.[15]

The disconnection between the Christian upper and lower classes was political and socio-economic. Numerous monasteries were constructed or significantly redeveloped during the Ottoman period in rural areas, for example St Minas near Kato Drys in Larnaca, St Panteleimonas at Myrtou, Kyrenia, St Nicholas of the Cats at Akrotiri, Limassol, St Thekla at Mosfiloti, Larnaca, and others.[16] In the nineteenth century the church also took the lead in running schools in the towns and some regional centres for Orthodox Christians. Yet its power in collecting and imposing taxes resulted in a dilution of religiosity as the peasant and labouring classes saw them as overlords.[17] Some Christians (originally mostly Roman Catholics) were 'linobambaki' (linen-cottons): publicly Muslim and privately Christian, developing their own hybrid religion, confusing practices, traditions and rituals of both.[18]

By the last decades of Ottoman rule, the rise of a middle class of merchants and professionals disturbed Ottoman Cypriot society. Many of the merchants and professionals, namely money-lenders, advocates, doctors and teachers, were 'Hellenised': some were Cypriots educated abroad and introduced to Greek national identity and the project of the Greek state for a 'Greater Greece'; or Greek citizens, especially from the Ionian Islands.[19] Yet not all foreign-educated Cypriots were Hellenised, Sophronios being an example.[20] The development of Greek nationalism in Cyprus was elitist. For it to resonate with the majority of the Orthodox Christians it needed institutionalisation at various levels, especially in education, and a liberal constitution so the Hellenised professional and middle classes could work in it. British rule provided such an environment, so much so that by 1914 the British had aided the Greek nationalist Bishop of Kitium to win the disputed (since the death of Sophronios in 1900) archiepiscopal throne.[21]

These changes and challenges to the previous order help explain the passive role of the political elites in recruitment efforts, yet were not developed enough to have a significant influence on the formation of the Cypriot Mule Corps. The British understood that for the majority of the population (i.e. peasantry and unskilled labourers) religion and nationalism would not be a barrier to volunteering, and targeted them appropriately.

The impact of British rule on socio-economic conditions
In June 1878 Lord Beaconsfield's government demanded and received from the Ottoman Sultan, Abdul Hamid II, the right to occupy and administer Cyprus. Beaconsfield and Lord Salisbury, the Foreign

Secretary, wanted to balance Russian gains from the Russo–Ottoman War of 1877–8, which they perceived as threatening British financial, economic and strategic interests in the Ottoman Empire, Egypt and India. In the Anglo–Turkish Convention they promised to militarily support the Ottoman Empire if Russia ever threatened it again and to do so they needed to make Cyprus into a place of arms.[22] Beaconsfield's government justified selecting Cyprus against the advice of the army and navy experts, who wanted Stampalia, because they believed Cyprus was the right size and location to base an army, it had a harbour (at Famagusta) which they would make world-class, plentiful water, an agreeable climate and docile Christian and Muslim inhabitants. Cyprus would be an experiment in how British modernity and Occidentalism could transform a premodern Oriental Ottoman space into an oasis of enlightened government, with its people bathed in the wealth generated by British industry and investment.[23]

The British confidence in 'renewing' Cyprus to its 'formerly glorious days' was misplaced. The island was unhealthy, with marshy grounds and filthy towns, it lacked water, and had virtually no internal and external communications. Cyprus was as mythical an 'El Dorado' as the Amazonian one.[24] Beaconsfield's government knew it, indefinitely postponing the redevelopment of Famagusta Harbour. Then the Liberal opposition, which had strongly opposed the occupation of Cyprus, won the 1880 election and transferred the island from the Foreign to the Colonial Office, slowing further British development. They slashed the public works budget, while Cypriot revenue was hampered by the imposition of a tribute to the Ottoman government that the British retained in lieu of Ottoman Crimean War debt.[25] Yet British rule changed Cypriot political and socio-economic conditions and set Cyprus on the road towards modernisation, even if this road was long and bumpy.

British rule encouraged and even supported the importing of rival Greek and Turkish nationalisms into the island. The Liberal government introduced a legislative council with a local majority and rejected the introduction of English-language instruction alongside the Greek and Turkish languages because they considered the Cypriots, at least the Orthodox Christians, as Europeans that belonged to the broader Greek family and enlightened enough to develop without English. This contradicted the views of most men on the ground, some of whom considered the Cypriots as their own group. It also ignored the Muslim community. Clearly for the British, Cyprus, unlike most other British possessions, was primarily 'Christian' and thus perceived as being, at least partly, 'European' and would be treated within the framework of modernity. This eventually allowed for the development of Greek (and Turkish) nationalism after 1910, when the decade-long dispute over who would succeed Sophronios resulted (through British intervention) in the victory for the Greek nationalists and the uniting of the two sides behind *enosis*. Their wish was granted, but rejected by their 'mother' during the Great War.[26]

The nature of British colonial rule in Cyprus and the imperial status of the island as a backwater had two pivotal results: (1) the limited extension of political modernity, which allowed for the development of a new nationalised, specifically Hellenised (and later Turkish), Cypriot elite, which the British did not check because they considered Cyprus a backwater and the Christians as Greeks;[27] (2) the British improvements in internal communications, public hygiene, and medical services and practises, resulted in a significant increase in the population from 186,173 in 1881 to 274,108 in 1911, a 47% increase, which meant change across Cypriot society especially in relation to living standards, occupations and the nature and character of the middle and lower classes.

With the exception of the small professional and merchant classes, most Cypriots worked in agriculture, either as peasants or labourers, or sometimes as both, depending on the season. Some agricultural labourers worked on large estates, *chefliks*.[28] Each village had its own pastures and, depending on location, its own woodlands for fuel. The Karpas peninsula grew cereals and summer crops, and most notably cotton and tobacco. In the non-irrigated low-lying Mesaoria (between the Troodos and Kyrenia Mountain ranges) cereals were primarily cultivated, while in the flood-irrigated areas of the Mesaoria summer crops were also grown. In the Paphos and Limassol Districts, where rocky hills predominated, vines were cultivated. In the *Kochino-chorka* (red-villages) of the Famagusta District, where a terracotta-coloured clay soil prevailed, potatoes, colocasi (taro) and onions were grown. Only in the well-irrigated areas west of Limassol, south of Famagusta town, and in Lefka, Morphou and Lapithos, could citrus and pomegranate be grown.[29] Harvest and therefore profit depended on the climate, which often turned bad, with frequent droughts and locust plagues. Although British reforms improved agricultural production and conditions for the peasants, Nicholas Lanitis, who reported on rural indebtedness in Cyprus in the 1940s, argued that in the early twentieth century there was still little fertile land under irrigation, little knowledge in modern cultivation methods and not enough credit available beyond the usurer.[30] Usury, being unregulated by the Ottoman and British governments (at least until the Usury (Farmers) Law of April 1919, which made it illegal to impose interest on loans to farmers above 12% per annum),[31] meant very high interest rates and the obligatory sale of land, dwellings and/or animals to repay loans.

British modernising reforms increased life expectancy and lowered infant mortality rates by improving public health and medical facilities; securing food supplies from locust destruction; and by developing internal communications, allowing for faster access to trade and medical facilities. The last two developments have been discussed elsewhere,[32] but little has been written about public health and medical facilities. British reforms to eradicate various diseases met with some success, yet in the absence of studies comparing policies and outcomes across the British Empire it is not clear how this success measures comparatively. With malaria Cyprus compares favourably with its neighbours: it was totally eradicated in Cyprus by 1949;[33] in Palestine by 1947;[34] Italy not until 1962;[35] and Greece in 1974.[36] This, of course, has no bearing on efforts to eradicate diseases during the first decades of British rule, although the evidence suggests that the British introduced important measures. A report in 1879 revealed that the diseases in and around the town of Famagusta included typhoid, smallpox and malaria, and advised that much work was needed to prevent the formation of marshes, which were blamed for the prevalence of these diseases.[37] Another report costed the recommendations to remedy the insalubrity of Famagusta at over £100,000.[38] By this time the Cypriot government had created a medical department and employed medical officers at the six districts. Within three years of British rule, hospitals and/or dispensaries had been established and/or pre-existing ones redeveloped in all the district towns, though some relied on voluntary contributions.[39] In 1892 a new government hospital was opened in Nicosia, while the Cyprus Society, a group of High-Church Anglicans in Britain, opened a new district hospital in Kyrenia, which eventually came under government control because of little funding. By 1914 the island had a government-administered central hospital in Nicosia, which included consumptive wards, a dispensary and a maternity block,[40] and others in Famagusta, Larnaca, Limassol, Paphos and Kyrenia. The rise in the number of doctors reflects the improved medical facilities, with 27 in 1891 rising to 70 in 1911.[41] The colonial medical department embarked upon vigorous and partially successful campaigns to alleviate the 'fevers', trachoma and leprosy. They implemented an extensive campaign to vaccinate and revaccinate as many people as possible and planted Australian eucalyptus to deal with the stagnant waters.[42] Yet malarial fever was still common. High Commissioner Sendall informed Lord Ripon, the Colonial Secretary, in October 1894 that he and his party could not conduct affairs because they were ill with malaria after returning from the Paphos District.[43] Initiatives were also undertaken to alleviate blindness caused by trachoma ophthalmia, with a successful reduction from 2,238 cases in

1881 to 1,415 in 1911, and syphilis and gonorrhoea, although many did not seek treatment for these diseases because of stigma and conservative attitudes.[44]

The first major imperial investment occurred when Joseph Chamberlain was Colonial Secretary from 1895 to 1903. He managed to convince a parsimonious treasury to offer generous loans to the underdeveloped parts of the British Empire.[45] Chamberlain, with the support of High Commissioner Sendall, wanted to encourage agriculture and sericulture, redevelop internal and external communications and undertake irrigation works with the £314,000 loan under the 1899 Colonial Loans Act: £60,000 for irrigation in the Mesaoria; £124,000 for the redevelopment of Famagusta Harbour, completed in June 1906; and £130,000 for the construction of a railway between Nicosia and Famagusta, finished in October 1905.[46] These works created new local employment (both temporary and permanent) and contributed to the increase in agricultural production and trade by 1914. The tonnage of imports and exports at Famagusta Harbour increased from 45,752 in 1905–6 to 95,032 in 1911–12. To be sure it took the railway until 1913–14 to post a profit and it never kept up with the loan interest and the sinking fund charges, yet the tonnage of goods to and from Famagusta Harbour on the railway steadily increased.[47]

The 'inconsequential possession' was never more felt than with the lack of concrete legislative reforms to facilitate economic growth, particularly finance for all sections of Cypriot society. For example, the British introduced the Companies Act of 1862, which was amended in 1900 and 1907 and then consolidated in 1908, to most overseas possessions by 1917, but Cyprus (along with Bermuda, Gibraltar, Malta, Newfoundland, The Seychelles, and Egypt) was left out.[48]

An analysis of the increasing population and where it was increasing, geographically and across the rural and urban divide, allows for an understanding of the socio-economic changes. The censuses for 1881, 1891, 1901 and 1911 show a significant increase in population, from 186,173, to 209,286 (rise of 12.75%), to 237,023 (13.25%) and 274,108 (15.65%), respectively.[49] British rule created the right conditions for the Cypriot population to increase: life expectancy and birth rates rose, while infant mortality rates fell because of improved hygiene and medical care. But to understand the implications of the nature of this growth it is important to understand at what rate the population increased across the six districts, and across the urban and rural spectrum.

Famagusta district had the most population growth between 1891 and 1901 at 17.1%, and between 1901 and 1911 at 20.66%, growing from 41,423 in 1891 to 58,530 in 1911. The town (Old Famagusta and Varosha) grew 23.85% between 1881 and 1891, down to 13.6% between 1891 and 1901, and by a huge 39.3% between 1901 and 1911, with the population rising from 3,367 in 1891 to 5,327 in 1911.[50] There are two reasons to account for these fluctuating levels of growth: (1) a factor in the growth of 23.85% between 1881 and 1891 was the famine that had gripped the Karpas Peninsula in the late 1880s, necessitating internal migration from those rural areas to the town, while the improvement in rural conditions by the mid-1890s saw some movement from the town back to the rural areas; (2) the incredible rise of nearly 40% between 1901 and 1911 must be attributed to the various works in and around the town, necessitating much local labour, as well as to an increase in trade towards the end of the decade owing to more production and better communications (reflected in the significant rise in revenues, from an average of £197,889 between 1899 and 1903, to an average of £271,851 between 1904 and 1908, increasing further to £318,539 between 1909 and 1913).[51] The breakdown across rural areas also tells an interesting story. In the 1901 Census the increase in population in certain rural areas (where the population was above 1,000) in the ten-year period was mostly around the district average of 17.1%, such as Trikomo 16.7%, Marathovouno 18.4%, Vatili 19.4%, Akanthou 19.1% and Asha 16.3%, with Lefkoniko being the lowest at 13.2%, with the exceptions being the last two villages at the tip of the Karpas Peninsula, Rizokarpaso at 32.6% and Yialousa at 41.5%.[52] These sharp increases for the last two cases can be attributed to former inhabitants returning after the famine: indeed Rizokarpaso had a drop in population of 7.2% between 1881 and 1891. Another reason for the rise was the British investment in the sericulture and tobacco industries in these regions.[53] From 1905 to 1910 exporters of cotton, silk cocoons and tobacco made good profits.[54] The population growth of the Karpas continued between 1901 and 1911, despite the massive increase in the population of Famagusta town, with Rizokarpaso on the district average (which was 20.66%) at 20.1% and Yialousa above it at 23.84%.[55] This explains the high enlistment of these places in the Cypriot Mule Corps.

The increase in population of the other districts tells a different story. Nicosia district ranked second in 1901 and fourth in 1911. The growth was around the national average (13.25% and 15.65%, respectively) at 15.6% and 14.3%, respectively, but in 1901 it was primarily in or around the town, with Nicosia town increasing by 23% from 1891, the highest of the towns. Kaimakli, today a suburb of Nicosia, grew by 27.4%. But in 1911 the increase in Nicosia town was the lowest of all the towns, at 8.8%, with significant growth (likely internal migration) in nearby villages, large villages and regional centres, with Kaimakli growing 22%, Strovolos 24%, Athienou 22%, Palaiochorio 21% and the Muslim village of Lourougina by 18.2%. Therefore the trend in relation to Nicosia district was in the reverse to that of Famagusta, excepting the Karpas: more urban growth between 1891 and 1901, and more rural growth between 1901 and 1911.[56] There were two reasons for this: the expansion of Nicosia towards Kaimakli (which had a railway branch) and Strovolos (near Government House) can be characterised as semi-urban sprawl owing to the smallness of the town and its proximity to Kaimakli and Strovolos; and better agricultural prospects saw people moving to places between Nicosia and Famagusta, such as Athienou, Dhali and Lourougina. These places were not the main recruiting grounds for the Mule Corps.

Proportionally, Kyrenia was the most important district for recruitment in the Mule Corps, yet it was the smallest in population and land. It ranked third in population growth between 1901 and 1911 (rising 17.5%). The villages with 1,000 or more inhabitants, Lapithos, one of the largest in the island, and Karavas, grew well below the district average, at 5.3% and 0.8% in 1901, and 7.3% and 6.4% in 1911, reflecting the growth in the town which rose from a 9.8% increase between 1881 and 1891, 16.9% from 1891 to 1901, and 29.2% from 1901 to 1911.[57] Unemployment drove the movement from Lapithos, Karavas and other villages to the town and this was reflected in the high numbers that enlisted from these places in the Mule Corps.

The other districts show similar connections between their population ebbs and flows and enlistment into the Cypriot Mule Corps, although that they did not have the same access to the rail transport that the three other districts had. Limassol district followed a similar pattern in growth to Famagusta, but on a smaller scale, with enlistment into the Mule Corps driven by the presence of the British garrison at Polymedia. Paphos and Larnaca consistently had the lowest growth, with both lacking agricultural land and its people migrating to other districts, namely Famagusta, for work. Paphos was the poorest and most isolated of the districts.[58] Despite the lack of communications, all these districts significantly contributed to the Mule Corps.

Population growth meant more housing, more jobs, a greater diversification in employment and a greater demand for finance. It also meant that more jobs needed creating. During the first four decades of British rule, most Cypriots remained small-scale cultivators, herders and labourers, although with the rise in population and its redistribution across the urban and rural spectrum, other careers became feasible. The 1891 Census was the first time that occupations were counted. Out of the population of 209,286, 68,010 (32.5%) stated an occupation, in addition to 35,748 (17%) claiming to be landowners as well as having a second occupation. At the top of the list of occupations were farmers with 15,605, followed by scholars and students at 13,196, labourers 8,476, herders 4,705, domestic servants 3,745, weavers 3,424 and shoemakers 1,840. In the 1901 Census, 86,905 people, out of 237,023 (36.7%) stated an occupation, in addition to 35,338 (15%) stating that they were landowners, in comparison to 1911 which saw an increase to 103,352 stating an occupation, in addition to 44,055 claiming to be landowners as well as a second occupation, while only 631 stated that they were only landowners. The increase in employed people seems commensurate with the population increase, but the increase to landowners seems disproportionate, and must be due to more people owning land or not stating in the 1901 Census that they were landowners as well as having another occupation. In the 1901 Census 14,642 claimed to be farmers, but in 1911 it doubled to 29,363. This increase in farming and land ownership was also reflected in the significant increase in agricultural labourers and ploughmen, at 16,080 in 1911, while the figures in 1901 show 1,162 ploughmen and 12,862 labourers (in 1911 2,000 were also counted as 'day labourers').[59] The increase in farming and agricultural labouring was reflected in the decrease in domestic service from 4,050 in 1901 to 2,532 in 1911. This meant that more people needed finance to achieve their dream of owning property, enough animals, farming equipment or a spinning wheel, evidenced by the increase in clerks from 282 in 1901 to 1,218 in 1911, bank employees from 11 in 1901 to 57 in 1911 and 25 bankers or brokers. This increase in the private sector was mirrored in the government sector, with the civil service growing from 500 in 1891 to 847 in 1911.[60]

The development of savings and cooperative banks before 1914 reflected these increases in population and occupations, and was an important step in mitigating the social and economic issues that arose out of them. In January 1899 a group of Greek Cypriot political elites, headed by Ioannis Economides, a Hellenised Cypriot nationalist and a merciless usurer, started the Nicosia Savings Bank. Based on Italian Popular Banks, it aimed to mobilise the savings of small depositors, attracting deposits from the middle- and lower-class urbanites in and around towns and regional centres, mostly housewives, shopkeepers and clerks, and investing into the private sector, especially small businesses. Other savings banks followed.[61] The establishment of the Nicosia Savings Bank prompted the Cypriot government to pass the Government Savings Bank Law in 1900.[62] By 1903 each of the principal towns had a Government Savings Bank, but the private banks offered better rates and the Government Savings Bank did not lend to the private sector, investing its funds in the London money market, so by 1929 it had a mere £841 in deposits, while the Bank of Cyprus (formerly, Nicosia Savings Bank) had £122,000.[63] The establishment of savings banks provided the financial security and opportunities for the expansion of the professional and middle classes – groups not especially represented in the Mule Corps – but also helped finance the cooperative movement.

The development of the cooperative movement aimed to help cash- and credit-starved peasants and labourers. The first cooperative society was founded in Lefkonico, Famagusta, in November 1909, named 'Lefkoniko Communal Bank', under the directorship of Economides. Its charter stipulated that its members (initially 23) were jointly responsible for the liabilities (without any limit) of the society. The bank provided loans to new members with credit at reasonable terms.[64] Economides figured that there was more money to make (by comparison to usury) by making credit more readily available and on better (though not overly generous) terms, through loaning the money of small savers (invested in the Savings Banks) to farmers through the cooperative. By loaning more at relatively high interest rates to more people, he would increase his profits. He established the cooperative society as another source of credit, beginning the important step of ending the stranglehold of the usurer. Soon, other societies were created and these became regulated in 1914 with the Cooperative Credit Societies Law.[65] Yet the cooperative movement was still in its infancy and peasants saw the Mule Corps as a golden opportunity for fast money.

The British arrival slowly 'modernised' Cyprus, even if this was inconsistent, especially politically.[66] Important improvements were in public hygiene and health, which led to the rapid population growth, which in turn resulted in a surplus of the lower classes looking for work by 1914. The Cypriot Mule Corps came along at exactly the right moment for them.

Cyprus, 1914–18: beyond the Cypriot Mule Corps

The service of the Cypriot Mule Corps from summer 1916 until April 1920 was not the only role played by Cypriots during the Great War. This section outlines this wider contribution, since there are important political and socio-economic implications from this on the Cypriot Mule Corps.

From a backwater to a pawn

By the end of October 1914 the Ottoman government of the Committee of Union and Progress had joined the Central Powers. On 5 November

Whitehall reacted by annexing Cyprus.[67] This meant that the British Empire and Cyprus were at war with the Ottoman Empire.

From a strategic point of view, the island remained insignificant for at least the first 18 months of the war, when it was primarily a pawn. When the war began in August 1914 there were less than 150 troops forming the garrison: one company of infantry and a few details of the Army Service and Army Medical Corps, all deriving from the Egyptian Command.[68] This reflected the strategic inconsequence of the island. At the time, the military police (*Zaptieh*) were responsible for internal security. C.W. Orr, the Chief Secretary from July 1911 to May 1917, claimed in the annual report for 1914–15 that the Ottoman entry into the war and the annexation 'created a new situation for Cyprus, but in practise the results were little felt'.[69] He was not wrong. For the first 18 months most British military and political planners saw Cyprus as insignificant, of value only as a pawn that could be ceded to Greece in exchange for that country joining the war. The British acknowledged that in a war against another major power they were unlikely to defend Cyprus. In 1912 the General Staff and Field Marshall John French, Chief of Imperial General Staff, reported that in a war with Austria-Hungary and the British having lost command of the Eastern Mediterranean Sea for the first two months of the war, the defences of the island would not withstand an invasion. If the Ottoman Empire was also aligned with the Triple Alliance, the invasion could not be stopped.[70] That Cyprus was inconsequential was further reflected in the decision to put it in the French naval patrol sphere at meetings in December 1915 and March 1916 which delineated French, British and Italian naval patrol zones in the Mediterranean.[71] The British wanted to patrol areas in and around Malta and Egypt where they had strategic and military interests.

The idea of Cyprus being a pawn had a long historical context, dating back to its controversial occupation in 1878 when leading Liberals opposed the Conservative government's policy.[72] Then in October 1908 the French and Russian governments, both British allies, suggested returning Cyprus to Ottoman rule if the Porte accepted the cession of Crete to Greece. Whitehall rejected this, yet privately the Foreign Secretary, Sir Edward Grey, argued,

> I believe Cyprus is of no use to us and the Convention respecting it an anachronism and encumbrance, I would therefore give the island away in return for any better arrangements we could obtain. Indeed bargain or no bargain we should be better without Cyprus.[73]

This resonated with David Lloyd George, the Chancellor of the Exchequer since April 1908, and Winston Churchill, the First Lord of the Admiralty since October 1911. Churchill, who had coolly brushed off the fanatical *enosis* party when he visited Cyprus in 1907 as the Under-Secretary of State for Colonial Affairs, by referring to the protection of the Muslim Cypriots,[74] was in 1912 so absorbed by the naval arms race with Germany that he set aside the welfare of Muslim Cypriots. Along with Lloyd George, Churchill proposed in December 1912 to the Pro-Entente Greek Prime Minister Eleftherios Venizelos that in exchange for Athens granting Whitehall the right to use Argostoli harbour on Cephalonia, one of the Ionian Islands, in time of war and peace, the British government would cede Cyprus to Greece. Churchill, who claimed to have had the approval of both Prime Minister Asquith and Grey, was thinking pre-emptively: in a war against the Central Powers the British from Argostoli could block the Austro-Hungarian Fleet from exiting the Adriatic and menacing British shipping in the Mediterranean, while Cyprus would become a Greek responsibility to defend. A deal could not be worked out before the war started in August, when the benefits to the British had become redundant, after they and the French occupied Corfu.[75]

Cyprus remained a pawn, now as part of the allied game of enticing the Balkan states into the war. Within weeks of the war starting, the Cabinet agreed to cede Cyprus to Greece at the first chance.[76] Chances came and went; the best was in October 1915 after the failed Gallipoli landings and Bulgaria's entry and quick successes against Serbia. Whitehall was concerned at the resistance of the King of Greece, Constantine I, to adhere to the Greco–Serbian Treaty of 1912 that stipulated that a Bulgarian attack on either Greece or Serbia would mean that the other had to attack Bulgaria. Constantine's position had resulted in the resignation of the popularly elected Anglophile, Venizelos.[77] Whitehall decided to test the new royalist government, offering to cede Cyprus to Greece forthwith if Athens aided Serbia against Bulgaria. The elaborate plan was never implemented properly, and was also stalled by the high commissioner of Cyprus, Sir John Clauson, but in any event the pro-royalist Greek government of Alexander Zaimis rejected it.[78] So even as a pawn Cyprus had failed.

From backwater to bustling

The rejection was a wake-up call for the British and the French to realise their common aims; this was not simply a reflection of the Gallipoli failure, but also of failures on the Western Front. This meant pressuring neutral states, such as Greece, by consolidating their position in Macedonia. They also decided that they needed to focus their military effort on their imperial aims after defeating the Ottoman Empire. British and French aims were captured in the Sykes–Picot

Agreement in May 1916. Devised by Mark Sykes, a Conservative MP and 'Middle East' expert, and Francois Georges-Picot, a French diplomat, the agreement divided the Ottoman provinces from Cilicia to Mesopotamia into either direct or indirect (where an Arab state would be created) French or British control.[79]

The structures and infrastructure to achieve these aims now needed conceptualisation and implementation. Cyprus was important to these aims, as they now centred on its adjacent mainland, rather than the distant Ottoman capital and the Balkans, which, in the case of the latter, continued as a secondary theatre on a more defensive strategy. Cyprus was valuable enough for the British to agree in Clause 4 of the Sykes–Picot Agreement that they would not cede it to another power without consulting the French government.[80] Suddenly, the geographic location of Cyprus made it important as a military and humanitarian base. It played an important role as an intelligence base for the Middle East campaigns (namely Palestine), as a military base for the French trained Legion d'Orient, as a place to house POWs, and as a place for refugees. The Troodos Hill Station and the Polymedia Garrison Camp in Limassol served as bases for British and Commonwealth convalescents from Gallipoli and Egypt, although playing second fiddle to Malta, even though Troodos had more space and a cooler hills climate.[81]

Cyprus had an important role in gathering intelligence and counter-intelligence. The Eastern Mediterranean Special Intelligence Bureau (EMSIB) operated on the southern shores of Anatolia and the northern Syrian coast out of Cyprus (with southern Syrian intelligence out of Port Said). Cyprus was used as the base for human and electronic intelligence gathering. Both proved unreliable. Electronic intelligence, which necessitated the construction of wireless stations (namely direction finders) in Cyprus, was in its infancy, and while obtaining credible information was one thing, it needed deciphering and communicating to the front, and action taken accordingly. Human intelligence was even more unreliable. Although Jewish agents proved good, Cypriot agents were unreliable. There was a risk that vital military information about troop movements and military plans in Cyprus and Egypt could be leaked via Cyprus. There was a disagreement between the military intelligence officers and the colonial government as regards counter-espionage. After martial law was declared, progressively new regulations were added, but these did not satisfy EMSIB, who demanded that martial law in Cyprus be brought into line with the tougher one in Egypt. Sir John Clauson, who replaced Goold-Adams within weeks of the war beginning, refused. Ultimately, the repeated threats posed by disloyal Cypriots and the pressure from military intelligence forced

Clauson's hand in April 1918.[82] EMSIB had been right to worry: some Muslims tried to break-out Ottoman POWs and another group stole a boat and at Antalya revealed numerous military secrets.[83]

Cyprus served as a location for various military and humanitarian camps during the war. Karaolos, a few miles north of Old Famagusta, served as a major Ottoman Prisoner of War camp from October 1916 to February 1920. By May 1917 the camp housed 3,500 prisoners, rising to 5,400 in early 1918 and to 10,000 by the end of the war.[84] As mentioned, disloyal Cypriot Muslims attempted to 'break-out' Ottoman POWs in what was one of several breaches that forced Clauson to implement the tougher restrictions.[85] Also in October 1916, French army officers established a camp at Monarga, 12 miles north of Famagusta, to train Armenian volunteers in the Legion d'Orient. Over 4,500 Armenian volunteers from genocide survivors to those of the diaspora, especially from the USA, trained at the camp, which disbanded in February 1919. The Legion d'Orient, renamed the Armenian Legion in 1919, served in the Palestine Campaign, namely at the Battle of Arara, and in the French army of occupation of Cilicia and other Ottoman Armenian-populated provinces.[86] The Cypriot government attempted to keep the Legion a secret, but this was not easy because some of the Armenians misbehaved and caused problems for locals and because Cypriot Muslims revealed the existence of the Legion at Antalya and the Ottomans sent surveillance planes, which photographed the camp.[87] Cyprus also provided asylum to many groups fleeing Ottoman dominions, namely from Cilicia and Syria. The Cypriot government formed a special committee to arrange for their housing, care, education and employment.[88] Indeed a number of refugees from Syria arrived in Cyprus both before and after the Ottoman declaration of war. A critical evacuation was that of Ruad Island, which the French had occupied in August 1915, after the Ottoman army threatened to bombard it in November 1917. The women, children and elderly, numbering 761, were housed in the quarantine station at Dhekelia, Larnaca. After the armistice they were repatriated.[89] As for Armenian refugees fleeing the genocide, they were less welcome, such as those from the Musa Dagh resistance in July 1915, but later Armenians were settled in the island in the 1920s.[90] All these camps were provisioned and maintained entirely from local resources.[91]

Cyprus, being geographically located and its primary industry being agriculture, served as an important supplies base for the Allied forces in the Near and Middle East. As the *Handbook for Cyprus* in 1920 stated, 'it is probably true to say that at no time for many hundreds of years has there been so great a demand as during the war for the various products of the island'.[92] A number of commissions from the

Expeditionary Forces in Egypt, Salonica and France visited/had representatives in the island and purchased supplies, such as grain (wheat, barley and oats), carobs, potatoes, onions, eggs, various vegetables and fruit, cheese, dried fruits, wine and brandy, and chopped straw. The war diary of the Director of Supplies and Transport, Salonica, Brigadier-General Arthur Long, shows how valuable Cyprus was for allied supplies in Egypt, Salonica and France. Long started buying Cypriot products in summer 1916, when he started to procure mules and enlist muleteers.[93] The most important products from Cyprus were potatoes, carobs (locust beans) and wood. Thousands of tons of potatoes were exported from Cyprus to Salonica during the war for both consumption and as seed. As early as May 1917 Long decided that he did not need Italian potatoes or potato seed because he could obtain requirements from Cyprus.[94] He was also planning to grow the entire vegetable ration from July onwards, with the exception of onions, which would be obtained from Cyprus.[95] But he soon conceded that Macedonian conditions were too harsh and as early as October 1917 he wired Sisman that Salonica needed all the potatoes Cyprus could produce in 1918 and to ask Clauson to 'induce Cypriots to increase potato cultivation'.[96] Cypriot potatoes became imperative to Salonica when in January 1918 Long could no longer procure potatoes from France.[97] Carobs were just as important and Long purchased them for Salonica and France to feed horses and mules.[98] In 1917 Sisman purchased 30,000 tons of carob beans, 20,000 tons for France and the rest for Salonica.[99] In October 1917 Long purchased another 12,000 tons.[100] Then in 1918 about half the 1917 harvest (over 40,000 tons) was purchased for France and Salonica.[101] Cyprus also supplied wood to the army, especially in Egypt, which entirely relied on fuel from abroad. In 1916 Cyprus donated more than 2,000 tons of fuel for the Egyptian Expeditionary Force. Subsequently, the General Officer-Commanding-in-Chief in Egypt requested a regular supply of wood fuel from Cyprus. Until 31 March 1919, about 75,000 tons of fuel costing about £80,000; 200,000 cubic feet of sawn timber valued at £23,000; 410,000 pickets costing £7,000; and 36,000 telegraph poles valued at £13,000 were supplied.[102]

The Cypriot government implemented policies to increase the production of food-stuffs. For example, good prices were paid for potatoes, thus encouraging more cultivation, while the government also provided generous grants of seed corn to farmers. More significantly, perhaps, were the restrictions placed on the cultivation of 'non-essential products'. A labour shortage especially impacted upon the government departments engaged in the provision of transporting supplies to the army. The Railway Department was already disadvantaged

Table 2.1 Cypriot revenue, 1909–25

Year	Revenue (£)
1909–10	309,775
1910–11	286,848
1911–12	319,572
1912–13	334,685
1913–14	341,816
1914–15	290,110
1915–16	363,692
1916–17	332,584
1917–18	498,460
1918–19	610,499
1919–20	602,927
1920	668,518
1921	682,374
1922	668,294
1923	567,389
1924	593,318
1925	668,130

Source: Cyprus Annual Reports for the respective years.

because of the shortage of rolling stock, which consisted of a mere nine locomotives and 72 wagons. This was 'barely sufficient for the ordinary requirements of the island in normal times', so the task of transporting war materials in addition to internal needs 'imposed a very severe strain on the resources of the railway'. Consequently it was difficult to keep the rolling stock in order, especially since it was 'practically impossible to obtain renewals or spare parts from the outside world'. The Forestry Department was arguably the most impacted since the need to provide timber and fuel was so great, and necessitated the undertaking of additional works because the existing infrastructure was insufficient. Three new saw-mills were built, while 28 miles of road and 102 miles of forest tracks were created to transport the timber and fuel from the places where they were felled to the railway or sea. Various means were used to transport the timber aside from the railway, including native boats, some of which were sunk by enemy submarines. Owing to the constant damage to roads and culverts from the heavy military lorries and carts moving supplies, the Public Works Department had considerable work repairing roads and building new ones.[103]

The requirements of the war and the action taken by the authorities dramatically increased government revenue. The first boom year was 1917–18 with £498,460, a massive increase from the previous years, while the following year the revenue collected skyrocketed to £610,499, and continued to be consistently at about this amount into the 1920s.

In November 1920 the Treasury in London, having noted the excellent state of Cypriot finances and having accumulated a reserve fund of £200,000, wrote to the Colonial Office about how Cyprus should contribute to the cost of the war. Claiming that the island had not made any contribution it asked whether it could 'offer any relief to the sorely burdened British taxpayer'.[104] The Colonial Office replied that 'the political reasons against making any demand upon her [Cyprus] at the present time are ... conclusive'.[105]

Cypriot society and the Great War

Various sections of society, across class and religion, reacted differently to the war. Overall, Cypriot society was loyal, yet not monolithic. The peasant and labouring classes were the most loyal. Many educated elites supported the 'neutralist' King Constantine of Greece or the Ottoman enemy, even if there were only a few acts that threatened the war effort.

The British watered down the disloyal elements of the local population and the impact of the war on society. Sir Charles Prestwood Lucas, a civil servant in the Colonial Office and later head of the Dominion Department, claimed in his official account of the British Empire during the Great War that 'the body of Moslems in Cyprus, as elsewhere in the British Empire, showed no desire to follow the lead of Turkey, and were all content with British citizenship'.[106] This was a generalisation and some Cypriot Christians were also disloyal, despite Muslims and Christians enlisting in the Mule Corps in droves. Lucas exaggerated when he claimed that

> No inconvenience was ... caused to the civil and industrial life of the community, and the existence of martial law made it unnecessary to pass the manifold war enactments which kept the local legislatures busy in most colonies.[107]

He neglected that martial law placed many limitations on the population, while the military intelligence authorities constantly wanted the Cypriot government to upgrade it to match Egypt's. Stevenson echoed Lucas, claiming in his report on Cyprus during the war that

> all classes of the community combined in a cheerful and resolute manner to assist the Government of the island by willingly meeting the many demands made on them and by readily submitting to the restrictions imposed by the various regulations which military exigencies necessitated.[108]

These rosy assessments imply a loyal population, yet it was not so monolithic. Stevenson's use of the word 'all' should be replaced with 'most'. There is much evidence to suggest that the loyalty of some of the Cypriots, especially of the political, professional and business elites, across the 'religious divide', was dubious, yet most of the peasant and labouring classes were loyal.[109]

One reason for the educated classes being less loyal was, in Lucas's words, the fact that the war, like elsewhere in the world, 'brought high prices and great increase[s] in the cost of living'.[110] The political, professional and business classes made much money through lending it but since the peasant and labouring classes were making money through the Cypriot Mule Corps and the nascent cooperative movement they were losing out. So, most of the political, professional and business elites were economically adversely affected, especially in conjunction with the rising living costs and the lack of a corresponding rise in income from their fixed salaries. Politically the educated classes were either pro-British status quo or followed the divisions in Greece and the Ottoman Empire. Some Cypriot Christians and Muslims, especially civil servants, were pro-British and supported the status quo. A smaller group of Cypriot Orthodox Christians were Anglophile supporters of Venizelos, yet still Greek nationalists. The British questioned their loyalties to British rule because they supported *enosis* and so the British rejected an offer from one of them to create a Cypriot fighting force for the war.[111] More of the Cypriot Orthodox elite were Royalists and supported Greek neutrality. An illustrative example was the incident on 12 February 1917 when the firebrand Greek-born nationalist Dr Philios Zannettos interrupted a speech by the Venezelist Bishop of Kitium, Metaxakis, at the Girls School, Larnaca when Metaxakis expressed sorrow at the massacre of British troops in Athens on 1 and 2 December 1916. Zannettos angrily shouted that the massacre was a British lie, betraying his anti-British sympathies. Denying his intervention, Zannettos was contradicted by a stream of witnesses, while the Royalist newspapers criticised Metaxakis for blindly following Venizelist and British positions. The incident, one of many, highlighted the political divisions within the Christian political elites across Venizelist and Royalist lines.[112] This disloyalty, however, did not threaten the British war effort as some Muslim acts did. A small group of Muslims were fanatically loyal to the Young Turks,[113] such as those groups that attempted to break out Ottoman POWs and that fled to Antalya and revealed vital intelligence to the enemy.

On the other hand, during the war the peasant and labouring classes were substantially better off. They were able to off-set the rise in living costs by selling more products than before the war, and producing more vegetables and grains for their own use. Moreover, there was a significant increase in labouring jobs, aided by the fact that so many able-bodied men enlisted for the Cypriot Mule Corps, reducing competition.[114] There was also more money for those with an allotment or those muleteers returning with their pockets full to invest back into the Cypriot economy. The 'loyalties' across the class and religious divide must therefore take into account political and socio-economic considerations. Peasants and rural labourers were too busy trying to feed their families to care about local politics or a world war and had less knowledge about such matters. Yet they knew that the Mule Corps was a unique opportunity for well-paid work and their loyalty to the British cause was inherent in their enlistment.

Conclusion

Two British approaches to Cyprus dictated the transition in society from the premodern to the modern: the first was the British breaking of the traditional Ottoman system of co-opting the local elite, namely the higher clergy of the Cypriot Orthodox Church, and instituting a limited introduction of political modernity; the second was to regard Cyprus as an inconsequential possession, which meant little imperial and private investment, necessitating the colonial government trying to do its best with the limited finances to develop the island and increase productivity and revenue. There were a number of repercussions from these two approaches.

The failure to co-opt local elites left a political and social power vacuum at the top. New social and political elites emerged from the introduction of political modernity, such as the legislature. One group, although not homogenous, were the outgrowth of the British modernist path that the British were closely controlling. These were mostly educated elites who were soon joined by the rising middle class to slowly adopt a new ideology – nationalism. This was not, however, a Cypriot nationalism that included Muslims as well as Christians, or a 'state' nationalism, but an exclusive nationalism that identified Cypriot Orthodox Christians as Greeks and the 'motherland' as Greece, thus necessitating the creation of a selective and nationalised script of the Greek nation in Cyprus. This left the traditional elite out in the cold, until they assimilated into the movement. Ultimately, British modernisation led to the development of a pro-British group, mostly civil servants, and two nationalist groups, one closely tied to the Greek monarchy and the other to the liberal movement in Greece. The Muslim elite were also divided between those supporting the British, those who supported the British but also had ties with the old order in the Ottoman Empire, and those supporting the Young Turk Movement. In any event, the nationalisation of the peasantry and working classes did not occur before the Great War and therefore did not deter them from attempting to enlist in the Cypriot Mule Corps.

Cypriot government efforts to develop society resulted in a significant rise in population and a corresponding rise in men seeking work, some of which was alleviated by an increase in traditional and non-traditional employment, which had an important impact on socio-economic structures. Although it did not produce a politicised or nationalised polity, it did mean that there were more economic opportunities for the lower classes, namely in agriculture and construction, necessitating the need to obtain finance so more land could be cultivated and homes built. There were only two ways to obtain funds: borrow it from money lenders or from the few cooperative banks. The alternative was to emigrate. For this reason the offer to work as muleteers in the British Army offered significant financial incentives to those peasant and rural labouring men and their families.

The Cypriot Mule Corps was not the only contribution made by Cyprus. In July 1919 High Commissioner Stevenson sent Milner, the Colonial Secretary, a statistical breakdown of the contribution of Cyprus during the Great War, broken down into five sections, men, animals, money, foodstuffs and timber.[115] Except for the first, all have been discussed above. Even without the Cypriot Mule Corps, it was a significant contribution, yet it was the enlistment of men into it that was the most impressive.

Notes

1. Captain L.B. Weldon, *'Hard Lying': Eastern Mediterranean, 1914–1919*, Herbert Jenkins, London, 1925, 97.
2. Ibid., 20.
3. See Varnava, *British Imperialism in Cyprus*.
4. For a broader context see Michalis N. Michael, Tassos Anastassiades and Chantal Verdeil (eds), *Religious Communities and Modern Statehood: The Ottoman and Post-Ottoman World at the Age of Nationalism and Colonialism*, Klaus Schwarz Verlag, Berlin, 2015.
5. Varnava, *British Imperialism in Cyprus*, 152–201; Varnava, 'Sophronios III, 1865–1900: The Last of the "Old" and the First of the "New" Archbishop-Ethnarchs?' in Andrekos Varnava and Michalis N. Michael (eds), *The Archbishop's of Cyprus in the Modern Age*, Cambridge Scholars Publishing, 2013, 106–47; Andrekos Varnava and Irene Pophaides, 'Kyrillos II, 1909–16: The First Greek Nationalist and *Enosist*', ibid., 148–176.
6. Costas Kyrris, 'The Role of Greeks in the Ottoman Administration of Cyprus', *Proceedings of the First International Conference on Cypriot Studies*, 3(A), 1973, 149–79; Nicholas Coureas, 'The Cypriot Reaction to the Establishment of the Latin Church: Resistance and Collaboration', *Sources Travaux Historiques*, 43/4, 1995, 75–84.

7 See generally Varnava and Michael (eds), *The Archbishops of Cyprus in the Modern Age*.
8 Achilles Aimilianides, 'Η Εξέλιξει του Δίκαιου των Μικτών Γάμων εν Κύπρω' ('The development of the Law of Mixed Marriages in Cyprus'), *Kypriakai Spoudai*, 2, 1938, 197-236 (209); Paschalis Kitromilides, 'From Coexistence to Confrontation: The Dynamics of Ethnic Conflict in Cyprus', in Michalis Attalides (ed.), *Cyprus Reviewed*, Nicosia, 1977, 35-70; Paul Sant Cassia, 'Religion, Politics and Ethnicity in Cyprus during the Turkocratia (1571-1878)', *European Studies of Sociology*, 1986, 3-28; Kemal Cicek, 'Living Together: Muslim-Christian Relations in Eighteenth-Century Cyprus as Reflected by the Sharia Court Records', *Islam and Christian-Muslim Relations*, 4(1), 1993, 36-64; Theodore Papadopoullos, *Δημώδη Κυπριακά Άσματα εξ Ανεκδότων Συλλογών του ΙΘ'Αιώνος* (Cypriot folk Songs on unpublished collections of the nineteenth century), Nicosia, 1975, 63, 151-7, 213-16, 220-5, 239-41, 243-50; K. Giagoullis, 'Ο Χριστοφής τζε η Εμινέ' ('Christophis and Emine'), *Laographiki Kypros*, 23, 1972, 15-21.
9 N. Kizilyurek, 'The Turkish Cypriot Upper Class and Question of Identity', *Turkish Cypriot Identity in Literature*, Fatal, London, 1990, 21.
10 FO 198/13, consular report, 1858.
11 Richard A. Patrick, *Political Geography and the Cyprus Conflict: 1963-1971*, Ontario 1976, 12; Census, 1891.
12 Michalis N. Michael, *Η Εκκλησία της Κύπρου κατά την οθωμανική περίοδο (1571-1878): Η σταδιακή συγκρότηση της σε θεσμό πολιτικής εξουσίας* (The Church of Cyprus during the Ottoman period (1571-1878): the gradual establishment of an institution of political power), Cyprus Research Centre, Nicosia, 2005, 215-40; Varnava, *British Imperialism in Cyprus*, 153-5.
13 John Kakridis, 'The Ancient Greeks and the Greeks of the War of Independence', *Balkan Studies*, 4(2), 1963, 251-64; Victor Roudometof, 'From Rum Millet to Greek Nation: Enlightenment, Secularisation, and National Identity in Ottoman Balkan Society, 1453-1821', *Journal of Modern Greek Studies*, 16(1), 1998, 11-48.
14 Sophronios autobiographical note, 1868, Theodore Papadopoullos, 'Εθναρχικός Ρόλος της Ορθοδόξου Ιεραρχίας' (Ethnarchic Role of the Orthodox hierarchy), *Kypriakai Spoudai*, 35, 1971, 95-141 (115).
15 Varnava, 'Sophronios III'.
16 Demetrios Kappae, *Τα Μοναστήρια της Κύπρου* (The monasteries of Cyprus), 3rd edition, author, Limassol, 1998.
17 Rolandos Katsiaounis, *Labour, Society and Politics in Cyprus in the Second Half of the Nineteenth Century*, Nicosia, 1996, 72-7; Varnava, *British Imperialism in Cyprus*, 167.
18 Roland L.N. Michell, 'A Muslim-Christian Sect in Cyprus', *The Nineteenth Century and After*, 63, May 1908, 751-62; R.M. Dawkins, 'The Crypto-Christians of Turkey', *Byzantion*, 1933, 247-75; Costas M. Constantinou, 'Aporias of Identity: Bicommunalism, Hybridity and the "Cyprus Problem"', *Cooperation and Conflict*, 42(3), 2007, 247-70.
19 Varnava, *British Imperialism in Cyprus*, 163-4, 294.
20 Varnava, 'Sophronios III'.
21 Varnava, *British Imperialism in Cyprus*, 185-6.
22 Ibid., 75-87.
23 Ibid., particularly chapters 3 and 4.
24 See Andrekos Varnava, 'El Dorados, utopias and dystopias in imperialism and colonial settlement', in Andrekos Varnava (ed.), *Imperial Expectations and Realities: El Dorados, Utopias and Dystopias*, Manchester University Press, 2015, 1-25.
25 Varnava, *British Imperialism in Cyprus*, 93-126.
26 Ibid, 172-5, 152-201, 272-80.
27 Varnava and Yakinthou, 'Cyprus: Political Modernity and Structures of Democracy in a Divided Island'.

28 *Cyprus: Report of the Commission Appointed to Enquire into the Extent, Causes and Effects of Indebtedness in the Island*, Government Printing Office, Nicosia, 1918.
29 Nicholas Constantine Lanitis, *Rural Indebtedness and Agricultural Co-operation in Cyprus*, Limassol, 1945 (revised, Proodos, Limassol 1992), 8.
30 Ibid., 10–12, 34, 41.
31 Stanley Fisher, *The Statute Laws of Cyprus, 1878–1923*, I–II, Waterlow & Sons, London, 1923, I, 906–7.
32 For the locust campaigns and internal communications, see Varnava, *British Imperialism in Cyprus*, 132–45, 155.
33 Morgan, *Sweet and Bitter Island*, 197–8.
34 Sandra M. Sufian, *Healing the Land and the Nation: Malaria and the Zionist Project in Palestine, 1920–1947*, University of Chicago Press, 2007.
35 Frank M. Snowden, '"Fields of death": Malaria in Italy, 1861–1962', *Modern Italy*, 4(1), 1999, 25–57.
36 A. Vakali et al., 'Malaria in Greece, 1975 to 2010', *Euro Surveillance*, 17(47), 2012, pii=20322. Available online: http://www.eurosurveillance.org/ViewArticle.aspx?ArticleId=20322.
37 CO67/10, General Report on Famagusta District by Civil Surgeon, Dr C. Irvine, 20 November 1879. See further Varnava, *British Imperialism in Cyprus*, 118.
38 *Report on the Sanitary Condition and Drainage of the District of Famagusta and the Mesaoria in Cyprus*, the Chevalier David Bocci, Chief Engineer, RE, Parma, 5 June 1880, CO, November 1881; Varnava, *British Imperialism in Cyprus*, 97–107.
39 For example with the new hospital in Larnaca being built on land donated by the Cypriot landowner Richard Mattei.
40 The maternity block struggled to attract women, with only 13 admissions in 1913–14.
41 *Second Annual Report of the Sanitary Commissioner with the Government of Cyprus for the Year 1881*, CO Confidential Print, Mediterranean, No. 12, April 1883; Varnava, *British Imperialism in Cyprus*, 169–71; Censuses 1891 and 1911.
42 *Second Annual Report of the Sanitary Commissioner with the Government of Cyprus 1881*.
43 CO 67/87/19066, No. 305, Sendall to Ripon, 20 October 1894.
44 Censuses of 1901 and 1911; *Second Annual Report of the Sanitary Commissioner with the Government of Cyprus 1881*.
45 Robert Kubicek, 'Joseph Chamberlain, the Treasury and Imperial Development, 1895–1903', *The Canadian Historical Association*, 44(1), 1965, 105–16.
46 Varnava, *British Imperialism in Cyprus*, 142–3.
47 Ibid., 142–5, 289; *Annual Report for Cyprus, 1913–14*, 38–41.
48 Andrekos Varnava and Peter Clarke, 'Accounting in Cyprus during Late Ottoman and Early British Rule, 1840–1918', *The Cyprus Review*, 26(2), 2014, 33–55.
49 Census Reports 1881, 1891, 1901, 1911.
50 Ibid.
51 Diamond Jenness, *The Economics of Cyprus: A Survey to 1914*, McGill University Press, Montreal, 1962, 198.
52 Census Reports 1891, 1901 and 1911.
53 Jenness, *The Economics of Cyprus*, 187.
54 Ibid., 206; Fisher, *The Statute Laws of Cyprus*, 259.
55 Census Reports 1901 and 1911.
56 Census Reports 1881, 1891, 1901 and 1911.
57 Census Reports 1901 and 1911. From 1901 to 1911 Kyrenia must have received people from Nicosia, the closest town, probably because the redevelopment of the small harbour at Kyrenia (completed in the early 1890s) improved trade between Cyprus and Anatolia. Varnava, *British Imperialism in Cyprus*, 135–9.
58 Sir Charles R. Tyser, *Cyprus: Extract from the Annual Report of the Chief Justice Sir Charles Tyser for the Year 1913–14*, Government Printing Office, Nicosia, 1914, 1, 6–7.

59 The other occupation to drastically increase between 1901 and 1911 was weavers, from 6,034 to 10,121, tripling since 1891. The increase was linked to the greater production of cotton and silk and so was directly related to cultivation. As Katsiaounis also showed, the relative poverty of the first decade or so of British rule was gradually changing by the turn of the century. Katsiaounis, *Labour, Society and Politics in Cyprus*, 119–37.
60 Census Reports 1881, 1891, 1901 and 1911; Varnava and Clarke, 'Accounting in Cyprus during Late Ottoman and Early British Rule'.
61 Kate Phylaktis, 'Banking in a British Colony: Cyprus 1878–1959', *Business History*, 1987–8, 416–31; Varnava, *British Imperialism in Cyprus*, 135–9, 179.
62 Fisher, *The Statute Laws of Cyprus*, 850–6.
63 Phylaktis, 'Banking in a British Colony', 421. Phylaktis argued that the growth of the Nicosia Savings Bank was largely due to the decision of the Cypriot government in 1912 to allow it to change its status into a *Societe anonyme*, on the basis of the Ottoman Commercial Law. Thus the Bank of Cyprus enjoyed the rare privilege of limited liability before the 1922 Companies (Limited Liability) Law. See Varnava and Clarke, 'Accounting in Cyprus during Late Ottoman and Early British Rule'; and Peter Clarke and Andrekos Varnava, 'Accounting in Cyprus during British Rule, Post-World War I to Independence', *Accounting History*, 18(3), 2013, 293–315.
64 Kevork K. Keshishian, *Famagusta Town and District Cyprus*, Limassol, 1985, 103; *The Co-operative Movement in Cyprus*, Public Information Office, 2004, 25–8.
65 Fisher, *The Statute Laws of Cyprus*, 170–80; Aristedis Koudounaris, Βιογραφικόν Λεξικόν Κυπρίων, 1800–1920 (Biographical lexicon of Cypriots, 1800–1920), Nicosia, 2001, 267–8; Varnava and Clarke, 'Accounting in Cyprus during Late Ottoman and Early British Rule'.
66 Varnava and Yakinthou, 'Cyprus: Political Modernity and Structures of Democracy in a Divided Island'.
67 See the following files on why Cyprus was annexed rather than made a protectorate, and for matters relating to Cypriots becoming British subjects. FO371/2143/56311, FO371/2143/62037, FO371/2143/65473, FO371/2143/65957, FO371/2143/67613, FO371/2143/67712 and FO371/2143/67792.
68 Sir Charles Lucas, *The Empire at War*, V, Royal Colonial Institute, Oxford University Press, 1926, 21.
69 *Annual Report on Cyprus for 1914–15*, Cd-7662, HMSO, London, 1915, 40.
70 CAB 38/20/13, Attack on Cyprus by Austria; Defence of Cyprus, 9 May 1912; CAB 38/20/16, Note by the Chief of the Imperial General Staff covering the following papers prepared by the General Staff on the attack and defence of: Malta (92C); Cyprus (93C); and Egypt (149B), 9 May 1912.
71 *Mediterranean Staff Papers Relating to Naval Operations from August 1917 to December 1918*, C.B. 1546, compiled by staff of the Commander-in-Chief Mediterranean, Admiralty, January 1920.
72 Varnava, *British Imperialism in Cyprus*, 97–100, 246–7.
73 Ibid., 248–9; FO800/172, private, Grey to Bertie, 29 October 1908.
74 Varnava, *British Imperialism in Cyprus*, 183–6.
75 Ibid., 250–61.
76 FO800/91, Grey to Harcourt, 19 January 1915; Philip Magnus, *Kitchener*, London, 1958, 313–14.
77 See George B. Leon, *Greece and the Great Powers*, Institute for Balkan Studies, Thessaloniki, 1974.
78 Varnava, *British Imperialism in Cyprus*, 261–6.
79 See file FO371/2767/23579; Andrekos Varnava, 'French and British Post-War Imperial Agendas and Forging an Armenian Homeland after the Genocide: The Formation of the *Légion d'Orient* in October 1916', *The Historical Journal*, 57(4), 2014, 997–1025.
80 For text of the Sykes–Picot Agreement, see *Documents on British Foreign Policy 1919–1939*, First Series, IV, London, 1952, 241–51.

81 Lucas, *The Empire at War*, V, 21; Andrekos Varnava, 'Recreating Rural Britain and Maintaining Britishness in the Mediterranean: The Troodos Hill Station in Early British Cyprus', *The Cyprus Review*, 17(2), 2005, 47–80.
82 Varnava, 'British Military Intelligence in Cyprus during the Great War'.
83 Ibid.; for the stolen vessel see SA1/806/1917. This was revealed to the Cypriot authorities after the war by a Cypriot Muslim asked to interpret for the men.
84 CO67/182/61931, secret, Clauson to Bonar Law, 11 December 1916; *Annual Report for Cyprus, 1916–17*, 17; Lucas, *The Empire at War*, V, 21; Danny Goldman, 'Famagusta's Historical Detention and Refugee Camps', *Journal of Cypriot Studies*, 11, 2005, 29–53, 32.
85 Varnava, 'British Military Intelligence in Cyprus during the Great War'.
86 Varnava, 'Imperialism First, the War Second'; Varnava, 'French Imperialism, Armenian Autonomy and Anglo–French War Aims'.
87 SA1/780/16; Andrekos Varnava, 'Famagusta during the Great War: From Backwater to Bustling', in Michael Walsh (ed.), *Famagusta: City of Empires, 1571–1960*, Cambridge Scholars Publishing, Newcastle upon Tyne, 2015, 91–111; Ulvi Keser, *Kıbrıs 1914–1923: Fransız Ermeni kampları İngiliz esir kampları ve Atatürkçü Kıbrıs Türkü* (Cyprus 1914–1923: French Armenian camps, British prisoner camps and Kemalist Cypriot Turks), Akdeniz Haber Ajansı Yayınları, Istanbul, 2001, photos 234–6 and 243–5.
88 *Annual Report for Cyprus, 1914–15*, 41; *Annual Report for Cyprus, 1919–20*, Cmd. 508–29, HMSO, London, 1920, 4; Lucas, *The Empire at War*, V, 21.
89 Lucas, *The Empire at War*, V, 21.
90 Andrekos Varnava and Trevor Harris, '"It is quite impossible to receive them": Saving the Musa Dagh Refugees and the Imperialism of European Humanitarianism', work in progress; For Armenian population statistics see Andrekos Varnava, 'The minorities of Cyprus in the history of Cyprus textbook for Lyceum students: a critique', in Andrekos Varnava, Nicholas Coureas and Marina Elia (eds), *The Minorities of Cyprus: Development Patterns and the Identity of the Internal-Exclusion*, Cambridge Scholars Publishing, 2009, 299–313.
91 CO67/192/37309, Stevenson memorandum, 3 June 1919; see SA1:1068/1916 and SA1/1184/1915; Varnava, 'Famagusta during the Great War: From Backwater to Bustling'.
92 Luke and Jardine, *The Handbook of Cyprus*, 293–4.
93 WO95/4790, WDSA, DSTS, 23 and 24 July 1917; ibid., 8 August 1917; ibid., 15 December 1917; from May 1918 Cyprus came under the administration of Egyptforce. WO95/4791, WDSA, DSTS, 26 May 1918; ibid., 12 June 1918.
94 WO95/4790, WDSA, DSTS, 12 May 1918.
95 Ibid., 17 May 1917.
96 WO95/4791, WDSA, DSTS, 26 May 1918; WO95/4790, WDSA, DSTS, 11 October 1917.
97 WO95/4791, WDSA, DSTS, 5 January 1918.
98 Ibid., 17 January 1918.
99 WO95/4790, WDSA, DSTS, 12 January 1917; ibid., 13 January 1917; ibid., 15 January 1917; ibid., 18 January 1917; ibid., 12 February 1917; ibid., 7 March 1917; ibid., 29 March 1917.
100 Ibid., 20 October 1917.
101 WO95/4791, WDSA, DTS, 16 February 1918 and 22 April 1918.
102 Lucas, *The Empire at War*, V, 21.
103 Ibid.
104 CO67/201/54305, Upcott, Treasury, to Fiddes, CO, 3 November 1920.
105 CO67/201/54305, Fiddes, CO to Upcott, Treasury, 12 November 1920.
106 Lucas, *The Empire at War*, V, 21. Muslims in India were not all loyal. See Philip Stigger, 'How Far Was the Loyalty of the Muslim Soldier in the Indian Army More in Doubt Than Usual throughout the First World War?' *Journal of the Society for Army Historical Research*, 87(351), 225–33.
107 Lucas, *The Empire at War*, V, 20.

108 CO67/192/37309, Stevenson memorandum, 3 June 1919.
109 Varnava, 'British Military Intelligence in Cyprus during the Great War'.
110 Lucas, *The Empire at War*, V, 21.
111 Varnava, 'The Politics and Imperialism of Colonial and Foreign Volunteer Legions during the Great War: Comparing Proposals for Cypriot, Armenian and Jewish Legions'.
112 See FCO141/2373, which includes police reports, witness statements and newspaper articles.
113 See also Altay Nevzat, *Nationalism amongst the Turks of Cyprus: The First Wave*, Oulou, 2005, 218–55.
114 CO67/192/37309, Stevenson memorandum, 3 June 1919.
115 CO67/192/44124, Stevenson to Milner, 15 July 1919.

CHAPTER THREE

The formation of the Cypriot Mule Corps

In summer 1916, the British authorities established the Cypriot Mule Corps for service in the British army at the Salonica Front. Officially styled the Macedonian Mule Corps, the majority of the men were Cypriots, not Macedonians. This chapter deals with its formation, answering why and how it was formed, why Cypriot mules and men were selected, and outlining the roles of the various authorities involved. Soon after establishing themselves in Salonica, the British, realising the harsh conditions, especially the terrain, turned to procuring Cypriot mules and enlisting Cypriots to drive them. In the absence of a document that discloses why Cypriot mules and drivers were chosen, this chapter suggests prior British experiences. By integrating the local with the global, this chapter shows how the British Empire operated and how Cypriot mules and muleteers were selected for this important war service.

On 6 October 1915 French and British forces established the Salonica Front after their failed Gallipoli landings to aid Serbia against the combined German, Austro-Hungarian and Bulgarian forces.[1] The French and British forces were sent north of Salonica, but failed to prevent the fall of Serbia. Greek political divisions did not help. The pro-Entente prime minister, Eleftherios Venizelos, resigned at the stubborn (perceived as pro-German) neutrality of King Constantine.[2] Subsequently the new Royalist government rejected the British offer to immediately cede Cyprus to Greece in exchange for militarily aiding Serbia.[3] Allied troops, numbering 600,000, under French Commander Maurice Sarrail, withdrew to the Salonica town area and established strong defensive positions from the Albanian Adriatic coast to the Struma River through an extensive system of trenches. Limited allied attacks near Monastir in Serbia in 1916 and 1917 led in September 1918 to the breakthrough into Bulgaria and the armistice.[4]

The campaign was fought in difficult climatic and physical

THE FORMATION OF THE CYPRIOT MULE CORPS

3.1 'Fed No Complaints', contained in Canon Newham's trunk.

conditions, which the allies had not properly prepared for. Diseases, particularly malaria, were prevalent. In the winter the winds were fierce and freezing, while in the summer the heat was unbearable and filled with malarial mosquitoes. All-year round the allied forces dealt with the barren mountains filled with treacherous ravines. Good roads were sparse; most were dirt-tracks in the mountains used by goats, donkeys, mules and the occasional bullock and old cart. Roads needed construction and serious resources devoted to transportation of all kinds in order to traverse the difficult mountains.[5] In the first months the British, who were making their way to Doiran, found the roads congested. It was not until after 24 April 1916 that General Sir Bryan Mahon, the commander of the 10th (Irish) Division and then the head of the British Salonica Force, upon being ordered to march to the Greco–Serbian border claimed that to succeed he immediately needed an additional 1,676 pack animals and 1,232 drivers per division.[6] This is when and why Cypriot mules (and from many other parts of the world) and Cypriot muleteers became pivotal.

Formation

The origins of the formation of the Cypriot Mule Corps lie with a 24 May 1916 enquiry from the British Minister in Athens, Sir Francis

Elliot, to the High Commissioner of Cyprus, Sir John Clauson, asking if 7,000 Cypriot muleteers could be raised for service in the British army in Salonica.[7] Three days later Lieutenant-General George Milne, the Commander of the British Salonica Forces, asked Clauson if 3,000 Cypriot muleteers could be furnished at once.

> I am anxious to raise [a] corps [of] muleteers for service in this area. I understand that some reliable Cypriots might be forthcoming. Daily pay [is] approximately three Drachma with higher rates for foreman [and] certain articles of clothing and fixed rations [provided free]. Could employ at once 3,000 and as many more later. Would you kindly inform me what numbers would be forthcoming from Cyprus and [the] time necessary to enrol.[8]

It is unclear what evidence they had that Cypriots were expert muleteers and 'reliable'. Clauson replied on 29 May that 3,000 muleteers could be raised in three weeks.[9]

The Salonica authorities initially attempted to recruit Macedonians as muleteers and to procure Cypriot mules. The involvement of mules was pivotal in all theatres in the Great War. In comparison to horses the importance of mules was most evident in the 'Eastern' Theatres, Salonica, Mesopotamia and Egypt-Palestine (see Appendix I), with the Macedonian and Mesopotamian theatres the only ones with more mules than horses. In March 1916 the Serbian army informed the French army that many of their horses had died during the bitterly cold winter and that they needed more animals than previously foreseen. The French asked the British to provide the Serbians with mules, and after much debate it was decided to procure mules from Cyprus.[10] On 14 June the British Salonica authorities enquired if 6,000 mules could be furnished from Cyprus, to which Clauson replied that 2,000 were available.[11] Also, Brigadier-General Arthur Long, the Director of Supply and Transport, had been trying to fill the want of mule drivers by recruiting Macedonians. As early as March, 25 had been recruited[12] and more followed, but on 9 May Long was advised that the Greek Royalist government had forbidden the Allies to recruit Macedonians, leading him to conclude that Athens 'wishes to place all possible obstacles in our way'.[13] The Venizelos government also disappointed him. Despite the first 100 Macedonian muleteers proving good and being doubled, Venizelos could not guarantee that they could remain in British service, so muleteers from Cyprus were finally sought.[14]

By 13 June the authorities in Salonica were negotiating with the Cypriot government on obtaining muleteers.[15] On 22 June the British Mission to the Serbian army at Famagusta informed Clauson that the War Office had approved the purchase of 2,000 mules and 500 men to conduct them. Clauson replied that the mules and muleteers had to be for the British and not the Serbian army. Milne replied that the muleteers would be for the British army, but most of the mules were for the Serbian army.[16] By 30 June, Major Lewis Collingwood Bearne,[17] who was in Cyprus to purchase mules for the Serbs, had been ordered to enlist 1,000 Cypriots.[18] Bearne advised Salonica on 1 July that the purchase of mules for the Serbian army was now under the General Officer Commanding Egypt, while he would assist him and also enlist the muleteers.[19]

It was not until the end of June that Clauson informed the Colonial Office of the details to enlist muleteers for service in the British army in Macedonia. On 26 June (and in a telegram on 28 June) Clauson opined to Bonar Law that

> The raising of a Cypriot transport corps for British army service is a measure from which excellent results may be hoped for, both politically and also, judging from the Military Report on Cyprus prepared by the General Staff in 1913, from the military standpoint. ... The Cypriots, both Christian and Moslem, are with insignificant exceptions keenly desirous of the success of the British arms, but in view of the mixed feelings with which the former section of the population regard the relations between Serbia and Greece it would be a mistake to send Serbians to Cyprus to collect mules for the Serbian Army.[20]

Clauson raised three points: (1) the political reasons in favour of an inter-Cypriot muleteer corps, because most of the Christian and Muslim population supported the British war effort; (2) the military reasons in favour, which centred on the Cypriot skills in driving mules; and (3) to not involve Serbs because many Cypriot Orthodox elites supported King Constantine's neutrality.[21]

The Colonial Office, although impressed with its officials in Cyprus, was none too impressed with the War Office. A 29 June minute stated, 'It is a great pity this is so late in the day – I can't imagine why the C-in-C Salonica did not think of it before.'[22] Two weeks later, the perceived military inaction saw the impatience of the Colonial Office increase, evident in the comment that there was 'a good deal of indecision and procrastination' from Salonica.[23]

The initial task of enlisting 1,000 muleteers was quickly doubled and then tripled. As early as 9 July 1916 the authorities in Salonica were preparing to receive the first batch of Cypriots.[24] On 13 July Bearne cabled Salonica that the enlistment of Cypriots was a success, and Egyptforce asked Salonica if it wanted more because it seemed possible that over 2,000 could be enlisted.[25] On the same day, Major-General Travers Clarke, Deputy Adjunct and Quarter Master General, wired Egyptforce that 600 Cypriot muleteers had been enlisted, 400 would follow, and 3,000 more were sought.[26] On 15 July the Salonica authorities asked Egyptforce to enlist 2,000 and Egyptforce immediately ordered Bearne to do so.[27] On 22 July Bearne informed Long that 150 muleteers were leaving Cyprus, and Long noted that they (153 in total) arrived on 25 July.[28] By 24 July the number wanted was increased to 3,000. Salonica wired Egyptforce that they were ready for the 2,000 mules from Cyprus, but they really needed the 3,000 muleteers and they could not take the mules before the muleteers or they should come together. They also requested one foreman for every 20 muleteers, with pay GDR 4 per day.[29] The Egyptian authorities queried the request for 3,000,[30] but on 27 July Egyptforce telegraphed Clauson that it was 'very urgent that 3,000 Muleteers from Cyprus should be obtained as soon as possible for Salonica. About 1,200 only secured up to date. Major Sisman is in charge. Hope you will give every assistance in your power.'[31]

L. Sisman, who was in charge of the Mule Purchasing Commission at Famagusta, had wired Long on 25 July that 1,050 muleteers were awaiting passage, but he needed Salonica to arrange it with Egypt.[32] On the day before Long had cabled Sisman to enlist 3,000 muleteers, with a ratio of one foreman to twenty mule drivers.[33] On the same day Salonica also cabled Egyptforce that the 3,000 being enlisted were sufficient, and should proceed to Egypt to accompany the mules with a ratio of one man to two mules.[34] On the next day the first instalment of Cypriot muleteers had arrived in Salonica.[35] Clauson replied, 'I am gladly giving every assistance in my power.'[36] As will be shown, to this end Clauson worked tirelessly as did his personnel.

Urgency now became paramount. The Army Council replied to the Colonial Office, which had been pressuring the War Office, on 1 August, that the Cypriot muleteers 'should be raised as quickly as possible', under the following conditions:

i. The Army Act should apply, without modification or exception, to these men whilst they are serving with troops subject to the Army Act, and that this should be clearly stated in the Local Act, or Imperial Order in Council, authorising their enlistment.
ii. The men should receive pay as Infantry at the rates laid down in Article 852, Royal Warrant for Pay, 1914, but would not be entitled to proficiency pay, corps pay or working pay.
iii. A free ration (scale to be fixed hereafter) should be provided.
iv. Separation allowance should be issuable at the rates laid down in para. 120, Allowance Regulations, 1914.
v. Disability pensions should be granted as provided for European soldiers in Article 1161, Royal Warrant for Pay, 1914.

THE FORMATION OF THE CYPRIOT MULE CORPS

Table 3.1 Distribution of Macedonian and Cypriot muleteers, 7 August 1916

Division	No. in divisional trains	No. in field ambulances	Total
10th Division	0	162	162
22nd Division	325	70	395
26th Division	253	202	455
27th Division	128	0	128
28th Division	79	0	79
7th Mounted Brigade	27	0	27
Total	812	434	1,246

Source: WO95/4790, war diary, Director of Supply and Transport, 7 August 1916.

vi. The widow of a soldier who died in the circumstances referred to in Article 1245, Royal Warrant for Pay, 1914, should be granted a gratuity of one year's pay at the rate at which the soldier was in receipt at the time of his death or discharge.

vii. The period of enlistment should be defined.[37]

These conditions were well thought out, so the War Office procrastination must have been merely bureaucratic. They reflected how, at least initially, the conditions of muleteers were closer to soldiers than to labourers, yet, as will be shown in subsequent chapters, this was not the case.

Meanwhile, the Cypriot government, along with Sisman, continued recruiting muleteers. Clauson advised Bonar Law on 5 August 1916 that 1,091 Cypriot muleteers had already left for Salonica and he was sending the agreement they had signed, covering them as campfollowers under the Army Act.[38] To this the Colonial Office minuted, 'I am very glad to find that while the WO was occupied in sweltering this proposal in red tape & working us ... The people on the spot were going ahead.'[39] Indeed on 2 August the second batch (796) of Cypriot muleteers arrived at Salonica and 500 were allotted to the 12th Corps and the rest to the 16th.[40] On 7 August Long devised this table (3.1) on the distribution of muleteers (297 Macedonians and 949 Cypriots) and added that another 851 were being trained. Almost two years later the number of muleteers had more than trebled, showing how important they were to the Macedonian Front (Table 3.2).

Why Cypriot mules and Cypriot muleteers?

Before exploring the organisation of the Cypriot Mule Corps it is important to digress in order to explore why Cypriot mules and

Table 3.2 Cypriot muleteers across various British units, 4 May 1918

British 12th Corps	Cypriot muleteers	Sick	Totals
British 22nd Division			
ASC train	412		412
British 26th Division			
ASC train	526		526
Other units – details	3	2	5
Total 12th Corps	941	2	943
British 16th Corps			
British 10th (Irish) Division			
British 27th Division			
ASC train	489	8	497
British 28th Division			
ASC train	482		482
228th Brigade	62		62
Other Units – details	119	9	128
Total 16th Corps	1152	17	1169
L of C & Base Camp			
ASC Supply	2011	119	2011
RE	10		10
RAMC	12	2	14
Total L of C & Base Camp	2035	121	2156
HT Units with Serbs	14		14
Grand total	4142	140	4282

Source: WO95/4768.

muleteers were sought. The archives do not provide the answers. The idea to raise Cypriot muleteers must have emanated from the British military authorities in Salonica because, as mentioned above, the Colonial Office wondered why the Commander-in-Chief of the Salonica Forces had not thought of it before and the initial contact with Clauson was from the British minister in Athens and not from the War Office. It must be assumed that there were members of the British military forces in Salonica with knowledge of the Cypriot mule and the capacity of Cypriots to be muleteers. For Cypriot rural society, beasts of burden, especially mules and donkeys, were important for their economic base and subject to various commercial transactions (individuals could own shares in them and other animals) and usages, as had been the case in Egypt into the early nineteenth century.[41] A historical survey, beginning from the mid-nineteenth century, shows that Cypriot mules and muleteers had good reputations. The British military authorities in Salonica must have thought to recruit them because of previous experiences in the Egyptian–Sudan campaigns, Anglo–Boer War and British India.

During the Crimean War, when Cyprus was a part of the Ottoman Empire, French merchants arrived in the island to buy mules for the French army in the Crimea. The subgovernor of Cyprus informed the Ottoman Foreign Ministry that mules would be sold to the French consul in Larnaca and that the local Mejlis would facilitate the consul's work.[42]

After the British occupation they too discovered the value of Cypriot mules and muleteers. Pivotal to British society in Cyprus was the six-month summer season when the central government left Nicosia and the garrison left Polymedia in Limassol for the Troodos Hill Station. There, one of the many sporting pursuits was polo and matches were played on mules.[43] In December 1880 High Commissioner Major-General Sir Robert Biddulph received a rude awakening to 'Greek' politics when he did not act to stop the Greek military purchasing mules in the island despite this being a breach of British neutrality since Greece was mobilising against the Ottoman Empire. He received a letter of thanks for 'his assistance' from the Greek Consul in Cyprus on behalf of King George of Greece for Biddulph's assistance in the matter. Biddulph denied to the Colonial Secretary, Lord Kimberley, that he or anybody in his government had offered any assistance.[44] The British realised the value of Cypriot mules and muleteers during the Egyptian Campaigns from 1882 to 1885 when Cypriot mules were prized.[45] An officer also recruited Cypriot Muslims for service under General Evelyn Wood on six-month contracts.[46] Hugh Sinclair, Biddulph's private secretary, claimed that Cypriot muleteers 'were famous for horse-mastership ... and the mules ... unequalled for docility and endurance'.[47] Muleteers died in the line of duty, but there was no compensation for their dependents.[48] Also the government awarded the medals at the Troodos Hill Station, although most veterans could not make it because they lived in other parts of the island and mainly in rural areas.[49]

By the turn of the century, the Indian government showed a great interest in the Cypriot donkey stallions, mules and jennets. From the mid-1880s the Indian government had been consistently purchasing Cypriot donkey stallions or jacks, reaching a high in 1897–8 with 21.[50] Then in 1898–9 the Indian government ordered a record 61 and followed this up the next year with 25.[51] In October 1898 Colonel A.E. Queripel, Inspector-General of the Civil Veterinary Department in the Indian government, visited Cyprus to purchase donkey stallions and report on the state of transport animals generally. Queripel established that the general state of transport animals on the European continent was very poor and that for a small island Cyprus was doing well. He saw in the island numerous pony mares with mules at their feet, whose height on average exceeded those bred in India. He revealed that the donkey mares were larger than the donkey stallions because the best mares were crossed with pony stallions to obtain mules (i.e. the jennet). Although this was not the norm in most parts of the world, this meant that the mules in Cyprus were of medium size, ideal for pack transport purposes. This also meant that there were not that many donkey stallions in the island, and indeed many were sold overseas (Bosnia-Herzegovina, Constantinople and Syria), although many were also crossed with horse mares. He approved of those donkey stallions for India, purchasing nine, and recommended that the Indian government enter into an agreement with the Cypriot government to purchase 25 to 30 donkey stallions aged about four per year, with a three-year warning of termination.[52] Queripel made some substantial recommendations for the Cypriot government to improve the breading stock of all transport animals:

a) The levying of a small tax on all donkeys exported;
b) Either the levying of a heavy tax on the importation of donkeys or the prohibition of importation altogether;
c) The awarding of prizes at all the large fairs to donkey stallions (fairs at Famagusta in March, Larnaca in April, and in September at Paphos and the Karpass);
d) The Cypriot government should maintain two indigenous donkey stallions in each district for breeding purposes;
e) To improve the breed of ponies there needs to be maintained a few good Arab pony stallions not exceeding 14 hands in size.[53]

The Indian government strongly endorsed Queripel's report, which it sent to the India Office on 9 March 1899. The cover letter agreed that it was highly desirable for the Indian government to enter into an agreement with the Cypriot government on purchasing 25 to 30 donkey stallions every year.[54] The recommendation was also supported by the under-secretary of state for India, Charles Leslie Sutherland, who claimed that Poitou was noted for its focus on mule breading, and Cyprus too could become noted for its donkey stallion breeding, to make Cyprus the breeding ground for Indian mules.[55] The India Office agreed with the proposal to formally have a contract with the Cypriot government to purchase donkey stallions, informing the Colonial Office of the offer in September 1899 and was pleased that some of Queripel's recommendations had been implemented.[56] Before the Cypriot government could respond, the India Office ordered 28 donkey stallions for 1900–1.[57] William Haynes Smith, the high commissioner of Cyprus, approved the offer of the India Office, only pointing out that prices needed to be reconsidered every three years because they were unstable and because he intended to encourage better breeding. Haynes Smith had already tried to improve quality, with the government stationing in some districts high-class donkey stallions whose services were offered for free and the offspring purchased by the Agriculture Department.[58]

The Indian government's interest in the Cypriot donkey encouraged Haynes Smith to offer the mule to the War and India Offices.[59] The fact that he waited over four months from the time that the Colonial Office had first informed him of the India Office offer on 15 September 1899 to when he accepted it on 24 January 1900 and first decided to write on the Cypriot mule indicates that Haynes Smith wanted to capitalise on the interest in Cypriot transport animals by pushing forward the claims of the Cypriot mule. He forcefully argued that the Cypriot mule was better than any other mule in the world because it: was more active than the Italian and American mule; could bear hard work better; could stand hardships better; was less prone to sickness; thrived on dry food; was more docile; was cheaper. Haynes Smith claimed that there were a considerable number sized 12.3 to 13.3 hands, and some 13.3 to 14.2 hands, but if larger animals were wanted they could be bred at 15 hands in a few years. But from his experience of the various sized mules in Cyprus, Haynes Smith believed that the medium-sized mule was just as strong and more mobile. In order to strengthen his argument, he referred to how Lord Kitchener had used the Cypriot mule to great advantage in the Sudan.[60]

The Colonial Office strongly endorsed Haynes Smith's proposal and referred to Queripel's report as more evidence.[61] This hit a chord with Lord Lansdowne, the War Secretary. Within a week he asked how soon 1,000 draught Cypriot mules aged five to nine and measuring 13.3 hands to 14.2 hands could be ready for shipment and at what price. The matter was so urgent he wanted communication via telegraph.[62] Seemingly satisfied that 1,000 mules could be purchased in no time, three days after his initial message he asked the Colonial Office to gather the mules at Larnaca for inspection by his purchasing officer.[63] Then on 17 February the War Office asked the Colonial Office to telegraph Haynes Smith that the purchasing officer was arriving on 1 March and wanted to ensure that the rejected mules would be disposed of without loss.[64] A week later the War Office became concerned about information that the majority of Cypriot mules were 'jennets' and therefore unsatisfactory compared to mules produced from a horse mare. It wanted most of the mules put up for inspection to be from horse mares.[65] The inspection officer, however, was dissatisfied, finding Cypriot mules too young and small.[66] A year later Haynes Smith tried again, this time he proposed a similar agreement over the mules to that agreed to with the India Office over the donkey stallions. He claimed that currently the average mule was 13.2 hands, but would be willing to implement policies to encourage the breeding of bigger animals, while he emphasised that Cypriots were experienced in raising docile mules.[67]

The War Office, however, did not believe that Cypriot mules, or 'jennets', were suitable. The War Office referred to the men sent to Cyprus to purchase transport animals for the Anglo–Boer War who mainly saw 'jennets'. Of the 590 mules examined, a mere 128 were deemed fit for army requirements and purchased at £UK19 per head. The War Office informed the Colonial Office that military requirements for mules were that they be aged between five and nine, with a height between 14 and 15 hands, trained to harness and not stallions or albinos. Lastly, the War Secretary was not interested in a continuing contract and any arrangement would be temporary.[68] If this was not the slap in the face for the proponents of Cypriot mules, it came when in May 1902 the War Office proposed to the Colonial Office that if the Anglo–Boer War continued they wanted to establish a horse and mule reception depot in Cyprus for animals purchased in Russia and Syria.[69] Clearly the Cypriot mule was being rejected.

Correspondingly, the Indian government had a different view of Cypriot jennets and donkey mares. In 1901 Captain Knapp visited Cyprus to report on the donkey and mule supply in the island for the 'Horse and Mule Breeding Commission' appointed by the Indian government in 1900. Knapp argued that Cypriot jennets and donkey mares were exceedingly fine and that the Indian government should purchase these animals until it produced its own. He was enthusiastic about using the jennet as an ordnance mule, as those in Cyprus were large enough and were purchased for this purpose by the Egyptian artillery. Knapp also argued that Cypriot donkey stallions, although few in number because many were sold to South Africa, Uganda, Egypt and Syria, were fine animals, and that the Cypriot government had established a 'Breeding Committee' which had stationed six donkey stallions at the district headquarters for breeders. Also Cypriot stallions were about a third of the price of Italian donkey stallions.[70]

To encourage agriculture the British invested in improving the Cypriot mule breeds without altering the attraction of Cypriot jennets. The Porte, which still had sovereignty over Cyprus, reacted to this in December 1910, when the British Embassy in Constantinople informed the Ottoman Foreign Ministry, which in turn informed the Grand Vizier, that the Cypriot government wanted to import horses

Table 3.3 Exports of mules and donkeys, 1905 to 1916

Year	Mules	Donkeys
1905	654	513
1906	675	430
1907	342	424
1908	162	564
1909	602	2,148
1910	1,305	3,256
1911	1,906	3,951
1912	1,486	2,420
1913	1,006	1,988
1914	676	2,197
1915	887	2
1916 (June)	323	

Source: SA1/758/1916, statement showing number of mules and donkeys exported from Cyprus from 1905 to end of June 1916.

Table 3.4 Number of muleteers across districts in Cyprus in 1901 and 1911 censuses

Year/place	Nicosia	Famagusta	Limassol	Larnaca	Paphos	Kyrenia	Total
1901	172	82	17	3	74	6	354
1911	246	62	44+1w	50	153+2w	172	730

Source: relevant Census reports.

and mules from Arabia to improve the quality of the horse and mule breeds. The Grand Vizier informed the Sultan that he initially wanted to oppose this, but realising that he had no right to do so he gave his 'consent'.[71] Mule and donkey exports grew from 1910 as breeding practices improved, as Table 3.3 shows.

Reflecting the government's success in encouraging mule breeding was the increase in the number of muleteers in the island between 1901 and 1911, particularly compared to camel drivers. In the 1901 Census 354 men were listed as muleteers, as opposed to 325 camel drivers.[72] In the 1911 Census muleteers were 730, while camel drivers remained static at 348 (see Table 3.4).[73]

Beyond the main point, namely that muleteers more than doubled in the ten-year period between 1901 and 1911, only one district had a decrease, and that was Famagusta, almost certainly because of the introduction of the train. This also explains why Nicosia had the least growth in this profession compared to all the other districts.

Someone in the British military force in Salonica may also have read the two War Office reports published before the Great War, one in 1907 and another in 1913[74]. They gave information on the characteristics of Cypriot pack animals and the martial qualities of Cypriots that, if read, could have led to the proposal to seek mules and muleteers from Cyprus.

The report from 1913 was positive on the value of Cypriot pack animals. With respect to horses, it stated that although small (mostly around 13 hands) they were hardy and docile. Larger horses were increasing thanks to crossing with English and Syrian stallions and the Athalassa stock-breeding farm had done much to achieve this. Nevertheless, only a small number were suitable for army work. Far more was said about Cypriot mules. The report stated that they were 'particularly fine and docile, and well adapted to mountain work', and therefore British military personnel in Salonica would have realised that they would be ideal for Macedonian conditions. More specifically the report added that the 'points of great importance in their suitability for mountain artillery work are the straight backs and well-arched ribs'. Additionally, the report clarified that mules bred from donkey mothers were preferred for pack, while the ones from pony mares were preferred for harness work. Larger mules were fewer in number, but the Egyptian artillery purchased theirs almost exclusively from Cyprus.[75] The report added that

> The weight-carrying powers of Cyprian mules are considerable, and it is not unusual to see them carrying from 350 to 450 lbs. of wheat from Nicosia to the mills of Kythrea, a distance of 8 miles, and return the same evening laden with flour. For harness purposes they are not less suitable, and are noted for their endurance, being capable of performing the journey from Nicosia to Larnaca and back (52 miles) in a day.[76]

The report also disclosed that the Cyprus Blue Books gave the total number of horses, mules and donkeys as 69,832 in 1911–12, and that at least half of these animals were mules.[77] The entire report can only, therefore, be taken as a very positive endorsement of the Cypriot mule, especially for mountainous work.

Equally important was that both reports claimed that the Cypriots had military potential, especially as muleteers. They mention that Cypriot Muslim muleteers showed considerable courage in the Sudan in 1885, while all Cypriot men were excellent horsemen and horsemasters. The report claimed that

> the desperate and gallant defence of Nicosia and Famagusta against the Turks in 1570 shows that the Christian inhabitants were not devoid of martial qualities; while the opinion held regarding the Cypriot Turk, by

those who have had the best opportunities of judging, are to the effect that he is probably as fine military material as his co-religionists on the mainland. In the operation against the Mahdists at Suakin in 1885 a number of Cypriot Turkish muleteers were employed, and were reported on as having shown, though unarmed, considerable courage during one or two night alarms, where their conduct was in marked contrast to that of other natives similarly employed. We have, however, no recent experience of their value as soldiers, though both Mohammedans and Christians are from their childhood fearless horsemen, as well as good horsemasters, and would appear to offer useful material for cavalry or mounted infantry.[78]

The statements about the Christian inhabitants were bizarre, not least because many Orthodox had welcomed the Ottoman invasion.[79] The perceived Muslim fighting abilities were enmeshed in martial races theory becoming a received wisdom: Clauson referred to them when he supported the raising of the mule corps in 1916; and these passages were repeated in the two subsequent reports.[80]

There is much evidence to prove that the British considered the Cypriots, both Muslims and Christians, as reliable and loyal. Sophronios promised Cypriot loyalty as far back as his welcoming address to Sir Garnet Wolseley in 1878; a loyalty that he maintained until his death and which was then taken up, even with increasing reference to *enosis*, by the Bishop of Kyrenia and his supporters during the archiepiscopal dispute.[81] The British government, both in the island and back in London, consistently believed that the Cypriots were reliable and loyal, using these characteristics to support their policy to reduce the British garrison during the 1880s and 1890s.[82] The police were especially praised for their loyalty and reliability, and racial and religious integration. This was evident when a group of *Zaptieh* volunteered in 1900 to serve in the Anglo–Boer War, or between 1899 and 1904 when the government promoted the idea of an inter-religious Cypriot regiment to garrison the island or even be used in other imperial stations, only for the War Office to reject both ideas.[83] The British observed this religious integration amongst the peasant and labouring classes, which comprised the vast majority of the population.

Organising the Cypriot Mule Corps

The organisation and running of the Cypriot Mule Corps was a complex endeavour involving three different authorities: the British military authorities in Salonica; the Cypriot government in Nicosia and Troodos; and the Mule Purchasing Commission, renamed in July 1917 the Muleteer Recruiting and Supply Purchasing Staff, at Famagusta.[84]

3.2 Cypriot muleteers 1917, Photo I, contained in Canon Newham's trunk.

Often the organisational structure worked well, but sometimes there was a breakdown in communication, methods and priorities.

Each authority, of course, had its own responsibilities. The authorities in Salonica and later in Constantinople were responsible for the day-to-day operational running of the Mule Corps and communicating

THE FORMATION OF THE CYPRIOT MULE CORPS

3.3 Cypriot muleteers 1917, Photo II, contained in Canon Newham's trunk.

with the other two authorities in the island over needs and problems. The two authorities in Cyprus where responsible for all matters relating to recruiting and repatriation, as well as for the running of the allotment scheme and treating those men returning with venereal and other diseases. The Cypriot government had much responsibility for running the Corps and dealing with the societal repercussions when, for example, problems arose with the allotment scheme, as well as with quarantining muleteers with venereal disease. It did well given the lack of resources and personnel. The Cypriot Mule Corps was a success for the vast majority of those involved, yet for any successful major operation there are always problems.

Conclusion

The British imperial family presented unique opportunities for those belonging to it. The Cypriot Mule Corps was formed in haste in summer 1916. The lack of British transport service personnel and the need to use them and other British forces in other capacities, coupled with the mountainous terrain and lack of roads, necessitated mules and mule drivers. Cypriot mules and muleteers, which had good reputations, were the answer. The Cypriot government took the organisation of the mule corps in their stride, working relatively well with the military authorities to bring it to fruition. The next chapter will explore the strategies used to recruit so many men and whether the Cypriots were pulled or pushed.

Notes

1. On the Greek seizure of Salonica during the First Balkan War see Richard C. Hall, *The Balkan Wars 1912–1913: Prelude to the First World War*, Routledge, London, 2000; and André Gerolymatos, *The Balkan Wars: Conquest, Revolution, and Retribution from the Ottoman Era to the Twentieth Century and Beyond*, Basic Books, New York, 2002.
2. There are many books on Greece's schism. The best remains Leon, *Greece and the Great Powers*.
3. Varnava, *British Imperialism in Cyprus*, 261–5.
4. For the latest account on the Salonica Front see Wakefield and Moody, *Under the Devil's Eye*.
5. Ibid.
6. C. Falls, *Military Operations – Macedonia*, I, HMSO, London, 1933, 112; see also Palmer, *The Gardeners of Salonika*, 63.
7. See CO67/181/32730, various minutes, summaries of correspondence between Salonica and Cyprus; SA1/722/1916, telegram, Elliot to Clauson, N/A, 1916.
8. SA1/722/1916, telegram, GHQS, to Clauson, 27 May 1916.
9. CO67/181/32730, telegram, Clauson to Milne, 29 May 1916; ibid., Clauson to Milne, 23 June 1916.
10. WO107/62, Colonel Le Vicomte de la Panouse, French Military Attaché, London, to Lieutenant-General Sir J. Cowans, WO, 21 March 1916; Ibid, 27 March 1916; ibid., Cowans to Panouse, 31 March 1916.
11. CO67/181/40421, secret, Clauson to Bonar Law, 7 August 1916, with enclosures; for early promises see CO67/181/32730, various minutes, summaries of correspondence between Salonica and Cyprus.
12. WO95/4790, WDSA, Long, DSTS, 7 March 1916.
13. Ibid, 9 May 1916.
14. WO95/4788, GHQS, Long, DSTS, October 1915–December 1916, 8 June 1916; WO95/4762, WDSA, AQMGS, June–July 1916, despatched messages, June 1916, G.I. Fraser, DAQMG, Salonica, to Egyptforce, 13 June 1916.
15. WO95/4762, WDSA, AQMGS, June–July 1916, despatched messages, June 1916, G.I. Fraser, DAQMG, Salonica, to Egyptforce, 13 June 1916.
16. See CO67/181/32730, various minutes, summaries of correspondence between Salonica and Cyprus; CO67/183/36388, A.S.C/958 (Q.M.G.5), WO to CO, 1 August 1916; SA1/722/1916, telegram, Elliot, Athens, to Clauson, N/A, 1916.
17. On 22 October 1916 a French motor lorry, loaded with 3,000 lbs of bombs, caught fire in the camp of the Serbian army. Efforts to beat out the flames with earth proved ineffectual and, after the fire had been burning for seven or eight minutes, Major Lewis Collingwood Bearne and Private Albert Edward Usher crawled under the lorry and extinguished the flames, thus averting a serious disaster at the risk of their own lives. Both were severely burnt on their hands and arms and were awarded the Albert Medal for their bravery. *London Gazette*, 28 December 1917.
18. WO95/4762, WDSA, AQMGS, June–July 1916, 30 June 1916; ibid., despatches, Lieutenant-Colonel, C.H. Furneaux, AQMG, to DQMG, 29 June 1916.
19. Ibid., 3 July 1916; ibid., despatch messages, Bearne to Salonica, 1 July 1916.
20. CO67/181/32730, secret, Clauson to Bonar Law, 26 June 1916; CO67/181/30717, telegram, Clauson to Bonar Law, 28 June 1916.
21. CO67/181/30717, telegram, Clauson to Bonar Law, 29 June 1916.
22. CO67/181/30717, minute, 29 June 1916.
23. CO67/181/32730, minute, 12 July 1916.

24 WO95/4833, WDSA, Divisional Train, 10th Division, 9 July 1916.
25 WO95/4762, WDSA, AQMGS, June–July 1916, despatch messages, Egyptforce to Salonica, 13 July 1916.
26 Ibid., Clarke, DQMGS, to Egyptforce, 13 July 1916.
27 Ibid., 19 July 1916; ibid., despatch messages, Egyptforce to Salonica, 15 July 1916; ibid., despatch messages, Salonica to Egyptforce, 15 July 1916.
28 WO95/4790, WDSA, Long, DSTS, 20 and 22 July 1916; ibid., 22 and 25 July 1916.
29 Ibid., 24 July 1916; WO95/4762, WDSA, AQMGS, June–July 1916, 24 July 1916.
30 WO95/4762, WDSA, AQMG, June–July 1916, despatch messages, Egyptforce to Salonica, 25 July 1916.
31 SA1/722/1916, telegram, Egypt Force to Clauson, 27 July 1916.
32 WO95/4762, WDSA, AQMGS, June–July 1916, despatch messages, Sisman to Long, 25 July 1916.
33 WO95/4788, WDSA, Long, DSTS, October 1915–December 1916, 24 July 1916.
34 WO95/4762, WDSA, AQMG, June–July 1916, despatch messages, Salonica to Egyptforce, 24 July 1916.
35 WO95/4788, WDSA, Long, DSTS, October 1915–December 1916, 25 July 1916.
36 SA1/722/1916, telegram, Clauson to Egypt Force, 27 July 1916.
37 CO67/183/36388, WO to CO, 1 August 1916.
38 SA1/722/1916, telegram, Bonar Law to Clauson, 4 August 1916; CO67/181/37153 and SA1/722/1916, telegram, Clauson to Bonar Law, 5 August 1916.
39 CO67/181/37153, minute, 7 August 1916.
40 WO95/4788, WDSA, Long, DSTS, 1 August 1916–31 August 1916, 2 August 1916; WO95/4790, WDSA, Long, DSTS, 25 July and 2 August 1916.
41 Mikhail, 'Unleashing the Beast', 326.
42 Bas.bakanlık Osmanlı Ars.ivleri (Prime Minister's Office Ottoman Archives), (BOA), Istanbul, HR.MKT/108/85, 27.Sh.1271, Subgovernor of Cyprus to Foreign Ministry, 27.Sh.1271; Subgovernor of Cyprus to Cyprus local parliament (Local Mejlis), 17 Rejep 1271; Subgovernor of Cyprus to Cyprus local parliament (Local Mejlis), 21 Rejep 1271.
43 Varnava, 'Recreating Rural Britain and Maintaining Britishness in the Mediterranean', 47–79.
44 CO67/13/277, 507, Biddulph to Kimberley, 24 December 1880, including letter from Ajax Caravias, Greek Consul, 22 December 1880.
45 G.C. Dawnay, *Campaigns: Zulu 1879, Egypt 1882, Suakim 1885: Being the Private Journal of Guy C. Dawnay*, Ken Trotman, Cambridge, 1989, 104; Lieut.-Colonel Hermann Vogt, *The Egyptian War of 1882*, Kegan Paul, London, 1883, 159, 166; Wolseley to Childers, 1 September 1882, Charles Royle, *The Egyptian Campaigns 1882 to 1885*, London, 1900, 165.
46 CO67/36/3748, 180, Sir E. Barring, Cairo, to CO, 29 February 1884; minute, Fairfield, 4 March 1884; CO to Biddulph, 7 March 1884; SA1:762/85, Muleteers application form, 19 February 1885.
47 Hugh Sinclair, *Camp and Society*, London, 1926, 130; Storrs, *Chronology*, 135.
48 SA1/1957/85, Michael Kyriako invalided from Suakin pleaded for the Cypriot government to pay £4 compensation to his wife, which was being paid by Brigade-Major E.E.S. Swaine, Famagusta's first Commissioner; SA1/2670/1885. A muleteer from Nicosia, Costi Hadji Yanni, was fatally shot.
49 See SA1/2549/1886; see also Varnava, 'Recreating Rural Britain and Maintaining Britishness in the Mediterranean', 47–79.
50 India Office (IO), British Library: IOR/L/MIL/7/1009, 1885–6; IOR/L/MIL/7/1013 1886–7; IOR/L/MIL/7/1015 1887–8; IOR/L/MIL/7/1022 1894–5; IOR/L/MIL/7/1024 1895–8; IOR/L/MIL/7/1029 1897–8; IOR/L/MIL/7/1033 1897–8.
51 CO67/121/8430, IO to CO, 30 March 1899.
52 CO67/121/24299, IO to CO, 9 September 1899, including Indian government to IO, 9 March 1899, signed by Lord Curzon and other members of council. This included Edwin H.H. Collen, who had written one of the reports that had been used to justify the choice of Cyprus in 1878; see, Varnava, *British Imperialism in Cyprus*, 84–6.

It also included the Veterinary Colonel A.E. Queripel's report, Simla, 30 October 1898, and also Charles Leslie Sutherland's report, 15 June 1899.
53 CO67/121/24299, Queripel's report, Simla, 30 October 1898.
54 Ibid., Indian government to IO, 9 March 1899.
55 Ibid., Sutherland's report, 15 June 1899.
56 Ibid., IO to CO, 9 September 1899.
57 CO67/121/33903, IO to CO, 5 December 1899.
58 CO67/122/3962, Haynes Smith to Chamberlain, 24 January 1900; CO to IO, 8 February 1900, formal CO acceptance of offer.
59 CO67/122/3962, Haynes Smith to Chamberlain, 24 January 1900; CO67/122/3000, Haynes Smith to Chamberlain, 17 January 1900.
60 CO67/122/3000, Haynes Smith to Chamberlain, 17 January 1900.
61 CO67/122/3000, CO to IO, 3 February 1900.
62 CO67/126/4415, WO to CO, 9 February 1900.
63 CO67/126/4856, WO to CO, 12 February 1900.
64 CO67/126/5439, WO to CO, 17 February 1900.
65 CO67/126/6187, WO to CO, 24 February 1900.
66 CO67/126/8013, WO to CO, 10 March 1900.
67 CO67/127/6025, Haynes Smith to Chamberlain, 7 February 1901.
68 CO67/129/8515, WO to CO, 5 March 1901.
69 CO67/133/21055, WO to CO, 28 May 1902.
70 *Cyprus: Horse, Mule and Donkey Breeding, 1901 and 1917*, HMSO, London, 1917.
71 I.HR/425/1, 4.M.1329, 1, Foreign Ministry to Grand Vizier, 10 December 1910; ibid., 2, Grand Vizier to Sultan, 4 January 1911.
72 Census Report, 1901, 54.
73 Census Report, 1911, 61. There were three women mule drivers and five camel drivers.
74 General Staff, WO, *Military Report and General Information concerning the Island of Cyprus*, London, 1907. Hereafter, *Military Report* (1907); General Staff, WO, *Military Report and General Information concerning the Island of Cyprus*, London, 1913. Hereafter, *Military Report* (1913).
75 *Military Report* (1913), 34.
76 Ibid.
77 Ibid.
78 *Military Report* (1907); *Military Report* (1913), 17.
79 Ahmet An, 'The Cypriot Armenian Minority and their Cultural Relationship with the Turkish Cypriots', in Andrekos Varnava, Nicholas Coureas and Marina Elia (eds), *The Minorities of Cyprus: Development Patterns and the Identity of the Internal-Exclusion*, Cambridge Scholars, Newcastle-upon-Tyne, 2009, 268–82; R.C. Jennings, *Christians and Muslims in Ottoman Cyprus and the Mediterranean World, 1571–1640*, New York University Press, 1992.
80 CO67/181/32730, secret, Clauson to Andrew Bonar Law, 26 June 1916; *Military Report* (1913), 17; *Military Report* (1936), 27; Varnava, '"Martial Races" in the Isle of Aphrodite'.
81 Varnava, *British Imperialism in Cyprus*, 152–201; Varnava, 'Sophronios III', 106–47; Varnava and Pophaides, 'Kyrillos II, 1909–16', 148–76.
82 Varnava, *British Imperialism in Cyprus*, 215–19.
83 CO67/122/1498, 5, Haynes Smith to Chamberlain, 4 January 1900, including letter signed by the men, 24 December 1899; CO67/126/2924, 079/917, WO to CO, 25 January 1900; see also Varnava, '"Martial Races" in the Isle of Aphrodite', 1058–9 for Anglo–Boer War.
84 SA1/722/1916, Sisman to Stevenson, 12 July 1917.

CHAPTER FOUR

Mule and muleteer recruitment: pushed or pulled?

In March 1920, Elias Christou, from Agios Theodoros, Karpasia, informed the government that he had served as a muleteer for three years but was owed £30 in wages. He claimed that he was 'a poor man and the head of a family', forced to borrow money to survive, and was 'ruined by the interest', and still his 'children remain[ed] day and night without food'. At length he revealed that 'I abandoned my family and my children for three years for the purpose of serving the glorious English army.' Christou, as with the vast majority of muleteers, was a peasant or an unskilled labourer, who, although loyal to the British Empire and the Allied cause, was really lured to enlist by the offer of secure and well-paying work.[1]

After a few early concerns, the British were mostly satisfied with these makeshift Cypriot muleteers. On 6 September 1917, a little over

4.1   Muleteers enlisting, with Canon Newman and *Zaptiehs*, contained in Canon Newham's trunk.

a year after the Cypriot Mule Corps was established, Major General Sir William Henry Rycroft, the Deputy Quartermaster General at Salonica, reported to General Milne, the Commander-in-Chief of the British Forces in Macedonia, that he was satisfied with training at Lembet Road. Although some men were too old, they could relieve British men, while new recruits would be better trained. 'I am certain we ought to encourage recruiting in Cyprus and try and increase output', with the desired age being 18–35, he opined.[2] Clearly the British authorities in Salonica were content with the Cypriot muleteers and so recruitment became even more paramount from mid-1917.

Procuring mules and recruiting muleteers were major jobs for the Cypriot government and for the military personnel in Cyprus and Salonica, needing much planning, organisation and coordination. A successful advertising campaign balanced the benefits the British were willing to offer, alongside the rights they did not wish to grant the muleteers. Ultimately, Cypriot men were both pushed by the conditions on the island and pulled by the allure of money into enlisting.

Recruitment into the Cypriot Mule Corps overtook the initial focus to procure mules, as reflected by the operation changing its name in July 1917 from 'Mule Purchasing Commission' to 'Muleteer Recruiting and Supply Purchasing Staff'.[3] It succeeded in attracting about 25% of the male population aged 18–35, based on the 1911 Census, about 12,200 men, owing to the Cypriot government's successful recruiting campaign and local push factors. Most muleteers, who were chiefly peasants and unskilled rural labourers, were effective and were valued. Yet many issues arose to threaten the Mule Corps and were the cause of complaints from muleteers and their families during and after their service. These issues were connected with the difficulty of running such a massive operation, across two geographical areas, with three different jurisdictions, and civil colonial staff thrown into the deep end.

This chapter contributes to the ongoing debates (Mansfield, Osborne, Pennell and McCartney) about enlistment in the Great War discussed in Chapter 1, by shifting the focus, as Smith did with the Jamaicans, onto a colonial context. It additionally contributes to the history of equines, also detailed in Chapter 1, and is the first study to explore the procurement of mules. The chapter attempts to answer, How and why were British procurement and recruitment methods so successful? This will necessitate providing statistical data on the number of mules procured and men enlisted and its analysis across typologies, for example the ethno-religious and urban-rural demographic breakdowns, as well as a discussion of the various British recruiting strategies. This chapter argues that mules were procured and muleteers were enlisted by using legal methods that left mule owners and men of military age with little alternative: a law to force owners to sell their mules; and another banning the emigration of men of military age. Additionally the British targeted the most vulnerable, peasants and labourers. Using Spivak's definition of the 'subaltern', the muleteers, who were the 'men and women among the illiterate peasantry, the tribals, the lowest strata of the urban subproletariat', had little agency.[4] This differs from Jamaica where the men were motivated to fight alongside their white overlords and not merely for the money.[5]

Mule purchasing and numbers

Before discussing muleteer recruitment, it is important to understand mule procurement because initially, as reflected in the name of the operation at Famagusta, the Mule Purchasing Commission, the focus was on purchasing mules. By July 1917 the focus had clearly switched to muleteers when the name changed to Muleteer Recruiting and Supply Purchasing Staff[6] and greater numbers of muleteers were recruited in comparison to mules.

Clauson, the high commissioner, advised Colonial Secretary Bonar Law, on 7 August 1916, that the Mule Purchasing Commission had been created to buy mules and enlist muleteers. Some 919 mules had been purchased in six weeks, yet he had promised 2,000.[7] A week later Clauson acted, issuing a proclamation under martial law to requisition mules for military purposes.

> Any person having in his ownership or under his control any mule when warned by public notice under this order signed by or on behalf of the District Commissioner and Provost Marshal and posted in the village or when notified by any member of the Cyprus Military Police produce such a mule at any place and time specified and shall deliver up such mule if required by the military purchasing officer on payment of such compensation as may be awarded by a Board appointed by the High Commissioner and Commander-in-Chief consisting of an officer of His Majesty's Military Service and an inhabitant of the Colony. In case of a difference of opinion the amount of compensation to be awarded shall be decided by the votes of a majority of the members and the award shall be final.[8]

The proclamation ended with a warning that any person who did not comply would be taken before the Provost Marshal (the commissioner of each district) and upon conviction would be 'liable to fine or imprisonment or both such punishments'.[9]

This was harsh, but reflected the government's desire to facilitate military needs. It also opened further opportunities for the development of a mule-breeding industry. No doubt, however, those without a means to breed and who merely had a mule or two for farming could be severely harmed, and the various district boards established did consider this. Initially, it was decided to purchase the mules by treaty, with the experiment first conducted at Platres on 17 August. Failure would lead to the commandeering as per the proclamation. The government had the district commissioner of Limassol, Wilfred Nash Bolton, warn all the villages around Platres to comply. The warning echoed Clauson's proclamation. Platres was chosen because it was close to the summer seat of the government at the Troodos Hill Station.[10] The board consisted of Captain T.P. Goodchild, from the Remount Department of the Egyptian Expeditionary Force, H. McLaughlan, a policeman, and the muktar of Platres, Ioannis Demetriou.[11]

The approach trialled in Platres was adopted throughout the island. Although the proclamation had been made, it was decided to purchase mules by treaty before commandeering them. Consequently, the structures for both approaches were in place and virtually identical, since the commandeering board in each district first tried to purchase mules by treaty, being conscious of not depleting mule stocks, damaging breeding programs, and harming the peasantry. Goodchild was a constant member of the boards, as the military representative and expert on the suitability of the mules. The government was represented by a policeman, such as McLaughlan in Limassol, M.C. Kareklas in Paphos[12] and inspector Alfred Wilson in Larnaca; by a civil servant, such as C. Barrett in Nicosia and C.M. Georgiades, Railway Department in Famagusta; or by a member of the judiciary, such as Michael John Lobarides, Mudir of Kyrenia. The local population was also represented, in Nicosia by Nicolakis Papadopoulos of Lacadamia, in Larnaca by Costis Aspri, in Famagusta by C. Constantinides, in Paphos by Yannakos Maltezos of Ktima, and in Kyrenia by N.K. Pyrgos, the mayor of Lapithos.[13]

The treaty approach did not work to the satisfaction of the authorities. In August 1916 numerous events were held where the purchasing of mules by private treaty was undertaken (see Table 4.1).[14] By 31 August a total of 2,208 mules (over 1,000 since Clauson's letter to Bonar Law on 7 August) had been purchased.

This was not enough, especially since the Mule Purchasing Commission now wanted larger mules for riding and draught.[15] So on 26 September Clauson authorised the compulsory acquisition of mules irrespective of size under his order of 14 August. All mule owners within a radius of 20 miles from the purchasing place had to produce their mules for inspection by Goodchild at various centres across the island, from 1 to 13 October.[16] This only resulted in the purchasing of slightly over 500 more mules. So from July to November 1916, 2,750 mules, 1,200 donkeys and 140 ponies embarked for Salonica.[17]

MULE AND MULETEER RECRUITMENT

Table 4.1 Mules purchased by 31 August 1916

District	Place	Number	Totals
Famagusta	Famagusta	96	96
Kyrenia	Kyrenia	40	50
Kyrenia	Myrtou	10	
Larnaca	Larnaca	176	203
Larnaca	Lefkara	7	
Larnaca	Kofinou	20	
Limassol	Limassol	357	1,087
Limassol	Troodos	113	
Limassol	Perapedi	124	
Limassol	Alektora	10	
Limassol	Omodos	12	
Limassol	Kilani	7	
Limassol	Platres	464	
Nicosia	Nicosia	429	547
Nicosia	Dali	16	
Nicosia	Kythrea	18	
Nicosia	Pedoula	15	
Nicosia	Morphou	69	
Paphos	Paphos	225	225
Total			2,208

Source: SA1/758/1916, numbers of mules purchased at various centres.

Cypriot mules purchased in 1916 were largely for the Serbian army. The British authorities in Salonica did not consider them suitable for the British army. But on 23 August 1916, Salonica wired Egyptforce that a better class of mule was available in Cyprus for £25–50 and that Colonel Holdsworth should find out how many were available.[18]

The purchasing and sending of mules and other animals to Salonica continued into 1917, although the recruiting of muleteers took precedence. From July 1916 to 30 September 1917 the Mule Purchasing Commission had purchased 5,881 transport animals, the majority being mules.[19]

In June and July 1919 the acting High Commissioner of Cyprus, Malcolm Stevenson, informed the Colonial Secretary, Lord Milner, that over 3,500 mules and over 3,000 donkeys had been exported for military purposes during the war (Table 4.2). He underestimated the mule numbers given that (see Table 3.3) in 1915 887 mules had been exported and he had left out 1914. This leads one to question the figures for the other years and to conclude that closer to 5,000 Cypriot mules were procured for military purposes.

Table 4.2 Transport animal exports

Year	Mules	Donkeys	Horses
1915	400	–	–
1916	2,750	1,200	140
1917	393	1,676	–
1918	–	373	–
Total	3,543	3,249	140

Source: SA1/910/1919, Stevenson to Milner, Colonial Sec., 3 June 1919 and 15 July 1919.

Goodchild was in Cyprus for several months in 1916 and 1917 and produced an important report on mule and donkey breeding on the island.[20] He claimed that Knapp's report of 1901 was

> so much to the point that very few new ideas can be put forward, even after the lapse of 16 or 17 years, during which time the conditions of road transport on the Island have considerably changed, and even also after the recent severe drain on animals caused by the purchase of mules made on a large scale for Army purposes under war conditions.[21]

Goodchild stated that mule and donkey exports from Cyprus were 'of considerable importance' and so 'the Government must decide which is of the most importance, the draught, the riding, or the pack animal' so it could focus on breeding the best of these. Because of the excellency of the Cypriot jennet, at size 13.1 hands to 14.1, an improvement from ten years earlier when most were 12.3 to 13.3 hands, they were ideal for army pack transport and according to Goodchild they 'cannot be surpassed in any country in the world'. Consequently, he recommended that 'it is to this class of animal that the most encouragement in breeding should be given'. In order to improve the jennet, it was important to develop the breeding of large donkey stallions, so that a plentiful supply of donkey mares was available. Thus, the Cypriot breed of donkey stallion would also improve and be sold to India. Equally important was to import a quality stallion breed, such as an English or Welsh variety. So, Goodchild concluded that 'when the excellency of the Cyprus donkey is maintained by selection, and the stamp of pony stallions is improved by importation, the production of that most useful and valuable pack animal – the Cyprus jennet – is sure to follow'.[22]

The district commissioner of Nicosia, C.S. Cade, and the principal forest officer, A.K. Bovill, agreed with Goodchild's recommendations, although Cade believed that the best locations for pony stallions were not the hills south of Mount Troodos (i.e. Platres, Fini, Omodos and Kilani), as Goodchild suggested, but on the plains at Morphou, Deftera, Lefkoniko and Vatili. It is not possible to determine from where the most mules were purchased, but it can be determined from where more muleteers were recruited, even though this is not an accurate representation of where better mules came from because many of the muleteers were inexperienced in handling mules. The results are instructive, since Morphou (11% of the 1911 male population), Deftera (12%) and Vatili (14%) had enlistment percentages well above district averages (Nicosia was 7.1% and Famagusta was 5.6%), while for Platres (0.8%), Fini (5.8%), Omodos (2.1%) and Kilani (6.7%) the averages were either on or below the district percentage (Limassol had 6.5% enlistment).

Goodchild's report had engaged Cypriot colonial service personnel and both contributed important recommendations on mule breeding. Not only were the Cypriot government and the British military authorities interested in breeding more mules, but they were interested in breeding better-quality mules, and these recommendations helped achieve this during the war, creating opportunities for Cypriot breeders to profit. A good example was the father of Dr Fazil Kuchuk (later the first Vice-President of Cyprus), who profited from breeding and selling mules to the British.[23] Yet the main game quickly shifted from procuring mules to enlisting drivers.

Muleteer numbers and composition

As already indicated, the number of Cypriot muleteers engaged for service in the British army in Salonica was staggering, as much as 25% of the male population aged 18 to 35 served at one time or another, meaning over 11,000 men, and most probably over 12,000, had served. Since Cypriots also served elsewhere in the British army, such as in Egypt and the Western Front, and in the merchant navy, they were, proportionally, the largest represented national group from the Empire serving in the British armed forces during the Great War, surpassing even the settler colonies and India. According to a note in the Cypriot State Archives, between July 1916 and March 1919, the period when recruitment was open, 12,288 Cypriots enlisted.[24]

This includes those who re-enlisted a second and sometimes a third time. These men can be determined from the Honour Roll in the War Office, which, however, ends in November 1918 with the armistice, because the Honour Roll was compiled in order to distribute the British War Medal and those enlisting after were ineligible. Also, because the mule corps was created in such a rush, records of those men enlisting in the early days are incomplete, with thousands of names missing.

Table 4.3 Enlistment numbers until March 1919

Date	Enlistment no.
4/7/16–24/1/1918	7609
25–31/1/1918	166
Feb 1918	734
March 1918	878
April 1918	248
May 1918	163
June 1918	170
July 1918	334
August 1918	161
September 1918	219
October 1918	235
November 1918	111
December 1918	198
January 1919	220
February 1919	345
March 1919	497
Total	12,288

Source: SA1/722/1916/1, note for Secretary of State by Chief Secretary, April 1919.

The Honour Roll contains 11,178 entries (including re-enlistments and hundreds of numbers missing); but more documents in the War Office and in the State Archives in Nicosia provide the names and numbers of other muleteers, several enlisting after the armistice, and others in the early days who were not on the Honour Roll. Once all the various lists were collated, the Honour Roll was consolidated, and 10,788 were found to be Cypriots. Then when those who re-enlisted were taken into account, 10,015 Cypriots were shown to have enlisted once (i.e. 775 re-enlisted), meaning that 19.5% of the male population (according to the 1911 census) aged 15–39 enlisted. Of these there were full addresses in Cyprus for 9,119, which still represents an average enlistment of 17.8% of the male population aged 15–39. The overall percentage (i.e. 19.5%) increases to 22.2% when it is considered that between December 1918 and March 1919 at least a further 1,371 men had enlisted according to the list in the State Archives in Nicosia, while it is possibly a higher figure since a muleteer has been found with the number 14,888, meaning an additional 1,580 enlisted. The 775 that re-enlisted represent 7.2% of the men (775/10,788). Taking 1,371 as the more accurate figure of enlistments after the armistice, it is logical that more of these men re-enlisted for a second and third time, and indeed of the 79 men for which there are details, 24 had enlisted before, representing 30%. If the average of the two percentages was taken, the average being 18.75% (257/1,371), this would provide an estimate of 1,114 Cypriots volunteering after the armistice, bringing the total estimate of Cypriots who enlisted to 11,129, representing 21.7% of the male population aged 15–39.[25]

This figure is likely even higher. First, there are still numerous regimental numbers missing, and indeed out of the first 3,000 numbers and names, over 1,400 are missing. To be sure many of these men would have re-enlisted a second time, while some of them were likely Macedonians, but no doubt the majority were Cypriots. In any event, it is not unreasonable to estimate the number of Cypriots at over 12,000. If the 18.75% was applied the number of men re-enlisting would be 262, while if the percentage of Macedonians were also applied, a further 140 would be factored out, bringing the total to 998 and the overall total to 12,127, making the average 24.1% of the male population aged 15–39. Second, the figure of 11,129 does not take into account that the Census figures for 1911 grouped age divisions thus: 15–19; 20–24; 25–29; 30–34; 35–39. Therefore, this takes into account boys aged 15, 16 and 17 who were mostly precluded. This would also increase the average, even if some men aged 40 initially did get through. Moreover, after the second wave of large recruitment in mid-1917, men aged over 35 were excluded, again increasing the percentage. It is therefore not unreasonable to claim that at least a quarter of the male population in Cyprus aged 18–35 volunteered.

The religious demographic composition of the Cypriot element reveals as much about urban and rural life on the island as it does about inter-communality. Some 90.4% of the Cypriot element were Eastern Orthodox Christians, 8.4% were Cypriot Muslims, and 0.77% were Maronite Christians, with smaller numbers of Armenians and others (Table 4.4).[26] This compares to the population distribution at the 1911 Census as follows: Eastern Orthodox Christians numbered 78.2%, Muslims were 20.6% and Maronites 0.4% (Table 4.5).

The religious distribution needs explanation. First, the percentage for the Orthodox Cypriots and Maronite Cypriots was not exact because the Maronites could only be determined from their villages (Kormakitis, Asomatos, Karpasha, all in the Kyrenia District, and Agia Marina, in the Nicosia District), therefore those living in towns, which numbered 64 in the 1911 Census, could not be identified. This would slightly reduce the Orthodox contribution to below 90% and slightly increase the Maronite enlistment. The 1911 Census, however, also has irregularities, since the number of Christians comes to 1,133 from the four villages of Kormakitis, Asomatos, Karpasha and Agia Marina, which were almost exclusively Maronite, and this figure was greater

Table 4.4 Religious/ethnic distribution of the Cypriot Mule Corps

Religion/ethnicity	Total enlisted	Re-enlisted	Total (excl. re-enlisted)	% Total (excl. re-enlisted)	% Cypriots
Orthodox/Cypriot	9,794	740	9,054	81	90.4
Muslim/Cypriot	875	29	846	7.57	8.45
Maronite/Cypriot	83	6	77	0.69	0.77
Armenian/Cypriot	25	0	25	0.22	0.25
Others/Cypriots	13	0	13	0.12	0.13
Orthodox/Macedonian	1,131	0	1,131	10.14	
Muslim/Macedonian	4	0	4	0.04	
Others/Non-Cypriots	22	0	22	0.2	
Total	11,947	775	11,172		10,015

Source: SA1/722/1916/1, note by Chief Secretary, April 1919, and WO405/1 and WO329/2357.

Table 4.5 Religious/ethnic distribution of population, 1911

Religion	Number	Percentage
Eastern Orthodox	214,280	78.2
Muslim	56,428	20.6
Maronite	1,073	0.4
Roman Catholic	815	0.3
Gregorian	549	0.2
Church of England	397	0.15
Jewish	193	0.07
Protestant	126	0.05
Presbyterian	25	0.009
Wesleyan	12	0.004
Catholic	9	0.003
Eastern Catholic	1	0.0
Total	274,108	

Source: Census report 1911.

than the total Maronites on the entire island, which is given as 1,073. This does not even include the few Maronites in Kambili village and those many more living in the urban centres, which according to the 1911 Census were 64, meaning that it was likely that there were 1,200 Cypriot Maronites in 1911. Ultimately, even at 0.77%, the Maronite enlistment was twice their population as an overall percentage of population.

A second issue is how to explain why the Muslim enlistment does not match their demographic representation on the island. It would be easy to assume that the comparatively lower Muslim enlistment was due to loyalties to the Ottoman Empire. Such assumptions would be readily made by Greek and Greek Cypriot nationalists, as well as by Turkish and Turkish Cypriot nationalists. As the work of Altay Nevzat and my own have shown, such assumptions are not black and white.[27] Indeed, there is a better explanation for the discrepancy. Cypriots, regardless of their religion, enlisted together. There are many examples on the Honour Role of Christians and Muslims from the same village enlisting on the same day. Given the distance from the villages to the recruiting centres, they probably travelled together.[28] Also, the tables below show that enlistment was greater in rural than in urban areas. This is indicated by the higher enlistment rates (almost 35%, when no other district had 20%) in the Kyrenia District, where there was little urbanisation (Table 4.6). II shows the average enlistment from the entire male population from across the districts, broken down into a selection of urban and rural centres, showing how rural areas had a

Table 4.6 Enlistment numbers and percentages across Cyprus

District	1911 Census – Males 15–39	Cyprus Mule Corps	% Males 15–39
Nicosia	15,366	2,909	18.93
Famagusta	10,658	1,570	14.73
Limassol	9,343	1,451	15.53
Paphos	6,842	1,274	18.62
Larnaca	5,669	737	13.00
Kyrenia	3,382	1,178	34.83
Total	51,260	9,119	17.79

Source: WO405/1 and WO329/2357.

Table 4.7 Distribution of population in urban centres, 1911

Municipality	% Orthodox Christians	% Muslims	% Other
Nicosia	58	37.6	4.4
Famagusta	77.6	20.7	1.6
Limassol	75	23	2.1
Paphos	51.4	47.9	0.7
Larnaca	68.3	25.4	6.3
Kyrenia	65	33	2

Source: Census 1911.

Table 4.8 Urban–rural spread in Cypriot Mule Corps

Urban–rural spread	No.	Percentage
Urban	1409	15.45
Semi-urban	306	3.36
Regional centre > 2,000	683	7.49
Village – large 900–1,999	1401	15.37
Village < 899	5240	57.47
N/A	79	0.87
Total	9,118	

Source: WO405/1 and WO329/2357.

much higher rate of enlistment. Table 4.7 shows that more Muslims lived in urban than in rural areas, hence their lower enlistment, while Table 4.8 shows that the Mule Corps was mostly composed of men from rural areas (almost 60%) and therefore mainly of peasants and rural labourers. Tables 4.4, 4.5 and 4.7 show that since the majority of the Cypriot population and muleteers were Orthodox Christians and more Orthodox Christians lived in rural areas compared to Muslim Cypriots, then most of the Mule Corps was bound to be Orthodox Christians. This argument is strengthened by Appendix II, which shows that, with the exception of Limassol, the percentage of enlistment across the rural areas of each district was always more than the percentage of the town. Additionally, villages (<900) had a much higher percentage of enlistment than urban (towns), semi-urban (villages near towns) and regional centres (2,000+ people and away from towns), and, with a few exceptions, also of larger villages (900+ population). Also noteworthy was the high enlistment rate of the two *chiftliks*, large rural plantations with rural labourers. The anomaly of Limassol can be explained by the fact that there were no semi-urban or regional centres and therefore the urban centre had a higher population of Orthodox Christian working class; nor did the large villages attract the same enlistment as other districts, thus they played the role of regional centres, but on a smaller scale. Again, as in the other districts, the bulk of the enlistment came from villages.

Proportionally, Kyrenia District, the smallest, with the town being less populated than the nearby regional centre of Lapithos, had the most enlistment. The district also had two large villages, Karavas, adjacent to Lapithos, and Dicomo, with high enlistment. Many of the villages were isolated from the rest of the island because they fell on the sea-side of the Pentadaktylos Mountain range. The district was primarily known for its citrus groves. It followed the national trend in terms of the town enlistment rates being less in larger and built-up areas, namely the towns, Lapithos, Dicomo and Karavas, compared to the villages, which had higher rates. What marks Kyrenia apart was the much greater rates generally, with numerous villages and large villages having more than 20% enlistment of men, and Lapithos over 15%, making it the largest regional centre. The lack of urbanisation and the growth in population meant a scarcity of work, which gave the mule corps an added importance for the people, even if Paphos was poorer.[29]

The numbers of foremen and interpreters also reveal much about the backgrounds of the men doing these jobs. It could be assumed that foremen and interpreters came from the urban centres, but this holds true only for the interpreters. Altogether 312 foremen were listed and since six are listed twice there were 306, and of these 95 were Macedonians, making the Cypriot element 211. Interestingly, the percentages across the various Cypriot groups mirrored the findings overall, with Orthodox Cypriots making up 90% and Muslim Cypriots 8.5%. There was one overseer of the foremen, a Macedonian named Ioannis Koupsanis, but it is not clear what his actual role as overseer

Table 4.9 Ethno-religious composition of foremen

Ethnic/religious	No.	Overall percentage	Cypriot percentage
Orthodox Cypriots	190	62.1	90
Muslim Cypriots	18	5.88	8.53
Maronite Cypriots	2	0.65	0.95
Latin Cypriots	1	0.33	0.47
Macedonians	95	31	
Total	306		
Total Cypriots	211		

Source: WO405/1 and WO329/2357.

Table 4.10 Urban–rural composition of Cypriot foremen

	No.	Percentage
Urban	51	24.2
Semi-urban	5	2.4
Regional centre	15	7.1
Village – large	12	5.69
Village	48	22.75
N/A	80	37.9
Total	211	

Source: WO405/1 and WO329/2357.

was or for how long he served. The foremen came from various urban as well as rural parts of the island, as some were immediately accepted as foremen while others were promoted later. More foremen came from urban areas than the overall average for the mule corps, yet there was a sizeable rural component.

There were 87 interpreters – three were Macedonians and two Cypriots enlisted twice, making 82 Cypriots (see Appendix III). Of these, Polyvios Kyprianos from Nicosia was the Chief Interpreter. According to the war diary of the 10th Divisional Train, three Cypriot interpreters reported for work on 12 August 1916, yet they are not listed in the honour roll,[30] indicating that perhaps there were more, since Stevenson claimed 100.[31] Additionally in May 1918 the British Minister in Athens informed Long, Director of Supplies and Transport, that 'Cypriot students have declared that a majority of them are ready to volunteer for service in the British Army' and Long wanted 20 as interpreters.[32] It is doubtful if they were taken. The ethno-religious breakdown revealed 67 Orthodox, four Muslims and four Armenians, three Latin Catholics, and one Arab Christian, a Christian of unknown

Table 4.11 Ethno-religious composition of interpreters

Ethnic/religious	No.	Overall percentage	Cypriot percentage
Orthodox Cypriots	67	78.8	81.7
Muslim Cypriots	4	4.7	4.9
Armenian Cypriots	4	4.7	4.9
Latin Cypriots	3	3.5	3.7
Other Cypriots	4	4.7	4.9
Macedonians	3	3.5	
Total	85		
Total Cypriots	82		

Source: WO405/1 and WO329/2357.

Table 4.12 Urban–rural composition of Cypriot interpreters

	No.	Percentage
Urban	61	74.4
Semi-urban	1	1.2
Regional centre	4	4.9
Village – large	1	1.2
Village	13	15.9
N/A	2	2.4
Total	82	

Source: WO405/1 and WO329/2357.

denomination, an Anglican and a Scot. This shows that the Muslims were about half in representation as their overall numbers, reflecting the fact that Muslims were less likely to learn English than Christians, even though proportionally more Muslims lived in urban centres. The incentive for Cypriots with interpreting skills was also money, since they would earn GDR 5 a day, with rations and clothing as for muleteers.[33] Compared to foremen, interpreters were heavily drawn from urban places (Table 4.12). However, that 16% came from villages shows that rural families did send their children to schools to learn English.

Why were interpreters needed since there were Macedonian Grecophone Christians and Turko-phone Muslims? Cypriot interpreters provided translation that only they could, since the Cypriot languages, belonging to the Greek or Turkish family of languages, were different to mainstream Greek and Turkish, in a similar way that Maltese, which belongs to the Arabic family of languages, differs from mainstream Arabic languages, because of Italian influences.[34] Greeks and

Turks in Greece could not provide such a service because they did not understand Cypriot Greek and Turkish, and even the British who learned mainstream Greek and Turkish could not.[35] Interpreters could be placed in a position of harm and did travel to the front, since the General Routine Orders from June 1917 stipulated that they could be asked to carry arms if their commanding officer ordered them to do so for their safety.[36]

The civil status of the men in the Mule Corps reveals that men from all ages and situations were enlisted. Most men were single, but many were or had been married. There was next of kin information for 9,578 of them, a large sample and an excellent basis for analysis. Those that re-enlisted a second and third time have been counted for each time, because aside from the task of filtering them out the second and third time, often they gave a different next of kin. The breakdown shown in the next two tables reveals that 30.77% of the men put their father as next of kin, followed by their wife at 24.96% and then their mothers at 22.98%. Overall, as can be seen in Table 4.14, at least 27.53% of the men were married, had been married or were engaged. In Cyprus being engaged meant that a religious ceremony had been administered and it was very hard to 'back out' of such a commitment, and therefore was 'as good' as being married. The enlistment rate of married men was high even if it was short of the 40.36% of men (from age 15) in the 1911 Census that were married. Most of these men had children and therefore they had a greater financial responsibility. Furthermore, Cypriots often lived in extended families, taking care of parents and grandparents, with males, especially the first born, contributing towards dowries for their sister(s). This reinforces the argument that the need for money and the wages on offer (as well as free clothes and food) attracted them. Additionally, according to a report by Stevenson in March 1920, a much larger amount of land was under cultivation from 1918 than before the war, indicating that peasants were investing the wages of muleteers into their land to sell produce to the British.[37] Overall the statistics reveal an even spread across the age group 18–39, although there must have been a greater number of men between the ages of 18 and 25 because there were more single men and only a few listed their children (who needed to be 18) as next of kin.

The need to boost recruitment increased over time and, despite a number of threats, rates increased when needed. On 3 January 1917 Long advised Major-General Clarke, Deputy Adjunct and Quartermaster General, and Milne, that various matters connected with recruiting Cypriot muleteers needed resolving. He wanted to send Major I.M. Heilbron, ASC, to the island to improve matters.[38]

Table 4.13 Next of kin results for Cypriot Mule Corps members

Next of kin	No.	Percentage
Father	2,947	30.77
Wife	2,391	24.96
Mother	2,201	22.98
Brother	640	6.68
Sister	613	6.40
Uncle	194	2.03
Friend	89	0.93
Brother-in-law	76	0.79
Son	65	0.68
Cousin	54	0.54
Fiancée	46	0.48
Godfather	34	0.35
Aunt	32	0.33
Cypriot government	32	0.33
Daughter	29	0.30
Nephew	28	0.29
Grandmother	14	0.15
Church	13	0.14
Father-in-law	11	0.11
Niece	9	0.09
Sister-in-law	9	0.09
Grandfather	6	0.06
Master	6	0.06
Best man	5	0.05
Father (allotted)	5	0.05
Mother-in-law	5	0.05
Relative	4	0.04
Stepmother	3	0.03
Godmother	2	0.02
Guardian	2	0.02
Next of kin	2	0.02
Poor asylum	2	0.02
Stepfather	2	0.02
Godbrother	1	0.01
Godsister	1	0.01
Guardian (allotted)	1	0.01
Merchant	1	0.01
Mother (allotted)	1	0.01
Red Cross	1	0.01
Representative	1	0.01
Total	9,578	

Source: WO405/1 and WO329/2357.

Table 4.14 Next of kin breakdown of married men

Next of kin	No.	Percentage
Wife	2,391	24.96
Brother-in-law	76	0.79
Son	65	0.68
Fiancée	46	0.48
Daughter	29	0.30
Father-in-law	11	0.11
Sister-in-law	9	0.09
Best man	5	0.05
Mother-in-law	5	0.05
Total	2,637/9,578	27.53

Source: WO405/1 and WO329/2357.

Table 4.15 Civil status of men, 1911 Census

	Unmarried	Married	Widowed	Divorced	Total
Males aged 15+ 1911 Census	83,122	52,340	3,899	22	139,383
Percentage	59.64%	37.55%	2.8%	0.02%	

Source: 1911 Census.

Clarke's reply queried why he needed another representative since he had Major Sisman. Long believed that he should have gone to Cyprus personally or sent a representative to inspect the work there, but since Clarke thought it unnecessary he backed off.[39]

In January 1918 the Colonial Office informed Clauson and Sisman that the War Office wanted 4,000 more Cypriot muleteers in eight months at a rate of 500 per month. The Colonial Secretary, Walter Long, told Clauson that he was 'most anxious to meet War Office wishes'. He asked for information on how many had been recruited so far and at what rate per month.[40] Sisman reported that from 4 July 1916 to 24 July 1917, 7,609 Cypriots had enlisted (including those who had re-enlisted),[41] and the average per month for 1916 and 1917 was 398. When he was in Salonica in July 1917 Rycroft had 'impressed upon me [Sisman] the necessity of obtaining every available recruit', something Milne had also done.[42] On 10 September 1917 Brigadier-General Long received Rycroft report's from his visit to the Muleteer Depot and Training School on Lembet Road (see start of this chapter). Rycroft observed that training was going well and new muleteers would prove 'more satisfactory than has often been the case in the past, as they will join their units with a certain knowledge of how to harness or saddle animals and how to clean their harness'. Some of the older men could do other work, such as in remount depots or veterinary lines, where they could relieve British personnel. Rycroft recommended not only encouraging Cypriot recruitment, but increasing it. Long doubted that many more could be recruited because the system was voluntary, but would have Sisman try. Transport was a major problem, because often up to 400 men were awaiting shipment at Famagusta for three months. It was just as hard to repatriate the Cypriots and 'we have had hundreds of men in the Muleteer Depot here waiting for passage for weeks and months before shipping could be found for them' and it did not look like improving soon. A regular shipping service was necessary.[43] In Cyprus, Sisman, with Clauson's support, formed new depot under British and Cypriot officers. On 24 August Sisman wired Long that about 150 muleteers would be shipped to Salonica per month, increasing to 180 per month in four weeks and higher later.[44] By the end of 1917 the average rate had increased to on or above 400 a month. But the shipment problem continued. In October Sisman informed Long that 500 muleteers were awaiting shipment to Salonica.[45] Two weeks later they were still there, but had grown to 600 muleteers and 25 interpreters.[46]

In response to the request for 500 per month for eight months, in January 1918 Sisman reported that there was 'every chance of getting 450 per month for the next 3–4 months'.[47] The War Office, however, increased their demand. Long cabled Clauson on 11 March 1918 that the War Office wanted to know if contracts could be changed to lock muleteers in for the duration of the war and whether monthly recruiting rates could be increased to 1,000.[48] Clauson replied that 'enlistment for [the] period of [the] war would most seriously prejudice recruiting of Cypriots' and that the present monthly recruitment rate had increased to 700, but 500 was the maximum that could be maintained.[49] Indeed all concerned on the island had underestimated themselves: for the last week of January 1918, 166 men were recruited; for February there were 734, and for March 878, dropping to 248 in April.[50] These numbers merely represented those enlisted, since many more had volunteered, since Sisman noted that from 1 January to 6 March, 2,097 men had volunteered and 40.9% had been rejected.[51]

In May and June 1918 volunteers fell owing to the harvesting season. On 8 July Long noted that there were only 260 muleteers awaiting shipment. In Salonica contracts were ending and by the end of 1918, 2,684 were eligible for discharge. Long decided that the situation necessitated that he draw upon the reserve of 250 British Horse Transport Drivers until recruiting picked up again in Cyprus or a large number of Cypriots re-enlisted. If this did not happen 'the question of reinforcements is going to be acute ... [and] the general question of personnel for Horse Transport Units is worthy of immediate consideration as regards source of supply of reinforcements'.[52] In order to stimulate recruitment, a new poster (discussed below) was introduced.[53] This time the call for more recruits was only a moderate success. In November 1918 a mere 292 muleteers were awaiting shipment to Salonica to replace the 205 being discharged at the end of that month.[54] The situation was desperate enough for the authorities in Salonica to request 1,000 Indian muleteers (something that had been previously ruled out).[55] In December Long claimed that 855 Cypriot muleteers were due for discharge in that month and unless replacements were forthcoming or muleteers re-enlisted 'for further duty', it would be necessary to demobilise British personnel from various horse transport companies.[56] The 128 muleteers awaiting shipment at Famagusta were insufficient.[57] In January 1919 Sisman wired that there was one officer and nine other ranks of the Royal Army Supply Company and two officers and one other rank from the Royal Army Medical Corps working on muleteer recruiting, which was on average 225 per month, with potential to climb to 300.[58]

By mid-March 1919 Long informed Egyptforce of the imminent closure of the Salonica base.[59] On 28 March 1919 he contacted all concerned that the recruitment of Cypriot muleteers would cease, and those serving would be discharged as soon as their services were not required.[60] On the next day he asked Rycroft to arrange on the Asiatic side of Constantinople for the establishment of the Base Horse Transport and Base Muleteer Depots.[61] In September 1919, 600 Cypriot muleteers became surplus to requirements and were discharged.[62]

The effectiveness of the Cypriot muleteers

The need for Cypriot muleteers cannot be questioned, yet the effectiveness of their work was not always considered highly. Problems arose in July and August 1916 with the Macedonian and Cypriot muleteers. On 26 July 27 men of the 'Macedonian Mule Corps' joined the 31st Field Ambulance, Royal Army Medical Corps in the 10th Division.[63] These new men were Cypriots, since 153 Cypriots had arrived the previous day.[64] They were working well. On 3 August another 19 men joined them, likely Macedonians, since in refusing to work they asked to return to Salonica. The commanding officer duly put them under guard.[65] On the next day the Officer Commanding the Mule Corps hurried to the 31st Field Ambulance to deal with the matter, but there is no information on what was done, other than to note that muleteers were subject to field punishment.⁶⁶ On 5 September 1916 the authorities in Salonica informed London that it was unfeasible for one Cypriot or Macedonian muleteer to lead more than two large mules. In October the Commanding Officer of the divisional train of the 10th Division visited Long to discuss 'various points affecting [the] Macedonians and Cypriots and calculated to increase their efficiency'.⁶⁷ Yet there were still reports of Cypriot muleteers malingering.⁶⁸

In February 1917 Clarke cabled the War Office that 'Macedonian and Cypriot Muleteers [were] already employed to [the] fullest extent with Divisional Trains and Field Ambulances. Do not recommend any further employment'.⁶⁹ Long noted on 1 April that Divisional Trains had 50% Macedonian and Cypriot muleteers and would not recommend more. Days earlier he had rejected suggestions that Indian personnel could replace the Cypriots even though

> Indians might advantageously be employed to form the personnel of Divisional Trains (particularly in the Pack Echelons) and replace the Macedonians and Cypriots. It was pointed out, however, that it is not considered desirable to mix Indian personnel with white in one unit.⁷⁰

A year later the matter was raised again. This time Long rejected it because he preferred to increase Cypriot enlistment, which had restarted in earnest.⁷¹ Long revealed that

> Considerable difficulty is experienced with regard to Cypriot muleteers – both from the point of view of behaviour and venereal disease and the question of ceasing to recruit this class of man has been seriously considered, but it is not considered advisable to do this in view of the fact that we are ... unable to obtain Macedonians ... and the length of time it will take to get the Indian personnel introduced to the H.T. Units here. DAG writes with reference to a minute of the Provost Marshall concerning these men that they should be sent back to Cyprus at their own expense when discharged from the service and forfeiting their free passage to Cyprus, and that they should be handed over on to the ship under escort. This would prevent the undesirables still remaining in Salonica. I write to DAG that the one disadvantage of this scheme is that the Muleteers might try to 'work their ticket' if they know that they can get back to Cyprus.⁷²

Cypriots were a source of concern, but they were the preferred source because Indians were rejected on racial grounds and Macedonians, not much better, were unobtainable. On 6 August General Lawson visited various units for the Man Power Commission and suggested that the ASC horse transport drivers be replaced 'as far as possible by Macedonians and Cypriots who, although unaccustomed to "ride and drive" could be taught'.⁷³

Strategies of muleteer recruiting

Not all Cypriots were effective, but they were the best the British could get. How did they obtain so many volunteers? They needed to implement successful recruitment strategies in much haste in 1916 because the military authorities in Salonica needed the muleteers immediately and the request had come with little warning. Quick decisions were needed on the best strategies and how to implement these. The colonial government was not trained for such a task, but it knew the Cypriot peasant and labouring classes well, and had personnel who spoke the Cypriot language. Three decisions proved decisive: the prevention by law of the emigration of Cypriot males of military age; the appropriate use of communication methods to deliver the message to the peasant and labouring classes; and the various benefits, especially monetary, that were offered.

The first decisive decision that resolved the falling off of Cypriot enlistment was the passing of a regulation on 19 October 1916 forbidding the emigration of males of military age.[74] Clauson claimed that the impediments to enlisting Cypriots as muleteers was competing with the emigration of men to the USA, or their engagement as seasonal workers in Egypt and for the French armed forces.[75] He revealed that between 1 January and 21 October 1916 940 passports had been issued to Cypriots for the USA. The average Cypriot immigrant commanded two or three dollars a day and could live on half a dollar, while those knowing some English could earn up to five dollars a day. He was equally worried about Cypriot labourers being offered employment in France for an incredible £6 to £8 a day. Both options were 'adversely affecting the recruitment of transport drivers'.[76]

This justified Clauson's decisive action, which was sparked when on 15 August 1916 Long cabled Sisman asking when the 1,500 muleteers would be furnished to make up the 3,000 promised.[77] Sisman cabled the next day that enlistment was 'falling off'. Long noted that counting the 550 arriving tomorrow only 1,600 would have arrived from Cyprus and 'it seems unlikely that our demand for 3,000 will be realised'.[78] It was then that the Salonica authorities asked Venizelos if they could recruit in Crete, which he agreed, but doubted that they would obtain anywhere near the 1,000 they wanted.[79] On 21 August Sisman wired Long that the remainder of the 3,000 muleteers would be available before the end of September when the harvest was over.[80] It was not until 29 August that Sisman informed Salonica that 500 mules and donkeys and 300 muleteers should be ready to send by 6 September.[81] On the next day Long wired that he also needed 30 interpreters, who would be paid at foremen wages.[82] Sisman next confirmed that another 500 muleteers would be ready to embark for Salonica on 11 September.[83] Yet these, along with the 410 muleteers that had arrived from Cyprus on 6 September,[84] still meant a 1,200 shortfall and on 7 October Long asked Sisman when these men could be furnished.[85] Two days later Sisman cabled that the 1,200 would be available by 20 November,[86] but nothing was said about how they were going to get them until 1 November when Sisman informed Long that upon his representations Clauson had issued a proclamation forbidding emigration and that enlistment was improving.[87] Indeed, on 24 October Clauson had published in the *Cyprus Gazette* the following proclamation of five days earlier: 'From the 19th October, 1916, and until further order, no person deemed fit for Military Service will be allowed to leave Cyprus without special permission.'[88]

This decisive step worked. Without any chance of leaving the island for work abroad, Cypriot men had little alternative but to volunteer as muleteers in the British army. Long noted, as of 6 November 1916, 3,496 Cypriot muleteers, foremen and interpreters had enlisted.[89] On 2 December 1916 Sisman informed Long that 600 muleteers would be ready to embark from Cyprus on 15 December (637 arrived on 19 December) and wanted to know how many more were wanted.[90] Long needed another 1,000 to complete establishments in Salonica and another 500 to replace 'wastages'; those killed or discharged because they were unsuitable, diseased or injured. He added that since volunteering was strong, only the best men should be enlisted.[91] A further 863 muleteers were to leave Cyprus on 5 January, which Long told Sisman would complete existing deficiencies, but he should maintain the enlistment of 300 muleteers per month to replace wastage.[92] This was done, since on 10 February 1917 another 700 were ready.[93]

The Cypriot government correctly decided that posters were the best method of communicating the offer to the Cypriots. The posters did not only serve as a source of information, but also as a source for attracting curiosity, since, as Table 4.16 shows, over 73% of the population was illiterate in 1911, and over 60% of the male population was illiterate and therefore could not read the posters or leaflets produced. Given that the majority of these men lived in rural areas, the proportion of illiterate was therefore greater in the villages, from where the vast majority of the muleteers were recruited. This means that most men who enlisted needed a literate person to explain the posters and leaflets.

The first poster was rushed out in summer 1916. At the top in the largest font and decreasing in size it stated: 'Muleteers wanted for the British Armies advancing in Macedonia and Bulgaria, splendid opportunity for the Cypriot young men to see the world and take

Table 4.16 Literacy in Cyprus, 1911 Census

Sex	Read and write	Read only	Illiterate	Total pop.
Males	53,841 = 38.63%	1,012 = 0.73%	84,530 = 60.65%	139,383
Females	17,044 = 12.65%	1,519 = 1.31%	116,162 = 86.22%	134,725
Total	70,885 = 25.86%	2,531 = 0.92%	200,692 = 73.22%	274,108

Source: 1911 Census.

part in the Great War'. Next the poster outlined the wages: £4.15.0 to £6.0.0 for foremen; £4.15.0 for saddlers, farriers and coach-makers; and £3.12.0. for muleteers. It also added that food and clothing were provided free of charge. Lastly, in small print, the poster detailed the allotment scheme, free repatriation at the end of the war, and that applicants needed to be aged 19–40 and present themselves to the Mule Purchasing Commission at Famagusta.[94] Recruitment numbers show that the poster and leaflet strategy worked.

The main incentive was money. In the 1913 edition of the *Handbook of Cyprus* produced by the Cypriot government the wages of agricultural labourers were put at 3 to 18 Cypriot Piastres (Grosha locally) a month and between £CY 2 and £CY 20 a year, depending if board and food were included.[95] Nothing had changed in the 1920 edition, except that it was added that during harvest such workers could earn up to 36 Cypriot Piastres a month with food.[96] This was a pittance in comparison to the wages offered in the mule corps.

As the first year of service was drawing to a close, the Cypriot colonial authorities embarked upon a new advertising campaign after the military authorities in Salonica wanted more muleteers. Again posters and leaflets were the preferred method of communication, despite the low literacy rates. In what was either a draft of a leaflet or poster (none was found in the archives), probably from Salonica because there was a lack of knowledge on muleteer recruiting in Cyprus, the handwritten notice fixed the age range at 18–35, following Rycroft's recommendation and Long's orders to Sisman on 9 September.[97] The only other important point about it was that it invited all those who would 'like to see Greece and the world' to volunteer, but the Cypriot authorities never mentioned Greece in any of the posters, probably because for political reasons it was inappropriate or because they did not consider it an inducement for the peasantry and labouring classes.[98]

The draft notice influenced the poster produced and distributed at the end of 1917.[99] At the top it announced in large capital letters that 'all healthy men aged 18–35, all volunteers to obtain huge wages' should read on. The notice began with, 'Food, clothes and 90 Drachma a month', which was clarified in small print as £3.12.0. It then asked, 'if you want to see the world' go to one of the recruiting camps in Famagusta, Limassol and Paphos to become a muleteer in the service of the British army. The third strategy to attract the Cypriot was to claim that they would 'not be in any danger', explaining that service as a muleteer was not military service and that it would be far from the front. The next move was to promise free repatriation and that their pockets would be full of money. Finally, the last strategy was to offer to pay up to GDR 50 a month to relatives. What was proposed followed the same approach and virtually the same content as previous posters, excepting the lowering of the age from 40 to 35 and 19 to 18.

The posters were clearly the primary source of advertising, since a survey of the Cypriot newspapers found that the Mule Corps was seldom mentioned. Only one article advertised recruitment. The author, Evagoras Savvides, who worked as a clerk for the Mule Purchasing Commission, later enlisted as an interpreter, 13308. In the article he revealed that he was the director of the recruiting station at Kalo Chorko near Lefka, and that there were additional stations in the area (north-western district of Nicosia) at Pyrgo Tyllirias and Morphou. The enlisted men remained at the stations for as long as it took to arrange for their transportation on the train to Famagusta, meanwhile receiving free food. Savvides claimed that 'this is the most opportune time ... because of the lack of work opportunities to think about enlistment, because aside from the stable wage and clothing, food was free'. Savvides argued that the £3.15.0 per month, in wages could never be earned in Cyprus from agriculture, especially with the bad harvest in 1916 leaving some 'close to suffering from hunger'. He reassured those thinking about enlisting that their lives would not be in any danger since they would be nowhere near the frontline.[100] Savvides, as the Cypriot government did, appealed to the labouring and peasant classes, promising them a secure wage, food and clothing, safety, and that they would not be subjected to military law. This last promise was of course inaccurate.

The British understood that most Cypriot peasants and labourers were poor and illiterate and in some cases did not have access to newspapers. They appealed to what they needed, money and clothes, and used them as models to attract others. It was proposed to have muleteers surrender their old clothes and a sum given to them upon repatriation to purchase new ones.[101] Sisman argued that there may not be enough clothes at Famagusta for 300 or so men and if they were given such an allowance they might waste it. Sisman revealed that

> From the report of the Officer in charge of discharged muleteers, it appears that a great deal of gambling is indulged in on board the transport, although every effort is made to prevent it. Thus it is that many of the men arrive destitute, and beg to be taken in to the Depot at Famagusta for food and billets.

Their failure to return as 'rich men' and the poverty of the village pushed many into re-enlisting after a few weeks in their villages, but only the most fit were retaken, and those rejected hung around the depot to offer their services in exchange for food. Sisman believed that 'Apparently the village diet to which they return does not come up to their army rations.'[102] Clearly Sisman feared that an allowance would either be gambled away or used to purchase food, but he recognised that there was no alternative.[103] On 4 January 1918 Long noted that it had been decided that muleteers would be clothed during training at Famagusta so they could be seen in public and thus create a sense of pride in them and those seeing them, and that their old clothes would be given to local tailors who would sell clothing to time-expired muleteers up to 10 shillings, including a jacket, trousers and cap.[104] Sisman made these arrangements by 19 January and Salonica sent 500 sets of uniforms monthly.[105]

Conclusion

Can the Cypriot muleteers be considered 'subaltern'? The British colonised the Cypriots and although they considered the Cypriot Christians as 'European', within the British imperial project the Cypriots (as a whole) occupied a space on the fringes of Orientalism.[106] Using Spivak's definition of the 'subaltern' (via Gramsci and Guha), the muleteers that enlisted (and their families) were indeed the 'men and women among the illiterate peasantry, the tribals, the lowest strata of the urban subproletariat'[107] and lacked agency in the relationship between the all-powerful coloniser and disempowered colonised. In the case of the Cypriot Mule Corps the peasant and labouring classes were given little option but to enlist to serve in the British army, as the British were able to play on local push factors to pull in volunteers. These push-and-pull factors revolved around money and other material incentives, because the majority of the men being peasants and rural or urban labourers meant that they were attracted by the financial and material rewards, especially given the few opportunities on the island and the banning of emigration. Being a part of the British Empire presented, in this case, a unique opportunity, but it was subject to British control.

Notes

1   1 SA1/978/1916, Christou, no. 3743, to Fenn, CSC, 7 March 1920.
2   SA1/722/1916, Rycroft, DQMGC, to Milne, 6 September 1917.
3   SA1/722/1916, Sisman to Stevenson, 12 July 1917.
4   Spivak, 'Can the Subaltern Speak?' 283.
5   Smith, *Jamaican Volunteers in the First World War*.
6   Ibid.
7   CO67/181/40421, secret, Clauson to Bonar Law, 7 August 1916, with enclosures; for early promises see CO67/181/32730, various minutes, summaries of correspondence between Salonica and Cyprus.
8   SA1/758/1916, Copy of Clauson's Proclamation, 14 August 1916.
9   Ibid.

10   For the Hill Station see Varnava, 'Recreating Rural Britain and Maintaining Britishness in the Mediterranean'.
11   SA1/758/1916, telegram, Fenn, ACSC, to Bolton, DCLi, 14 August 1916; letter, Fenn, ACSC, to Bolton, DCLi, 14 August 1916; telegram, Fenn, ACSC, to Kyriakides, 14 August 1916; Bolton, DCLi, to Fenn, 15 August 1916; copy of notice put up at villages.
12   Kareklas was noted for later researching and writing the report on the notorious Hassanpoullia crime gang. M.C. Kareklas, *The Criminal Activities of the Hassanpoulia*, Government Printing Office, Nicosia, 1938.
13   SA1/758/1916, Fenn, ACSC, to Colonel G. Holdsworth, 14 August 1916; Fenn, ACSC, to Cade, DCNi, 19 August 1916; ADCLa to Fenn, ACSC, 25 August 1916; Fenn, ACSC, to Goodchild, 31 August 1916; Fenn, ACSC, to all commissioners and treasurer, 2 September 1916; Fenn, ACSC, to Goodchild, 2 September 1916.
14   SA1/758/1916, list of villages from which to commandeer mules; Fenn to Bovill and Cade, 31 August 1916.
15   Ibid., Goodchild to Orr, CSC, 19 September 1916.
16   SA1/758/1916, Fenn to all district commissioners, 26 September 1916.
17   SA1/722/1916 Clauson, notes for Secretary of State, 5 June 1917.
18   WO95/4763, despatch messages, AHQ, Salonica, to Egyptforce, 23 August 1916.
19   SA1/758/1916, Sisman to Stevenson, 22 October 1917.
20   *Cyprus: Horse, Mule and Donkey Breeding, 1901 and 1917*, 4–6.
21   Ibid., 4.
22   Ibid., 5.
23   I thank Mete Hatay, PRIO Cyprus Centre, Nicosia, for this information.
24   See SA1/722/1916/1, note for Secretary of State, by CSC, April 1919.
25   Ibid; also, WO405/1 and WO329/2357.
26   See WO405/1 and WO329/2357.
27   Nevzat, *Nationalism amongst the Turks of Cyprus*; Varnava, 'British Military Intelligence in Cyprus'.
28   Using WO405/1.
29   Tyser, *Cyprus*, 1, 6–7.
30   WO95/4833, WDSA, Divisional Train, 10th Division, 9 July 1916.
31   CO67/192/44124, Stevenson to Milner, 15 July 1918.
32   WO95/4791, WDSA, Long, DSTS, 15 May 1918.
33   WO95/4790, WDSA, Long, DSTS, 28 August 1917.
34   C.M. Bowra, 'Homeric Words in Cyprus', *Journal of Hellenic Studies*, 54, 1934, 54–74; K. Hatziioannou, Περί των εν τη Μεσαιωνική και Νεωτέρα Κυπριακή Ξένων Γλωσσών Στοιχείων (On the medieval and modern Cypriot foreign language data), Athens, 1936; R.M. Dawkins, *The Nature of the Cypriot Chronicle of Leontios Machaeras*, Oxford 1945; G. Horrocks, *Greek: A History of its Language and its Speakers*, Longman, London, 1997, 298–333; C. Giakoullis, Θησαυρός Κυπριακής Διαλέκτου (Thesaurus of the Cypriot dialect), Nicosia, 2002.
35   D'Abernon Papers, British Library, 48928, 113–14, Cobham to D'Arbernon, 4 January 1881. D'Arbernon (Vincent) had been offered a student dragomanship at Constantinople.
36   WO95/4766, WDSA, GRO, by Milne, 10 June 1917.
37   CO67/197/17873, Stevenson to Milner, 26 March 1920.
38   WO95/4790, WDSA, Long, DSTS, 3 January 1917.
39   Ibid., 4 January 1917.
40   SA1/722/1916/1, Telegram, Long, Colonial Sec, to Clauson, 22 January 1918.
41   Ibid., Sisman to Stevenson, CSC, 24 January 1918.
42   Ibid., Sisman Memorandum on Muleteer Recruiting, 24 January 1918.
43   WO95/4790, WDSA, Long, DSTS, 10 September 1917.
44   Ibid., 24 August and 20 September 1917.
45   Ibid., 11 October 1917.
46   Ibid., 25 October 1917.
47   SA1/722/1916/1, Sisman Memorandum on Muleteer Recruiting, 24 January 1918.

MULE AND MULETEER RECRUITMENT

48 Ibid., telegram, Long to Clauson, 11 March 1918.
49 Ibid., telegram, Clauson to Long, 12 March 1918.
50 Ibid., note for Secretary of State by CSC, April 1919.
51 Ibid., Sisman to Stevenson, 7 March 1918.
52 WO95/4791, WDSA, Long, DSTS, 8 July 1918.
53 Ibid., 10 August 1918.
54 Ibid., 12 November 1918.
55 Ibid., 25 November 1918.
56 Ibid., 16 December 1918.
57 Ibid., 27 December 1918.
58 Ibid., 25 January 1919.
59 Ibid., 13 March 1919.
60 Ibid., 28 March 1919.
61 Ibid., 29 March 1919 and 14 April 1919.
62 WO95/4952, WDSA, DSTBS, 24 September 1919.
63 WO95/4833, WDSA, 31st Field Ambulance, RAMC, 10th Division, 26 July and 3 August 1916.
64 WO95/4790, WDSA, Long, DSTS, 22 and 25 July, 1916. See Table 3.1.
65 WO95/4833, WDSA, 31st Field Ambulance, RAMC, 10th Division, 26 July and 3 August 1916.
66 Ibid., Divisional Train, 10th Division, 4 August 1916.
67 Ibid., 10 October 1916.
68 WO95/4790, WDSA, Long, DSTS, 16 November 1916.
69 WO95/4763, WDSA, 22 February 1917.
70 WO95/4790, WDSA, Long, DSTS, 1 April 1917.
71 WO95/4791, WDSA, Long, DSTS, 21 March 1918.
72 WO95/4790, WDSA, Long, DSTS, 29 April 1917.
73 Ibid., 6 August 1917.
74 *The Cyprus Gazette*, 1252, 24 October 1916.
75 SA1/1083/1916/1, General Agent Cyprus, Elias Papadopoulos, advertisement, translated 17 October 1916; ibid., Carauna Fils to High Commissioner of Australia in the UK, 24 September 1916; ibid., Caruana Fils to Secretary of Emigrants' Information Office, London, 24 September 1916; ibid., T.C. MacNaghten, Chairman, Emigrants' Information Office, to CO, 11 October 1916; ibid., Bonar Law to Clauson, 19 October 1916; ibid., CO to Chairman, Immigrants Information Office, 19 October 1916; ibid., Clauson to Bonar Law, 6 November 1916; ibid., HM Consul, Lyons, to Clauson, 19 October 1916; ibid., ACSC to HM Consul, Lyons, 8 Nov 1916; ibid., Caruana Fils to CSC, 1 September 1919.
76 Ibid., Clauson to Bonar Law, 6 November 1916; Sisman agreed that the French were paying Cypriots more, making it harder to enlist muleteers. WO95/4790, WDSA, Long, DSTS, 1 November 1916.
77 WO95/4788, WDSA, Long, DSTS, 15 August 1916.
78 Ibid., 16 August 1916.
79 WO95/4763, Salonica Army, despatch messages, August 1916, Elliot to Milne, 23 August 1916; WO95/4790, WDSA, Long, DSTS, 13 September 1916.
80 WO95/4790, WDSA, Long, DSTS, 21 August 1916.
81 WO95/4788, WDSA, Long, DSTS, 29 August 1916.
82 WO95/4790, WDSA, Long, DSTS, 30 August 1916.
83 Ibid., 10 September 1916.
84 WO95/4788, WDSA, Long, DSTS, 6 September 1916.
85 Ibid., 7 October 1916.
86 Ibid., 9 October 1916.
87 Ibid., 1 November 1916.
88 *The Cyprus Gazette*, 1252, 24 October 1916. Passports already issued had to be returned.
89 WO95/4788, WDSA, Long, DSTS, 6 November 1916.
90 WO95/4790, WDSA, Long, DSTS, 2 December 1916; ibid., 19 December 1916.

91 Ibid., 3 December 1916.
92 Ibid., 23 December 1916.
93 Ibid., 10 February 1917.
94 SA1/722/16, 65, poster in Greek with English translation in pencil.
95 Harry Charles Lukach and Douglas James Jardine, *The Handbook of Cyprus*, Edward Stanford, London, 1913, 275.
96 Harry Charles Luke and Douglas James Jardine, *The Handbook of Cyprus*, Macmillan, London, 1920, 278.
97 SA1/722/16, 122, notice, hand-written, undated; WO95/4790, WDSA, Long, DSTS, 9 September 1917.
98 SA1/722/16, 122, notice, hand written, undated.
99 SA1/722/16, 330, poster.
100 *Eleutheria*, 9/26 December 1916, 3.
101 SA1/722/1916, Stevenson to Duton, 7 September 1917; ibid., Lethbridge to Stevenson, 10 September 1917.
102 Ibid., Sisman to ACCPC, 14 September 1917.
103 Ibid., ACCPC to Stevenson, 17 September 1917; ibid., Rycroft, DQMGS, to Stevenson, 8 October 1917; ibid., Stevenson to Rycroft, DQMGS, 30 October 1917.
104 WO95/4791, WDSA, Long, DSTS, 4 January 1918;
105 Ibid., 19 January 1918; SA1/722/1916/1, CSC to Clauson, 24 January 1918; ibid., Sisman to Stevenson, CSC, 24 January 1918; ibid., telegram, Clauson to Long, 24 January 1918; ibid., Walker, for AQMG, to DOSS and DSTS, 1 February 1918; ibid., DOSS to Clauson, 10 February 1918; WO95/4767, WDSA, AQMG, 9 January 1918
106 Varnava, *British Imperialism in Cyprus*, 152–201
107 Spivak, 'Can the Subaltern Speak?' 283.

CHAPTER FIVE

Contracts, challenges, hardships and the 'liminal space'

Several months after the Cypriot Mule Corps was formed it was thrown into jeopardy when the British authorities failed to get the allotment scheme running. Wilfred Nash Bolton, the district commissioner of Limassol, informed Sir Charles Orr, the Chief Secretary, about the distress.

> I have the honour to request that if possible something may be done to relieve the distress caused by the nonfulfilment of the promises made to the villagers when they were enlisted as volunteers for Muleteers at Salonica. All sorts of men left their homes and those dependent on them under an understanding that a portion of their pay in the form of allotments would be paid here to their wives, & etc. ... No real effort seems to have been made and these unfortunate people are now living on charity and money borrowed at exorbitant rates.[1]

This chapter outlines the issues that arose for the British in relation to the contracts they offered the Cypriots. The British needed to strike a fine balance between a contract that attracted the right Cypriot men and one which did not make them too many promises. This took time to perfect. As time progressed and more muleteers were needed, their contracts changed to reflect increased benefits, but fewer rights for them and fewer responsibilities for the British. The chapter also deals with the problems of implementing of one of the main British responsibilities, the promise of an allotment scheme. The initial delays in starting the scheme threatened recruitment (which was the main concern for the authorities) and caused many hardships for the recruits and their families (as seen by Bolton's stinging statements). In this sense Homi Bhabha's 'liminal space' in which 'negotiation' can take place between colonised and coloniser, seems applicable, even if dominated by the coloniser.[2] When it suited them, such as when recruitment was at risk, the British not only listened but attempted

5.1 'Mule-Panniers for the Transport of Wounded: Two Wounded Serbians Brought Down from the Mountains', *Illustrated London News*, 149, 4043, 14 October 1916.

to rectify the injustices, even showing flexibility; but when it did not they proved inflexible and oblivious to Cypriot claims.

Balancing the contracts

Pivotal to recruitment was the contracts offered to the muleteers, which defined their rights and responsibilities, and those of the British. In all, three different contracts were introduced, as well as revisions made to these, and continuing contracts for those staying on after 12 months. The introduction of new contracts that outlined new responsibilities for both parties reflected the unplanned formation of the Mule Corps and the experience of the first year, since they clarified controversies that arose and reduced the rights of the muleteers and the responsibilities of the British to them, while retaining the incentives for Cypriots to volunteer. The comparisons between the advertising and contracts reveal the realities behind the façade of the propaganda.

The first contract offered was in August 1916 and was by far the most minimalist and least concerned with reducing their rights. Clauson sent copies of the agreement to Bonar Law on 7 August 1916.[3] The agreement had five headings: period of the agreement; discipline; scale of pay and fines; leave; and repatriation. Under 'period of the agreement' it was stipulated that the undersigned agreed to 'serve' in the British army for one year or for the duration of the war. As already mentioned, the use of the word 'serve' later became contentious. Also contentious was the implication that the muleteer had the option, after one year, to stay on or be repatriated for free. This section also stipulated that muleteers had to obey all commands, including from native foremen, except to carry arms. If the work ceased before the termination of one year, the undersigned accepted seven days' notice. Also, they agreed to be inoculated against cholera. Under the heading of discipline, the muleteer agreed that he would be subject to British military law like any other British soldier, and accepted that for spying for the enemy he could be executed. As discussed in the previous chapter the pay was very attractive by Cypriot standards. Various incidentals, such as food, clothing, and a brassard, were provided free. Payment of wages would always be one week in arrears, while fines could be deducted for misconduct and 'irregularity' in their work (ranging from GDR 2 to GDR 10) and they could even be dismissed. Muleteers and foremen were not entitled to any pay if they fell sick. With respect to leave, this would be possible if they had not received any orders, while they would not receive any pay when on leave. If leave was exceeded they would be considered a deserter and accordingly punished. Finally, the agreement obligated the British to repatriate the men for free.[4]

5.2 'Light Railways Used for Bringing In Wounded: Two Stretcher-Cases on a Horse-Drawn Truck', *Illustrated London News*, 149, 4043, 14 October 1916.

As various problems arose in Salonica, muleteer contracts were modified or replaced. Minor modifications were first made in autumn 1916 and muleteers already enlisted under the old contract were not asked to sign it.[5] Yet the changes were important. Distinctions in pay were clarified: grade A and B foremen (GDR 5 and GDR 4 respectively) and muleteers GDR 3 per day (as opposed to GDR 90 a month).[6] The most significant change was that 'no compensation shall be payable by the British Government in respect of my death, wounds or incapacity while in their service'.[7] The use of the word service in the contract meant little to the British. They had realised that some muleteers would be in harm's way and therefore they wished to not be responsible for their welfare or that of their dependents in the event of death or incapacity. This contradicted conditions V and VI provided by the Army Council to the Colonial Office on 1 August 1916 when the Cypriot Mule Corps was being formed, which stipulated that disability pensions should be granted as provided for European soldiers in Article 1161, Royal Warrant for Pay, 1914, and the widow of a soldier who died in the circumstances referred to in Article 1245, Royal Warrant for Pay, 1914, should be granted a gratuity of one year's pay at the rate at which the soldier was in receipt at the time of his death or discharge.[8] Although this was unbeknown to the Cypriot muleteers, the denial of compensation in case of incapacity or death became a major source of complaint for incapacitated veterans and for dependents (see Chapter 8).

CONTRACTS, CHALLENGES, HARDSHIPS

In autumn 1917 this agreement was replaced after two controversies arose. One related to the differing interpretations on the 'period of agreement'. The first and subsequent amended agreements to date stated that the undersigned muleteer agreed 'to serve his Britannic Majesty's Government (British army) for a period of one year or the duration of the War, and for such period thereafter as ... services may be required by the British Army in the Balkans'.[9] On 26 May Long noted that the muleteers believed that they had signed a contract for one year, but the British in Salonica thought they would serve until the duration of the war if necessary.[10] Indeed the war diary of the 10th Division divisional train shows on 29 September 1916 that the British genuinely believed this, since 'of the 730 muleteers only 60 were under agreement to serve for a period of 6 months. All others are secured for duration of war.'[11] Long argued that 'In view of the trouble we have had with the Cypriot muleteers, I am strongly in favour of allowing these men to return to Cyprus when they have completed one year's service.'[12]

5.3 'Light Railways Built for Supply Transport: Truck-Loads of Provision Drawn by Mules Going Up to the Front', *Illustrated London News*, 150, 4062, 24 February 1917.

Long was unsure how he would replace them. There were currently 3,753 muleteers serving and those who enlisted early would have served their year in July, and most of the others would soon thereafter. However, if muleteer numbers decreased to 3,000, there was no way of replacing the Cypriots. Long tried again to recruit Macedonians,[13] but this did not work and on 11 June he issued a circular that

> it is necessary for the present to retain in this country Muleteers who will have completed 12 months service. Each man has signed a contract to serve for twelve months or duration of the war, and the Deputy Adjutant General, GHQ, instructs that all Muleteers should be informed that any attempt to strike on their part will be put down with strong disciplinary action. The question of granting a bonus to Muleteers on the completion of twelve months service is still under consideration, as also is the question of granting furlough.[14]

To compound the problems in Salonica, Long wired Sisman that muleteer recruiting had to cease for now because there was no freight available from Cyprus to Salonica.[15]

On 4 July 1917 Rycroft minuted that a decision had been taken to permit the termination of all Cypriot and Macedonian muleteers on the conclusion of 12 months' service, with Cypriots repatriated as soon as possible. The Cypriots would continue to serve at the agreed pay rates until shipping was available. But if any Cypriots agreed to serve a further year they would be offered a 10% raise and furlough to Cyprus as soon as possible.[16] Long clarified that two lists would be made: one with those continuing and another with those to be repatriated.[17] On 16 July Rycroft and Long attended a meeting at GHQ that discussed the muleteer question. It was revealed that up to 25% of Cypriots wanted to re-engage and so they would be given a 10% bonus and signed up for another year. The Cypriots opting to not continue would be given two options: (1) continue under the same conditions until passage to Cyprus was available, with these men given preference over the others who (2) refused and would be interned at base in a 'concentration camp' under supervision of the provost marshal where they would not work and receive no pay and be charged rations from arrears of pay due to them or from money in their possession at GDR 1 per day.[18] On 19 July Long accordingly told Sisman that it was 'necessary to reopen recruiting in Cyprus on the original lines' and to re-recruit ex-muleteers.[19] Indeed Sisman went into action and 301 were immediately prepared to embark by 30 July.[20]

A decision may have been taken, but the British continued to experience problems with the Cypriot muleteers. On 3 August Long informed Rycroft that in the next days there would be 860 muleteers

5.4 'The Sleigh as a Transport Vehicle for Crossing Deep Mud: An Improvised Method of Carrying Timber', *Illustrated London News*, 150, 4062, 24 February 1917.

at base, for which transport had been requested for 600, but there was a delay and within weeks the 500-odd men discharged in August would join them.[21] Long claimed that

> Trouble is arising with these men who came down from their Division to the Base Muleteer Depot and refused to work, although they did not refuse to work with their Divisions ... It is becoming an urgent matter, for many reasons, to get these men away lest they create further trouble and require further disciplinary action, to which we do not wish to proceed.[22]

Long implied that disciplinary action had already been taken against muleteers refusing to work.

On 5 August Milne informed Clauson of what was happening, asking for any observations, while also disclosing that the decision was based upon the dissatisfaction of muleteers after having served a year and

5.5 'The Mule as Locomotive on a Light Railway: Giving the Animals a Push-Off with Their Ten-Ton Load', *Illustrated London News*, 150, 4062, 24 February 1917.

believing that their period of service had ended only to be told that they had misconstrued the agreement.[23] About a month later, Milne added that he believed that various Cypriot muleteer contracts had not treated leave well. One contract gave leave without pay and more recently leave was dispensed with altogether. Milne proposed that muleteers receive leave to Cyprus with pay provided they agreed to re-engage for another year.[24] To this last proposal Clauson immediately agreed.[25]

Receiving no reply to his more substantive concerns and solutions, on 18 October 1917 Milne reminded Clauson about the problem. He revealed that Cypriot muleteers referred to a proclamation distributed in the island that their service would be only for one year. Milne claimed that what was putting some of them off from continuing was their periodic exposure to shell fire. In any event, Milne had decided for the immediate future to 'hold them to serve', offering them a 10% pay raise as soon as they had completed one year of service, until they could be replaced and then repatriated – an improvement for muleteers from his earlier offer to continue with the same wages. For the future Milne asked Clauson to consider three options: compulsory service, as suggested in the report by Lieutenant-General H.B. Lawson;[26] voluntary enlistment for the period of the war, thus muleteers would take the oath of allegiance as soldiers; and to continue the present system. Milne argued that the first option was preferable, because the supply of men would be assured, but recognised that compulsion was difficult to implement and a political question and therefore beyond his capacity to comment on. The second option was also preferable to the current system. This option would require 'an appeal to the patriotism of the Cypriots, and thus cause an improvement in the type of man enlisted'. Additionally, the muleteer would have 'the right to call himself a soldier and his periodic exposure to danger would cease to be a grievance'. The possible problem, however, was a decrease in numbers and it was 'a matter of very great importance that no such decrease should take place'.[27] Clearly his least preferred option was to continue the current system because it gave him the least control.

Clauson replied on 12 November that 'the present system of engagement under agreement is, in existing circumstances, the most satisfactory'. He rejected compulsory service, although he gave no reasons to justify his claim that there were 'several reasons' that made it impracticable to implement. He also rejected, again without reason, a system of voluntary enlistment for the duration of the war, because it would 'have the effect of retarding recruiting to a considerable extent'. He mounted a strong argument to retain the current system. First he clarified that the current agreement was for one year and that upon termination of that year the British government was responsible for repatriating the muleteers. According to Clauson, experience had shown that most of the men had returned after serving for a year and therefore a 'withdrawal of this concession would have a most prejudicial effect upon recruiting'. Clauson outlined a series of facts to support how the current system was an overwhelming success.[28]

> During the period of fifteen months from July 1916 to September 1917 inclusive, a total number of 6,599 muleteers entered into agreement to serve in the Mule Corps, and I understand that, at the present time, no great difficulty is being experienced by the Officer Commanding the Muleteer Recruiting Staff in obtaining men in spite of the fact that all those who have been recently engaged have, in the course of their ordinary daily life, been in close contact with returned muleteers and must accordingly be fully cognisant of the conditions under which the work is carried out and the risks to which they will be exposed. In addition, a considerable number of ex-muleteers of the Mule Corps have ... reenlisted.[29]

5.6 'With the Greek Soldiers in Macedonia: Muleteers', *Illustrated London News*, 150, 4063, 3 March 1917.

For Clauson devising and implementing a new system would have been exhaustive. Moreover, given Milne's preferred alternatives, a new system would be politically fraught given the position of most of the political elites from the two main communities.

Milne was bound to consider Clauson's views and the same system was continued, although a new 'agreement' was introduced. It clarified the issue of period of service, which was now 'for a period of one year from the date of embarkation'.[30] The new contract also clarified what would happen to a muleteer while awaiting repatriation and also what would happen regarding repatriation in the event of misconduct.

> The cost of my passage shall be borne by me if such termination is due to my misconduct (including the contraction of venereal disease) but by the British Government if such termination is due to any other cause. During any such period as may elapse between the termination of this agreement and my repatriation, I agree to continue in the service of the British Government upon the terms of this agreement so far as the same are applicable.[31]

These additions show that the British wanted to cover every base and obtain as much as possible out of the muleteers. The new 'agreement' saw the muleteers working beyond the agreed one year indefinitely, until they could be repatriated. This could take weeks and months. Furthermore, the military authorities in Salonica and the Cypriot government would recoup any funds expended on muleteers dismissed for misconduct, including for venereal disease. Before the new contract, the Cypriot government was already inspecting the men upon arrival and providing treatment in the quarantine station in Larnaca, charging the men for treatment and upkeep. This addition to the contract had been first suggested as early as May 1917, when in response to the repatriation of 92 discharged Cypriot muleteers it was decided to keep their last wages to recoup repatriation costs, which were GDR 100 (a little over one month's wage). Long informed Sisman to credit the government with this amount in the case of each Cypriot being repatriated for misconduct.[32]

Clauson and Milne agreed that the running of the Cypriot Mule Corps was now, in December 1917, on the best footing yet.[33] The changes were perhaps accelerated by the execution of Georgos Haji Philipou on 5 December 1917. Haji Philipou from Kalopanayiotis, Nicosia, had served since 20 November 1916, and after completing a year he wanted to be repatriated. He and others were imprisoned and 15 days later he was shot for refusing an order of his superior officer. His parents' letter to Clauson is the only surviving evidence. In it they pleaded for his money, over £30, and for compensation. His money was returned, but no compensation, or an apology, was offered.[34] The extremity of this act indicates that other violent episodes against Cypriots refusing to serve beyond their one-year contract were possible.

Despite what Clauson and Milne believed about the second contract, in May 1918 a third one was introduced, adding a section on allotments, another issue that risked recruitment.[35] The new clause made an allotment compulsory if a muleteer was married or had children. 'During the term of this agreement, I shall be bound to contribute to the support of my wife and/or children to the extent of one drachma per day.'[36] The clause then covered what would happen to the allotment in case payments were interrupted.

> Should my pay be stopped for any reason for a period not exceeding 7 days, the allotment shall continue to be paid and shall be recovered out of any pay which has then already accrued or shall thereafter accrue due to me. Should the period during which my pay is stopped continue for more than 7 days the allotment shall cease for a period of the same duration as that for which my pay shall have been stopped.[37]

Clearly the British considered an allotment vital.

In addition to the revision and replacement of the contracts, the British also introduced 're-engagement contracts' for those muleteers re-signing. As shown above, the British authorities in Salonica were so desperate to retain the Cypriot muleteers that they offered them a 10% bonus if they re-signed and a two-week fully paid furlough. The first such re-engagement contract, introduced in August 1917, merely repeated the ordinary contract, while adding the 10% bonus.[38] A new one was introduced at the same time as Agreement C in May 1918, clarifying that the 10% bonus meant that a foremen grade A would get GDR 5.5; foremen grade B GDR 4.4; and GDR 3.3 for muleteers.[39] The offer of the furlough was not added, possibly because the British could not commit to it, though they did implement it from time to time. Those re-signed muleteers on furlough in September 1917 looked, in Sisman's words, 'very smart and clean [and] when questioned upon arriving they appeared to be well satisfied with their treatment'. After a few days in their villages they 'returned to the Depot at Famagusta, requesting to be allowed to remain there until the next transport arrives'.[40] No doubt the offer of furlough was a winner.[41]

There were two issues that the British authorities had to resolve in order to prevent any threat to enlistments. One, as previously discussed, was the time served. But the most serious risk to recruitment was the early delays to implementing the allotment scheme.

The allotment scheme

Running the allotment scheme was one of the most important tasks of the Cypriot government. It had agreed with Sisman on 24 July 1916 that it would distribute muleteer allotments to their dependents if the military provided the amounts, names, addresses and conditions under which the allotments were payable. The District Paymaster Cyprus would reimburse the treasury monthly. There would be a nominal roll of Cypriot muleteers making allotment payments to their dependents, which included their number, rank, name, amount and the name and address of the recipient.[42] Long agreed on 4 August 1916, so long as the Cypriot authorities handled it.[43] Walter Andrew Bowring, the treasurer, took the matter in hand, and on 25 August advised district commissioners that allotments would be paid at their treasuries, from 'Form B', but that irregular lists would initially apply.[44] The military authorities in Salonica were pleased given that they could not run such an operation. The maximum allotment was fixed at GDR 50 per month.[45]

From the beginning serious problems delayed implementation. The first problem revolved around disagreements between the civil administration running the scheme and the military authorities. On 9 August Bowring informed Orr, the Chief Secretary, that he had no information on the allotment scheme from the military authorities and that Francis Baxendale, the district commissioner of Famagusta, had been given a cheque for £251.16.0 worth of allotments.[46] A week later Bowring had Baxendale return the cheque because the government was still considering which system to adopt.⁴⁷ On the same day Bowring informed Major J.G.B. Lethbridge, the Officer Commanding the Troops in Cyprus and District Paymaster, that the forms were ready and that they should prepare duplicate lists at district treasuries, while the district commissioners had been informed to notify payees to visit their treasuries on pay dates to obtain their allotment. Bowring added that there could be no changes to the allotments unless death occurred and even then the Cypriot government could not be responsible for overpayments.⁴⁸ On 18 August Bowring informed Orr that the irregular lists had many errors, it was labour intensive and he was short of skilled staff.⁴⁹ A week later Bowring expressed concerns to Orr that it would be several weeks before the regular monthly allotments were arranged. Until then, he reluctantly accepted the irregular lists. He was more concerned that on the list given to Baxendale (with the £251.16.0) there were 160 names from Nicosia and that 2,000 more muleteers were being sought with compulsory allotments contemplated, meaning that district commissioners could be dealing with 1,000 allotments: 'far greater work than first contemplated'.⁵⁰ Clauson acknowledged the difficulties and suggested on 2 September that all parties begin discussions.⁵¹

But the conflict only worsened. Lethbridge informed Sisman on 21 September about the conditions of the Cypriot government: that he should duplicate allotment lists (made out by districts on form B) and certified by an officer representing the Director of Transport, Salonica and send them to Lethbridge; and allotments should be paid at a monthly rate, in Cypriot currency, and commence from the first day of the calendar month. Lethbridge reminded Sisman that Bowring was 'very under staffed, therefore lists must be as simple as possible'.⁵²

Sisman was not pleased: 'It is regretted that the Cyprus Treasury cannot see its way to facilitate the disbursement of allotments to the needy dependents of Muleteers, as arranged with the Chief Secretary.' He added that because 'War exists, the needs of the Army under active service conditions are immediate and imperative'. He claimed that because the Cypriot treasury did not institute form B until recently all previous lists should be honoured. Sisman refused to make lists by districts and to duplicate them, and claimed that allotments should not be referred to Lethbridge (the Acting Paymaster) because he represented the Command Paymaster, Egypt, so only the Cypriot Treasury and the Command Paymaster, Salonica were responsible. For Sisman the crisis was urgent:

> Considerable trouble and distressing scenes are witnessed here [Famagusta], by these delays being made to an early payment of allotments, causing families in sore need to visit the Depot Camp here,

and is putting officers concerned to considerable personal expense to relieve such cases.

Sisman implied that officers were digging into their pockets and he was upset that he was being forced by the Cypriot government to return the first allotment lists to Salonica and have muleteers send postal orders. He reminded the Cypriot treasury that 'the allotments are to the benefit of Cyprus, and that from the Chief Secretary's letter of 25 July 1916 the obstructions to disbursements raised by the treasurer were not anticipated'. He finally added,

> The delay in the payment of less than three thousand muleteers dependents here in Cyprus may give cause for unpleasant comment at home, where allotments are paid to millions upon the same rolls as those previously submitted to the Cyprus Treasury. Without doubt the War Office will eventually take the matter up with the Colonial Office.[53]

Lethbridge confirmed that because he represented the Command Paymaster, Egypt, the issue of muleteer allotments should not go through him.[54] Bowring had to deal with this locally and in cooperation with the Command Paymaster, Salonica.[55] This made matters worse for the Cypriot government, which informed Sisman that to deal with this matter swiftly it urgently required the allotment amounts in Cypriot currency, the names and addresses (including districts, because many villages had the same name across districts) of the muleteers.[56] The government told Sisman, 'As you are aware the dependents of the muleteers have been thronging the various Government officers in order to obtain the allotments promised them in the posters issued by the military authorities and otherwise.'[57]

Indeed, this was the corollary of this mess – the impact on dependents. C.S. Cade, the district commissioner of Nicosia, was irate, writing to Orr on 3 October that something had to be done to expedite the payment to the wives and families of muleteers,[58] because many 'women complain to me that they and their children are starving, and it seems to me highly important that the matter should be settled without further delay, and these unfortunate people given the money so long overdue to them'.[59] Cade knew that the men who first went to Salonica had given money for their families and he could not understand why this had not been distributed. To prove his point he enclosed a recruiting poster, showing that dependents would be properly cared for.[60] The district commissioner of Paphos was also concerned, informing Orr that the complaints were negatively impacting recruiting.[61] This was the main British concern.

Sisman sent a stinging rejoinder on 10 October. He reminded Orr that allotments were sent to the government (via Baxendale) and these were returned. Then form B did not exist and normal War Office protocol was followed in preparing early rolls, which the government rejected. Duplicate rolls were being prepared to satisfy the government, but Sisman believed that the treasury should have been doing this, because its 'routine duties may be scarcely affected by the war'. Moreover, he had no authority to make allotments in Cypriot currency and Bowring should deal with this too.[62] At length he went to the crux of his letter:

> The military authorities are in no way to blame for the painful scenes witnessed daily at this depot, and at the Commissioner's Offices. The responsibility for the delays in payment and obstructions lies with the Treasury. It is a matter for regret that the allotments could not have been paid out by the Commissioners as previously arranged; and who apparently do not share the Treasurer's fears as to disbursement.[63]

Sisman also informed Lethbridge that the allotments of muleteers sent to Salonica before 14 August had been prepared, but had not yet been paid.[64]

Despite the 'blame game', all were trying to resolve the mess throughout October because of the negative ramifications on recruitment. On 10 October Lethbridge informed Orr that he was no longer involved with the administration of the Mule Corps and that he was forwarding letters from the Command Paymaster Egypt and the Command Paymaster Salonica together with nominal rolls of muleteers.[65] The latter stated that he had made the rolls according to districts, but because Cyprus was unknown to him and some of the men were unsure of which district their village was in, errors were likely.[66] Orr had received the first allotment rolls from Salonica and would work with the District Paymaster Salonica.[67] From 12 to 23 October a number of matters were settled: the exchange from drachma to sterling was set at GDR 5 to four shillings; allotments were converted to a monthly rate on the basis of a 30-day month; the Command Paymaster Salonica would do the conversions and notify the Cypriot government when an allotment had been stopped; and the District Paymaster Cyprus would communicate with Bowring on all matters relating to the scheme.[68] On 24 October the government informed the Command Paymaster Salonica that the allotment scheme was in place. The rate was set at GDR 25 to £1, and since Sisman had set the rate of pay for a muleteer at £3.12.0 per month, this was equal to GDR 90 per month.[69] Bowring informed all the district commissioners that the scheme was set and provided them with full instructions and particulars on 25 October 1916.[70]

But just when the issue seemed resolved, it again became acute in January 1917. In December 1916 Bowring informed the district commissioners that muleteer allotments would no longer go through his office, but through them and the district paymaster at army headquarters in Nicosia.[71] Ostensibly this was a good decision, yet on 20 January 1917 Sisman informed Long that muleteer allotments had been stopped, and that families 'were in a state of destitution' because allotments were four months overdue.[72] Lists were sent to the Command Paymaster Salonica on 19 and 27 December for allotments up to 30 November, but the District Paymaster Cyprus had no reply.[73] The military authorities in Salonica informed Orr on 29 January that muleteers were upset that allotments had again been delayed.[74] On 31 January Cade revealed that allotments were stopped on 28 November, causing a very serious problem for families reliant on it: 'The payees pester me with applications for the sums due to them, and I fear that many of them are undergoing great hardship for want of money.'[75] Clauson telegraphed Salonica that 'delays and suspension [of] allotments have caused great distress and serious effects politically and on recruiting', and 'hope[d] [that the] situation can be alleviated and not repeated'.[76]

Lethbridge clarified matters to the new Officer Commanding the Troops. He had authorised the payment to dependents of muleteers totalling £2,761.12.2, but before doing so he had witnessed how many 'dependents of the muleteers were on the verge of starvation'. Yet the Command Paymaster Salonica rejected these lists and held him responsible for the amount paid out. Therefore Lethgridge had no alternative but to suspend further payments on 28 November.[77] He revealed that the destitution he witnessed compelled him to make 'small advances out of my own pocket in cases of urgent need, and I know that other English civilians in the Island have also advanced money to certain dependants who are in a state of destitution'.[78] He warned that the District Paymaster Cyprus needed more authority to deal with this matter, since the lists could be lost and the Command Paymaster Salonica was not passing allotments. 'I do not think it can be understood what terrible hardships are being endured by many families in Cyprus owing to the holding up of money which should, undoubtedly, be paid to them without any delay.'[79]

The new District Paymaster, J.E. Parry, defended Lethbridge. He claimed that the problem started only when the Command Paymaster Salonica had refused to recognise the rolls made in Cyprus and on 28 November suspended allotments. Attempts to resolve the issue had failed because the Command Paymaster Salonica did not receive the rolls, while sending duplicates had wasted much time. Parry warned the Command Paymaster Salonica that the matter was urgent owing to 'the hardship of those expecting an allotment'.[80] For its part the Cypriot government offered to write to Salonica in support of Lethbridge.[81]

For a second time this had serious consequences for recruitment and families. Bowring wanted to suspend the special staff working on allotments,[82] but the real issue was the widespread socio-economic distress caused by the delays. Men were unlikely to enlist if they had no confidence in the allotment system. As shown at the start of this chapter, Bolton informed Orr about the distress.[83] This was a stinging attack on the failure to implement a scheme promised to the muleteers. Bolton's criticism may or may not have jolted the respective authorities into action. Within a few months the allotment scheme was up and running and for the most part worked well thereafter.

Yet there still were problems, namely the lack of clerical staff in the district commissionerships. As early as August 1916 Cade warned that more staff were needed to deal with allotments, which was a lengthy process because most dependents were illiterate.[84] The Cypriot government acted. On 24 and 25 October 1916 it informed the district commissioners of changes to staffing. In Nicosia, Larnaca and Kyrenia division III or IV clerks were moved from the district courts to the district treasuries.[85] This worked well. In Limassol there was an overload in the district treasury and a clerk was also moved from the district court on 13 November.[86] In Paphos an extra clerical assistant was appointed to work on allotments.[87]

The only problem arose in Famagusta. From 27 October the services of Hassan Shevket Effendi, clerk III division, were placed at the disposal of the Famagusta district treasury to work on allotments.[88] But Shevket reverted to his former duties on 18 December and M. Orfi Effendi, a clerk IV division from the district court of Nicosia, worked in the Famagusta treasury for three hours a day on allotments.[89] Thus the Famagusta district treasury had less clerical staff for allotments. On 29 March 1917 Bowring advised that Baxendale was struggling to rectify M. Orfi Effendi's many mistakes. Bowring claimed that Famagusta was the only problem.[90] The government transferred George G. Papapetrou, a clerk IV division from the Agricultural Department to the Famagusta district treasury,[91] and problems persisted. In May Parry informed Baxendale that the allotments for January and February had not been made.[92] Then on 1 June Parry complained to Baxendale that the allotments from January had not been paid for Famagusta and the muleteers were very concerned for their families.[93] Parry, receiving no reply from Baxendale, complained to Bowring on 8 June,[94] who then scolded Baxendale:

> I regret to say that the work at Famagusta does not give satisfaction, in fact it is really the only place the Acting District Paymaster has trouble with and this is all the more remarkable as, unless I am mistaken, it was you who impressed on Major Sisman how simple and easy this work would be even before any details had been worked out.[95]

Baxendale was apologetic but deflected blame onto the lack of a qualified accounting clerk because he had more pressing work. He criticised the choice of Papapetrou because he had no accounting skills and because of his weak English.[96] Bowring immediately accused the Famagusta district treasury of 'want of method and supervision' because instead of paying families for three months only one had been paid. Bowring believed that the current treasury clerk, Theodoulos Montis,[97] was 'willing and painstaking', but not 'quite the right type to run a large office like Famagusta'. Bowring did not know if Papapetrou was unsuitable, but did state that he had recommended that only clerks of Third Division or higher be appointed.[98] Clauson swapped Montis with Michael John Michaelides, a division II clerk at Limassol, and Papapetrou with Philip A. Sinasian, who worked at the Larnaca postal department.[99] This showed how the Cypriot civil service lacked trained staff at the III or IV divisions with the accounting skills to run the allotments scheme.[100]

For the most part thereafter the allotment scheme ran well, but the muleteers and their dependents did not forget the stress and hardship caused. It subsequently became difficult to recruit muleteers when an allotment was made compulsory.[101] In May 1918 H.V. Gorlie, Commanding 238th Company, informed Base HQ at Salonica that the muleteers did not want an allotment and preferred to send their remittances by registered mail after each pay day:

> Muleteers in this company have been interviewed and the advantages of making an allotment have been explained. But none of them want to take it up because they claim that a year ago an allotment scheme was instituted whereby the Cyprus police authorities were to pay allotments to their wives and other dependents. But when they went to collect money they were molested by the police and had too much difficulty getting their money and many did not bother thereafter. Whether this is true or not is unclear, but these are the reasons offered.[102]

Milne, in sending Gorlie's report to Clauson, added that muleteers complained that their families were destitute, but the earlier allotment problems were hampering efforts to induce them to agree to a compulsory allotment of GDR 1 per day. Also, some muleteers knew that their families had to travel long distances to obtain their allotments and this was not always possible.[103] Clauson agreed to a compulsory allotment,[104] which, as stated above, was introduced in the final contract. This had a negative impact on recruitment, although this was not as imperative as the first months of 1918, since numbers fell from the high in March of 878 (see Table 4.3).

The most tragic story from the failure to properly implement the allotment scheme was the case of Christodoulos Onoufriou. He had arranged for a £24-per-year allotment for his wife Athena Alexandrou, but when he returned to Yeroskipou, Paphos, on 23 April 1920 he had found his wife dead and he was told that she did not receive any money.[105]

Meningitis outbreak, 1918

The other significant threat to recruitment was the outbreak of cerebrospinal meningitis in muleteers at the Famagusta Mule Depot in April 1918. On 2 April Harry Lukach (Luke), Famagusta's district commissioner since January, telegraphed Stevenson (Orr's replacement) that two cases of cerebrospinal meningitis had been diagnosed at the Mule Depot, three new cases at Peristeronopigi and another at Agios Sergios. Schools at Peristeronopigi were closed, and medical staff were coming to Nicosia to confer with the government and sanitary department on closing the depot.[106] Sisman informed the Salonica authorities who telegraphed Clauson that they would accept the muleteers exposed and would arrange for their disinfection on the ships and at Salonica because 'it is of the greatest importance that the despatch of these muleteers be not delayed' and 'on no account should recruiting of muleteers be suspended'.[107]

The Chief Medical Officer advised Stevenson that such an outbreak was common, but this was particularly bad. In February three cases were reported, one in Limassol and one each in Vogolia and Gastria, villages in the Karpas. The cases were isolated and disinfection was successful. But the disease had spread and from March there were ten cases under treatment at Spathariko, Arnadi and Peristeronopigi (x2), in the Famagusta District; Pervolia and Hirokitia in Larnaca District; and Morphou (x2), Linou and Agii Omologites in the Nicosia District. Three had thus far died in Peristeronopigi, Leonariso (in the Karpass) and Athienou (Nicosia).[108] Numerous other cases were reported, including three at Peristeronopigi and two at the Mule Depot on 2 April. The main reason why the disease had spread so much was because the serum to treat it had run out, and they were trying to obtain more from Egypt.[109] The Chief Medical Officer recommended that because of the latest reports from Famagusta, it was desirable that the entire district be declared infected under the provisions of the

Infectious Disease Prevention Law 1883, to empower medical officers to prevent an epidemic.[110]

Muleteer recruitment was in jeopardy for the first time and immediate action was needed. The Cypriot government decided, after consulting the military and medical authorities, to segregate infected muleteers at a new camp near Salamis.[111] On 8 April this camp was pitched 200 metres from the old one.[112] But the epidemic was spreading. The Chief Medical Officer reported more cases on 13 April, one at Millia, Famagusta, Maroni and Agios Theodoros, in Larnaca, and in Larnaca town itself. Meanwhile, a further two had died at Agios Sergios, Famagusta and another at Agios Loukas, a suburb of Famagusta. He claimed that the disease would shortly disappear, but that it had caused a number of deaths, and problems would continue since he could not secure the serum from Egypt and had to order it from England.[113] The British authorities in Salonica took precautions to not risk recruiting. This worked. They informed Clauson on 27 April that 300 muleteers were examined and all were fine.[114]

Yet in Cyprus the damage had been done. The threat to life was real. The deaths forced school closures, thus the crisis was impacting on the broader community.[115] A return of cases and deaths for 17 February 1918 to the end of April produced by the Chief Secretary showed 35 cases and 14 deaths, mostly in the Famagusta District. Subsequent reports showed the disease disappearing[116] and eventually the crises abated. Most importantly the British managed to avert the ending of their recruitment drive, although enlistment dropped in April 1918.

Conclusion

Within Bhabha's 'liminal space' the Cypriot muleteers had limited agency. They successfully challenged the British military authorities in Salonica when they believed their rights were being disregarded as regards their period of service. Their challenge succeeded because Clauson supported it and because, if rejected, it would have threatened recruitment. Similarly, the British scrambled to resolve the initial failure to implement the allotment scheme. The British need for Cypriot muleteers gave the peasant and labouring men who enlisted some room to speak with their coloniser, but there was no real discussion. The British dictated the terms of the contracts offered and therefore the relationship. They introduced a raft of measures to entice them to enlist, while with the other hand removed obligations they should have had to them. Ultimately the contracts paid the Cypriots very well, but left them (and their dependants) unprotected and vulnerable, especially after their service. These subalterns could speak and were listened to, but they had limited control over what the British did with what they heard.

Notes

1. SA1/722/1916, Bolton to Orr, 14 February 1917.
2. Homi Bhabha, *The Location of Culture*, Routledge, London, 2008, 5.
3. CO67/181/40421, secret, Clauson to Bonar Law, 7 August 1916, with enclosures; contract also in SA1/758/1916.
4. Ibid.
5. WO95/4790, WDSA, Long, DSTS, 9 December 1916.
6. SA1/722/1916, 321, agreement signed by Cypriot muleteers.
7. Ibid.
8. CO67/183/36388, WO to CO, 1 August 1916.
9. SA1/722/1916, 321, agreement signed by Cypriot muleteers.
10. WO95/4790, WDSA, Long, DSTS, 26 May 1917.
11. WO95/4833, WDSA, Divisional Train, 10th Division, 29 September 1916.
12. WO95/4790, WDSA, Long, DSTS, 26 May 1917.
13. Ibid.
14. Ibid., 11 June 1917.
15. Ibid., 27 June 1917.
16. SA1/722/1916, 252, Rycroft minute, 4 July 1917.
17. WO95/4790, WDSA, Long, DSTS, 7 July 1917.
18. Ibid., 16 July 1917; SA1/722/1916, 253, Rycroft minute, 16 July 1917. Macedonians not wanting to continue would be released, but those of military age would be handed over to the Greek army.
19. SA1/722/1916, 254, Long to Sisman, 19 July 1917. Sisman sent these to Clauson on 3 August 1917; See also WO95/4790, WDSA, Long, DSTS, 18 July 1917.
20. WO95/4790, WDSA, Long, DSTS, 30 July 1917.
21. Ibid., 3 August 1917.
22. Ibid.
23. SA1/722/1916, 264–5, Milne to Clauson, 5 August 1917.
24. SA1/722/1916, Milne to Clauson, 7 September 1917. Macedonian members of the mule corps were denied leave to the Aegean Islands. See WO95/4790, WDSA, Long, DSTS, 10 November 1917.
25. SA1/722/1916, Clauson to Milne, 20 September 1917.
26. This report was not found.
27. SA1/722/1916, 322–4, Milne to Clauson, 18 October 1917.
28. SA1/722/1916, 325–7, Clauson to Milne, 12 November 1917.
29. Ibid. Sisman agreed with Clauson on the risk that compulsion might damage food supplies, so pivotal now with the various troops in Cyprus and in neighbouring places that were being fed by Cypriot produce. See SA1/722/1916/1, Sisman Memorandum on Muleteer Recruiting, 24 January 1918.
30. SA1/722/1916/1, 388, agreement.
31. Ibid.
32. WO95/4790, WDSA, Long, DSTS, 12 and 17 May 1917.
33. SA1/722/1916, Milne to Clauson, 11 Dec 1917.
34. Christos Eliophotou, *Ο Πρώτος Παγκόσμιος Πόλεμος και η Προσφορά της Κύπρου* (The First World War and the participation of Cyprus), Nicosia 1987, 39–41. Haji Philipou had no. 5624.
35. SA1/722/1916/1, 401, agreement (C Revised).
36. Ibid.
37. Ibid.
38. WO95/4790, WDSA, Long, DSTS, August 1917.
39. SA1/722/1916/1, 399, Re-engagement Contract (Revised).

40 SA1/722/1916, Sisman to ACCPC, 14 September 1917.
41 See WO95/4809, WDSA, 854 Auxiliary Pack Company, part of 27th Division Train before November 1917, 29 March, 6 August, 18 August and 6 September 1918.
42 SA1/722/1916, CSC to OCMPC, 25 July 1916.
43 WO95/4788, WDSA, Long, DSTS, 4 August 1916.
44 SA1/722/1916, Bowring to All District Commissioners, 25 August 1916.
45 Ibid., Colonel Holdsworth, OCMPC to Orr, 24 June 1916, sending telegram, WDSA, Long, DSTS, to OCMPC, undated.
46 Ibid., Bowring to Orr, 9 August 1916.
47 Ibid., Bowring to Baxendale, 16 August 1916.
48 Ibid., Bowring to OCTC, 16 August 1916.
49 Ibid., Bowring to Orr, 18 August 1916.
50 Ibid., 25 August 1916.
51 Ibid., Clauson memorandum, 2 September 1916.
52 Ibid., Lethbridge to Sisman, 21 September 1916.
53 Ibid., Sisman to Lethbridge, 23 September 1916. The less than 3,000 names were not on the Honour Roll and some of these were added once found in the Cypriot States Archives.
54 Ibid., Lethbridge to Bowring, 29 September 1916.
55 Ibid., telegram, Thompson, Command Paymaster Egypt, to OCTC, 30 September 1916.
56 Ibid., ACSC to Sisman, 4 October 1916.
57 Ibid.
58 Ibid., Cade to Orr, 3 October 1916.
59 Ibid.
60 Ibid.
61 Ibid., telegram, DCPa to Orr, 9 October 1916; ACSC to Cade, 4 October 1916; ACSC to DCPa, 10 October 1916.
62 Ibid., Sisman to Orr, 10 October 1916.
63 Ibid.
64 Ibid., telegram, Sisman to Orr, 12 October 1916.
65 Ibid., Lethbridge to Orr, 10 October 1916.
66 Ibid., DPS to Lethbridge, Cyprus, 27 September 1916.
67 SA1/722/1916, telegram, Orr to Sisman, 12 October 1916.
68 Ibid., ACSC to Lethbridge, 17 October 1916; ACSC to Lethbridge, 18 October 1916; Lethbridge to ACSC, 20 October 1916; ACSC to Lethbridge, 23 October 1916; DPS to Orr, 12 October 1916.
69 Ibid., ACSC to DPS, 24 October 1916.
70 Ibid., Bowring to All Commissioners, 25 October 1916.
71 Ibid., 13 Dec 1916.
72 WO95/4790, WDSA, Long, DSTS, 20 January 1917.
73 Ibid., 23 January 1917.
74 SA1/722/1916, ACSC to OCTC, 31 January 1917.
75 Ibid., Cade to Orr, 31 January 1917.
76 Ibid., telegram, Clauson to Britforce, 3 February 1917.
77 Ibid., Lethbridge to OCTC, 5 February 1917.
78 Ibid.
79 Ibid.
80 Ibid., Parry to OCTC, 5 February 1917.
81 Ibid., Orr to OCTC, 7 February 1917.
82 Ibid., Bowring to Orr, 13 February 1917.
83 Ibid., Bolton to Orr, 14 February 1917.
84 Ibid., Cade to Bowring, 21 August 1916.
85 Ibid., ACSC to President of Nicosia District Court, 24 October 1916; ACSC to President of Larnaca District Court, 24 October 1916; ACSC to President of Kyrenia District Court, 24 October 1916; ACSC to President of Larnaca District Court, 24 October 1916; ACSC to President of Kyrenia District Court, 24 October 1916.

CONTRACTS, CHALLENGES, HARDSHIPS

86 Ibid., ACSC to President of Limassol District Court, 10 November 1916.
87 Ibid., ACSC to DCPa, 25 October 1916.
88 Ibid., ACSC to Baxendale, 24 October 1916; ibid., 25 October 1916.
89 Ibid., President District Court Nicosia to Orr, 6 December 1916; Orr to Baxendale, 9 Dec 1916.
90 Ibid., Bowring to Orr, 29 March 1917.
91 Ibid., Orr to Baxendale, 2 April 1917.
92 Ibid., Parry to Baxendale, 15 May 1917.
93 Ibid., 1 June 1917.
94 Ibid., 8 June 1917.
95 Ibid., Bowring to Baxendale, 9 June 1917.
96 Ibid, Baxendale to Treasurer, 14 June 1917.
97 Theodoulos Montis was the father of the Cypriot poet Costas Montis.
98 SA1/722/1916, Bowring to CSC, 15 June 1917.
99 Ibid, Stevenson to Baxendale, 22 June 1917; Stevenson to Bolton, 22 June 1917; Stevenson to Baxendale, 4 July 1917; Stevenson to Island Postmaster, 4 July 1917.
100 Varnava and Clarke, 'Accounting in Cyprus during Late Ottoman and Early British Rule, 1840–1918'.
101 SA1/722/1916/1, H.V. Gorlie, Commanding 238 Company, to Base HQ, Salonica, 20 May 1918; Milne to Clauson, 2 June 1918.
102 Ibid., Gorlie to Base HQ, Salonica, 20 May 1918.
103 Ibid., Milne to Clauson, 2 June 1918.
104 Ibid., Clauson to Milne, July 1918.
105 SA1/978/1916, Christodoulos Onoufriou, 14280/14039, Yeroskipou, Paphos, to Fenn, 26 April 1920.
106 SA1/625/1918, telegram, Luke, to Stevenson, 2 April 1918.
107 Ibid., telegram, British forces Salonica, to Clauson, 3 April 1918; WO95/4768, WDSA, Rycroft, DQMG, 3 April 1918.
108 SA1/625/1918, CMOC to CSC, 3 April 1918.
109 Ibid.
110 Ibid.
111 SA1/625/1918, Minute, Stevenson, 3 April 1918; Minute, Stevenson, 3 and 5 April 1918.
112 Ibid., 8 April 1918.
113 Ibid., CMOC, to CSC, 13 April 1918.
114 Ibid., telegram, British force Salonica, to Clauson, 27 April 1918; WO95/4768, WDSA, Rycroft, DQMG, 27 April 1918.
115 SA1/625/1918, telegram, Luke to Stevenson, 13 April 1918.
116 Ibid., note CSC, undated.

CHAPTER SIX

Conditions for mules and muleteers

Christos Komodromou, my father-in-law, relates how his father Nicholas would occasionally discuss his experiences in Salonica. Nicholas, a blacksmith who probably worked as such during his service, related how the muleteers had great hardships transporting goods to and from the front with their only entertainment being the occasional movie. He also learned to speak some Slavic-Macedonian and to read and write in English, becoming a life-long Anglophile. The conditions he described were harrowing. On one of their many outings into the Rizokarpaso countryside, Nicholas told a thirsty Christos to drink from the stream and that in Macedonia he and other muleteers would drink from streams which had bones in them.[1] These bones were the remains of men killed during the Balkan Wars and were taken by allied soldiers as souvenirs.[2]

What were conditions like for the mules and the Cypriot muleteers? Chapter 1 outlined how this book will contribute to the growing literature on equines in war and the experiences of men serving in British uniform. This chapter explores what conditions were like in the Cypriot Mule Corps, the health and working conditions of the muleteers and mules, and how the muleteers treated their mules. The chapter argues that conditions were harsh: the climate, terrain and nature of the work challenged the men and impacted on their welfare and that of their mules. The health of muleteers was pivotal. The high rate of venereal disease threatened to derail their service and thus their ability to capitalise on this job opportunity and correspondingly threatened the British need to use them for this important war service.

Asses at war

Initially mule procurement was just as important as muleteer recruitment and perhaps even seen as more significant because the name of the operation at Famagusta was the Mule Purchasing Commission. By July 1917 the focus had clearly switched to muleteers, as reflected in the name change to Muleteer Recruiting and Supply Purchasing Staff[3] and the greater numbers of muleteers recruited in comparison to the mules purchased. Nevertheless, a significant number of mules were procured in Cyprus; around 5,000, as previously shown. It must be noted that Cyprus was not the main supplier of army mules during the war, with thousands procured from India, China, Argentina, Canada and the USA,[4] although Cyprus was a notable supplier, so much so that in September 1919, when the Colonial and War Offices were putting together a dossier on the importance of Cyprus remaining British to counter *enosis* supporters in the Foreign Office and Prime Minister Lloyd George, Admiral John de Robeck, the then Commander-in-Chief of the Mediterranean Fleet, argued that one of the benefits of the British possessing Cyprus was their access to its mules, which were enduring and docile, and had been supplied to the army during the Crimean War, the Abyssinian Campaign, the Egyptian Campaign and the Great War.[5]

Mules in Salonica were worked hard. Their main task was to haul supplies to the front and return with the wounded and dead. Loads for pack mules were on average 160 lbs in December 1916, depending on the size of the mule.[6] The weight was not only great, but traversing the narrow mountain tracks, which had steep ravines, was hazardous. In June 1917 the Director of Remounts noted in his diary that eight strong Carter Mules had no trouble moving a 60-pound gun and a 6-inch Howitzer from the Ordnance to the Artillery Training School, up a steep hill.[7] Mules had it tough if a truck or tractor broke down, since it would fall to them to do the work.[8] Additionally, in the first 12 months mules were also used to carry stone for road building, which was hard work. Rest was the best medicine for overworked mules.[9] Major Black, a veterinarian in the 10th Irish Division, claimed that the making of enclosures (*kraals*) by some of the companies in his divisional train should be adopted by all companies because 'a few days rest in a kraal will ... restore an animal to working condition, which, if left at work, will fall away further in condition, and eventually have to be evacuated to hospital'.[10]

Caring for mules was pivotal and both the British and the Cypriots lacked the expertise, but soon found that the mule was not the difficult beast to look after. To be sure feeding mules was not easy. It was not until early 1918 that the system adopted of driving them to the troughs to feed so that they were packed as close as possible (four mules to a trough), was adopted. It reduced the number of accidents from kicks and ensured that timid mules ate their fair share.[11] There was some controversy on the clipping of mules.[12] The authorities in Salonica were adamant that it had been beneficial. Major Black argued that the advantage was that their skins could be kept clean, they were unlikely to contract mange, and it was easier to detect and cure it.[13] Indeed Black argued that mange was 'one of the most serious diseases on Active Service, as it spreads rapidly, and, in one form especially, is extremely difficult to cure'.[14] Milne argued that clipping in winter 1916–17 had reduced the amount of mange and vermin, as well as chills.[15] All animals were clipped by mid-November 1917, except those being sent to Egypt.[16]

Mules were immune from many equine diseases. In July 1916 Colonel F. Eassie, Army Veterinary Corps, reported that more mules than normal were suffering from biliary fever (Piroplasmosis), which was carried by a tick, because of the extreme heat.[17] Fortunately, the disease abated in August as the weather cooled, but it had meant that 8.1% of mules were sick, either in hospital or in their units, a percentage that increased in October to over 10%.[18] Mules were less likely to contract biliary fever, since in March 1917 horses at Arakli Farm had contracted it, but the mules were practically immune.[19] Another disease that mules were not immune to was glanders, caused by infection with the bacterium Burkholderia mallei, usually by ingestion of contaminated food or water. Signs of glanders included the formation of nodular lesions in the lungs and ulceration of the mucous membranes in the upper respiratory tract. The acute form results in coughing, fever and the release of an infectious nasal discharge, followed by septicaemia and death within days. In the Irish Division there was an outbreak of glanders amongst the horses and mules of 'B' Battery in October 1916 and some were destroyed,[20] a measure that a few weeks later became a requirement for all horses and mules cast from the army.[21] Another outbreak occurred in the 840th Company in May 1917 and in July another in the 841st Company, with several mules destroyed.[22] In August 1917 the Salonica authorities cabled the War Office that their veterinary hospitals had twice the authorised number of animals.[23] Procedures were introduced to fully investigate the cause of death of an animal. Whoever found the animal had to cut its ear off, place it in a tin box and deposit it with the veterinary unit, providing the particulars on its unit. The carcass had to be buried six feet deep and away from any water supply. Before burial the nostrils needed plugging and a sack tied over the head.[24]

The Macedonian climate also affected mules, who were accustomed to the hotter Mediterranean and North and South American climates. To face the winter mules needed to be fatter, but this was difficult since they were worked hard.[25] Mules began to suffer in November

1918 because of the harsh weather and the lack of food.[26] In winter 1918 the wet conditions affected them badly because the blankets on their backs became wet and they got sore backs.[27]

Mules were often caught in the firing line. For example in August 1916 as the 7th Battalion Oxford and Buckinghamshire Light Infantry were taking Horseshoe Hill in the Kalinova ravine, the enemy aeroplane spotted the animals and bombs killed 12 mules and wounded six men.[28]

There is much information on the condition and treatment of mules in Salonica. Eassie regularly inspected them and produced lists with information on their condition for the British XVI Corps. From correspondence and the lists showing muleteer numbers in their units (Table 3.2) it is possible to determine the units in which Cypriots served.

The condition of the mules in the units with Cypriots was good but not as good as the permanent mule corps from India, such as the Indore Imperial Service Mule Transport and the 31st Indian Mule Corps in the 16th Corps.[29] Eassie opined that the best supervised unit in the 10th Division train was the 841st Army Supply Company, Pack Echelon,[30] in which Cypriots served, such as Ioannis Haji Georji, from Livadia, Larnaca.[31] Eassie reported that this company, which in April 1917 had 152 mules, had only 30 mules evacuated for debility during the last six months, and that the 'Greek personnel [were] better trained than in other Units of this Train',[32] 'Greek' being mistaken for 'Cypriots'. It was not so good in the 840th Army Supply Company Pack Echelon in the same train where Cypriots served, such as Andreas Sava, who later died in Constantinople serving in the 121st Company.[33] Eassie observed that most of the mules were good, but several were poor and a third were unclipped and needed attention. In the last six months 70 mules had been evacuated for debility, a large number because there were 400 mules in this company in April 1917.[34] The other two companies, the 842nd and 843rd had 147 and 169 mules, respectively and so were about as large in size as the 841st. The mules in 842nd were generally in a good condition, although more attention was required with the unclipped mules, and there were several which had long feet and were dumped. A large number, 64, had been evacuated for debility in the last six months.[35] By comparison the 843rd only had 46 evacuated but according to Eassie it was 'the worst company in the Pack Echelon', because too many mules were too thin, their feet needed clipping and they were dumped, and many had marks of lice infection.[36]

The condition of the mules in the units of the 27th Division in which Cypriots served were generally better. Cypriots served in the 852nd Army Supply Company Pack Echelon, such as Kyriacos Pavlou[37] and Ioannis Constantinou.[38] In March 1917 it had 276 mules. Eassie reported that the section of this company at Kopaci were mostly very good, with only one evacuated in six months.[39] But the detachment from this company at Tashli was not as good. Several mules there were too light, their grooming needed attention, there was some dumping on their feet and their lines needed repair, while 55 were evacuated for debility in six months, and a further 34 were grazing at Monuhi and needed care.[40] The 855th Company, Army Supply Company, Pack Echelon, at Kopaci, which had Cypriots serving, such as Costis Nicola, a foreman,[41] George Georgiades[42] and Michalis Sava,[43] was as good as the 854th Company at the same place, with only two mules evacuated for debility in six months.[44] The other two pack echelons in this train, the 853rd and 854th, were equally as good.[45]

The mules in the 28th Divisional units did not fair as well. In the 122nd Army Service Company in which Cypriots served, such as Nicholas Zachariades,[46] the 154 mules in March 1917 were mostly fair in condition, with some being too thin. Grooming was poor and several needed clipping for lice. Their feet were lowered well enough, but there was some dumping to toes. Forty had been sent to the valley for rest and grazing, while 90 had been evacuated for debility in the last six months. Eassie believed that the wheel-train units, of which the 122nd belonged, had suffered working in the winter on wet roads, 'but even so their condition should have been better', attributing this to a lack of supervision.[47] Yet this unit was probably the best of the group, since the 125th and 120th had had 108 and 160 mules evacuated for debility in the last six months, while the 125th had several lice-infested mules due to 'defective animal management'.[48]

Cypriots also served in the 16th Corps, which was spread across the 10th, 27th, and 28th divisional areas. The condition of the mules in these units depended on which divisional area they were stationed at. Those with the 16th Corps serving in the 10th divisional area were a mixed bag. The mules in the 16th Corps Signal Company, which had 118 mules, were 'fairly good' in April 1917,[49] while the 222 in the 16th Corps Provisional Combined Horse Ambulance Convoy were well supervised and in good condition in March 1917, although in winter, when the roads were heavy, they had been returned to the Field Ambulance in a poor condition.[50] But those in the other units did not fair as well. The 295 mules in the 799th Convoy Army Supply Company were too thin in April 1917, their grooming needed attention, especially since some were unclipped and these and recently clipped ones showed signs of lice infection. Eassie attributed their condition to them carrying heavy loads of stone at the quarries and only had Sunday to rest and graze.[51] Those mules in the 16th Corps with the

27th Division were much better as these were serviced by professional muleteers of the 31st Indian Mule Corps and the Sharatpur Imperial Service Mule Transport.[52] Those mules in the 16th Corps serving in the 28th divisional area were mostly with the 'C' Section 16th Corps Ammunition Column, and therefore had much hard work, with their condition being only fair and 148 evacuated for debility in the last six months.

Clearly the condition of the mules depended on a number of variables. These variables were how many were in one unit, where the unit was serving, the nature of its work, and the abilities and experience of the supervision and the mule handlers. Most mules were overworked and though efforts were made to keep them in good condition, this was easier said than done.

By 1917 the condition of the mules improved slightly because much of the hard road building had finished[53] and because the Cypriot muleteers were better trained and more knowledgeable. In his September 1917 letter to Milne, Rycroft claimed that after visiting training at Lembet Road he was satisfied with the Cypriot muleteers and that new muleteers would be better trained and more capable of harnessing and cleaning animals.[54] This implied that the earlier muleteers had lacked adequate training in caring for mules.

Cypriots improved in how they treated their mules, but this varied depending on their training and their unit. For example, in March 1918, Lieutenant-Colonel P.J. Harris, Eassie's assistant, reported that at Arakli Farm he 'witnessed the [Cypriot] men grooming ... in a half-hearted way'.[55] This was saying much since their officers would have informed them of the need to do this well given the inspection, so clearly it was more to do with skills than aptitude. Harris added that he had only inspected this unit a month before and was annoyed that his recommendations to improve the treatment of the mules had been ignored.[56] On 19 March Harris inspected the mules of 209th Army Supply Company, which were also handled by Cypriots. These were in a slightly better condition, except for those mules carrying heavy loads of stone up to 25 kg. These were not doing well, especially the lighter mules. Harris revealed that the new arrivals 'had no knowledge of riding, driving or grooming and have had to be taught and the welfare of the animals, in my opinion, has not benefitted thereby'.[57]

After their service ended, mules had varying fates. Some were sold to local slaughterhouses or as beasts of burden, upon a guarantee that they would be well treated and subject to periodic inspection.[58] Indeed until July 1919 nearly 30,000 mules were sold in Macedonia at prices varying from £33 to £46, compared with 22,196 camels at an average price of £22, 11,101 horses at prices varying from £17 to £42, and 11,046 donkeys sold at prices varying from £8 to £9.[59] Cypriot mules did not return to the island. Mules serving in Macedonia were transported to other areas of conflict and imperial interest, such as Egypt. In February 1919, following the decision of the War Cabinet in November 1918 to provide all assistance to Anton Denikin, the commander of the anti-Bolshevik volunteer army at Novocherkassk in the Northern Caucasus, two shiploads of mules from Salonica were sent to him.[60] In August 1919 the War Cabinet agreed to send a further 4,000.[61] Mules continued to serve in Constantinople. According to Eassie's diary in June 1919 there were 20,797 mules and horses in Constantinople with a sick rate of merely 3.23, while 4.57 per 1,000 had died or been destroyed.[62]

Cypriot muleteers at work

The work of muleteers differed in Salonica compared to Constantinople and depended on which unit they served. In Macedonia life was harsher because a war was raging and the terrain and climate were hard. In Constantinople a 'war' of sorts was being fought as the British army was an army of occupation amongst a sometimes hostile (mostly Muslim) and sometimes favourable (mostly Christian) population and therefore tensions existed amongst the religiously diverse group of communities which were increasingly being nationalised.[63]

In Salonica the majority of Cypriot muleteers transported supplies (weapons, ammunition and food) to the front, and wounded and dead back to base, mostly at night, across barren mountains that had poor roads and treacherous ravines. Indeed, many times, especially in the early months when the forces were getting accustomed to the steep terrain, wagons and pack mules were lost down ravines.[64] The work was hard and never-ending. In September 1918 the Cypriot muleteers in the 854th Company had much work loading and unloading mules and now handling three mules per man, but their officer was pleased that they 'all responded well to the extra calls made on them'.[65] The climate added to the difficult task, since in the winter the winds were fierce and freezing, while in the summer the humidity and heat were unbearable and filled with malarial mosquitoes. The first muleteers arrived in summer 1916, a summer that had come earlier than usual, was hotter than normal and included thunderstorms.[66] When it cooled down in September, the change to winter was acute.[67] The end of January 1917 saw more cold and much rain.[68] In the following winter, snow posed a problem, not merely because of the drop in temperature, but also because mules replaced trucks.[69] In November 1918, about a week after the armistice was signed, there was a blizzard.[70] In the summer months water was scarce, as there was not enough for the personnel and animals.[71] Muleteers were well fed by comparison to home and rations were constantly revised to their benefit and in line with what was seasonal.[72]

The primary complaint of Cypriot muleteers in Salonica was their periodic exposure to shellfire. Milne informed Clauson in October 1917 that the Cypriots were not re-signing because of this.[73] The undertakings that they would be safe and away from the front were untrue. Cypriot muleteers continued their work despite the trying climate, terrain and conditions of the front, although several were killed and wounded because of shellfire.[74]

Many men discussed their experiences with their families. They emphasised the hardships they endured endlessly driving their mule at night up and down narrow and winding dirt tracks carrying heavy loads, as shown by the example of Nicholas Komodromou at the start of this chapter. Many of these stories have been captured by the Europeana project. Several muleteers, such as Demetris Alexandrou Proxenos from Yialousa and Nicholas Pittas from Asha, claimed that service was hard.[75] Pittas would say, 'I hope you never see what I have seen.' The fear and horror were conveyed by Sophocles Loizou Panteli from Kathikas, Paphos. On 1 September 1918 his unit went to the front for the first time to take food and he saw a great fire caused by the war and heard much canon and bullet fire, which scared them. He also disclosed how he and others witnessed much carnage on the Bulgarian side and were particularly affected by the killing of a small boy.[76] There was little relief when the men slept, since at night they would hear jackals howling in the mountains.[77] The work conditions, as discussed elsewhere, could be hazardous and trying. Damianos Styllis from Paleohori Orini, Nicosia, a veteran of the Balkan Wars, related to his children how the transporting of goods was mostly done at night, which was incredibly tiring. Many muleteers and mules became caught in swamps and they would go back to find them, while sometimes the mule would remain with or even manage to find his handler. He also discussed how many of his colleagues died before his eyes, including one from an enemy bullet and another after stepping on a landmine.[78] Kyriakos Riri Chichi from Lefkonico told his grandson stories of carrying food and ammunition through icy rivers, and once when his mule had been killed he had to carry the supplies on his shoulders.[79] Similarly, Savas Toufexis from Lithrodonta transported wounded from the front and once after his mule was killed and he had been wounded, he had to carry a wounded soldier on his back, and was cheered upon reaching the hospital.[80] There were other heroic acts of self-sacrifice. Georgios Louka Ttakkas from Tripimeni saved numerous mules that had wandered into enemy lines.[81]

The experience of the muleteers in Constantinople was different, because the work, terrain, climate and political conditions differed. With the exception of those muleteers serving in the Army of the Black Sea, who had a harder time being in a war zone, the majority of the Cypriot muleteers served as part of the auxiliary forces of the British Army of Occupation of Constantinople, based at Bostancı, a neighbourhood of Kadıköy on the Asian side of Constantinople. The task was to assist in police transportation, thus the work was less physically demanding, yet it still had its difficulties given the tense atmosphere and heated feelings of a population under occupation.[82] Meanwhile there was a greater opportunity to have time away from work and be more involved with the life of the city. Savas Toufexis related how one day he escorted Cypriot Muslim muleteers to Ayia Sophia Mosque to celebrate Ramadan. Knowing Turkish well, Toufexis tried to enter the great church/mosque, but the caretaker barred him. He raised money from his Muslim compatriots and bribed the caretaker, who gave him the full tour.[83] Clearly service for Cypriot muleteers in Constantinople meant greater opportunities for adventure and intermingling with locals.

In Constantinople the various allied forces (British, French, Greek and Italian) with Red Cross and local Ottoman officials formed a committee which met weekly to discuss sanitary matters. The committee was most concerned at the exposure of men in service to infected prostitutes. In the 16th meeting held on 9 June 1919 the Assistant Director of Medical Services, 28th Division, Haidar Pasha (Asiatic Constantinople), reported that infected women handed over to the Ottoman police with venereal disease were being released within 48 hours. This had to stop. The women needed a medical examination and treatment. The situation in Galata (in the heart of European Constantinople) was particularly worrisome. The Ottoman Inspector of Police reported that about 400 brothels and numerous drinking houses employed such women, who went undetected. He recommended that women working in brothels and drinking houses be medically examined, the sale of alcohol be banned from brothels and fines levied on those who did not comply. The committee recommended that Galata be divided into zones, with a local sanitary inspector assigned to each to report and for police to act.[84]

The health of a muleteer

A muleteer's health was pivotal to the success of the corps. Sick muleteers could not work, impacting on the work of a unit, the welfare of mules, and those back in the island dealing with allotment payments, which ceased during the period of recuperation or repatriation, greatly affecting dependents. The British and French forces were susceptible to malaria, by comparison to the Cypriots who were not and had a problem with venereal diseases.[85] As early as 20 September 1916 Brigadier-General Long advised that arrangements were being made for the disposal of muleteers suffering venereal disease or any other disease likely to be long-lasting.[86] In November Major Lethbridge decided to establish a successful system of monitoring muleteers discharged because of disease or other incapacities in order to suspend allotments. The Cypriot government agreed that the Famagusta police should take the names, numbers and addresses of discharged muleteers, to stop allotments.[87] But it made it clear to Lethbridge that it was not responsible for notifying him of the arrival of muleteers.[88] Indeed in January 1917 it was decided that Salonica would cable Egypt, where the repatriated muleteers were stopping first, with a list of muleteers with venereal disease.[89]

By February 1917 the arrival of unhealthy Cypriot muleteers to Salonica was upsetting Long. He wrote to Rycroft and Milne on 27 February that in the last batch of muleteers, which numbered 660, 90 were unfit and would be returned. He was upset because this had happened before and he had asked that an army medical officer be sent to examine all potential recruits, but was told that the local medical officers could do it. Long thought they could not and it was costing Salonica too much money, about GDR 14,392 since these men were being paid their wages, given food and being repatriated. He wanted an army medical officer stationed at Famagusta to examine muleteers before they were enlisted, even though venereal disease may not have been detectable until they got on the ship or even later in Salonica.[90]

> About a year ago, a Medical Officer was sent to Cyprus on duty in connection with the examination of Muleteer recruits. This officer has been the means of saving the public a great deal of money since we are now certain of having rejections of unfit men made in Cyprus. Previously we had many men come here unfit for service and they often remained some considerable time before being sent back for discharge. We are now increasing the recruiting of Muleteers in Cyprus and have recruiting Depots at Limassol, Paphos, Polis, Pyrgo, Kalochorion, Nicosia and Famagusta, and it is found that one Medical Officer cannot cope with the duties. I therefore ask DAG if another Medical Officer may be sent to Cyprus on recruiting duty.[91]

In June 1917 Long was frustrated, this time by the slow pace of repatriating the medically unfit Cypriots. He noted that there were 386 awaiting repatriation (they arrived at Famagusta on the *Umballa* on 13 July 1917) and eating rations, and he was 'having considerable trouble with them'. The delay was because no ship would take them because of the risk of infection.[92]

As soon as muleteers reached Salonica some were deemed unfit and repatriated. Sisman informed Long as early as 24 November 1916 that about 100 had been repatriated already.[93] The first such muleteers for which there are records were the 410 on the HMS *Verbera* on 11 March 1917. Baxendale reported that all were dismissed because they were diseased or otherwise unfit. Sisman prepared a list of the reasons (Table 6.1).[94] The list shows that although there were numerous reasons to discharge muleteers, the majority (66%) had a venereal disease.

The incidence of venereal disease is further shown in Appendix IV, which shows why the men arriving on the HMS *Umballa* on 13 July 1917 were discharged. Unfortunately page 2 of the list is missing from the original document, but those men suffering from venereal disease were fortunately on another list, and so 51 out of the 66 names missing were identified. Four hundred ninety-five muleteers were repatriated on the *Umballa* – 100 had served out their contracts and had not been discharged and 395 were deemed medically unfit and discharged. Fifty-one out of the 66 discharged muleteers on the missing page were added, while a further 5 could not be found on the Honour Roll because their numbers were not given, therefore the data presented and analysed below is for 375 muleteers, with 20 missing. Of these seven were foremen.

The demographic distribution of these discharged muleteers closely corresponds to the overall enlistment. This indicates that there was no religious group that was more likely to be discharged for medical or other reasons, but especially venereal disease.

The urban and rural composition of those discharged reveals little difference compared to overall enlistment percentages. Villages were slightly lower, while large villages higher. This indicates that there was no social group more likely to contract venereal disease (or other diseases), and that generally across the island there was a lack of knowledge of venereal disease.

The figures on the civil condition of the men indicate that a married muleteer was more likely to contract venereal disease than a single one. This shows that the younger men, although well represented, were more timid than the married men, who were accustomed, according to a report on venereal disease in 1929, to prostitutes with the knowledge of their wives.[95]

Table 6.5 clearly shows that there were many diseases and defects, some which existed before going to Salonica, but venereal diseases were the most prevalent. The percentage of men suffering from venereal disease from both cohorts compares well. In the first the 270 represented 66%, while in the second the 262 represented 70%.

CONDITIONS FOR MULES AND MULETEERS

Table 6.1 Reason for Discharging muleteers on HMS Verbera, 11 March 1917

Reason for discharge	No.
Gonorrhoea	270
Vermin	29
Rheumatism	12
Hernia	10
Venereal sores	12
Debility	12
Weak eyes	9
Spleen trouble	8
Syphilis	8
Epilepsy	8
Old age	4
No disease	4
Senility	3
Old fractures	3
Dislocated elbow	2
Bronchitis	2
Old wounds	2
Mental deficiency	2
Orchitis	1
Pleuresy	1
Conjunct	1
Epidymitis	1
Muscular astrophy	1
Urethritis	1
Neuritis	1
Migraine	1
Hydrocele	1
Mule kick	1
Total	410

Source: SA1/722/1916/1, Sisman to CSC, 13 March 1917.

Table 6.2 Ethno-religious composition of discharged muleteers

Ethnic/religious	No.	% Discharged Umballa	% Overall Cypriots
Orthodox Cypriots	337	89.87	90.4
Muslim Cypriots	36	9.6	8.45
Maronite Cypriots	2	0.53	0.77
Total	375		

Source: WO405/1 and WO329/2357.

Table 6.3 Urban–rural composition of those discharged

	No.	% Discharged	% Overall CMC
Urban	59	15.73	15.45
Semi-urban	12	3.2	3.36
Regional centre	37	9.87	7.49
Village – large	42	11.2	15.37
Village	209	55.73	57.47
N/A	15*	4	0.87
Total	375		

Source: WO405/1 and WO329/2357.

* Includes one who resides in Alexandria, Egypt, and another with address given as Salonica.

Table 6.4 Next of kin results for repatriated muleteers suffering venereal disease

Next of Kin	No.	% VD	% Overall
Father	75	20	30.77
Wife	112	29.87	24.96
Mother	79	21.07	22.98
Brother	22	5.87	6.68
Sister	15	4	6.40
Uncle	8	2.13	2.03
Friend	4	1.07	0.93
Brother-in-law	4	1.07	0.79
Son	2	0.53	0.68
Cousin	5	1.33	0.54
Fiancée	4	1.07	0.48
Aunt	3	0.8	0.33
Daughter	2	0.53	0.30
Nephew	2	0.53	0.29
Grandmother	1	0.27	0.15
Father-in-law	1	0.27	0.11
Niece	1	0.27	0.09
Grandfather	1	0.27	0.06
Stepfather	1	0.27	0.02
N/A	33	8.8	N/A
Total	375		

Source: WO405/1 and WO329/2357.

CONDITIONS FOR MULES AND MULETEERS

Table 6.5 Reasons for discharge of muleteers on HMS Umballa, 13 July 1917

Reason for discharge	No.
Gonorrhoea	262
Debility	20
Bronchitis / bronchitis and debility	10
Mentally deficient	8
Myalgia – chronic	7
Senility	7
Sight defect/ sight defect and debility / night blindness	6
Rheumatism	5
Age and debility	5
Hearing defect / deaf / deaf and debility	4
Soft chancre	4
Anaemia	2
Liver	2
Conjunctivitis	2
Tuberculosis	2
Pneumonia	1
Old age	1
Old jaw fracture	1
Old fracture	1
Perforated wound – abdomen	1
Pleural effusion	1
Tachycardia	1
Lame	1
Weak chest	1
Whitlow left thumb	1
Inguinal hernia – left	1
Vential hernia	1
V.D.H.	1
Inefficiency	1
Hydrocele	1
Malaria	1
Epilepsy	1
Fainting fits	1
Floating kidney	1
Gastritis	1
Frostbite	1
Fever	1
Intellectual weakness and debility	1
Scrotal swelling	1
Appendicitis	1
Corneal ulcer	1
Arthritis of elbow	1
Adherent operation scar	1
Total	375

Source: SA1/722/1916/1, Sisman to Orr, 13 March 1917.

Venereal disease

In his 1930 report on rural life in Cyprus, Brewster Joseph Surridge claimed that it was

> well known that during 1918 and 1919 a large proportion of Cyprus muleteers drawn from villages all over the island were returned from the Salonica Expeditionary Force suffering from venereal disease and infection must have spread.[96]

Surridge had an intimate knowledge of the crisis. As the local commandant of police in Larnaca he had prepared the lists of muleteers with venereal disease at the quarantine station. Clearly it was well known throughout the island that muleteers returned with venereal disease and that they spread the infection. It had spread so much that in 1926 the British Social Hygiene Council reported on stemming what had become a serious problem.[97]

Some threats to recruitment were discussed in the previous chapter, but another was the high incidence of venereal disease. Many muleteers were found with venereal disease in Salonica and repatriated before their one-year contract ended, while some were detected with venereal disease upon repatriation. In both cases they were charged for their recuperation in the Larnaca quarantine station. Some muleteers, especially those who did bring back some money, may have been put off by the experience, thinking that it was not worth going again if they were merely going to give their hard-earned over to the British; but others decided to re-enlist in order to bring back more money and hopefully avoid quarantine. For example, of those 375 muleteers repatriated between 31 March and 7 July 1917, 40 re-enlisted, or 10.7%.

Treating muleteers with venereal disease was another drain on the resources of the Cypriot government. It had both a medical and a financial aspect, and required changing the contract, as discussed before, and significant police work. Based on the experience of those returned in March, the government informed Bayly, the chief of police, that 300 or so discharged muleteers were expected at Famagusta, of whom it was 'probable that a large number will be suffering from venereal disease or vermin'. Clauson authorised under martial law to have them conveyed to the Larnaca quarantine station until the health officer at Larnaca recommended their release. Any funds in their possession would be seized and placed on deposit at the district treasury at Larnaca, and all expenses including transport from Famagusta to Larnaca, quarantine fees, cost of drugs, food allowance and other expenses incurred would be defrayed from the amount taken from the individual or from pay withheld.[98] Clearly the financial cost of treating those with venereal disease had been considered and the Cypriot government would not be financially liable unless the muleteer returned with little or no money.

The police made all the arrangements to implement the policy to separate the men as soon as they landed. Bayly informed Orr that upon landing at Famagusta the men had been searched, their money taken, clothes fumigated, hair cropped, and made to bathe in the sea. Their pay had not been settled and so most had little if any money. He arranged for each man to receive one *okka*[99] of bread, some cheese or olives, and some fruit and vegetables daily for 5cp or 6cp. Those with money were allowed to use 3cp a day for extras and a grocer could sell them more produce. A local inspector, A.J. Wilson, took charge of them, opening a ledge account showing the amount expended on them. A police guard was placed over the quarantine station and the muleteers were cautioned not to escape or they would be dealt with under martial law.[100]

Many muleteers who did not have the money to cover the quarantine costs were covered by the Cypriot government through 'vote 27 war expenditure'. As early as 17 April 1917 the district commissioner of Larnaca charged £26.3.3 to that vote,[101] while as late as July 1919, Panayi Haji Nicola from Akanthou, Famagusta, was discharged from the quarantine station and hospital and his balance owed, £5.2.6, was charged to it.[102]

It did not help that the men returned with Greek drachmas. After the *Elele* arrived on 11 March with muleteers largely infested with venereal disease, it returned again on 3 April with another 301, 184 with venereal disease or vermin. They were separated from those not infected and taken to the Larnaca quarantine station. There was no trouble confiscating their money, £541.10.0 in total, but Wilson found that most only carried drachmas, which needed exchanging into Cypriot currency. Most were dirty and unhealthy, 33 were penniless, and all were housed at the quarantine station under armed guard in case of trouble.[103] Clauson authorised that food be given to those without money and that enquiries be made in their villages or towns to see if they had the means to pay this debt.[104]

For as long as men returned with venereal disease the Cypriot authorities maintained lists of those quarantined. Numerous men often had less than £1, which, depending on the length of their stay, might not have been enough.[105] With the 184 quarantined on 3 April 1917, by 27 April 29 were still being treated.[106] By 14 May only two remained.[107] For those repatriated on the *Umballa*, detailed lists were made on their finances, with particular focus on those men whose funds proved insufficient to cover their quarantine.[108] It is no wonder that the British authorities had decided to deduct money from outstanding pay.[109] This meant keeping lists of those men who had an outstanding allotment.[110]

Milne and Clauson agreed to deduct money from outstanding pay and allotments in May 1917. After the first experiences of discharged muleteers with venereal disease, they discussed how to better deal with this. Milne informed Clauson on 6 May that there were nearly 100 time-discharged muleteers still in Salonica, many with venereal disease and needing examination upon repatriation.[111] Indeed several men were detected on arriving at Famagusta when they were subjected to a medical check by the Chief Medical Officer. For example, on 5 April Bayly informed the government that four more men were found with venereal disease at Famagusta depot from those arriving on the *Elele*, bringing the total to 188. Two of them were penniless, bringing the total to 35. Clauson replied on 25 May that he had taken

> drastic action in placing in confinement at their own expense the large numbers of Cypriots already returned ... suffering from venereal disease (self-induced in many cases, it is said) and I will continue to take such action against offenders as may be calculated to deter others without discouraging further recruiting.[112]

Clauson blamed the men for contracting venereal disease (that it was 'self-induced'), likely a moral view on the problem, and in quarantining and confiscating their money, he acknowledged that it could impact upon recruiting. Therefore, in order to cover the costs of treatment and to limit the stress for all concerned, he asked Milne that any balance of pay due to muleteers discharged at Salonica be given to the Cypriot government so that the costs of treatment at the quarantine station could be defrayed, before final payment could be made.[113]

This may have seemed prudent theoretically, but in practice it was difficult to implement. There were numerous cases where the money was recovered because it was simply taken from outstanding wages or the allotment and credited to 'overpayments Recovered' vote 27 'War Expenditure'.[114] But many men, until the new 'withholding of pay' contract was introduced, had been paid and they either did not have an allotment[115] or their dependents had received it.[116] Where debts could not be recovered the Cypriot government called upon those who owed money to pay their debts.[117] To determine whether they had the means to pay, the Cypriot government examined the assets of indebted muleteers. There is no evidence that any had assets seized to cover quarantine costs, but the British tried. The case of Adamos Stavrinou, from Mosphiloti, Larnaca, was an example. Quarantined on 3 April 1917 and hospitalised on 9 May, he was released on 7 August owing £6.16.0.[118] Within days Stevenson, recently appointed Chief Secretary, had the police investigate whether he had any property from which the debt could be recovered.[119] Bayly reported that his only property was a one-fifth share in two olive trees, valued at 190cp, adding, 'this man is poor and has no other property of any description'.[120] This would have been laughable were it not that it was common for Cypriots to own 'shares' in trees.[121] This tough stance to recuperate funds risked re-enlistment. For example, Wilson noted that 24 muleteers wanted to send money to their families for Easter, but the government rejected this because most if not all of their money would be needed to cover their quarantine costs.[122] The main problem was the need to suspend the allotment payments of those who had insufficient funds to pay their quarantine costs, which was first done in April 1917.[123] For example, it ordered the suspension of allotment payments to Christo Nicola from Lania, Limassol.[124] But the efforts to suspend allotments came to nothing with those muleteers who had been 'time-discharged' and found with venereal disease after being repatriated when Sisman revealed that all accounts for such men had been settled before leaving Salonica.[125]

Wilson, in charge of the financial aspects of the venereal cases at the quarantine station, struggled without suitably skilled accounting staff.[126] In January 1918 the Chief Auditor's office found that muleteer records at the Larnaca quarantine station were defective. 'There is a mass of literature in the shape of correspondence, lists, etc., which might on examination and lengthy analysis throw light on obscure questions, but I submit they are not suitable for audit.'[127] The Chief Auditor argued that Wilson had a tough job, made harder because there was no cash book and the original lists of muleteers and their money, prepared at Famagusta by Bayly, were

> most confusing, and, unless the sums (a jumble of Greek and English currency) handed over by the latter to Inspector Wilson were cautiously verified and agreed with the total represented by the lists in question, some subsequent muddle was bound to happen.[128]

The discrepancy with muleteer money, although in favour of the government, needed resolving, and the only remedy was to use a cash book.[129]

Bayly accepted the auditor's advice. He claimed that the current system, which consisted of a register of muleteers with their number, name, village and district, date of his entry into and discharge from quarantine, money seized, his costs and money returned on discharge, with receipt, could be improved. The system, he claimed, was born in much haste. On 2 April 1917 he was ordered to Famagusta to meet the ship returning muleteers, seize the money from those with venereal disease and send them to the Larnaca quarantine station. The men, however, began passing their money to their friends, becoming necessary to take it immediately because

> had this work been left till next morning when we could have opened a Cash Book, Ledge, etc ... there would probably have been no money to take over, and the whole expense of keeping these ex-muleteers in Quarantine would have fallen on the Government.[130]

Moreover, he reminded the government 'that we are not dealing with disciplined troops, but with a howling, disorderly mob, devoid of any sort of discipline, or order'.[131] He worked with Inspector Televantou and Wilson until 2:30 a.m. and there was no time to open books or ledgers because the HMS *Kosseir* was leaving for Larnaca before daylight.

> I see that the Auditor takes exception chiefly to the way ... the original list was made out by me, [but] he must be entirely unaware of the difficulties one has to content with in dealing with men of this discipline. It is I submit a very easy thing for him to sit in his office 10 months after the event and say what books should have been opened at the time, possibly he is right from an Accountants point of view, but it is almost impossible under the circumstances, and with the very short time at our disposal for my officers and myself to do more than we did.[132]

The Chief Auditor acknowledged the difficulties, but they were irrelevant in moving ahead. He asked that in future Wilson open a cash book showing foreign money in a separate column pending its exchange, when an adjustment entry could be made and the sum in Cypriot currency entered.[133] Stevenson duly informed Baxendale, now the district commissioner of Larnaca, that Bayly would give these new instructions to Wilson.[134]

Another significant problem was exchanging the drachmas. The director of the Imperial Ottoman Bank found that Alexandria would not buy them and they would need to be sent to Salonica.[135] From £566.4.1½ found on the muleteers in April 1917, £428.4.0 were in drachmas, presuming an exchange rate of GDR 25 to £1. After some discussions, the Bank of Athens accepted the drachmas at GDR 28 to £1, much less than first hoped, amounting to a mere £385.[136]

This problem resurfaced several months later, since GDR 1,070 and £110.6.0 had been taken from the 267 muleteers suffering venereal disease arriving in July 1917. The drachmas were exchanged at the Imperial Ottoman Bank at the rate of GDR 28 to £1, which the bank admitted was a low rate.[137]

An even more serious problem was muleteers resisting quarantine. On the afternoon of 5 April 1917 the 188 repatriated muleteers at the quarantine station became restless. In the morning 'a very large percentage of them broke through the guard and forced the door and broke quarantine'. Police forced them back and Baxendale threatened to punish them under martial law. After this 'the men now appear very quiet'.[138] Another incident occurred on 2 September 1917, when nearly 1,000 muleteers returned. Baxendale reported that the police tried to remove 223 muleteers (corrected to 207) with venereal disease into lighters to convey them to the Larnaca quarantine station, but the men knew their fate and resisted. The 12 police were powerless, as the other ex-muleteers were sympathetic and 'a big disturbance [was] brewing'. When the infected men could not be separated, the names of the others, nearly 700 time-expired and 75 on furlough, were called and landed. They were medically examined and another 20 cases (corrected later to 14) of venereal disease were added to the others. The Officer Commanding the Royal Scots sent 50 men to assist, which improved the situation and at 1:30 a.m. the infected men were towed off to the Larnaca quarantine station. What made the task harder was that nearly 100 names and numbers were wrong on the lists from Salonica.[139]

For much of 1917 the dismissal of large numbers of muleteers because of venereal disease was a serious problem, but by October 1917 the problem virtually disappeared. In August 1917, when 1,017 muleteers were repatriated on the HMT *Huntsgreen*, not one had venereal disease.[140] In March 1918 Bayly countered the proposal to introduce a cash book by showing that few muleteers were returning with venereal disease (see Table 6.6).

The significant reduction continued. On 1 August 1918 the HMT *Maghda* arrived with 150 muleteers, only two with venereal disease. One of the men, Vasilis Michael, from Agios Elias, Famagusta, had no money and took a loan to pay his 13 shilling debt. The other man, Pavlos Georgiou, from Kalavassos, Larnaca, had his £0.5.4½ taken to

Table 6.6 Numbers with venereal disease from 31 October 1917 to 1 March 1918

Arrival date	No. of muleteers	VD cases
31/10/1917	116	1
13/11/1917	91	1
21/12/1917	212	0
20/2/1918	266	1
1/3/1918	174	0
Total	859	3

Source: SA1/607/1917, CCPC to Stevenson, 9 March 1918.

pay his costs.[141] On 2 May 1919 five ex-muleteers were admitted to the Larnaca quarantine station with venereal disease: one, Mentesh Ali from Fallias, Paphos, had £38.18.0, while the rest had probably lost all their money to him in gambling since they were penniless.[142] In June 1919 a further eight were sent to the Larnaca quarantine station: six had no money, one had 0.1.1, while one had, once again, probably beaten them at cards, since he had £19.13.0.[143] In July 1919 the number of men returning with venereal disease was down to four, all of whom had no money.[144]

Finally, in April 1920, when the Cypriot Mule Corps was formally disbanded, Stevenson ordered repatriated muleteers not be detained under martial law for quarantine purposes against venereal disease or vermin, and that no further charges should be incurred in this connection under vote 28 'war expenditure'.[145] Ships repatriating muleteers were returning with fewer and sometimes no cases of venereal disease. For example on 27 February 1920 the SS *Panama* arrived with 295 muleteers and no cases.[146] Then on 30 December 1920 the HMT *Huntscastle* repatriated 181 muleteers, with only two with venereal disease.[147]

The sharp decrease in venereal disease amongst Cypriot muleteers can be explained and the answer also explains how and where they contracted it. To be sure, as Wakefield and Moody showed, venereal disease was mostly imported to Salonica, but it is questionable, given the Cypriot case, that venereal disease was not a major issue. Venereal disease was serious enough for the British to establish a venereal disease hospital near Karaissi village.[148] Before and during the war, numerous advancements were made in the prevention and treatment of venereal diseases.[149] Members of the Mule Corps were not treated at this hospital. The reason for the dramatic reduction of venereal disease in the Mule Corps was that it was contracted at Famagusta. In May 1919 the Cypriot government informed the military authorities that only eight muleteers with numbers higher than 7600 had returned with venereal disease and owed quarantine dues.[150] Thus the men with venereal disease were the earliest to enlist.

So what was the source of the venereal disease problem at Famagusta and what policy stopped muleteers contracting it? On 19 September 1916, Dr Pavlides, the district medical officer at Famagusta, suggested to Baxendale, then still the district commissioner of Famagusta, a solution to the threat posed to the war effort by prostitution at Famagusta. Pavlides observed that this was an important question in peacetime, but more important in wartime, with the frequent visits of British and French war ships to Famagusta resulting in the accumulation of prostitutes. Currently there were about 30, which was proportionate to the amount of sailors and soldiers, but if the number of soldiers and sailors increased, the number of prostitutes would too. Few of these women were free from venereal disease and the Municipality of Varosha wanted the industry regulated. Pavlides told Baxendale that he would help so long as those infected were isolated and treated. But after two months of discussions the municipality was powerless to carry out his proposals. He asked Baxendale if the government proposed to allow these women to infect people and undermine public health, or treat them to clean up the industry? He recognised that the traditional solution was to send the women away, but this only exported the disease elsewhere.[151] Pavlides was not proposing a new approach, since his method had been used in the British army for 50 years under the Contagious Diseases Act 1864,[152] yet it was too progressive for the conservative Cypriot government.

The ensuing debate veered from Pavlides's progressive solution, towards seeing the problem as a crime and thus as a police rather than a social and health problem. Baxendale sent Pavlides's report to Captain G.A. Williamson, the senior medical officer at the Ottoman POW Camp, informing him that several men of the 22nd Battalion of the Rifle Brigade had contracted venereal disease when stationed at Famagusta and so had 30 men under Lieutenant-Commander de Rubet, who was commanding the French Syrian patrol. In addition to British and French troops, Baxendale reminded Williamson of the 3,000 muleteers training at Famagusta. 'A large number of these men have developed venereal disease on the way to, or after arrival at Salonica, showing that the disease was contacted here.'[153] Baxendale was worried about the muleteers and the Ottoman POW camp since there were many ways of entering the old city besides the main entrances. He added, 'it seems to me that some drastic measure is necessary'.[154]

Williamson sent all the correspondence to his superior, the Officer Commanding the Troops Cyprus. He argued that the disease could not be stopped because Baxendale was sending the infected women away and the disease would be spread into the wider district, including to men who could be future recruits. Williamson placed Famagusta town out of bounds to all military personnel and argued that only if women were treated in a civil hospital, such as Pavlides had recommended, could it be restricted.[155] The Officer Commanding the Troops warned Clauson that it was 'imperative that drastic steps should be taken to prevent the disease increasing amongst the Soldiers and Sailors of our Army and those of our Allies'.[156] He knew that in Egypt 'lock hospitals', where women were treated by civil doctors, were working. This was needed at Famagusta because 'it is useless to shut one's eyes to the fact that unless women are kept in certain houses which are under constant Medical supervision and control, and all other public women's houses closed by Police, a very serious situation will arise here'.[157]

Clauson immediately sought advice from Egypt. Lieutenant-General Sir E.A. Altham, Inspector-General Lines of Communication, Egyptian Expeditionary Force, replied that there was much venereal disease in Egypt and to deal with the matter a committee was formed comprising the Bishop in Jerusalem, an army doctor, two civil doctors, the commandant of civil police, General Watson, commander of the Cairo District, and himself.[158] Egyptian law required compulsory registration and examination, but the committee decided that the examination of the women was ineffective without more time and the system deluded young men into thinking that these women were fine. It was finally decided to treat venereal diseases like other infectious diseases, freely providing examination and treatment. There was no doubt, however, that 'abstinence from immorality is the only real physical safeguard from disease'. Therefore, he opined, the moral standard of the men must be lifted.[159]

All advice pointed to treating the women, yet Clauson accepted the regressive recommendations of Bolton, Limassol's commissioner, which arrived on 20 December. Bolton revealed that in the winter he decided to act on the venereal disease amongst the garrison and young townspeople. He decided to place the brothels out of bounds and arranged for examinations at the cost of one shilling for each woman. A notice in red ink was placed on every infected house. Also, photos and descriptions of the women were kept. Almost at once venereal disease fell off.[160] Clauson warned Baxendale to banish all infected women from the town. 'Under martial law I authorise you to close any brothel and banish any prostitute, details of which should be given to Police Commandants and Commissioners of other districts. Follow Limassol model.'[161] Also prostitutes were to have an identity booklet, with examination notes, needed police permission to move to another district, and if they did had to present for examination.[162] Police were to keep a book with the addresses of brothels, name of the matron and two photos with a description of each woman, with the spare photo sent to another district if they moved. Medical practitioners would report if a woman gave 'a disease to any of their patients'.[163]

The instructions were sent to all parties,[164] yet there were still naysayers. Williamson argued that infected women would not be treated and would spread the disease.[165] The new district medical officer, Thompson, agreed that the system adopted was failing, but because drunken soldiers could not identify a photo to avoid visiting an infected woman, he wanted brothels closed and infected prostitutes sent to remote villagers so they could not come into contact with men in service.[166] This was more regressive than the approach adopted.

Baxendale disagreed with Thompson, informing Clauson that the system adopted had improved the situation. He clarified that Thompson was upset with him for arranging without consulting him to have the doctor at the Legion d'Orient camp, Major Mueller, examine suspect women at a municipality room after 24 Armenians were infected. Baxendale reported that Williamson had advised that venereal disease had decreased since February, with only three cases out of 1,000 a month in his camp, and sufferers were generally military police patrolling Famagusta to prevent soldiers from going there. Baxendale did not believe that Thompson's proposal was better.[167] The debate annoyed Clauson, who told Baxendale to verbally inform Thompson that

> the subject was not one to get onto paper and that he had better shut up. I also told the mayor that however praiseworthy his hygienic efforts were the subject was one which British public opinion was very touchy about, and that the next thing would be an article in English giving photographs of his hospital placard and his 'public house' notices with a question in the House of Commons on the top of it.[168]

Clauson was livid. He saw the matter as a moral and police matter. He did not want to end prostitution, because it 'satisfied the soldiers' masculine needs' and maintained the 'manliness' of the army, as Ballhatchet argued.[169] Yet he did not want to treat the women because he feared a backlash back home, although the Contagious Diseases Act 1864 allowed for 'lock hospitals'. Instead he decided to expel them to rural areas, spreading the disease.

The measures taken at Famagusta reduced venereal disease amongst Cypriot muleteers, yet spread it to rural areas. Surridge blamed this on the ex-muleteers, but the system adopted must also be blamed. Also, when the war ended and few prostitutes were needed at Famagusta, the women out of work must have spread the disease when moving to other parts of the island.

Deaths

Muleteer deaths in service have been alluded to and the impact on dependents will be discussed in Chapter 8. It suffices here to provide the statistics and statistical analysis and different causes of death. A total of 177 Cypriots were killed. The demographic breakdown indicates that fewer Muslims died than their overall representation. As might be expected, the urban and rural spread shows little difference to the overall representation. Being married did not make muleteers

Table 6.7 Religious breakdown of those who died

Ethno-religious	No. died	% Total died	% Cypriots died	% Overall Cypriots
Orthodox Cypriots	165	90.1	93.2	90.4
Muslim Cypriots	10	5.5	5.7	8.45
Maronite Cypriots	2	1.1	1.1	0.77
Macedonians	5	2.7		
Total	182			
Total Cypriots	177			

Source: WO405/1 and WO329/2357.

* One is from Alexandria, Egypt.

Table 6.8 Urban–rural spread of Cypriots who died

	No.	% Death	% Overall CMC
Urban	26*	14.69	15.45
Semi-urban	8	4.52	3.36
Regional centre	10	5.65	7.49
Village – large	22	12.43	15.37
Village	106	59.89	57.47
N/A	5	2.82	0.87
Total	177		

Source: WO405/1 and WO329/2357.

less carefree or lucky, since there was a high proportion of death with married men. The British did not record the causes of most deaths, but many died from diseases and enemy fire.

Conclusion

Most Cypriot muleteers, despite the conditions, got along well. Many continued beyond their 12-month contracts or re-enlisted soon after being repatriated. Most served their 12-month contract and earned good wages, much of it entering the Cypriot economy. The British valued their work, even if it was not always effective. But many did not have good experiences. Mules and men had to endure the harsh climate, terrain and work. The mules were treated relatively well given the lack of experience of the muleteers, yet many were overworked and suffered health problems. Some muleteers also had health problems, especially venereal disease. Many men, particularly those

Table 6.9 Next of kin spread of dead

Next of kin	No.	% Died	% Overall
Wife	46	25.27	24.96
Father	45	24.73	30.77
Mother	37	20.33	22.98
Sister	16	8.80	6.40
N/A	12	6.59	N/A
Brother	8	4.40	6.68
Uncle	4	2.20	2.03
Cousin	2	1.10	0.54
Nephew	2	1.10	0.29
Cypriot government	1	0.55	0.33
Daughter	1	0.55	0.30
Fiancée	1	0.55	0.48
Friend	1	0.55	0.93
Godfather	1	0.55	0.35
Grandfather	1	0.55	0.06
Grandmother	1	0.55	0.15
Niece	1	0.55	0.09
Relative	1	0.55	0.04
Son	1	0.55	0.68
Total	182		

Source: WO405/1 and WO329/2357.

enlisting early, contracted venereal disease at Famagusta, cutting short their service and having to cover treatment costs. Additionally, too many died given the British promises that they would be safe. Within Bhabha's liminal space the negotiation had become one-sided. The British did not want muleteers who had venereal disease, yet could have treated them in Salonica. While they had promised those enlisting that they would not be in harms way, they clearly were.

Notes

1 Interview Chris Komodromou, 19 December 2013. Nicholas had no. 8938.
2 Wakefield and Moody, *Under the Devil's Eye*, 56.
3 SA1/722/1916, Sisman to Stevenson, 12 July 1917.
4 CAB24/17, Secret, G.T. War Cabinet, 22 June 1917; CAB24/21, Secret, War Cabinet, memorandum circulated by the India Secretary, 23 July 1917; CAB24/21, G.T. 1563, Mesopotamia Animals; CAB24/22, Ministry of Shipping to the War Cabinet Secretary, 11 August 1917; CAB23/6, Secret, War Cabinet, 391, minutes, 15 April 1918; CAB/23/7, Secret, War Cabinet, 469, minutes, 4 September 1918.
5 CAB24/90, G.T. 8318, Memorandum by Admiral J.M. de Robeck, CICMF, 18 September 1919, provided to War Cabinet 13 October 1919.

6   WO95/4764, WDSA, Notes of conference held at General HQ, 20 December 1916.
7   WO95/4790, WDSA, DRS, June 1917.
8   See WO95/4809, Army Troops, Salonica Army, 854th Auxiliary Pack Company, part of 27th Division Train before November 1917, 7 and 8 June 1918.
9   See WO95/4808, WDSA, 14th Auxiliary HTC, 15 July 1917 and 2, 9, 11 September 1917; WO95/4827, WDSA, Mounted Brigade, 16th Corps Troops, 17 November 1918.
10 WO95/4830, WDSA, 10th Division, Major A.V.C. Black, ADVSS, 17 December 1916.
11 WO95/4790, WDSA, Dowell, DRS, 10 May 1918.
12 Andrekos Varnava, 'The Vagaries and Value of the Army Transport Mule in the British Army during the Great War', *Historical Research*, accepted February 2015.
13 WO95/4830, WDSA, 10th Division, Major A.V.C. Black, ADVSS, General Remarks, Clipping, 17 October 1916.
14 Ibid.
15 WO95/4766, WDSA, Milne to War Secretary, 3 May 1917.
16 WO95/4790, WDSA, DRS, 29 November 1917.
17 WO95/4762, WDSA, Eassie to HQ, 13 July 1916.
18 WO95/4763, WDSA, Casualty Returns: Animals, August 1916, Eassie to HQ, 10 August 1916; ibid., WDSA, Daily Meteorological Report, August 1916, Weather Report for August 1916; ibid., Return of Casualties of Animals for week ending 26 October 1916.
19 WO95/4790, WDSA, DRS, 11–12 March 1917; WO95/4863, WDSA, 26th Division, Major William A. Jelbart, ADVSS, Report on Biliary Fever, 21 June 1917.
20 WO95/4830, WDSA, 10th Division, Major A.V.C. Black, ADVSS, Report on Glanders, 9 October 1916.
21 WO95/4763, WDSA, despatch messages, Troopers to GHQS, 26 October 1916.
22 WO95/4830, WDSA, ADVSS, 10th Division, Glanders, 31 July 1917.
23 WO95/4766, WDSA, 2 August 1917.
24 WO95/4830, WDSA, 10th Division, Major A.V.C. Black, ADVSS, Circular Memo on Dead Animals, October 1916.
25 See WO95/4808, WDSA, 14th Auxiliary HTC, 22 September 1917.
26 WO95/4863, WDSA, ADVSS, 26th Division, 16, 20, 24 and 30 November 1918.
27 WO95/4827, WDSA, HQ Mounted Brigade, 16th Corps Troops, 29 November 1918.
28 WO95/4859, WDSA, Commander Lieutenant-Colonel A.T. Robinson report, 23 August 1916.
29 WO95/4788, WDSA, Eassie, 1–30 April 1917, Indore Imperial Service Mule Transport, 21 April 1917; ibid., 31st Indian Mule Corps, 24 March 1917.
30 Ibid., 841st Company, ASC, Pack Echelon, at Cope's Kop, 20 April 1917.
31 SA1/978/1916/3, Ioannis Haji Georji, no. 3796, to Stevenson, 15 November 1921.
32 WO95/4788, WDSA, Eassie, 1–30 April 1917, 841st Company, ASC, Pack Echelon, at Cope's Kop, 20 April 1917.
33 SA1/978/1916/1, Savas Georgiou and Despina Panayi to Colonial Secretary, 13 June 1924.
34 WO95/4788, WDSA, Eassie, 1–30 April 1917, 840th Company, ASC, Pack Echelon, at Mekes, 20 April 1917.
35 Ibid., 842nd Company, ASC, Pack Echelon, at Mekes, 19 April 1917.
36 Ibid., 843rd Company, ASC, Pack Echelon, at Mekes, 19 April 1917.
37 SA1/978/1916, Kyriacos Pavlou, no. 5838, Katydata, Nicosia, to Clauson, 14 March 1918.
38 SA1/1010/1917, Milne to Clauson, 27 December 1918. Constantinou was from Larnaca tis Lapithou, Kyrenia, no. 9451.
39 WO95/4788, WDSA, Eassie, 852nd Company, ASC, Pack Echelon, at Kopaci, 26 March 1917.
40 Ibid., 852nd Company, ASC, Pack Echelon, at Tashli, 26 March 1917.

CONDITIONS FOR MULES AND MULETEERS

41 SA1/978/1916/3, Costis Nicola, Foreman E.C., Agios Ermolaos, resident of Lapithos, to Fenn, 18 February 1922.
42 SA1/978/1916/2, George C. Georgiades, no. 3625, from Filia, Nicosia, now Piraeus, to CSC, 18 May 1938.
43 See SA1/1453/1920/1. Savas had no. 7737.
44 WO95/4788, WDSA, Eassie, 855th Company, ASC, Pack Echelon, at Kopaci, 26 March 1917.
45 Ibid., 853rd Company, ASC, Pack Echelon, at Tashli, 30 March 1917; ibid., 854th Company, ASC, Pack Echelon, at Merkes, 23 March 1917.
46 SA1/1453/1920/2, Nicholas Zachariades to CSC, 11 June 1923.
47 WO95/4788, WDSA, Eassie, 122nd Company, ASC, 3 March 1917; for heavy roads in 1916 see WO95/4809, Army Troops, 21st Auxiliary HTC (362nd Company, ASC), 7 September 1916.
48 WO95/4788, WDSA, Eassie, 120th Company and 125th Company, 3 March 1917.
49 Ibid., 16th Corps Signal Company, 22 April 1917.
50 Ibid., 16th Corps Provisional Combined Horse Ambulance Convoy, 21 April 1917. Ironically there were no horses in this unit.
51 Ibid., 799th Convoy, ASC, 22 April 1917.
52 Ibid., 31st Indian Mule Corps and the Sharatpur Imperial Service Mule Transport, 26 April 1917.
53 For road making and poor roads see, WO95/4808, WDSA, 14th Auxiliary HTC, 5, 7 and 25 September 1916.
54 SA1/722/1916, Rycroft to Milne, 6 September 1917.
55 WO95/4788, Harris to GHQS, 7 March 1918.
56 Ibid.
57 Ibid., 20 March 1918.
58 Butler, *The War Horses*.
59 Hansard, House of Commons, 1 July 1919, 117, 752–3.
60 CAB24/74, Secret, Ministry of Shipping, Memorandum on Assistance to General Denikin at Novorossik, 5 February 1919.
61 CAB23/11, Secret, War Cabinet, 613, minutes, 13 August 1919.
62 WO95/4790, WDSA, AVSS, 7 June 1919.
63 See Criss, *Istanbul under Allied Occupation*; Nicholas Doumanis, *Before the Nation*, Oxford University Press, 2012.
64 WO95/4867, WDSA, 78th Field Ambulance, 26th Division, 28 July 1916.
65 See WO95/4809, WDSA, 854th Auxiliary Pack Company, part of 27th Division Train before November 1917, 18 February and 29 March 1918.
66 WO95/4762, WDSA, Daily Weather Report, June 1916, Report for May 1916; ibid., WDSA, Daily Meteorological Report, July 1916.
67 WO95/4763, WDSA, Daily Weather Report, October 1916, Report for September 1916.
68 WO95/4813, WDSA, 31st Mule Cart Corps, Kopasi, 28 January 1917; WO95/4827, WDSA, Army Column, 16th Corps Troops, 31 January 1917.
69 See WO95/4809, WDSA, 854th Auxiliary Pack Company, part of 27th Division Train before November 1917, 18 February and 29 March 1918.
70 WO95/4827, WDSA, HQ Mounted Brigade, 16th Corps Troops, 21 November 1918.
71 WO95/4808, WDSA, 14th Auxiliary HTC, 27 August 1916.
72 WO95/4791, WDSA, Long, DSTS, 2 January 1918; ibid., 13 February 1918.
73 SA1/722/1916, 322–4, Milne to Clauson, 18 October 1917.
74 See WO95/4809, WDSA, 12th Auxiliary HTC, Report on Convoy from Hirsova to Swindon Ammunition Dump, 15 September 1918.
75 Europeana, entries/webpages for Demetris Proxenos and Nicholas Pittas, 9568. Proxenos is not on the honour roll.
76 Ibid., Sophocles Loizou Panteli, 9267.
77 Ibid., Demetris Georgiou, 9805, from Louvara, Limassol.
78 Ibid., Damianos Styllis, 5475.

79 Ibid., Kyriakos Riri Chichi, 6575.
80 Ibid., Savas Toufexis, 12435.
81 Ibid., Georgios Louka Ttakkas, 10902.
82 See Criss, *Istanbul under Allied Occupation*; Doumanis, *Before the Nation*.
83 Europeana, entries/webpages for Savas Toufexis. Toufexis also served in the Black Sea where he saved a Russian boy from being hit by a tram and was rewarded by the boy's father, an officer, with a medal, which is with the family.
84 WO95/4956, WDSA, ADMSS, 12th Corps, 16th Meeting of International Sanitary Committee, 9 June 1919.
85 Jacob Mikanowski, 'Dr Hirszfeld's War: Tropical Medicine and the Invention of Sero-Anthropology on the Macedonian Front', *Social History of Medicine*, 25(1), 2011, 103–21.
86 WO95/4790, WDSA, Long, DSTS, 20 September 1916.
87 SA1/722/1916/1, Lethbridge to CSC, 16 November 1916 and Fenn to CCP, 18 Nov 1916.
88 Ibid., Fenn to Lethbridge, 18 Nov 1916.
89 WO95/4790, WDSA, Long, DSTS, 16 January 1917.
90 Ibid., 27 February 1917.
91 WO95/4791, WDSA, Long, DSTS, 21 February 1918.
92 WO95/4790, WDSA, Long, DSTS, 3 June 1917.
93 Ibid., 24 November 1916.
94 SA1/722/1916/1, Sisman to CSC, 13 March 1917. Full information on who they were and were they came from is not available, making a full analysis impossible.
95 Reginald E. Hopton, *The Campaign against Venereal Disease in Cyprus: Review of the First Year's Work*, Government Printing Office, Nicosia, 1929.
96 B.J. Surridge, *A Survey of Rural Life in Cyprus*, Government Printing Office, Nicosia, 1930, 16.
97 CO67/220/5, *Advanced Report Presented by the Delegation of the British Social Hygiene Council to His Excellency the Officer Administering the Government of Cyprus*, signed by C. Neville-Rolfe, Secretary-General of the British Social Hygiene Council and Dr David Lees, Government Printing Press, Nicosia, 1926. The report did not connect the problem to the muleteers.
98 SA1/607/1917, Confidential, ACSC to CCPC, 2 April 1917.
99 Okka (often Oke) was an Ottoman measure of mass and, depending on where you were, was from 1.2 to 1.3 kg.
100 SA1/607/1917, ACCPC to Orr, 5 April 1917; SA1/607/1917/a, ACCPC to Orr, 17 July 1917.
101 SA1/607/1917, Woodhouse to Orr, 17 April 1917.
102 Ibid., Surridge, LCCMP, to CCPC, 22 July 1919; ACSC to CCPC, 19 August 1919. Haji Nicola had no. 12501.
103 Ibid, 3 telegrams, LCCMP, Larnaca, to Orr, 3 April 1917.
104 Ibid., pressing and confidential, ACSC to CCPC, 4 April 1917.
105 Ibid., confidential, ACCPC to Orr, 10 April 1917; ACSC to Sisman, 28 April 1917.
106 Ibid., CMOC to Orr, 27 April 1917.
107 Ibid., CMOC to Stevenson, 17 May 1917.
108 SA1/607/1917/a, ACCPC to Stevenson, 24 July 1917; 8 August 1917; 9 August 1917; Stevenson to ADPC, 29 August 1917.
109 Ibid., Stevenson to all District Commissioners, 13 August 1917.
110 Ibid., Stevenson to ADPC, 18 July 1917; ADPC to Stevenson, 20 July 1917.
111 SA1/722/1916/1, Milne to Clauson, 6 May 1917.
112 SA1/607/1917, Clauson to Milne, 25 May 1917.
113 Ibid.
114 See, SA1/607/1917/a, Cade, DCNi, to Stevenson, 15 September 1917; Baxendale, DCFa, to Stevenson, 19 September 1917; Baxendale, DCFa, to Stevenson, 2 November 1917; ADCPa, to Stevenson, 21 Nov 1917; Baxendale, DCFa, to Stevenson, 30 November 1917; Luke, DCPa, to Stevenson, 11 December 1917; Baxendale, DCFa, to Stevenson, 31 December 1917; DCPa to Stevenson, 8 January

1918; Luke, DCFa, to Stevenson, 1 February 1918; Luke, DCFa, to Stevenson, 1 March 1918.
115 Ibid., Cade, DCNi, to Stevenson, 29 August 1917.
116 For examples see, ibid., Bolton, DCLi, to CSC, 13 August 1917.
117 Ibid., Baxendale, DCFa, to Stevenson, 17 August 1917.
118 SA1/607/1917, Woodhouse, DCLa, to Stevenson, 16 Aug 1917. Stavrinou had no. 4735.
119 Ibid., Stevenson to CCPC, 21 August 1917.
120 Ibid., ACCPC to Stevenson, 8 September 1917.
121 See the various court cases on joint tree ownership in *The Cyprus Law Reports: Cases Determined by the Supreme Court of Cyprus on Appeal from the Daavi Courts and District Courts*, Nicosia, Cyprus, 1960.
122 SA1/607/1917, confidential, ACCPC to CSC, 7 April 1917.
123 Ibid., ACSC to Parry, 12 April 1917; Parry to CSC, 13 April 1917; ACSC to Parry, 25 April 1917; ACSC to CCPC, 13 April 1917; ACSC to district commissioners, 25 April 1917.
124 Ibid., CSC to Woodhouse, DCLa, 15 May 1917. Nicola had no. 5928.
125 Ibid., Sisman to Orr, 2 May 1917.
126 For lack of accounting staff, see Varnava and Clarke, 'Accounting in Cyprus during Late Ottoman and Early British Rule', 48–9.
127 SA1/607/1917, Auditor to Stevenson, 6 February 1918.
128 Ibid.
129 Ibid.
130 Ibid., ACCPC to Stevenson, 21 Feb 1918.
131 Ibid.
132 Ibid.
133 Ibid., Ed. Du Boulay, Auditor to Stevenson, 26 Feb 1918.
134 Ibid., CSC to Baxendale, DCLa, 1 March 1918.
135 Ibid., Director of Imperial Ottoman Bank, Larnaca, to CCPC, 5 April 1917.
136 Ibid., confidential, ACCPC to CSC, 16 April 1917; telegram, LCCMP to CCPC, 29 April 1917; ACCPC to CSC, 3 May 1917.
137 SA1/607/1917/a, ACCPC to Stevenson, 18 July 1917.
138 SA1/607/1917, confidential, Wilson, LCCMP, to CCPC, 7 April 1917.
139 SA1/607/1917/b, Baxendale, DCFa, to Stevenson, 3 September 1917; also, ibid., A.M. Fleury, LCCMP, to CCPC, 3 September 1917; For corrected numbers see, ibid., ACCPC to Stevenson, 19 September 1917.
140 WO95/4766, WDSA, 14 August 1917.
141 SA1/607/1917/c, Fleury, LCCMP, to CCPC, 1 August 1918; Wilson, inspector, LCCMP, to CCPC, 18 August 1918; Wilson to CCPC, 24 August 1918. Michael had no. 7238 and Georgiou had no. 10759.
142 Ibid., F. Braggiotti, I/C Police, to CCPC, 8 May 1919. Ali had no. 10347. The others were: Nicholas Ioannou, 10282, Vasilia, Kyrenia, Theodoulou Christofi, 10786, Kambi, Nicosia, Meletios Haralambou, 10703, Lapithos, Kyrenia and Ioannis Haji Sava, Omorfida, Nicosia.
143 Ibid., Surridge, LCCMP, Larnaca, to CCPC, 4 June 1919. Perhaps Costandi had won at cards.
144 Ibid., M. Ahmed, for LCCMP, to CCPC, 31 July 1919.
145 SA1/607/1917, Fenn to CCPC, 1 April 1920.
146 Ibid., S. Pavlou, NO for I/C of Police, Famagusta, to CCPC, 28 February 1920.
147 Ibid., Y.M. Tilliro, LCCMP, to CCPC, 31 December 1919.
148 Wakefield and Moody, *Under the Devil's Eye*, 174–5.
149 See Bridget A. Towers, 'Health Education Policy 1916–1926: Venereal Disease and the Prophylaxis Dilemma', *Medical History*, 24, 1980, 70–87; David Evans, 'Tackling the "Hideous Scourge": The Creation of the Venereal Disease Treatment Centres in Early Twentieth-Century Britain', *Social History of Medicine*, 5(3), 413–33; Philippa Levine, *Prostitution, Race, and Politics: Policing Venereal Disease in the British Empire*, Routledge, London, 2003.

150 SA1/607/1917, Fenn to Parry, 20 May 1919.
151 SA1/979/1916, Pavlides to Baxendale, 19 September 1916.
152 The legislation allowed police officers to arrest and have prostitutes in certain ports and army towns medically examined. Infected women were confined in 'lock hospital' until 'cured'. I thank Evan Smith for this.
153 SA1/979/1916, Baxendale to Williamson, RAMC, SMO, POW Camp, 22 September 1916.
154 Ibid.
155 Ibid., Williamson, SMO, to the OCTC, 19 November 1916.
156 Ibid., OCTC to Orr, 20 November 1916.
157 Ibid.
158 Ibid., Lieutenant-General Sir E.A. Altham, Inspector-General Lines of Communication, EEF, to Clauson, 5 October 1916.
159 Ibid.; also, Suzanne Brugger, *Australians and Egypt, 1914–1919*, Melbourne University Press, 1980.
160 SA1/979/1916, OCTC to Orr, 14 December 1916; Orr to OCTC, 17 December 1916; Bolton, DCLi, to Orr, 20 December 1916; confidential, ACSC to all Commissioners (except Famagusta), 27 December 1916.
161 Ibid., confidential, ACSC to Baxendale, 27 December 1916.
162 Ibid., Instructions as to Brothels and Prostitutes.
163 Ibid., confidential, Bolton to Orr, 4 Jan 1917.
164 Ibid., ACSC to Commissioners (except Limassol), 16 January 1917; confidential, Orr to OCTC, H.G. Dixon, 16 January 1917; ADCLa to Orr, 18 January 1917.
165 Ibid., Williamson to Dixon, 17 January 1917.
166 Ibid., Thompson, to Baxendale, 28 May 1917.
167 Ibid., Baxendale to Stevenson, 6 June 1917.
168 Ibid., Clauson to Stevenson, 1 September 1917.
169 Kenneth Ballhatchet, *Race, Sex and Class under the Raj: Imperial Attitudes and Policies and their Critics, 1793–1905*, Weidenfeld and Nicolson, London, 1980, 20. I thank Evan Smith for this source.

CHAPTER SEVEN

Muleteer behaviour during service

In December 1918 Loizo Costa was stabbed to death in broad daylight during a fight between him and another muleteer. His fellow muleteers had recently discovered that he had led an organised gang that had systematically stolen from them. Having gone undetected, it is unknown how many men were involved or for how long it had operated. This was not the only criminality recorded, but crime was not rife. Most muleteers were well behaved or got away with it. The nature and incidence of criminal behaviour reflected the harsh conditions in Salonica and the different circumstances in Constantinople, as well as the high rate of violence in Cyprus itself.

Chapter 1 showed how there is little literature on how and why soldiers misbehaved during their service, while there is nothing on the behaviour of auxiliary forces. This chapter argues that criminality, such as desertion, theft and violent crimes, did exist, and it must be understood in its appropriate social and economic contexts. The majority of Cypriot muleteers knew that this was a significant job opportunity and that their fidelity was paramount to them benefiting fully, yet as seen in the previous chapters they were not afraid to complain when they felt the harsh hand of British injustice.

Desertion

Behavioural problems one finds with military corps, such as desertion and crime, were not prevalent in the Cypriot Mule Corps. Desertion is faced by all military units, whether personnel were in a war because of conscription or because they volunteered, and usually it is the result of 'cowardice'.[1] In the case of the Mule Corps, there were a mere 117 desertions. Six were Macedonians, and one Cypriot enlisted two separate times and deserted both times. Clearly, for the majority of the muleteers, serving had benefits that far outweighed desertion.

Before exploring desertion of Cypriot muleteers in Salonica and Constantinople, it is important to understand that desertion occurred in Cyprus before service began. As early as a few weeks after the establishment of the Cypriot Mule Corps, several men had changed their minds. On 5 August 1916 the Cypriot police were informed of the desertion of Michael D. Ktori, 803, who was returned to camp and was punished. There was also a list of other deserters.[2] Then on 18 August Georgios Iacovou wrote to Clauson begging for the release of his son, Loucas Georgiou, Larnaca, aged 17, who had enlisted as a muleteer, but changed his mind. He was subsequently arrested on 17 August and marched to Famagusta from Larnaca.[3] Clauson demanded a full police report.[4] This clarified that in mid-July Georgiou went to Famagusta alone and enlisted, but left a few days later with his father who had come from Larnaca to fetch him. According to his statement he quit because he believed that the doctor had found him underage and his number had not been called out. The police claimed this was an excuse and he had set a bad precedent, with 30 others deserting in tow. Wanting to stop this, the military authorities had the police track the deserters back to their villages to apprehend and return them to the depot.[5] Georgiou was accepted back, despite his age, and he served for one year.[6]

7.1   Photograph of British War Medal I, Macedonian Mule Corps, Eraklis Theodorou, no. 5333, from Predori, Paphos.

MULETEER BEHAVIOUR DURING SERVICE

Some families opposed their sons enlisting in the Cypriot Mule Corps, mainly because their agricultural operations, which they perceived to be more financially profitable, would be damaged. For example the fathers of Christofis Sophianou, Rizokarpaso,[7] Michael Anastasi, Kato Dhri,[8] Andonios A. Stavri, Paralimni,[9] Raif Izzet, Komi Kebir,[10] and the mothers of Christodoulos Georgiou, Salaminou (a widow) and that of Christodoulos Yorgallis, Paleokythro, wanted them returned because their farms would suffer.[11] Andreas Stavri, Andonios's father, claimed that his agricultural business would stop and he (who was wounded in his hand), his wife and five younger children would 'all die of hunger'.[12] In all these cases the high commissioner was unwilling to intervene.[13] In the case of Christofis Sophianou, Sisman interviewed him and the 18-year-old was adamant that he wanted to continue serving.[14] Yorgalli's mother was 'weeping and lamenting and I entreat that my son may be exempted from the obligation of serving as a muleteer ... [because] we shall be reduced to poverty and our land will be left uncultivated and we shall have no support from anyone else'.[15] Clauson refused.[16] These cases suggest a generational gap and that these young men enlisted for the personal adventure of travelling abroad or because they did not like farming, unlike most men who enlisted because of the financial and material rewards, since their parents foresaw a financial loss for themselves.

One father objected to his son enlisting because he had spent a small

7.2   Photograph of British War Medal II, Macedonian Mule Corps.

[163]

fortune educating him, a rare example of someone from the growing middle-class. Costi Karageorgi from Nicosia objected to his son, Kypros Karageorghi, enlisting because of his poor health and education. Kypros had studied eight years in the Cypriot gymnasium, three years in a high school in Cairo and the last two years at the Nicosia English School under Canon Newman. Costi removed his son from school because of health reasons. He had no problems with his son working as an interpreter, but his health was not good enough to be a muleteer, while he had never ridden let alone had any knowledge of caring for mules. Costi also claimed that Kypros was underage (16½),[17] meaning that he was only 11 when sent to study in Cairo. Sisman was most satisfied with Kyrpos's work and the boy was happy, so he would not interfere unless Clauson ordered it, and he would not.[18] Interestingly, Canon Newman was an important figure in the training of Cypriot muleteers, as images found in his trunk show (see Figures 3.1, 3.2, 3.3 and 4.1).

There were many desertions in Salonica during the first nine months of the Mule Corps, that is, from March 1916 until December, when many Macedonians left the corps for numerous reasons. The authorities in Salonica only started listing desertions of muleteers in December 1916, so it is impossible to know about earlier desertions. Most of them during this period were Macedonians, who found better-paid work elsewhere or were forced to join Venizelos's National Defence Force. For this reason the figures that E.C. Boulter provided on desertions were incomplete because he did not take this earlier period into account.[19]

A close analysis of the data on desertions shows that there were three types of deserters, based on the full data, and enlistment and desertion dates, for 57 of the men.[20] There were those, ten in total (17.5%), who deserted within two months, usually within four weeks of arriving in Salonica. These men used their enlistment as an opportunity to work around the migration restrictions. A second group of eight (14%) deserted between two and six months, and usually around six months. It was likely that these men were also 'migrant deserters' who decided to make some money first before moving on to their desired destination. It was also likely that some of them included men who could not handle the conditions of war, either the work, terrain, weather[21] and/or treatment. Finally there was a larger group of 39 (68.4%) who deserted close to their discharge date (often after serving more than two years). These men were the strategic deserters, filling their pockets with money before deserting. Some of them, however, must have decided to not return to Cyprus after obtaining a taste for life outside the confines of the island, while for others it was planned,

Table 7.1 Demographic distribution of desertion

Ethno-religious	No.	% Total	% Cypriot deserters	% Overall Cypriots
Orthodox Cypriots	92	79.3	83.6	90.4
Muslim Cypriots	18	15.5	16.4	8.45
Latin-Catholic Cypriots	1	0.86	0.91	0.13 (others)
Non-Cypriots	6	5.2		
Total	117			
Total Cypriots	111			

Source: WO405/1 and WO329/2357.

Table 7.2 Urban–rural composition of Cypriot deserters

	No.	% Deserters	% Overall CMC
Urban	27	24.3	15.45
Semi-urban	7	6.3	3.36
Regional centre	6	5.4	7.49
Village – large	9	8.1	15.37
Village	39	35.1	57.47
N/A	23	24.3	0.87
Total	111		

Source: WO405/1 and WO329/2357.

having greater destinations in mind than Salonica or Athens, settling in other European cities. Of these 27 who deserted when serving in Constantinople, only three were Muslims. Moreover, the Ottoman authorities believed that locals, both Christians and Muslims, were helping Cypriot 'Rums' to desert.[22] This indicates that religion was no barrier in what was a collaborative effort to support deserters.

An analysis of the demographics of the desertions reveals that there was a higher proportion of Muslim Cypriot desertion compared to Christian when compared to overall numbers. They were spread across the various types of deserter and the only explanation is that the higher Muslim desertion rates correspond to the higher urban rates.

An exploration of the urban–rural composition of the deserters shows that fewer men from villages deserted than their overall representation (Table 7.2). This indicates that they had a greater need to make a go of the Mule Corps and that more men from urban areas were unwilling to return to the island.

The civil condition of the deserters indicates that married men were less likely to desert. This, again, reflects the motivations of married

Table 7.3 Next of kin spread of deserters

Next of kin	No.	% Deserters	% Overall
Father	31	26.5	30.77
Mother	18	15.4	22.98
Wife	12	10.3	24.96
Sister	12	10.3	6.40
Brother	8	6.8	6.68
Uncle	3	2.6	2.03
Friend	1	0.85	0.93
Cousin	1	0.85	0.54
Fiancée	1	0.85	0.48
Nephew	1	0.85	0.29
N/A	29	24.8	N/A
Total	117		

Source: WO405/1 and WO329/2357.

men to provide for their families. Younger men, although many having responsibilities to parents and siblings, were more likely to desert (Table 7.3).

Punishment of deserters was rare, since it was rare for the military authorities to catch a deserter, but also harsh, with a deserter at best being discharged or at worst gaoled. Incredibly, there are a few examples of discharged and repatriated muleteers who were accepted back into the Mule Corps. Indeed some were not even listed as deserted. In March 1919 in Constantinople three Cypriot muleteers, Demetris Christoforou from Larnaca, in 362nd Company, RASC, Constandinos Koulourou from Kato Lacadamia, also in 362nd Company, RASC, and Georgios Venedicto from Varosha, an interpreter in the 83rd Field Ambulance, absented themselves without leave and were gaoled, the latter the most severely for 56 days.[23] Another muleteer who left his compound without leave, Kyriakos Haji Elia from Yialousa, was given a six-month sentence.[24] An example of an official deserter who was caught and gaoled, admittedly for the additional crime of stealing public goods, was Haralambo Sofokli from Agios Amvrosios, of the 798th Horse Transport Company, who was sentenced to two years' hard labour on 19 May 1919.[25]

Ultimately, desertion was not a major problem. Cypriot muleteers were not motivated to dessert because they were mostly satisfied serving in their units. The mule corps satisfied their need to work and most returned to the island after their service and decided on their future then.

MULETEER BEHAVIOUR DURING SERVICE

Misconduct and criminality

All volunteer military units, even auxiliary types, contain criminal activity. As stated, most of the muleteers got along well with both their superiors and with each other. This was despite the power imbalances caused by army regulations and discipline, but also by imperial-colonial power imbalances. Statistically a small group, a mere 121, found themselves dismissed for 'criminal' misconduct, imprisoned for various crimes and even executed.

Violent crimes in Cyprus were a major problem. In the Annual Report for 1913–14 it was stated that criminal returns had slightly increased from the previous year and there had been six convictions for murder, fifteen for homicide and nine for assault with intent to kill. The report stated that 'the proneness of the Cypriote to have recourse to the knife is still a regrettable factor in the social condition of the country'. In total 18,814 persons were brought before the Magisterial Courts and 139 the Superior Courts,[26] a high number for such a small place. In 1914–15 those charged significantly increased. This included for homicide, with 35 charged, although the report stated that the 'character of the murders was of a less savage nature than in previous years'.[27] In the 1915–16 report there were no statistics for violent crimes, although it was reported that there was an increase to 8,206 convictions from the 5,579 of the previous year, with 66 per cent being for default of payment of fines, fees and taxes.[28] Crime was on the increase, especially financial crimes, indicating a lack of employment opportunities in Cyprus before the Mule Corps. The incidence of violent crimes and the use of the dagger or knife to commit violence indicate a strong sense of honour, pride and shame in crimes.[29] Appendix VIII shows that of the 121 Cypriots dismissed for misconduct, ten were dismissed on their first stint and then allowed to re-enlist; while seven were dismissed on their second stint, and one on his third. Although it cannot be assumed, some of the ten who re-enlisted may have slipped through undetected.

The demographics of those dismissed reveals that there was a lower misconduct rate for Muslim Cypriots compared to their overall enlistment percentage and especially by comparison to Muslim Cypriot desertion. The difference, however, is negligible, especially since not all cases of dismissal for misconduct are known, and there are many names missing. Nevertheless, the results show that there was not one religious group more likely to commit a crime or misconduct than another, which reflects that crime was a social rather than an ethnic condition (Table 7.4).

Table 7.4 Religious breakdown of those dismissed for misconduct

Ethno-religious	No. dismissed	% Dismissed	% Overall CMC
Orthodox Cypriots	109	89.3	90.4
Muslim Cypriots	9	7.4	8.45
Armenian Cypriots	1	0.8	0.25
Other Cypriots (undermined)	3	2.5	
Total	122		

Source: WO405/1 and WO329/2357.

Table 7.5 Urban–rural composition of Cypriots dismissed for misconduct

	No.	% Misconduct	% Overall CMC
Urban	21	17.2	15.45
Semi-urban	4	3.3	3.36
Regional centre	14	11.5	7.49
Village – large	16	13.1	15.37
Village	60	49.2	57.47
N/A	7	5.7	0.87
Total	122		

Source: WO405/1 and WO329/2357.

Indeed that crime is a social condition was reflected in the urban and rural distribution of those committing a crime, with proportionally less crime from villages. As with desertions there was greater restraint and discipline from the peasant and rural labouring men, who stood to lose more if they were dismissed than perhaps those from urban and regional centres (Table 7.5).

Married men were more likely to be dismissed for misconduct than single men (Table 7.6). This indicates again a greater sense of the 'honour' and 'shame' codes prevailing in the island, especially when it came to disobedience to a superior officer. With theft it may have been to obtain more money.

Appendix VIII shows how there was little information on why these men were dismissed, available only for a mere 23. A close analysis of these reveals that there were five main reasons for dismissal. The most common reasons were theft, both petty theft and armed robbery, and for violence against a colleague or a superior officer. More rare reasons were for sexual crimes, manslaughter and murder.

Before exploring these various crimes in detail, the issue of imprisonment must be addressed. In July 1918 Milne asked Clauson if the

Table 7.6 Next of kin spread for Cypriot muleteers dismissed

Next of kin	No.	% Dismissed	% Overall CMC
Wife	36	29.51	24.96
Father	30	24.59	30.77
Mother	23	18.85	22.98
Brother	7	5.74	6.68
Sister	6	4.92	6.40
Friend	4	3.28	0.93
Uncle	2	1.64	2.03
Brother-in-law	2	1.64	0.79
Aunt	2	1.64	0.33
Godfather	1	0.82	0.35
Cypriot government	1	0.82	0.33
Grandmother	1	0.82	0.15
Father-in-law	1	0.82	0.11
N/A	6	4.92	N/A
Total	122		

Source: WO405/1 and WO329/2357.

Cypriot government would accept those sentenced to serve their time in Cyprus.[30] Clauson replied that all cases would be judged individually.[31] But without prompting from Salonica, in February 1919 Stevenson, Clauson's replacement, informed Milne that he was 'now prepared to give you authority to send prisoners to Cyprus at your discretion'.[32] Stevenson was clearly putting the Clauson era of cautious accommodation of the military authorities behind him. His enthusiasm to help the military authorities this time locked Cyprus into paying for the expenses of imprisoning these military prisoners, although the auditor informed him that normal practice was for the military to pay.[33]

In Salonica muleteers did not frequent the city, so policing was mostly a military affair, but in Constantinople an inter-allied committee was formed to control the Ottoman Police Force under the presidency of Brigadier-General Fuller. The Ottoman police in Constantinople was separated into five areas: Pera, Galata, Stamboul, Scutari and Haji Pasha, and was controlled by the Director General, Colonel Halil Bey. Appointed soon after the armistice, Halil Bey immediately replaced numerous police and the committee commented that he was a Salonica Jew, which was good because the force was multi-religious, mainly comprising Muslims and Christians, with the population of Constantinople being 54% Muslim and 46% Christian. The allies proposed to control policing by separating the town into three sectors: Pera and Galata, Stambul, and Scutari, with each sector having three officers from each of the allied groups and ten police from each. These police would supervise the carrying out of orders by the Ottoman police and enquire into public complaints against the police and troops. Military policing would be carried out as before, with each ally responsible for their own forces.[34]

Theft and robbery

Theft and robbery were the more common crimes of the Cypriot muleteers. As mentioned at the start, there was the organised 'theft gang'. Stealing from a fellow muleteer was difficult to detect and prove. For this reason the majority of theft cases deal with the theft of public goods. Only one man was gaoled in Salonica for stealing public goods. Haralambos Sofokli, discussed above, was given two years' hard labour for his desertion and stealing of public goods on 19 May 1919.[35] In the absence of details for the majority of cases of dismissal for misconduct, and the prevalence of theft and robbery, it must be assumed that there were more cases.

There were several cases of robbery, receiving stolen goods and fraud. The following three in Salonica may have been working together, since the sentences took place less than a week apart, and two of the men enlisted at the same time. Aristides Ioannou from Limassol was sentenced to one year's hard labour for armed robbery on 3 July 1918 by the Commander of 22nd Division.[36] Six days later the Commander of 22nd Division sentenced two more men, Georgios Michael from Agia Phyla, Limassol, and Ioannis Petrou from Miliou, Paphos, this time for nine months' hard labour for robbery.[37] These men were all sent to serve their sentences in the Central Prison in Nicosia.[38] In Constantinople, Georgis Athanassis from Karmi, serving in the 29th Reserve Park RASC, was sentenced to six months for stealing public goods.[39] Georgios Yanni from Lithrangomi, serving in the RACC, was given 56 days for receiving stolen public goods.[40] Meanwhile, Kyriakos Haji Illia from Yialousa was charged with two counts of altering his pay book, and sentenced to three months.[41]

In Constantinople Cypriot muleteers became notorious for stealing from and damaging local vegetable gardens and orchards. On 16 May 1919 Nazim Agha petitioned the gendarmerie station at Icherenkoey in Constantinople, reporting that 'Cypriot Rums' and 'Negros' in the British army were constantly damaging his melons, and he had failed to sell any because of it. He claimed that the soldiers cried out, 'we will do this to all Turkish goods'.[42] The reported cries must not be attributed to a 'Greco–Turkish conflict', especially since these men, a mixed group of Cypriots, Africans, West Indians and men from the Subcontinent, were venting their anger at their former wartime enemy. By summer the frequency of the Cypriot muleteers drinking to excess in local pubs and damaging local gardens resulted in a delegation from Bashi-Büyük, Maltepe, to the Subgovernorship of Kartal.[43] Four days later the police reported that 'Cypriot Rums' in the British army were damaging and stealing produce (tomatoes, eggplants and cucumbers) from local farms in Bostancı.[44] The reports continued and were a source of concern for the Interior Ministry.[45] The investigation into Nazim Agha's case found that the Cypriots were accompanied by 'Negros' and that the damage to his farm in Kayishdaghi was estimated at about 5,000 kurush.[46] Although the British embassy was informed,[47] the attacks continued. Cypriot muleteers next damaged the garden of Shevki Effendi in Bashi-Büyük Village, causing an estimated 30,160 kurush damage.[48] Service in Constantinople offered greater opportunity to commit such crimes because of their peacetime role and the proximity to inhabited areas.

Finally, Miltiades Nicolaou from Gouri, Nicosia, was deported from Constantinople in 1922 after serving six months for theft. Nicolaou, with his uncle, a priest, Papandreas Haji Yorki, as his next of kin, had been a charge upon the British Relief Fund before being dismissed from his job at the veterinary hospital at Constantinople in late 1921 upon suspicion of theft. He confessed to breaking into the quarters of an officer of the Royal Army Veterinary Corps on 24 March 1922 and stole £135 and a pair of shoes. Nicolaou was sentenced to six months with hard labour and upon serving his time he was deported to Cyprus.[49]

Striking a superior officer or police

Another reason for dismissal was for striking a superior officer. It would be a generalisation to attribute this to Cypriots being 'hot-headed' and there are better explanations to account for this, for example the conditions that existed in their service in both Salonica and Constantinople.

The incidents of striking a superior officer or police occurred in Constantinople, further indicating the frustrating peacetime service there. On record, the first person convicted of striking his superior officer was Lucas Nicola from Strovolos, serving with the 115th Company, sentenced on 24 December 1918 to five years and sent to Cyprus in 1920 to serve his time.[50] There were numerous cases in March 1919 in Constantinople. Costis Stylianou from Agios Theodoros, Larnaca, serving in the 26th Division, was sentenced to 18 months in March 1919.[51] He should have known better since this was his second stint as a muleteer, having previously served for a year from September 1916, and a further eight months the second time. He was followed by three others who served in the 362nd Company,

RASC, Georgios Michael, who received four months for striking his forman;[52] Haralambos Stavrino from Larnaca, who received three months for throwing stones at his foreman;[53] Georgios Constantino from Varosha, also three months prison for using insubordinate language to his superior officer, inciting muleteers to overcome resistance of guard and escaping from arrest;[54] and Ioannis Loizou from Peristerona, Nicosia, serving in the 54th Brigade RFA, who received a six-month sentence for striking his superior officer, resisting an escort and escaping custody (i.e. a deserter).[55] In April 1919, Constandinos Illia from Goudi, Paphos, serving in the 163rd Company, RASC, was imprisoned for a day for using insubordinate language to his superior officer.[56] Next, in May 1919, Loucas Vassiliou was convicted for three months for assaulting police.[57] In June 1919 Andreas Georgiou (real name Gregoriou) from Limassol, was sentenced to two years on 24 June 1919 for striking his superior officer. Three days later Panayis Kyriakou from Agios Georgios, Famagusta, was given six months for offering violence to his superior officer, and on the same day Nicolas Vassiliou was sentenced to three months for conduct to the prejudice of good order and military discipline.[58] Gregoriou was one of the most experienced muleteers, having served three separate stints. Kyriakou also should have known better since he too had previously served. Finally Theofanis K. Floudiotis, serving in 121st Horse Transport Company, was sentenced on 20 February 1920 to six months' hard labour for striking his superior officer.[59]

The high incidence of Cypriots striking their superior officer illustrates the tough conditions faced by civilian volunteers, the obvious restlessness of men being subject to military control and discipline, especially in postwar Constantinople, and finally the differing codes of honour in the Mediterranean, particularly in Cyprus.[60]

Sexual crimes

Sexual crimes were quite uncommon.[61] Life in the military was obviously isolating, leading to sexual frustration, yet in the case of homosexuality there was greater opportunity. In the absence of any studies on homosexuality in Cyprus it cannot be assumed that it was any more taboo in Cyprus than in Britain. The one reported 'criminal' case involved Michael Lazari from Limassol, and Christodoulos Nicola from Emba, both serving in the 238th Horse Transport Company. They were sent to Cyprus to serve their three years' hard labour.[62] Christodoulos Nicola had served from 8 June 1917 until his official dismissal on 2 April 1919, meaning that he was approaching two years' service. On the other hand, Michael Lazari served two stints, first from 9 June 1917 to 2 July 1918, and then from 28 October 1918 to 9 May

1919. These men enlisted one day apart and therefore had probably met in June 1917. Without attempting to infer, it is possible that they had a relationship for some time. Indeed homosexuality would have been difficult to police and some men would have been sympathetic and not reported it. The fact that some men were clear of venereal disease in Salonica but found to be infected upon repatriation indicates some sexual activity at Salonica and/or on the ship.

Manslaughter and murder

Manslaughter and murder were not common and for some cases there is little information. Milne informed Clauson in December 1918, a few days before Clauson died, that he wanted to send to Cyprus two men, one convicted of attempted manslaughter and another of manslaughter. Ioannis Constantino from Larnaca tis Lapithou, Kyrenia, who had served with 852nd Company, was sentenced to 5 years for wounding with intent to do grievous bodily harm, while Georgios Theodosi from Agia Phyla, Limassol, was sentenced to one year for manslaughter.[63]

One of the more significant crimes and which revealed the existence of organised crime amongst the muleteers occurred in December 1918. In March 1919, Costas Panayi, Kato (Lower) Dicomo, informed Stevenson that his son Loizos Costa was stabbed and killed by Gregoris Jonis, Vatili, Famagusta, at Salonica. Gregoris had returned to his village and Panayi demanded that Stevenson have him charged.[64] Police enquiries into the death of Costa had found that on that fateful day he was with about a hundred muleteers in Salonica awaiting repatriation. Costa was with 16 others, many from Dicomo, in a tent. On the night of 26 December 1918, a muleteer Gregoris Nicola, alias Jonis, went into Costa's tent with a dagger and said to him, 'even you Loizo *Koumbaro*,[65] you do such things', referring to thefts which had taken place. Nicola then left the tent, but shortly afterwards some muleteers began cutting the tent ropes. Costa ran out and a group of muleteers chased him. A fight ensued and on being dispersed Costa was stabbed on his head and side, dying shortly afterwards. Despite a military investigation, there was no evidence to charge anyone. Veterans were interviewed in Cyprus and they confirmed that 'Loizo was a member of an organised gang of Muleteers who systematically robbed the others, who revenged themselves by murdering him.'[66] Panayi was duly informed that the military authorities had fully investigated his son's death and no further action would be taken.[67] The organisation of a gang of muleteers that robbed others indicates planned crime, yet given the lack of evidence it is unclear how many people were involved and for how long.

Muleteers committed several serious crimes in Constantinople.

In April 1919, Bakir Shoukri from Nicosia, serving in the 112th Company, RASC, was gaoled for six months for wounding a fellow muleteer.[68] The most serious crime saw the execution of four muleteers. This came to light in Cyprus only when Panayiotis Kalli Kallatta wrote to the government that his brother Kyriacos Kalli Kallatta, who left Cyprus in December 1918, was in October 1919 court-martialled and shot in Constantinople. Panayiotis wanted this confirmed and his belongings returned so he could give them to Kyriacos's two children.[69] The military authorities confirmed that the following men were convicted on 8 to 15 October on three charges of murder: Kyriakos Kalli; Yorkis Antonio from Agia Varvara; Yangos Haji Louka; and Georghis Simeoni from Sotira, Limassol. The Commander-in-Chief confirmed that the sentences were carried out at 07.14 hours on 31 October 1919.[70] Panayiotis was duly informed.[71]

The British and Cypriot archives have no further data. The story below is reconstructed from Ottoman archives, which provide contradictory evidence. The first report of the incident, which happened on 12 October, was prepared by Sargent Mustafa, Commander of the Gendarmerie station, and Lieutenant Izzet, on 12 and 13 October. The report reveals that two Cypriots, Ioannis son of Hajicosta, 13886 and Georgis son of Nikola, 14245, from 22nd division, were arrested for shooting Mustafa Baki, who died 24 hours later, while eight other Cypriots fled.[72] Another Ottoman police report on 13 October added that in all 18 shots were fired.[73] On the same day, Üsküdar police reported that the Cypriots shouted to Mustafa Baki 'down with Turks' and that local 'Rums' shot at Ottoman police from their houses.[74] Perhaps there were ethnic tensions between some Cypriot muleteers and local Muslims, although the Turks were the wartime enemy. The Ottoman interior ministry was immediately informed that there had been 30 Cypriots serving in the British army who had been causing trouble and had shot at an Ottoman policeman, Mustafa Baki.[75] Many other Ottoman police reports followed. One on 14 October clarified that altogether 12 drunken Cypriot 'Rums' attacked the Ottoman police. After drinking at Ligor's pub they entered a café and after leaving it they encountered an Ottoman soldier, Mustafa Baki, wounding him on his chest. Ottoman police arrested two of the Cypriots and two others were shot.[76] The Ottoman interior ministry was updated with a fuller report that mentioned the wounding of Baki and the killing of two Cypriots. A British military doctor examined the two Cypriots before they were buried and confirmed the rifle wounds. The British High commission would be informed about the incident.[77] An Ottoman Central Police report blamed the Cypriots who had been harassing civilians at Maltepe for some time.[78] An updated Ottoman police report added that the Cypriots 'were guilty' of attacking Baki and establishing relations with local 'Rums' after arriving at Maltepe.[79] This collaboration was clarified in a report for the Ottoman Interior Ministry, which claimed that the local 'Rums' had given weapons to Cypriots. There was concern that a conflict might result between Cypriots and local Turks.[80] The prosecutor at Üsküdar was ordered to investigate the incidents involving Cypriots at Maltepe.[81]

The concerns of the Ottoman Governorship of Constantinople were upheld, since a number of incidents followed after the conviction of the four Cypriots. The first, reported on 28 October, three days before their executions, was a fight between Cypriot muleteers and British gendarmerie in Maltepe.[82] Then, shortly after the executions, Cypriots at the British base at Bostancı stoned and robbed the house of Captain Bedreddin Bey, an Ottoman soldier. Muslim soldiers in the British army were also involved, and judging from the names provided they were likely to have been Cypriots: Hasan, Huseyin, Ramazan, Surur, Mevlud and Mustafa. The report recommended that the Cypriots be replaced with British personnel.[83] This was followed by another incident of Cypriots in Maltepe fighting with the British soldiers.[84]

The Cypriot Mule Corps was disbanded in April 1920, although the allied occupation continued until 1923. When this was decided and why is unclear, although it may be connected to the various incidents in the last months of 1919.

Life for colonial officials

Most Cypriot colonial officials involved in running the Mule Corps got along well. Undoubtedly its formation placed additional stresses on the work of the government and the civil service, beyond their ordinary war duties, yet at the same time it certainly provided them with a sense of contribution to the war effort far greater than any other war time task, with the exception of military intelligence.[85] In the same way as the work of military intelligence saw a sometimes fraught relationship between the civilian colonial government officials and the military, there were occasional tensions in relation to the Cypriot Mule Corps, and sometimes within the civil establishment in the island. But for the most part the system worked well.

After the high commissioner, mostly Clauson, and the three chief secretaries who served during the war and immediately after, Charles Orr, William Fenn and Malcolm Stevenson, who succeeded Clauson, the most important Cypriot colonial service official in relation to the Cypriot Mule Corps was Bowring the treasurer. In the months leading to the official disbandment of the Cypriot Mule Corps, Milne brought to the attention of the War Secretary, Winston Churchill, Bowring's voluntary work, the various district commissioners and treasury clerks in connection with over 25,000 allotment payments amounting to over £100,000.[86] This initiated a round of congratulations for all concerned,[87] highlighting the significance of the Cypriot Mule Corps.

Conclusion

The majority of muleteers did not desert their post or commit a crime. At most several hundred misbehaved in one way or another. Deserters were few, which was a surprise given the conditions, especially at Salonica, and the issues around contracts and the British implementation of the allotment scheme. Misconduct and crime (at least as far as can be determined from the records at hand) were also low. For those on the wrong side of the British, whether their actions were planned or not, they felt the full force of military law and regulations. Ultimately, most saw their service as hard for various reasons, yet financially beneficial, and so kept their heads down in order to not risk it. Some also felt a sense of loyalty to the British Empire and its cause in the war. What became of them after their service is, however, another matter.

Notes

1. In addition to the books discussed in Chapter 1, see William Moore, *The Thin Yellow Line*, Cooper, London, 1970.
2. SA1/722/1916, Lt. 2nd Bat., L.R. Maquire, Mule Depot, to CCPC, 5 August 1916. This list was not found.
3. Ibid., telegram, Georgios Iacovou to Clauson, 18 August 1916.
4. Ibid., Orr to CCPC, 18 August 1916.
5. Ibid., ACCPC to Orr, 31 August 1916.
6. Ibid., Louca Georgiou, 3791, Statement, 10 August 1916.
7. Ibid., Yianni Sophianou (Christofis no. 12681) to Clauson, 9 August 1918.
8. Ibid., Anastasis Elia (Michael no. 12575) to Clauson, 7 August 1918.
9. Ibid., Andreas Stavri (Andonios no. 13072) to Clauson, 1 October 1918.
10. Ibid., Izzet Mustafa, Mouktar of Komi Kebir (Raif no. 12627), to Clauson, 31 August 1918.
11. Ibid., Annou Michael (Christodoulos no. 12673) to Clauson, 16 August 1918; ibid., Katinou Haji Demetri to Clauson, 23 October 1918.
12. SA1/978/1916/, Andreas Stavri to Clauson, 1 October 1918.
13. Ibid., Stevenson to Izzet Mustafa, 13 September 1918; ibid., Stevenson to Andreas Stavri, 15 October 1918.
14. Ibid., Sisman to Stevenson, 28 August 1918.
15. SA1/722/1916, Katinou Haji Demetri to Clauson, 23 October 1918.
16. SA1/978/1916, Stevenson to Katinou Haji Demetri, 23 October 1918.
17. SA1/680/1918, Costi Karageorghi to OCMPC, 10 April 1918.
18. Ibid., Sisman to Stevenson, 22 April 1918; ibid., Stevenson to Sisman, 24 April 1918.
19. WO95/4827, WDSA, Report by E.C. Boulter, Officer in Charge of Macedonian Mule Corps Records, 12 December 1917.

20 The desertion figures are based on WO405/1 and WO329/2357. Unfortunately, too often the British did not record the full details of deserters. For further detail see appendices on website for Manchester University Press (www.manchesteruniversitypress.co.uk/serving-the-empire-in-the-great-war-appendix/).
21 See WO95/4809, WDSA, 854th Auxiliary Pack Company, part of 27th Division Train before November 1917, 20, 21 and 22 November and 2 December 1918.
22 DH.EUM.AYS/36/17/1338.B.4, 29, Governorship of Constantinople to Interior Ministry, 21 September 1919. 'Rums' simply means Romans or *Romiee* – Eastern Orthodox Christians.
23 WO154/234, Table showing convictions by courts-martial against persons other than British soldiers, 1–31 March 1919. Nos 11647, 11651 and 12253 respectively.
24 SA1/1010/1917, Stevenson to Milne, 15 May 1920. Haji Elia had no. 9000.
25 Ibid., D.K.E Hale (General Officer Commanding Lines of Communication, Black Sea Army) to Stevenson, 13 June 1919. Sofokli had no. 9042.
26 *Annual Report for Cyprus, 1913–14*, cd. 7643, HMSO, London, 1914, 22.
27 *Annual Report for Cyprus, 1914–15*, Cd-7622, HMSO, London, 1915, 21.
28 *Annual Report for Cyprus, 1915–16*, Cd-8172, HMSO, London, 1916, 14.
29 See J.G. Peristiany, 'Honour and Shame in a Cypriot Highland Village', in J.G. Peristiany (ed.), *Honour and Shame: The Values of Mediterranean Society*, University of Chicago Press, 1966 (repr. Midway, 1974).
30 SA1/1010/1917, Milne to Clauson, 9 July 1918.
31 Ibid., Clauson to Milne, 3 August 1918.
32 Ibid., Stevenson to Milne, 7 Feb 1919.
33 Ibid., Auditor to Fenn, 30 April 1919; ibid., Fenn to Auditor, 2 May 1919.
34 WO95/4956, WDSA, General Staff, HQ Allied Forces, 'Organisation of the Turkish Police and Proposed Method of Allied Control', 28 January 1919.
35 SA1/1010/1917, Hale to Stevenson, 13 June 1919.
36 Ibid., Milne to Clauson, 3 July 1918. Ioannou had no. 8419.
37 Ibid, 9 July 1918. With nos 8417 and 1770, respectively.
38 Ibid., Clauson to Milne, 3 August 1918; ibid., 5 August 1918; ibid., CCPC to Stevenson, 24 October 1918.
39 WO154/235, Table of convictions by courts-martial against non-British soldiers, 1–30 April 1919. With no. 10670.
40 WO154/234, Table of convictions by courts-martial against non-British soldiers, 1–31 March 1919. With no. 11415.
41 WO154/236, Table of convictions by courts-martial against non-British soldiers, 1–31 May 1919. With no. 9000.
42 DH.EUM.AYS/24/81/1338.M.26, 21, Nazim Agha petition to Gendarmerie station at Icherenkoey, 16 May 1919.
43 Ibid., 25, Delegation from Bashi Buyuk, Maltepe to Subgovernorship of Kartal, 8 July 1919.
44 Ibid., 23, Lieutenant Izzet, Central Division, report, 12 July 1919.
45 Ibid., 19, Subgovernor of Kartal to Subgovernorship of Üsküdar, 17 July 1919; ibid., 20, Deputy governor of Constantinople to Interior Ministry, 22 July 1919.
46 Ibid., 16, Investigation report, signed by witnesses and owner, 17 August 1919; ibid., 11, Subgovernor of Kartal note, 23 August 1919; ibid., 10, Constantinople Governorship to Interior Ministry, 24 August 1919.
47 Ibid., 8, Central Police Commissariat to Foreign Ministry, 28 August 1919.
48 Ibid., 6, Constantinople Governorship to Interior Ministry, 18 September 1919; ibid., 16, Investigation report, signed by witnesses and owner, 17 August 1919; ibid., 11, Subgovernor of Kartal note, 23 August 1919; ibid., 2, Deputy Governor of Constantinople to Interior Ministry, 18 October 1919; ibid., 1, Central Police Commissariat to Foreign Ministry, 20 October 1919.
49 See CO67/209/21161 and his no. was 5661.
50 SA1/1010/1917, Milne to Stevenson, 2 January 1920. Nicola had nos 10603 and 4700.

51 Ibid., Hale to Stevenson, 7 March 1919. Stylianou had no. 10601.
52 WO154/234, Table of convictions by courts-martial against persons other than British soldiers, 1–31 March 1919. There is no Georgios Michael on the honour roll under 10195.
53 Ibid. Stavrino had no. 7474.
54 Ibid. Constantino had no. 11019.
55 WO154/235, Table of convictions by courts-martial against non-British soldiers, 1–30 April 1919. Loizou had no. 4040.
56 Ibid. Ilia had no. 8065.
57 SA1/978/1916, Vassilis Haji Stylianou, Larnaca, to CSC, 20 June 1919; Surridge for DCLa, to Fenn, 30 June 1919.
58 SA1/1010/1917, Hale to Stevenson, 17 July 1919. Gregoriou had nos 5910, 7402 and 12264, Kyriakou 12745 and Vassiliou 13509.
59 Ibid., Milne to Stevenson, 28 Feb 1920. Floudiotis had no. 13705.
60 See Peristiany, 'Honour and Shame in a Cypriot Highland Village'.
61 One muleteer was convicted for bestiality with a Jenny mule, but his father questioned the decision, claiming that his son's enemies made false accusations. See SA1/1010/1917, Milne to Clauson, 14 September 1917; Clauson to Milne, 16 October 1917; telegram, Britforce, Salonica, to Clauson, 19 November 1917; Army Form C, committing to prison, signed by Milne, 11 November 1917; Stevenson to Provost Marshal, British forces Salonica, 11 December 1917; Christodoulos Haji Ioannou, Argaki to Clauson, 18 December 1917; Stevenson to Haji Ioannou, 31 December 1917; Milne to Clauson, 8 January 1918.
62 Ibid., Hale to Stevenson, 29 March 1919. Lazaris had no. 13290 and Nicola 7736.
63 Ibid., Milne to Clauson, 27 December 1918. Constantino had no. 9451 and Theodosi 9315.
64 SA1/978/1916, Costa Panayi, Kato-Dikomo (Loizos had no. 8608) to Stevenson, 8 March 1919.
65 *Koumbaro* means best man at one's wedding, but in Cyprus it is used as a term to connote 'mate'.
66 SA1/978/1916, CCPC to Fenn, 13 March 1919.
67 Ibid., Fenn to Costa Panayi, 15 March 1919.
68 WO154/235, Table of convictions by courts-martial against persons other than British soldiers, 1–30 April 1919. Shoukkri had no. 3222.
69 SA1/978/1916, Panayiotis Kalli Kallatta to Fenn, 2 February 1920.
70 Ibid., ABS, GRO, 7 November 1919. 3364 Court Martial. C.R. No. 29724. A.G. 3. Nos 13787, 1964, 13624 and 12911 respectively.
71 Ibid., CSC to Panayiotis Kalli Kalatta, Yialousa, 22 May 1920.
72 DH.EUM.AYS/36/17/1338.B.4, 23, Ottoman Police Investigation report, 12 and 13 October 1919. It may be that these were the two men killed not arrested.
73 Ibid., 22, Ottoman police report, 13 October 1919.
74 Ibid., 20, Üsküdar Police report, 13 October 1919.
75 DH.EUM.AYS/24/13/1338.M.17, 1, Governorship of Constantinople to Interior Ministry, 12 October 1919; DH.EUM.AYS/36/17/1338.B.4, 21, Governorship of Constantinople to Interior Ministry, 13 October 1919.
76 Ibid., 19, Ottoman Police officer report, 14 October 1919. Reports disagree if Baki was a soldier or policeman.
77 Ibid., 17, Constantinople governorship to Interior Ministry, 15 October 1919.
78 Ibid., 12, Central Police Commissariat to Foreign Ministry, 15 October 1919.
79 Ibid., 15, Ottoman Police report, dated 16 October, in addition to the report of 13 October 1919.
80 Ibid., 14, Governorship of Constantinople to Interior Ministry, 20 October 1919.
81 Ibid., 13, Governorship of Constantinople to Interior Ministry, 26 October 1919.
82 Ibid., 11, Central Police Commissariat to Constantinople governorship, 28 October 1919.
83 Ibid., 10, deputy governor, Constantinople to Ministry of Interior, 13 November 1919.

84 Ibid., 4, deputy governor, Constantinople to Ministry of Interior, 3 December 1919.
85 See, Varnava, 'British Military Intelligence in Cyprus during the Great War', 353–78.
86 SA1/722/1916/1, Milne, CCABS, to War Secretary, 19 February 1920.
87 Ibid., WO to CO, 30 April 1920; Milner to Stevenson, 8 May 1920; Fenn to Treasurer, 28 May 1920.

CHAPTER EIGHT

Veterans and their families after service

In autumn 1921 Varnavas Michael Varnava, dressed in his best garb, lined up with other veterans of the Cypriot Mule Corps in Famagusta to receive his British War Medal. With their families watching, the ceremony must have given them great pride. Such ceremonies as this, which was attended by my great-grandfather, were held across all the towns of the island in autumn 1921. Sadly my great-grandfather's medal was lost in the war in Cyprus of 1974, and few are around these days,[1] some being destroyed upon the orders of EOKA in the mid-1950s.[2] The medal was important, especially to those who emigrated because they were able to use it in their adopted countries as a means of social inclusion and mobility, even after the Second World War. Many were proud of their service and asked for the British Victory Medal, to which they were not entitled.

Despite the assurances that men would not be in harm's way in the advertising to lure them into enlisting, many were killed or incapacitated as a result of their service. This chapter explores the impact of death and incapacity on veterans and dependants. It also looks at issues that veterans faced after returning and resettling into Cypriot life, which had changed dramatically because of the Great War. It discusses what the Cypriot government and military authorities did to alleviate the social and financial difficulties of veterans and their families, and what private organisations, namely the British Legion, did to aid those in need. It also looks at one of the solutions found by the men, emigration. As shown in Chapter 1, there is a significant literature on the experiences of veterans and their families after the Great War, especially in the context of Australia, but also Jamaica. This chapter argues that many Cypriot veterans, as with other examples, fell on hard times after the war, especially those unable to work because of incapacity, and this impacted negatively upon their families. Those who lost loved ones were also severely affected, financially and psychologically.

Unlike the authorities in Australia and Jamaica, the government and military authorities did little, in some cases nothing, to ameliorate the situation. Men again turned to emigration as their only way out of the mire.

Cyprus immediately after the Great War

Before exploring the main themes of this chapter, it is important, albeit briefly, to understand the ways in which the war changed Cyprus. On 26 July 1920 Stevenson reported to Lord Milner, the Colonial Secretary, on whether Cyprus was a suitable place for British settlement. Stevenson argued that, 'as elsewhere', the war had shaken the old and inaugurated a 'new order of things'. Cyprus was more expensive because the 'peasant classes have become enriched by profits and exportation during the war at enhanced prices'. Thus the peasants have 'become accustomed to a higher and more luxurious style of living and now consume themselves produce which previously they brought about entirely for sale in the market of the towns'. The working classes were now 'pressed hard', because food and commodities were more expensive, and therefore many were emigrating to Europe, Egypt and the USA, resulting in a labour shortage and higher wages for unskilled labour.[3]

Stevenson's report was most revealing about postwar Cyprus. The war had improved the lives of some peasants, but not all, and unskilled labourers were hit hard. Veterans were some of the hardest hit, since many belonged to the peasant and labouring classes.

Grieving and abandoned families

Some families were left broken by their men serving in the Cypriot Mule Corps. As shown previously some men died and others deserted, while others did not return, abandoning wives, children and other dependants. This section deals with the social and economic issues that arose from such broken families and the response of the various authorities to deal with them.

Death

For families who lost husbands, sons and brothers it was not only a great shock, especially since they had been led to believe that they would be away from the front, but also left a great financial hole. Bart Ziino has shown that in the Australian context, grieving was a communal response.[4] In Cyprus the grieving was not so communal, as the Mule Corps faded from memory and did not enter the national consciousness, while the immediate economic hardships of those left behind took precedence. There was a sense of injustice since the men had volunteered to serve in the British armed forces, yet they were, contractually, not considered as *serving*, but rather as *contract labour*, even though the contract used the word service. From the second contract it stipulated that there would be no compensation for an invalid muleteer or to families who had a muleteer die, even though this was not the original advice of the British military authorities. The cases discussed below are a selection of those for which families appealed to the government. There must have been many more (since 177 died) where appeals were not made, or in some fortunate cases where they received aid from family, friends or other organisations such as the Red Cross.

The appeals started in 1919 with Petros Haji Loizos, from Yialousa in the Karpas, informing Stevenson that his son, Loizos Petrou, had died from pneumonia while serving. Petrou had worked for 14 years as a labourer on the public roads before becoming chief labourer. 'He then listened to the voice of the respected government and abandoned his regular work ... and enlisted himself in the service of the English army.' Petros now demanded a government allowance to support his large family, since his son had been their only support.[5] The authorities confirmed that Petrou had died of pneumonia on 21 November 1918, but 'Under the terms of contract the British Military Authorities do not assume any responsibility for loss of life of muleteers while in their service, and the claim has therefore been rejected.'[6] This was the standard response from the British military authorities.[7]

In January 1920, Elengou Toouli Pezidianou, from Yeroskipou, Paphos, appealed to Stevenson for compensation for the death of her husband. An enemy shell had killed Yenethlis Ioannou on 15 July 1917 while he was performing his duties. She claimed that he was her only protector and she was now an 'orphan widow', thus associating herself with her two orphaned children. Due to her poor eyesight she could not work and they were therefore 'entirely destitute'. She wanted compensation through the War Orphans Fund so that she could maintain her children such as the families of the three sailors lost on the HMS *Kosseir*.[8] This showed that Pezidianou knew about the compensation given to the families of the HMS *Kosseir*, the government mail service, sunk by enemy fire on 12 August 1917.[9] The military authorities confirmed that a bomb/shell had killed Ioannou while on duty and he was buried at Karasouli Cemetery.[10] There were no further documents on the case, but it must be assumed that if Pezidianou received any reply it was along the same lines as the other appeals for compensation.

One applicant received small monetary relief, but not from the Cypriot government. Rodou Stylianou, from Anavargos, appealed to Thomas James Greenwood, the district commissioner of Paphos, on 3 May 1920, for compensation for the death of her husband, Michael Christodoulou. She had been told that he was leading mules carrying ammunition and other supplies for the front and the animals, frightened by motor cars, threw him into their path. Rodou was now left 'unprotected' with two infant children and with a father who was paralytic. She wanted compensation or a pension so they could maintain themselves.[11] Greenwood corroborated her story and recommended aid, revealing that her husband was a dyer who left her four jars, which were sold to pay his debts, forcing her to labour to maintain her children and disabled father.[12] Sisman claimed that Rodou's case had already been handled.[13] She had received £10, but it had not been enough to compensate her for her loss and she needed further welfare.[14] Sisman advised the government that it was pointless reapplying to the military authorities.[15] A year later Rodou and Arthur Marlay Fleury, the new district commissioner of Paphos, tried again, this time requesting a pension.[16] But the military authorities informed Stevenson that 'Under the terms of the contract signed by her husband, no compensation, pension or gratuity is payable by the British Military Authorities.'[17] So in the end Rodou was also given the standard response to stop her appeals.[18] The only difference was that the military authorities had given her £10.

There were several cases of widows claiming compensation or a pension when their husbands had died of 'natural' causes only to be told they were not eligible because they had not died on duty, implying that had they died on duty they would have been compensated. Patrou Theoharous of Tris Elies, Limassol, informed Stevenson on 30 May 1921 that her husband, Savas Theohari, died while serving as a muleteer, leaving her and their four children orphaned, with the eldest having since died. She claimed that she had no means of support and wanted compensation or a pension.[19] The military authorities informed Stevenson that Savas had died serving in the 27th Division on 16 August 1920 from tuberculosis, so not on the battlefield, and therefore 'the WO regret that nothing can be done for [his] wife'.[20] Another case was Fanou Haralambou, of Lefka, who wanted a pension because she was being forced to work as a labourer to maintain her orphaned children. In an emotive letter to Stevenson in September 1921, she asserted that her husband had given his life for the honour of England and his family deserved a pension.[21] But the military authorities revealed that Christos Ktori had died of erysipela in the 20th Stationary Hospital on 26 February 1917, and therefore of a 'natural death not caused by

Active Service in the Field', so no pension or compensation could be made.[22] Similarly, Susanna Eleftheriou, of Asgata, Limassol, asked for a pension in October 1921 because her husband Kleopas Christophorou had died serving as a muleteer. She had an underage child and could not earn a living.[23] Christophorou died in the 20th Stationary Hospital Salonica on 3 October 1918 of pneumonia and, as with the other cases, from 'a natural death not caused by Active Service in the Field', so no pension or compensation would be entertained.[24]

Then there were cases when an appeal for aid was rejected because the file had been destroyed. Theonou Toouli, of Agios Photi, Paphos, lost her husband Christos Yanni and was left with five minors.

> My deceased husband left no property whatever to maintain his children who are without clothes and are in the streets, therefore I beg Your Honour to recommend to the proper quarters for a subsidy to be given to them, because I too, have nothing by which to be able to support my children.[25]

The district commissioner of Paphos, Arthur Charles Tompkins, emphasised her poverty.[26] But the authorities in Constantinople could not trace Yanni as deceased because of 'all records of muleteers having been destroyed'.[27] But Tompkins had documents showing that Yanni had enlisted at Limassol, left in November 1917, died on 24 February 1918, and his wife had his medal.[28] Stevenson advised the military authorities to contact the War Office,[29] but there is no further correspondence, likely indicating that nothing further happened.

Muleteers who died left a massive hole for families. Not only were they mourned over, but they were also fought over, as their families, now destitute, sought some means of welfare to maintain themselves. When this was not forthcoming or was miniscule, they gave up. The British military authorities were slightly more flexible than the Cypriot government, once offering a 'one-off' payment, but this was not enough. The government could have done more, but failed to look after families who lost husbands and sons, devastating and impoverishing families.

Abandonment

Some muleteers abandoned their families, which, as with those that had died, left a terrible social and economic hole for them. The British authorities would not force men to return, or provide welfare to their dependents, yet they could have done both if they wanted. The cases below are a selection of those where families appealed to the Cypriot government for aid, and there must have been many other such cases where appeals were not made.

There was a case of abandonment as early as February 1918. Erato C. Lanitis enquired about the whereabouts of her husband Costas Lanitis of Limassol, since he had not returned after his service.[30] Erato did not ask for anything, but Panayiotou Georgi, from Karavas, Kyrenia, did. She claimed that her husband Solon D. Solou had informed her that he would not return to her and she appealed to the government to compel him to do so because she was unprotected and destitute.[31] Solou was discharged in Constantinople on 14 August 1920 and his address was unknown.[32] Even if the government knew where he was it would not interfere to bring him to Cyprus. This is what Myrianthi Kleovoulou was also told. Her husband Nicholas Kleovoulou of Tala, Paphos, enlisted in 1918 and she had not seen him again. Her two children and herself were left 'unprotected' and destitute. She asked the government to compel him to return or to provide them with a pension.[33] But the government was not prepared to intervene.[34]

When husbands abandoned dependent wives and children their allotments were ceased. Procopios Haji Georgiou Moustrides, of Malounda, made a £25-per-year allotment to his wife Maria, but she had not received it. With six underage children, Maria had borrowed money to survive and in May 1918 she informed Clauson that she desperately needed her allotment to pay her creditors.[35] Moustrides had an allotment under his first contract, but cancelled it as from 31 December 1916.[36] Maria had received no payments for 1917 because her husband had abandoned her and their children.[37] Another case was that of Christos Antonopoulos, from Arminou, Paphos. His wife Irene Georgiou had stopped receiving her allotment on 8 January 1919, as her husband had been hospitalised.[38] Irene desperately needed the balance of his allotment because she had five underage children.[39] By 1922 clearly Antonopoulos had left them (he had deserted in December 1919) and she was demanding the balance of his allotment to help raise their children.[40] She was told to visit the district treasury to obtain her money.[41]

Sons were just as missed as husbands. In March 1920 Solomis Romani from Karpasha, Kyrenia, had not heard from his son, Antoni Solomou, for seven months, and wanted to know if he was still serving or had been demobilised.[42] Solomou had been discharged in Constantinople on 3 December 1919, but was not repatriated and his current address was unknown.[43] In February 1924 Havva Jemal, from Nicosia, wanted to know the whereabouts of his son Ali Riza, who had enlisted seven years previously as an interpreter and from whom he had not heard in two years.[44] Charles Henry Hart-Davis, Nicosia's district commissioner, discovered that he was last at Chanak, where he was still serving.[45] The government informed Jemal that it could do nothing to help him.[46] These men, the first a Maronite and the second a Muslim, had clearly lost touch with their concerned parents, but the Cypriot government was unwilling to assist them.

Life for invalid veterans and their compensation struggles

As frequently discussed in this book the British also absolved themselves of any responsibility for compensating invalid veterans. This section discusses the experiences of four men who were incapacitated while serving in the Cypriot Mule Corps and their struggles for compensation. The men have been selected because they are different cases. The first case is Haris Panaou, selected because his was a more standard case of having lost a leg and received no compensation from the military or Cypriot authorities, although it was unique because it attracted the attention of the Archbishop of Cyprus. The second case is Yannis Panayi, which stands out because of his horrific accident and because he received a military gratuity and help from a non-government welfare organisation, St Dunstans. The third case is that of the legless Agathocles Haji Christodoulou, selected because he was the only case to receive a military payment and Cypriot government assistance. The final example was the unique case of the memory loss of Stavros Kojambashi, which the Cypriot authorities questioned and refused his demands for welfare.

Haris Panaou (Panayi), Rizokarpaso, Famagusta

The case of Haris Panaou (sometimes Panayi) is a good example of a disabled muleteer not compensated. In November 1919, a year after the armistice, Panayis Panayi from Rizokarpaso informed Stevenson that about a year previously his son Haris had enlisted, but six months later, while serving in Alexandria, accidently fell from a train and had his leg amputated from the knee. 'This unexpected accident of my son has plunged me into a very great despair: it has deprived myself, my wife and my family of our only support.'[47] Panayis wanted an artificial leg and a pension for his son, who was still under medical treatment at the British Red Cross and Order of St John, 21st General Hospital, Alexandria.[48]

When no answer was received, Haris, who had returned to Cyprus on 25 January 1920,[49] wrote to Arthur Fleury, Famagusta's district commissioner, who forwarded it to the chief secretary and onto Sisman, giving his story and his demands. Haris was only 20 when he enlisted and left Cyprus on 17 September 1918. After serving against the Bulgarians, in April 1919 he went to Alexandria with the 79th Field Ambulance Royal Army Medical Corps. At Alexandria a tram hit him when he was off duty and he was taken to a Military Hospital, where part of his leg was amputated. Meanwhile, his unit was ordered to Constantinople, so his commanding officer could not institute proceedings against the tram-way conductor. A military doctor took measurements, leading Haris to believe that he would receive an artificial leg. He pleaded that

> my father and mother are in very indigent circumstances. I am the eldest in a family of nine, which I was helping to support. I wish my case be brought before the proper authorities so that a pension or compensation may be awarded me for the loss of my leg on active service. Also I am helpless without my leg and wish if possible to obtain an artificial leg ...[50]

He added that he was also owed £40 in back pay.[51] Two days later, Haris wrote to Stevenson, repeating much of what he had given in his statement, adding that 'In the condition I am now, your excellency, I am unable not only to help my parents in the support of our large family but also to earn my own daily bread.'[52] He was appealing to the 'benevolent feelings of the English government' to provide him with an artificial leg and a monthly pension so that 'I may not die of starvation'. The Archbishop of Cyprus, Kyrillos III, wrote to Stevenson on his behalf, 'a youth of Rizokarpaso', who was fit and able-bodied, but now could not even earn 'his own daily bread'.[53]

The Cypriot government did not reply to father or son, but immediately replied to the archbishop that the matter was being considered.[54] Major G. Sims-Marshall, Deputy Assistant Adjutant General, Army of the Black Sea, wrote on 19 March 1920 that 'this man has no legal claim upon us of any sort' and 'had such an accident ... happened in civil life there is no one to whom he could look for compensation [and] I fail to see that this is even a case for an ex-gratia payment and cannot advise that the British Public should pay anything'.[55] The Military Claims Commission at Constantinople ruled that because Haris 'fell from a tramcar whilst out of camp without leave ... that no responsibility or liability devolves upon the British Military Authorities'.[56] Stevenson waited another month before advising Panayis that his claim had been rejected for the same reasons given.[57]

Six months later, Haris tried again. In a letter to the Cypriot government he demanded an artificial leg and a pension.[58] Sisman opined that no good would result if the matter was again referred to the Military Claims Commission. He suggested that

> the Authorities of the British Red Cross and Order of St John [should] be approached with a view to granting this man an artificial leg, but such application would, of course, carry more weight if it emanated from His

Excellency the High Commissioner, than would be the case if it were forwarded from this office.[59]

It is unclear if these organisations were approached, but in reply to Haris, Stevenson said nothing about them.[60] Haris did receive a leg, but not from the government or military authorities.[61]

The contracts were clear on the question of compensation. On this occasion the military authorities argued that because Haris was not on duty when he was injured that they were not liable. This was a poor excuse since he would not have been in Alexandria if he was not serving.

Yannis Panayi, Kouklia Paphos

On the other hand Yannis Panayi did receive some aid from the British military authorities. On 17 September 1920 the Finance Secretary in the War Office asked the General Officer CCABS to have Yannis Panayi, Kouklia, Paphos, medically examined and to award him a gratuity according to his degree of disablement corresponding with the scale already in force for the Greek Labour Corps and to deal with all future applications for compensation in the same way.[62] It is unclear who contacted the War Office on behalf of Panayi. The War Office decision showed some clarity in the matter and coming as it did in September 1920 suggests that they considered it to have been worthwhile to revisit the case of Haris Panaou.

Panayi was examined in November 1920 by S.J. Vassiliades, the District Medical Officer in Nicosia, who found both his hands were amputated from the middle of his arms, his eyes were removed and he had a large cicatrix on the right side of his abdomen. These injuries 'correspond with his statement that they were caused some time ago by the explosion of a hand bomb while he was in the service'.[63] The report was sent to General Officer CCABS,[64] and there is no record of a decision. Panayi tried again in May 1922. He informed Stevenson that he enlisted as a muleteer in 1918 and went to Salonica and Constantinople. 'While being at Agios Stephanos, I accidentally found on the ground a shell which blew up and entirely destroyed both my eyes and cut off my two hands and wounded much of my face and chest.'[65] Rushed to hospital, he was sent to England for treatment. He was repatriated in 1920 and until August 1921 he claimed to have received £8 per month from the British government. Then from August 1921 to January 1922 he was only paid £7.7.5 from the garrison headquarters in Limassol. He wanted a more regular payment because he was 'in a destroyed and crippled state and entirely useless and incapable for any work whatever so as to be able to support my family which consists of my wife and four children, the eldest of which is nearly eleven years old'.[66]

His case was taken up again in 1927, when the governor, Sir Ronald Storrs, toured Paphos and received a petition on behalf of Yannis Panayioti (Panayi). The petition claimed that he was receiving a pension of £8 per month, but this was cut to £2.5.0, which was not enough to feed his family of seven.[67] Heidenstam, the acting district commissioner of Paphos, had visited Yannis, and another source had informed him that he had received a lump sum of £400 from some 'Hellenic society' and an allowance of £8 per month, but this was stopped. He also revealed that his children, despite chances to work, preferred to stay home and live off their father's misfortune. Heidenstam could not find out where the £2.5.0 was coming from. Surridge, the new district commissioner of Paphos, tried to obtain more information from N.K. Lanites, an advocate and nationalist politician, from Limassol.[68] Surridge discovered that the £2.5.0 was from St Dunstans, a charitable organisation founded in 1915 by Sir Arthur Pearson, the owner of the *Evening Standard* and founder of the *Daily Express*, to help those who had lost their vision in the Great War.[69] For this reason, the Cypriot government declined to proceed any further,[70] not even to advocate to St Dunstans to increase the allowance.

Agathocles Haji Christodoulou

The only invalid to receive significant compensation from the military authorities and the Cypriot government was Agathocles Haji Christodoulou from Polistipos, Nicosia. According to the honour roll, he served from 16 February 1918 to 27 April 1919. He first appraised the Cypriot government on 16 May 1919 that on 7 December 1918, while serving at the Rupel fortifications, both his legs were broken and he was carried to the British military hospital near Salonica where in January 1919 they were amputated because of gangrene. Haji Christodoulou wanted the Cypriot government to forward his petition to the military authorities so he could receive his outstanding wages until 31 October 1918, which amounted to £11, and any reasonable sum from 1 November 1918 to 27 April 1919. He also asked for artificial legs and a small pension, because 'I am quite unable to do any work having been crippled for life.'[71]

The government, however, did nothing about his petition for at least four months. According to the General Routine Orders from March 1917 all muleteers would be paid their wage if hospitalised,[72] but this does not seem to have been followed all the time. It was not until 25 August that Sisman became aware of the case.[73] Meanwhile Haji Christodoulou addressed a second petition to Stevenson repeating his demands. He revealed that he was tormented, felt useless to society because he could not work, and that he would have been better off dead.[74] On 22 September 1919, over four months after his initial petition, the government informed Haji Christodoulou that his case was still being considered.[75] In reply, Haji Christodoulou asked for a speedy and satisfactory decision because he was destitute.[76] Finally the government wrote to the Black Sea Force on 4 October 1919. Two months later it was decided that because Haji Christodoulou was merely in the 'employ' of the British military authorities, they had 'no responsibility' and 'consequently reject the claim'. But the General Officer CCABS authorised an 'ex gratia' grant of £40.[77] The British military authorities continued to claim that the men in the Mule Corps were not in the 'service' of the British army, as their contracts stipulated, but in its 'employ', and therefore not liable to compensation. Haji Christodoulou was to receive compensation only because the CCABS pitied him.

But Haji Christodoulou remained unsatisfied and depressed. On 15 August 1920 he addressed an emotional letter to Winston Churchill, the War Secretary. He was 'a native of Cyprus (Christian Orthodox) and [the] son of poor old parents [who were] almost unable for work'. He related that he left them to enlist as a muleteer to better support them and his younger siblings and how he lost his legs, adding the obvious that 'since then I regret to say I remain footless'. Pleading for empathy, he claimed that he could not work, the £40 would soon run out and he needed a pension. He begged Churchill to 'please take pity on me and my poor old parents'.[78] Churchill acted. The CCABS asked Stevenson to have a surgeon report on the measurements required for providing artificial legs.[79] Finally in October 1920 Haji Christodoulou had got somewhere,[80] but the efforts to make his legs dragged on for 18 months as he was hauled from his village to Nicosia four times before the job was done, reflecting the inexperience of the Chief Medical Officer, F.B. Thompson, and the lack of instructions from the British military and medical authorities of the Black Sea Army. Thompson's first report on 18 November 1920 was insufficient.[81] So in January 1921 Haji Christodoulou visited Nicosia for a second time.[82] Then J.G. Ashley, for the Finance Secretary of the War Office, wanted better measurements of the stumps and a solid cast sent to the Director General of Medical Services, Ministry of Pensions.[83] So for a third time Haji Christodoulou visited Nicosia in May 1921 and the plaster casts were sent in July 1921.[84] But then the Cypriot government was informed that further measurements were needed, so Haji Christodoulou visited Thompson a fourth time.[85] Thankfully this was the last time and his legs were finally fitted on 27 July 1922, with the District Medical

Officer, C.H.D. Ralph, claiming that they fitted perfectly.[86] Ralph examined Haji Christodoulou again in October and he was surprised to find him 'walk[ing] without any form of assistance and able to go up and down stairs which in my opinion is very satisfactory'.[87]

Less than a year later, in April 1923, Haji Christodoulou claimed to Stevenson that he could walk only with sticks and, 'unable to carry out any sort of work' to maintain himself, needed a pension.[88] Stevenson wrote to the General Officer Commander-in-Chief Turkey relating Haji Christodoulou's story and mentioning that artificial limbs were provided from public expense.[89] The reply was predictable: Haji Christodoulou had already received £40 'as an Act of Grace' and no further aid was 'thought necessary'.[90] But Haji Christodoulou persisted. A year later he appealed for a pension to the Colonial Secretary, J.H. Thomas.[91] Thomas investigated, but the War Office claimed that he got the maximum gratuity and was not entitled to a pension.[92] Thomas suggested to Stevenson that the Legislative Council vote to give him a small pension,[93] but instead an 'ex gratia' gratuity of £20 was voted against vote 28 'gratuities and charitable allowances', which Haji Christodoulou received in July 1924.[94]

This money lasted for a few years, until Haji Christodoulou again fell on hard times. In October 1927 he petitioned the Cypriot government for a pension and new legs. His were worn out and he had 'became a rhapsodist going round the villages and town and singing my poverty and misfortune', but this was not enough to survive.[95] Governor Storrs investigated and the War Office agreed to provide new legs.[96] Equally important, Haji Christodoulou obtained a job at the Forestry Department in May 1928 as a telephone operator at Stavros tis Psokas Forest Station, while also repairing shoes – ironically the legless Haji Christodoulou had become a cobbler. Then in June 1931 the government started paying him £2 per annum to maintain his legs.[97]

Haji Christodoulou's life had been transformed, from a singing disabled man barely making a living to a telephone operator for the Forestry Department. Yet his legs continued to trouble him. He asked the government for steel legs and a promotion in August 1932.[98] After a medical check, his legs were repaired in Nicosia.[99] But in July 1934 a chance conversation with someone from the Paphos district commissionership led to another medical check and new legs.[100] Although it took over a year to arrange, the government bent the law, compensating him for his travel and loss of wages.[101] In 1939, several years after the British Legion in Cyprus became active in the welfare of Cypriot muleteers, it took an interest in why Haji Christodoulou had not received a pension, but the government claimed that the military authorities had 'no responsibility' and a gratuity was given out of pity.[102]

A few months later, life again changed for Haji Christodoulou when he wrote to the government requesting new legs. His boss, the Conservator of Forests, claimed that

> I experience considerable difficulty from the employment of this man. As you know he is a legless cripple dating from the 1914–18 war. Government supply and maintain his artificial legs, but he continually complains that his artificial limbs are most unsatisfactory. I have spoken to doctors ... and it appears that his complaints are in fact well founded, and ... there is a certain Jew living at Kouklia who makes artificial limbs, and it is thought he could make a new pair of legs which would be very much more satisfactory than the present ones.[103]

His employment in the Forestry Department as a telephone operator and night guard had not worked out, because 'his crippled condition makes him incapable of attending to any duty actively, and, secondly, because he is a rather lazy and quarrelsome fellow who does not intend to do too much'.[104] He was currently employed as a night guard at the timber depot at Xeros, but as with most night guards he slept soundly at night. The Conservator added that 'I regard his employment merely as a form of charitable pension ... for the reason that I have no suitable light work to offer him. In order to perform forest work a man *must* be active.'[105] The Conservator added that if no other department could offer him more suitable work, the government should give him new legs and discharge him with a sum so he could become a cobbler.[106] So after 12 years Haji Christodoulou's days as a civil servant were ending.[107]

Consequently, the government informed Haji Christodoulou that it would provide him with new legs, but no job. His employment with the Forestry Department ended on 1 December 1940 and he accepted £50 so he could start a cobblery. His new legs were made and the Chief Medical Officer was satisfied.[108]

Stavros Petrou Kojambashi, Palaeometocho, Nicosia
The case of Stavros Petros Kojambashi of Palaeometocho, Nicosia was perhaps a good reason why the British authorities were wary of providing welfare to injured muleteers. His was a fascinating story of claiming to have lost his memory from wounds received while serving as a muleteer. In 1936, Maroulla Kojambashi, his wife, suddenly wrote to the Cypriot government appealing for aid for her husband. She claimed that he recently regained his memory and told her that he was a Cypriot who had enlisted as a muleteer and had been wounded by a bombshell near Skra. He stayed a year at the Salonica British Hospital near White Tower. Because of his memory loss and partial insanity he

destroyed the papers related to these events and so never approached the British government for aid or protection and now they were 'very destitute'.[109]

The local enquiries of the Cypriot government found evidence that challenged her story. Stavros Petrou Kojambashi was born in Palaeometocho in 1899, yet he had not enlisted in the Cypriot Mule Corps, having gone to Greece in 1915 in search of work. The Cypriot government wanted the Greek Embassy to confirm if Maroulla's story had any basis.[110] The Greek Embassy in Athens investigated, but could not confirm Maroulla's story. C.N. Ezard, the Vice Consul at Piraeus, informed the Consul in Athens, that Maroulla and Stavros Kojambashi had asked Anastasios Kyrpoglou[111] to write the letter to the Cypriot government. Stavros and Maroulla lived on Kyrpoglou's farm at Neapolis Vion. Stavros had lived in Piraeus after the war and was kept alive through the generosity of a tradesman, since he had amnesia and a speech impairment. About three years previously he married Maroulla, a servant of the Kyrpoglou family. Ezard also found a note from Kojambashi's sister, possibly from 1923, that the Cypriot government was looking for him. This note would question the amnesia story.[112] The Greek Consul in Athens informed the Cypriot government that an acquaintance of Kojambashi claimed that he had enlisted at Limassol in 1915 and was despatched to Salonica. Other men from his village did the same, and also two other persons, Stavros Kavadias and Christos Demetrakopoulos, both of Karavas, were also included in the same draft.[113] Since the Mule Corps was not formed until 1916 this was either a lie or he had confused the year.

The Cypriot government ignored the case, but Kojambashi tried again in 1946. The British Consul in Athens informed him that too much time had passed to apply for a pension for the Great War, but to try the War Office.[114] Kojambashi informed the War Office of his earlier claims, adding that he had left an allotment to his brother, Kastlios Petrou Kojambashi.[115] The authorities in London decided that too long had passed.[116] But Stavros persisted, expressing his disappointment in a letter to the Cypriot government, disclosing that he was now on harder times since during the Second World War he had helped British soldiers escape and the Italians burnt his house and farm. He demanded compensation having been injured while serving in the British army during the Great War.[117] But the British repeated their original decision.[118] The War Office thought that the Colonial Office could help.[119] The Colonial Secretary, Arthur Creech Jones, corresponded with the Cypriot government,[120] but it could only offer to repatriate Kojambashi, but not his wife, as he was informed in 1936.[121] But Kojambashi persisted, next appealing to Prime Minister Clement

Atlee in April 1947.[122] This time the Foreign Office intervened, claiming that it was too late, yet it did ask the British Embassy in Athens to confirm his story.[123] A member of the Embassy in Athens reported that there were various inconsistencies in the story and that 'this man is a halfwit and illiterate and there is nothing to show that his disability was caused by service with the British Forces in the war of 1914–18'.[124]

The British authorities did not make the connection, but the case of Stavros Kojambasi is thrown on its head by his own application in 1923 for a medal, claiming that he had served with the no. 14084 – meaning that he had enlisted late or re-enlisted a second time in 1919.[125] At the time the authorities dismissed his claim because no. 14084 was not on the list.[126] In any event this proves that in 1923 he knew that he had served in the Mule Corps.

Veterans in Cyprus: poverty and aid

Veterans had to deal with numerous socio-economic problems. Delays in paying allotments affected many families, while veterans were also owed wages. Numerous other problems arose as the interwar years found Cypriot peasants and labourers struggling, particularly as the Great Depression hit. Poverty was one reason for enlisting and its persistence after the war compelled veterans to seek government and non-government welfare.

Allotments and outstanding pay, again

The unpaid wage claims of veterans dominate the files in the Cypriot State Archives. In summer 1917 it was decided that the final settlement of muleteer accounts would be made in Cyprus because the government wanted to recover quarantine costs.[127] This, unhappily for the veterans, led to significant delays in settling accounts, and some made claims of non-settlement. Veterans with outstanding pay claims fall into various categories: those who were discharged with illness; others who did not return immediately to Cyprus; and those who slipped through the cracks.

Veterans needed their wages and welfare because times were tough. Stevenson discouraged prospective British and European settlement because the cost of living had increased during the Great War by almost 300% and,

> whereas before the war Cyprus could be boasted as one of the cheap places of the world now though it is still on the whole ... slightly less expensive than the United Kingdom, yet the settler who pictures that he is coming to the land of cheapness and plenty will be sadly disappointed and find that in some respects Cyprus has been even more affected by

the changes of war than countries more nearly situated to the field of action.[128]

If Stevenson thought Cyprus was unsuitable for settlers, one can only wonder how hard it was for the veterans returning to their peasant and labouring lives.

For those discharged owing to illness, outstanding pay claims began before the system changed in summer 1917. In September 1917, Ioannis Georgiou from Astromeritis, Nicosia, informed Clauson that he was discharged on 30 April 1917 owing to illness and needed the balance of his salary because he was 'hard up'.[129] Three months later he repeated his letter, having received no satisfaction.[130] He was not paid until February 1918.[131] Panayis Haralambou also informed Clauson that after serving for six months and two days he was discharged owing to sickness, but was owed nearly £9. His account book was detained at the military offices at Salonica and later he was told that it was lost and that he would be paid in Cyprus. He complained to his district commissioner, but was told he had nothing to receive.[132] Mustafa Ahmed from Larnaca was in a similar situation. He had enlisted on 5 August 1917, but served only 47 days before being repatriated because of ill-health. After two months recuperating, he served out his contract, being discharged on 15 October 1918. He claimed that he was still owed £5.6.0.[133] Kyriacos Pavlou from Kadythada, Nicosia, had served for a year in the 852nd Company, 27th Division, and was detained at base for 28 days when he refused to renew his contract. His money, £16.8.0, was confiscated and he demanded it to maintain himself 'in these hard times'.[134]

The policy to withhold the last pay, introduced in summer 1917, increased the claims for outstanding wages in 1918, which were driven by the poverty of the men and their families, and a sense of injustice. One of the first to complain was Costas Petrou from Athienou in April 1918. He expected his wages seven months previously and was desperate: 'I am poor, ill and the head of a family, and cannot afford to have myself tended.'[135] Many claims were made from October 1918. The first was by Mehmet Moulla Mustafa from the small and poor village of Anadiou, Paphos.[136] Often the amount claimed to be owed was significant. Haji Ioannis Haji Protopapa from Leonariso, Famagusta, claimed that he was owed £15. 'It is unjust for me, Honourable Sir, to lose so many days wages as it was owing to poverty that I had to expatriate myself. In truth I feel proud of having served the glorious British army, but it is not right that I should lose my wages.'[137] Afxentios Loizou, also of Leonariso, protested that he was owed £12. 'It is unjust, Honourable Sir, for me to lose £12, to earn which I experienced so many privations.'[138] Nicholas Costanti from Limassol was clear: 'I am poor and I have a family, and therefore I am in great need of this money.'[139] Ali Sami, from Larnaca, was owed £12 and 'belong[ed] to a poor family who are now in great distress.'[140] Yiannis Michael from Yialousa was probably as poor as Ali Sami when he demanded his pay because he was 'very poor'.[141] Ioannis Christodoulou, originally from Geroskipou, now of Varosha, was a glutton for punishment, since in March 1919 he claimed that had served twice and was owed £20 from his first service: 'I owe money and my properties will be attacked on 1 April 1919, hence my present request for this money to be paid to me at once.'[142] In June 1919 Georgios Haji Demetriou from Ktima, Paphos, who had served with the 80th Hospital, 26th Division, claimed he was owed £20.[143]

The problem had become so widespread that veterans started writing in groups to claim unpaid wages. The first came from Kyriacos Haji Demetri, Efrem Zachariou, Eraclis Papadopoulos and Koumis Maryialos, from Agios Theodoros, Larnaca. They demanded their wages, claiming that they had 'sacrificed our blood in favour of the noble English government, from which we claim the justice that characterises it'.[144] Then followed an identical appeal from Anastassis Panjarou and Georgios P. Mouyiaris, from Athienou, and Constantinos Nicola Kalapodas, from Nicosia,[145] and then another from Rifat Kiamil, Ahmed Omer, Salih Subhi, Ali Faik and Emin Mehmed, from Kalo Horio, Nicosia, who stated that because 'our claims have not been paid to us makes us suffer wrong in as much as we are in great need of what is due to us, especially as long as poverty and the rise in the prices of commodity are prevalent.[146] The appeals from veterans to receive their pay continued on an individual and group basis throughout 1919, 1920 and 1921, pushed by their acute poverty.[147] Oulfet Haji Mustafa from Agios Andronicos, Karpas claimed in February 1920 that he was still owed £14 and was in 'a condition of poverty and distress'.[148] Mehmed Emin, from Vretcha, Paphos, was equally feeling the pinch, since after serving for nine months he was hospitalised and was unable to complete his contract, and was only paid £10 of his wages.[149] Others were told that there numbers could not be found, even when this was untrue, such as Salih Subhi Ali Faik, from Kalo Horio, Nicosia, who was begging for his pay because 'my poverty compels me to do so'.[150] Prodromos Petris, from Argaka, and Christoforos Haji Haralambou, from Akourdhalia, both in Paphos, claimed that they were discharged because of incapacity, and greatly needed their outstanding wages because they headed poor families.[151] Costas Haralambou from Agios Athanasios, Limassol, claimed £20 and he was in great financial difficulty.[152] Then in August 1921 Hassan Mehmet appealed for his outstanding £20 because his five children were orphaned and he had served two years as a muleteer to support them.[153] The poverty, clearly evident from the many cases above, was perhaps best reflected by the case of Christos Haralambou from Kato Platres. Informed to go to Limassol to collect his £10, someone impersonating him had already done so: his brother.[154]

Poverty had led most men to enlist in the Cypriot Mule Corps and its persistence after their service was made harder by outstanding wages, which they had to chase up. Their cries of injustice, however, went on deaf ears, as the British closed the already restricted liminal space.

The British Legion in Cyprus

The work of the British Legion has been mentioned in relation to incapacitated muleteers. Founded in 1921, it became a voice for the ex-service community after four earlier organisations merged.[155] The Cypriot branch appeared before 1937, even though its first chairman, Rupert Gunnis, had been in the island since 1926.[156] Later in 1937 William Battershill, the Colonial Secretary, 1935-37 (and later governor 1939-41), took over.

The British Legion in Cyprus was first mentioned in January 1937 in a note stipulating that Gunnis was providing a wounded veteran 5/- a fortnight until his case was resolved.[157] The Cypriot branch was small and lacked funds. In a note to the district commissioner of Famagusta, B.J. O'Brian, the unknown writer claimed that 'They have done and are doing what they can to help the ex-service men who are in want, but the funds are very limited.' The Cypriot branch was receiving a paltry £100 annually from London, most of which was immediately disbursed to those in need. O'Brian was told to write to Battershill about anyone who needed its aid.[158] In June 1937 O'Brian duly sent him a list of claims because of poverty. He investigated and recommended assistance for the following: (1) Nicholas Argyrou, from Aphania, Famagusta, who was nearly blind, married with five children, the eldest a daughter aged 13; (2) Angeli Michael Matsakary, from Yenagra, Famagusta, aged 67, who owned a small house, one *donum*[159] and one *evlek*[160] of land, which were all mortgaged. His seven children were only now able to support themselves and his age prevented him from doing enough work to survive; (3) Maria Demetri, from Prastio, Famagusta, whose son, Petros Demetriou, died while serving. Her husband was 70 and too old to work. They had three married sons, all labourers unable to support them and their own families and two unmarried daughters maintained themselves but could not assist their parents.[161] Battershill referred O'Brian to J.A. Bevan, the secretary of the Cypriot British Legion.¹⁶² Bevan claimed that times were tough for veterans and the committee only had limited funds.

> It is no exaggeration to say that the Benevolent Committee is overwhelmed with appeals for relief from ex-muleteers in Cyprus and in existing circumstances it is only possible to give casual relief to some of the worst cases of acute poverty, and then only to disabled persons or persons who, owing to some disability or old age, are positively unable to work. It is always a matter of extreme regret to the Committee that its activities in the relief of distress are so restricted through lack of funds, and every effort is being made to obtain further grants from the Central Committee in London in order to widen the scope of its relief.¹⁶³

The British Legion continued to support veterans after the Second World War. In 1945 John Demosthenous from Kaminarka, Limassol, appealed to the Cypriot government for aid and was referred to the British Legion. While serving as a muleteer he had injured his head and hand, and could not work properly since. In 1936, when Governor Palmer had visited his village, Demosthenous had told him of his service and injuries. From 1936 to 1940 the British Legion gave him an allowance and he wanted this restarted. Both his sons served in the Second World War and he tried to enlist, but was too old.¹⁶⁴ The district commissioner of Limassol confirmed that after Palmer's visit in 1937 the British Legion had paid Demosthenous 15/- a month until 1939. He did not know why it was stopped, but Demosthenous's right wrist was fractured and so he could only do light labouring work, while from his property he might make £5 per year. He asked that the British Legion resume payments, which it agreed at 20/- per month.¹⁶⁵

The Second World War, which saw the Cypriot Regiment serve in a similar capacity, yet receive far more rights, triggered a mass petition of First World War veterans on 27 April 1946. The petition was organised by Angelis Haji Gregory, originally from Gypsou, Famagusta, but now of Dali, Nicosia, who had served as a muleteer on two occasions. Some 552 men signed the petition. It is unclear how Haji Gregory had obtained so many signatures from across the entire island. His cover letter incorrectly stated that the signatories were 'ex-soldiers' of the Great War and asked for any government financial assistance because the veterans, who were over 45, were 'starving'. He pointed out that the soldiers of the Second World War all received gratuities and those released on medical grounds a pension, but they had not.¹⁶⁶ The district commissioner of Nicosia received it on 27 July 1946 and opined to the Cypriot Colonial Secretary that no gratuities could be entertained for the Great War now. He added, 'I presume the reason for the petition is that the ex-servicemen of 1914–1918 see gratuities and benefits on a very much larger scale being given to the ex-servicemen of this war, and that has made them jealous.'[167] The government advised that they should apply to the British Legion.[168]

Unemployment and poverty was widespread in interwar Cyprus. Veterans needed their wages paid and as time went by they also needed welfare, which the Cypriot government was unwilling to countenance. The Cypriot branch of the British Legion did what it could, but it was not enough. The government again ignored the voices of veterans.

Medals and migration

Emigrating was one way out of the poverty. Military service had given the men a taste of working overseas. Many veterans were repatriated only to soon emigrate, while others stayed behind. The evidence that many veterans emigrated comes from their hundreds of letters from the USA, France, Australia, Egypt, Greece and Turkey, requesting their medals and papers. Some examples are discussed below, but there must have been many who did not seek their medals or had received them before they emigrated, such as Stavros Georgiou, the father of Yusuf Islam / Cat Stevens, who left Cyprus for Egypt, then the USA, and finally London.[169]

Veterans who enlisted during the war were entitled to the British War Medal. On 5 October 1920 the Army Council informed the Colonial Office that the personnel of 'the Cypriot and Macedonian Mule Corps' would be awarded the British War Medal in bronze. The Army Council prepared the honour roll and asked Stevenson to distribute the medals.[170] Ceremonies were held across the island in 1921.[171] Many men living in Cyprus and abroad who did not attend the ceremonies asked for their medal and received it by post, while many also requested the British Victory Medal, to which they were not entitled. This shows their pride in serving. The medals and service papers of those living in Cyprus meant little when it came to employment, social mobility or welfare. The British Legion did attempt, even into the 1940s, to distribute medals to those who had not received them.[172] For those abroad, their medal and service papers were important for employment, social mobility and social inclusion.

Several men settled in Greece, either remaining or moving there after their service, or after being repatriated to Cyprus. George Constantinou Georgiades served (June 1916 to September 1917) with the 855th Company, 27th Division in Salonica and then (1918 to 1920) with the 386th Company Field Ambulance and the 84th Horse Transport Hospitals. From October 1922 to August 1923 he served as an interpreter with the Black Sea Labour Corps, in the 3rd Heavy

Battery, 1st Heavy Brigade, in Gallipoli. In 1938 he asked for his medal and papers because for 15 years in Greece he could not obtain a secure job. As a Cypriot British subject there were work restrictions and he wanted to now register with the British Association of Ancient Combatants in Athens.[173] Georgiades believed that membership in this elite club would secure him a job and social inclusion. The Colonial Secretary was, however, not sympathetic, asking him to approach the British Consul in Piraeus.[174]

Many members of the Cypriot Mule Corps remained in the Ottoman Empire/Turkey to continue to serve or had settled in Constantinople and wanted their medals. Kyriacos Pandelis Kakos from Omorphita, Nicosia, who had served in the 844th Company, 22nd Division, and now resided in Galata, Constantinople, wanted his medal.[175] It is unclear if he was still working for the British authorities, but the others were: Costas Argyriades, formerly a *Zaptieh* in Nicosia (with no. 3700), enlisted as an interpreter in August 1917 and served in Salonica until 4 November 1919 with the 86th Field Ambulance and then as an interpreter with the Allied Police Commission in Constantinople;[176] Ali Riza, also an interpreter from Nicosia and now in Chanak and still working for the British army;[177] Ramis Mehmet, also from Nicosia, who was still with the 83rd Infantry Brigade, DD Forces, Chanak;[178] Georgios Panayotopoulos from Vatili, Famagusta, and now the chief interpreter with Detachment 121st Horse Transport Company, RASC, at Harbie, Constantinople;[179] and Andreas Haralambou, from Larnaca, and serving with the British army at Base Supply Depot off the Straits Kilia.[180] Clearly working in the British army was a good job and the medal was a source of pride for these men, but after service few remained in the Ottoman Empire/Turkey because of employment restrictions.

Several veterans settled in Egypt, a traditional place of settlement and seasonal migration for Cypriots looking for work because it was close to home. In June 1923 Nicholas Zahariades (listed as Zaharia) from Komi Kebir, who served with the 80th Field Ambulance, 26th Division, and then with the 122nd Transport Co., 28th Division, Bostancı, wanted his medal.[181] In February 1925 Christodoulos G. Theodoriades informed Stevenson that he wanted a recommendation so he could obtain work in Alexandria because he was in poverty and needed to support his parents too.[182] Then in September 1926 three veterans, the interpreter George Ellinas from Kilinia, Paphos, Constantinos Christoforou Katekos from Larnaca and Georgios Economides, from Ktima, now in Alexandria, requested their medals, which were sent.[183] Finally, though not the last example, we note Michael Ioannou Annas, who in 1935 requested a replacement medal because he considered it 'holy'.[184] Not all of these men said why they wanted their medal or papers, yet most must have felt the pinch, as Theodoriades did, and thought it would help them obtain work. Others wanted their medals because they were proud of their service, such as Zahariades and Annas. Group letters indicate a Cypriot community in Alexandria, which was not so easy to create in the USA and Australia where they were spread thin across various states and cities.

Continuing on from 1916, when emigration was frozen, the USA re-emerged after the war as the favoured destination of Cypriots,[185] until the UK (specifically London) took over late in the 1920s[186]. In December 1922, M.R. Flynn, an attorney in Danville, Virginia, requested from Stevenson the medal for Pedros Nicola from Gypsou, Famagusta, who served with the 78th Field Ambulance, 26th Division. Nicola left Gypsou six months before medals were distributed and now resided in a cotton-mill town near Danville.[187] Then in January 1923 the British Vice Consul in Minneapolis informed Stevenson that Kyriakos Michael Konizou from Aglanja, Nicosia, wanted his discharge certificate and medal. Konizou had served with 304th Company, 79th Regiment; then with the 110th Infantry Company; then re-enlisted and served at the Struma River until April 1919. The British Vice Consul had informed Stevenson that he had a letter from the non-commissioned officer in charge of his company, Sergeant Walter Holt, corroborating Konizou's story. Konizou needed his discharge certificate and medal to prove that he had served.[188] Both these men wanted to prove their service probably to feel included within US society and to increase their employment prospects. Based on the letters requesting their medals, veterans settled in various parts of the USA, such as New York,[189] Ohio,[190] Wheeling, West Virginia,[191] Keesport, Pennsylvania,[192] and, amongst others, Gary, Indiana.[193]

Australia was another popular destination, although during the interwar years it did not reach the popularity of the USA or the UK. In July 1926 Costas Adamou, a resident of Melbourne, requested from the Cypriot government his service certificate.[194] The Cypriot government claimed that his number was not on the list and would not look into producing his papers.[195] In April 1930 George Ioannou Florides, originally from Agii Omologites, Nicosia and now of Sydney, served with 844th Transport Company and wanted his medal.[196] The government told him to write to the War Office.[197] It was not clear why after so many years Florides wanted his medal, but two years later Nicholas Yiasemi, from Yialousa, Famagusta and now in Orbost, Victoria, made it clear why he needed his certificate and medal: he was unemployed and desperate to support his family back in Cyprus.[198] He received the same reply.[199] Then in July 1937 Abraham Christofi from Agios

Amvrosios, Kyrenia, had his lawyer, H.V. Harris, Wheeler & Williams, Solicitors and Notaries, Newcastle, NSW, ask for his discharge papers because it was important for applying for jobs in Australia. The letter claimed that the military authorities in England were unable to trace his name in their records because he was demobilised at Famagusta in November 1918, even though he carried two medals.[200] The reasons for Nicholas Liassi, originally from Tripimeni, Famagusta and now of Perth, who served with the 28th Company in Salonica and Constantinople until 1920, wanting his discharge papers in 1940 were altogether different. With little English, his friend, Sargent A.D. Hunt, no. 76, 1st Field Company Engineers, 1st Australian Imperial Force, wrote to the Cypriot government asking for his discharge papers so he could join the local ex-serviceman's organisation.[201] The Cypriot government had sent the registers to the War Office in 1929 and so he needed to apply to them.[202] Had it kept the registers it would have found that Liassi had deserted. Finally, there was Paul Michael, originally from Akapnou, Limassol, but since 1925 residing in Berri, South Australia. In 1926 he had his medal sent to him,[203] but in 1944 he engaged lawyers in Adelaide to chase up his British Victory Medal.[204] The government replied that he was not entitled to it.[205] Michael wanted this medal, 25 years after his service, because of his pride in his service.

Many veterans emigrated during the interwar years. Unemployment drove them from Cyprus and it often pushed them to seek their medals and service papers for employment and social inclusion in their new homelands.

Conclusion

Veterans experienced mixed results after their service. Many who fell on hard times, however, were left in the lurch for one excuse after another. The Cypriot government and military authorities provided little if any welfare to those invalided or in poverty, or to those families who lost loved ones. Some men even claimed to not have been fully paid. Many men (and their families) complained about one injustice or another, but their voices were mostly ignored. The liminal space had become more liminal, as the military and civil authorities refused to budge on compensation and welfare, pushing the Cypriots to look for help from private charities. One solution was to emigrate, which often resulted in different hardships. For these men obtaining their medal was important for social inclusion and job prospects. Generally there was a sense of achievement and pride in their service, hence the many men who additionally requested the British Victory Medal. With the exception of the few men who obtained jobs as *Zaptiehs*, for most veterans remaining in Cyprus their medal meant little for job prospects, social inclusion and social mobility. Most veterans must have felt abandoned and even betrayed given their loyalty and contribution to the British war effort. The Cypriot government lost an opportunity to win veterans over by not introducing any work or land scheme to help them into work, as the governments in the settler colonies and the West Indies did. This is one reason why the Cypriot Mule Corps did not enter the public consciousness.

Notes

1   Fortunately, I was gifted a medal by Taff Williams from the Stoke Newington Police Station. See Figures 7.1 and 7.2.
2   Europeana, entries/web pages for Panay Polycarpou and Michael Michaelides, both from Palaiohori.
3   CO67/198/39099, Stevenson to Milner, 26 July 1920, 'Cyprus and Immigration: Report on the Openings and Prospects for Settlers from Overseas'.
4   Bart Ziino, *A Distant Grief: Australians, War Graves and the Great War*, University of Western Australia Press, Perth, 2007.
5   SA1/978/1916, Petros Haji Loizos to HCC, 28 May 1919. Loizos Petrou served with the no. 11755.
6   Ibid., Director of Claims and Customs, GHQC, to Sisman and Fenn, 17 October 1919.
7   Ibid., Fenn to Petris Haji Loizou, 10 December 1919.
8   Ibid., Elengou Toouli Pezidianou to Stevenson, 24 Jan 1920. Ioannou had the no. 6556.
9   Varnava, 'British Military Intelligence in Cyprus', 366–7.
10 SA1/978/1916, Sisman memo on Yenethlis Ioannou, undated, must be between 6 and 14 April 1920. He is no. 3537 at the cemetery.
11 Ibid., Rodou Stylianou to Greenwood, 3 May 1920. Christodoulou had no. 13613.
12 Ibid., Greenwood to Fenn, 12 May 1920.
13 Ibid., Fenn to Sisman, 22 May 1920; ibid., Sisman to Fenn, 17 July 1920.
14 Ibid., Fenn to Greenwood, 24 July 1920; ibid., Greenwood to Fenn, 31 July 1920.
15 Ibid., Sisman to Fenn, 10 August 1920.
16 Ibid., Fleury to Fenn, 28 November 1921.
17 Ibid., CCABS to Stevenson, 7 January 1922.
18 Ibid., Fenn to Fleury, 18 January 1922.
19 Ibid., Patrou Theoharous to Stevenson, 30 May 1921. Theohari had the no. 9404.
20 Ibid., CCABS to Stevenson, 30 August 1921; ibid., Fenn to Patrou Theoharous, 15 September 1921. Savas must have been ill at the time that the corps was disbanded, since it had been disbanded several months before his death.
21 Ibid., Phanou Haralambou to Stevenson, 12 September 1921.
22 SA1/978/1916/3, CCABS to Stevenson, 13 October 1921; Fenn to Phanou Haralambous, 27 October 1921. Ktori had the no. 3173.
23 Ibid., Susanna Eleftheriou, to Stevenson, 17 October 1921. Christophorou had no. 9713.
24 Ibid., CCABS to Stevenson, 22 November 1921; Fenn to Susanna Eleftheriou, 14 December 1921.
25 Ibid., Theonou Toouli to Tompkins, 12 October 1922. Yanni served with no. 8239.
26 Ibid., Tompkins to Fenn, 16 October 1922.
27 Ibid., for CICAOA, to Stevenson, 18 November 1922.
28 Ibid., Fenn to Tompkins, 6 December 1922; Tompkins to Fenn, 9 January 1923.

29 Ibid., Stevenson to CICAOA, 18 January 1923; CICAOA to War Secretary, 7 February 1923.
30 Ibid., Stevenson to Sisman, 8 February 1918. Lanitis had no. 6890.
31 SA1/978/1916/3, Panayiotou Georgi to Fenn, 1 August 1920. Solou had no. 14460.
32 Ibid., Sisman to Fenn, 18 October 1920.
33 Ibid., Myrianthi Kleovoulou to Stevenson, 3 January 1921. His no. was 6723.
34 Ibid., Fenn to Myrianthi Kleovoulou, 11 January 1921.
35 SA1/978/1916, Maria Procopiou–G. Moustrides, to Clauson, 26 May 1918. Moustrides served twice, first with no. 2458 and then 8429.
36 Ibid., Parry to Cade, DCNi, 17 June 1918.
37 Ibid., Stevenson to Maria Procopiou, 24 June 1918.
38 Ibid., Greenwood, DCPa, to Stevenson, 7 June 1919. Antonopoulos served twice, with no. 5454 and then 13386.
39 Ibid., Irene Georgiou to Fenn, 19 September 1920.
40 Ibid., to Stevenson, translated 24 February 1922; SA1/978/1916/3, Tompkins, DCPa, to Fenn, 22 July 1922.
41 SA1/978/1916, Greenwood to Fenn, 19 November 1920.
42 Ibid., Solomis Romani to Fenn, 18 March 1920. Served with no. 13091.
43 Ibid., Sisman to Fenn, 6 May 1920.
44 SA1/978/1916/1, Havva Jemal to Fenn, 18 February 1924. With no. 8131.
45 Ibid., Hart-Davis to Fenn, 3 March 1924.
46 Ibid., Fenn to Havva Jemal, 6 March 1924.
47 SA1/978/1916 Panayis Panayi to Stevenson, 26 November 1919. Haris served with no. 12887.
48 Ibid.
49 SA1/607/1917 B.J. Surridge, LCCMP, to CCPC, 31 January 1920.
50 SA1/978/1916 Haris Panayi Statement, February 1920, forwarded by Fleury, DCFa, to Fenn, 16 February 1920.
51 Ibid; SA1/978/1916 Fenn to Sisman, 20 February 1920.
52 SA1/978/1916 Haris Panayi to Stevenson, 22 February 1920.
53 Ibid; SA1/978/1916, Archbishop of Cyprus, Nicosia, Kyrillos, to Stevenson, 6 March 1920.
54 Ibid., Fenn to Kyrillos, 10 March 1920.
55 Ibid., Captain W.G. Horn for ADST, ABS, to Sisman, 19 March 1920.
56 SA1/978/1916/3, Director of Claims and Customs, GHQC, to Fenn, 19 April 1920.
57 Ibid., Fenn to Panayis Panayi, 22 May 1920.
58 Ibid., Haris Panayi to Fenn, 25 November 1920.
59 Ibid., Sisman to Fenn, 22 December 1920.
60 Ibid., Fenn to Haris Panayi, 5 January 1921.
61 Some of Haris Panaou's family migrated to Adelaide, but they did not know who had provided his leg.
62 SA1/978/1916/3 Finance Secretary, WO, to CCABS, 17 September 1920.
63 Ibid., CCABS, to Stevenson, 7 October 1920; Fenn to Yannis Panayi, 23 October 1920; S.J. Vassiliades, DMO, Nicosia, to Fenn, 6 November 1920.
64 Ibid., Stevenson to CCABS, 14 November 1920.
65 Ibid., Ioannis K. Pellides, for the illiterate, Yannis Panayi, to Stevenson, 4 May 1922.
66 Ibid.
67 SA1/978/1916/1 Petition presented to HCC when on tour in Paphos District, 10 April 1927.
68 Ibid., Surridge to CSC, 29 August 1927, includes Heidenstam report, formerly ADCPa, 22 August 1927.
69 Ibid., Surridge to CSC, 8 November 1927.
70 Ibid., CSC to DCPa, 2 December 1927.
71 SA1/978/1916, Haji Christodoulou, 10020, to Fenn, 16 May 1919.
72 WO95/4763, WDSA, GRO, 189, note 936, Pay of Muleteers, 18 March 1917
73 SA1/978/1916, Sisman to Fenn, 25 August 1919.

74 Ibid., Haji Christodoulou to Stevenson, 31 August 1919.
75 Ibid., Fenn to Haji Christodoulou, 22 September 1919.
76 Ibid., Haji Christodoulou to Stevenson, 2 November 1919.
77 Ibid., Director of Claims and Customs, GHQC, to Fenn, 17 December 1919; Fenn to Bayly, 22 January 1920; Bayly to Fenn, 24 February 1920.
78 SA1/978/1916/3, Haji Christodoulou to War Secretary, 15 August 1920.
79 Ibid., CCABS to Stevenson, 8 October 1920.
80 Ibid., Fenn to Haji Christodoulou, 22 October 1920.
81 Ibid., Stevenson to CCABS, 18 November 1920; CCABS to Stevenson, 4 January 1921.
82 Ibid., Fenn to CMOC, 24 January 1921; Fenn to Haji Christodoulou, 25 January 1921.
83 Ibid., J.G. Ashley, for the Finance Secretary, WO, to CCABS, 24 March 1921; CCABS to Stevenson, 14 April 1921.
84 Ibid., Fenn to Haji Christodoulou, 5 May 1921; ACMOC, to Fenn, 28 May 1921; Fenn to ACMOC, 6 June 1921; ACMOC, to Fenn, 6 June 1921; Stevenson to CCABS, 11 June 1921; CCABS to War Secretary, copy to Stevenson, 9 July 1921.
85 Ibid., CCABS, to Stevenson, October 1921; Fenn to Haji Christodoulou, 10 November 1921; CMOC to Fenn, 9 December 1921.
86 Ibid., CCABS, to Stevenson, 15 June 1922; Ralph to CMOC, 27 July 1922.
87 Ibid., Ralph to CMO, 26 October 1922.
88 Ibid., Haji Christodoulou to Stevenson, 24 April 1923.
89 Ibid., Stevenson to CICAOA, 3 May 1923.
90 Ibid., CCABS to Stevenson, 26 May 1923.
91 SA1/978/1916/1, Haji Christodoulou to Thomas, 3 March 1924.
92 Ibid., Thomas to Stevenson, 15 April 1924; Cubitt, WO, to CO, 26 May 1924.
93 Ibid., Thomas to Stevenson, 4 June 1924.
94 Ibid., Fenn to Hart-Davis, 26 June 1924; Hart-Davis, to Fenn, 24 July 1924.
95 Ibid., Haji Christodoulou to Storrs, 9 October 1927; Hart-Davis, the district commissioner of Nicosia supported his claim. See, ibid., Hart-Davis, to CSC, 25 October 1927.
96 Ibid., Storrs to Leo Amery, Colonial Secretary, 30 November 1927; WO to CO, 23 January 1928.
97 Ibid., Principal Forest Officer to CSC, 15 May 1931; Treasurer to CSC, 22 May 1931; ACSC to Treasurer, 4 June 1931.
98 Ibid., Agathoklis Haji Polistipiotis (changed name) to Storrs, 27 August 1932.
99 Ibid., ACFC to CSC, 4 October 1932; Acting Director of Health to CSC, 19 October 1932.
100 Ibid., DCPa to CFC, 5 July 1934; ACFC, to CSC, 20 July 1934; ACMO to CSC, 11 September 1934; WO to CO, 11 October 1934.
101 Ibid., W.H. Flinn, Treasurer and Overseas Pension Agent, to Ministry of Pensions, 6 June 1935; SA1/978/1916/2, Battershill to CFC, 8 November 1935; ibid., CFC to Battershill, 27 February 1936; ibid., Battershill to CFC, 29 February 1936.
102 Ibid., M.P. Kyriakides, Secretary of the Benevolent Committee, British Legion, to Wright, 29 May 1939; ibid., A.F.J. Reddaway, CSC, to Kyriakides, 26 August 1939; ibid., J.A. Greenwood, Acting Secretary, British Legion Cyprus, to CSC, 24 November 1939; ibid., Reddaway, CSC, to Greenwood, 1 December 1939.
103 Ibid., CFC to CSC, 10 April 1940.
104 Ibid.
105 Ibid.
106 Ibid.
107 Ibid., Printing Office, to CSC, 25 May 1940; Acting Director of Antiquities to CSC, 25 May 1940; Water Supply and Irrigation Department to CSC, 25 May 1940; Auditor to CSC, 25 May 1940; CCPC to CSC, 25 May 1940; Postmaster-General to CSC, 25 May 1940; Railway Department to CSC, 27 May 1940; Customs Department to CSC, 27 May 1940; Treasurer to CSC, 27 May 1940; Director of Education to CSC, 27 May 1940; Department of Cooperation, Registrar, to CSC,

27 May 1940; Attorney General to CSC, 27 May 1940; DCNi and DCKy, to CSC, 27 May 1940; DCLi to CSC, 28 May 1940; Paphos District Court to CSC, 28 May 1940; Limassol District Court to CSC, 29 May 1940; Medical Department to CSC, 28 May 1940; Director of Public Works to CSC, 29 May 1940; DCKy to CSC, 29 May 1940; DCPa to CSC, 28 May 1940; DCFa to CSC, 29 May 1940; Famagusta District Court, to CSC, 30 May 1940; Nicosia and Kyrenia District Courts to CSC, 1 June 1940; Director of Land and Surveys to CSC, 1 June 1940; Director of Agriculture to CSC, 1 June 1940; DCLa to CSC, 4 June 1940.
108   Ibid., CFC to Haji Christodoulou, copy to Secretary of Ex-service men League, Nicosia, 22 June 1940; ibid., CFC to CSC, 18 September 1940; W.H. Covington, CSC, to CFC and Treasury, 23 September 1940; ibid., Director of Medical Services, to CSC, 8 February 1941.
109   Ibid., Maroulla Kojambashi, Piraeus, to Palmer, undated letter, translated 8 July 1936.
110   Ibid., ACSC to British consulate Athens, 17 May 1936.
111   Based on his surname, Kyproglou must have had Cypriot heritage on his father's side.
112   SA1/978/1916/2, C.N. Ezard, Vice Consul, Piraeus, to Consul, Athens, 3 August 1936.
113   Ibid., Consul, Athens, to CSC, 4 February 1937. These names do not appear on the honour roll, but they may have adopted surnames in the meanwhile.
114   Ibid., British Vice Consul to Koutsambashis (writing his name in 'proper Greek'), 12 March 1946.
115   Ibid., Stavros Koutsambashis, Kampos, Vion, Greece, statement, 29 March 1946.
116   Ibid., L.M. Warren, London, to Koutsambashis, 30 September 1946.
117   Ibid., Stavros Koutsambashis to CSC, 3 November 1946.
118   Ibid., F.W. Uppinton to Stavros Koutsambashis, 25 November 1946.
119   Ibid., WO to Military Department, CO, 5 December 1946.
120   Ibid., Colonial Secretary to Officer Administering Cypriot government, 9 January 1947.
121   Ibid., Acting Governor to Colonial Secretary and British Embassy, Athens, 4 February 1947.
122   SA1/978/1916/3, Stavros Koutsambashis to British PM, 10 April 1947.
123   Ibid., FO, Southern Department, to The Chancery, British Embassy, Athens, 22 May 1947.
124   Ibid., British Embassy, Athens, Memo on Stavros Koutsambashis, 28 May 1947; British Embassy, Athens, to Southern Dept, FO, 28 May 1947.
125   SA1/1453/1920/2, ADCNi to Fenn, 14 September 1923.
126   Ibid., CSC to DCNi, 14 April 1924.
127   SA1/722/1916, DQMGS to Clauson, 9 August 1917.
128   CO67/198/39099, Stevenson to Milner, 26 July 1920, including Stevenson's report.
129   SA1/978/1916, Ioannis Georgiou, 3030, to Clauson, 10 September 1917.
130   Ibid., 6 December 1917.
131   Ibid., DCFa to Stevenson, 19 February 1918.
132   Ibid., Panayis Haralambou, 2321, to Clauson, 18 April 1918.
133   Ibid., Mustafa Ahmet, 5384, to Clauson, undated.
134   Ibid., Kyriacos Pavlou, 5838, to Clauson, 14 March 1918.
135   Ibid., Costas Petrou, 1901, to Clauson, 4 April 1918.
136   Ibid., Mehmet Moulla Mustafa, 3214, to Clauson, 28 October 1918, written in Greek.
137   Ibid., Haji Ioannis Haji Protopapa, 3706, to CSC, 22 November 1918.
138   Ibid., Afxentios Loizou, 3630, to CSC, 22 December 1918.
139   Ibid., Nicholas Constanti, 8619, to CSC, February 1919.
140   Ibid., Ali Sami, 8717, to CSC, 10 February 1919.
141   Ibid., Yiannis Michael, 5291, to Stevenson, 19 Feb 1919.
142   Ibid., Ioannis Christodooulou, 9943 and 14724, Geroskipou, now Varosha, to CSC, 22 March 1919.

143 Ibid., Georgios Haji Demetriou, 8648, to CSC, 26 June 1919. For more claims see ibid., Theodoros Evas to CSC, 2 July 1919; Theodoros Christodoulou to CSC, 28 August 1919; Dervish Ahmed to CSC, 1 July 1919; Gavrilli Pieri to CSC, 15 July 1919.
144 Ibid., Kyriacos Haji Demetri, Efrem Zachariou, Eraclis Papadopoulos, Koumis Maryialos, to CSC, undated, June 1919.
145 Ibid., Anastassis Panjarou, 9964, Constantinos N. Kalapodas, 5805, Georgios P. Mouyiaris, 9965, to Stevenson, 4 June 1919.
146 Ibid., Rifat Kiamil, 11100, Ahmed Omer, 10430, Salih Subhi, Ali Faik, 11162, Emin Mehmed, 11970, Kalo Horio, Nicosia, to Stevenson, 30 August 1919. Letter written by them in English.
147 Here are some representative examples: Theodoros Christodoulou, 10871, Yialousa, appealed twice for his pay, asserting that he was 'very poor'. His fellow villagers, Kyriacos Haji Loizou, 11774, Panayis Michael, 10868, and Marcos Yiasemi, 10869, followed. Ibid., Theodoros Christodoulou to CSC, 28 August 1919. In December 1919, ten veterans from Morphou complained that they had not been paid and were 'in great misery'. Ibid., Michael Haji Toffi, 13046; Petros Haji Olympios, 11281; Yiannis Haji Kyprios, 11051; Chrisatos Louka, 12550; Christos Stavrou, 12030; Yiannis Andrea, 11283; Matheos Haji Michael, 11630; Kyriacos Lambrou, 7746; Avraam Loizou, 11267; Yiannakos Haji Haralambou, 11267. Morphou, Nicosia, to CSC, 30 December 1919. In May 1920 three men from Rizokarpaso, Nicolaos Panayi 12867, Georgios Andrea 12864 and Demetrios Achillea 12888, claimed that they were owed their pay. SA1/978/1916/3, Nicolaos Panayi 12867, Georgios Andrea 12864 and Demetrios Achillea 12888, to CSC, 17 May 1920.
148 Ibid., Oulfet Haji Mustafa, no. 12242, to Stevenson, 25 February 1920.
149 Ibid., Mehmed Emin, 13167, to Stevenson, 26 February 1920.
150 Ibid., Salih Subhi, Ali Faik, 11162, Kalo Chorio (also Tsamli Keoi), to Stevenson, received 17 January 1920.
151 Ibid., Prodromos Petris, no. 14373, to CSC, received 9 July 1920; ibid., Christoforos Haji Haralambou, no. 10584, to CSC, 2 July 1920.
152 Ibid., Costas Charalambous, no. 12720, to CSC, 21 July 1920.
153 Ibid., Hassan Mehmet, Stavrokoko, no. 14298, Paphos, to Stevenson, 28 August 1921.
154 SA1/978/1916, Christos Haralambou to Stevenson, 30 March 1920; ibid., DCLi to CSC, 14 April 1920; SA1/978/1916/3, DCLi to CSC, 31 May 1920.
155 These were: the 'Comrades of the Great War', the 'National Association of Discharged Sailors and Soldiers', the 'National Federation of Discharged and Demobilized Sailors and Soldiers' and the 'Officers' Association'. The British Legion is known as the Royal British Legion since it was granted a Royal Charter in May 1971. See George Wootton, *The Official History of the British Legion*, Macdonald and Evans, London, 1956; Antony Brown, *Red for Remembrance: The British Legion, 1921–1971*, Heinemann, London, 1971; Brian Harding, *Keeping Faith: The Royal British Legion*, Leo Cooper, London, 2001.
156 First as the private secretary to Governor Storrs, 1926–32, and then as Inspector of Antiquities for the Cypriot Museum, 1932–5.
157 SA1/978/1916/2, Minute to CSC, 3 January 1937.
158 Ibid., Unknown, to B.J. O'Brian, DCFa, 12 February 1937.
159 An Ottoman unit of area, in Cyprus the *donum* is 14,400 sq. ft (1,338 m2) and is referred by the Cypriot word, σκάλες (*skales*).
160 Another Ottoman unit of measure, one *evlek* is equal to 3600 sq. ft (334 m²).
161 Ibid., O'Brian to CSC, 7 June 1937. Demtrious had no. 9256.
162 Ibid., R.J. Thorne to DCFa, 14 June 1937.
163 Ibid., Bevan to DCFa, 21 June 1937.
164 Ibid., John Demesthenous, 5328, Kaminarka, to Gov. of Cyprus, 30 November 1945.
165 Ibid., DCLi to CSC, 27 December 1945; CSC to D.M. Skettos, Honorary Sec., British Legion, Nicosia, 23 March 1946; British Legion Cyprus to CSC, 16 April 1946.

166 Ibid., Ex-Soldiers of the Great War, 1914–18, petition, to Governor of Cyprus, 27 April 1946. Haji Gregory served with nos 3178 and 12946. The list was made to look longer because 84 men signed two times, two signed three times, and there were signatures on behalf of two dead veterans (in all there were 640 signatures).
167 Ibid., DCNi and DCKy to CSC, 7 August 1946.
168 Ibid., ACSC to DCNi, 14 August 1946.
169 Yusuf / Cat Stevens revealed at his Philadelphia concert on 4 December 2014 that his father had been to Philadelphia before he had settled in London. A bootlegged video of his concert is on YouTube.
170 CO67/201/49076, Army Council to CO, 5 October 1920.
171 See SA1/1380/1921; SA1/1453/1920/3, DCNi to CSC, 15 September 1921.
172 SA1/978/1916/2, Cyprus British Legion to CSC, 10 February 1939; Chairman, British Legion, Cyprus Branch, Major-General Sir Courtenay Manifold, to CSC, 22 March 1939; Palmer to Macdonald, Secretary of State for Colonies, 6 April 1939; Macdonald to Officer Administering the Cypriot government, 20 May 1939; Reddaway, ACSC, to Manifold, 14 June 1939.
173 Ibid., George C. Georgiades, 3625 and 13311, Filia, Nicosia, now Piraeus, to CSC, 18 May 1938.
174 Ibid., ACSC to Georgiades, 28 June 1938.
175 Ibid., Kyriakos Pandeli Kakos, no. 6566, to CSC, undated.
176 SA1/1453/1920/2, Costas Argyriades, 8121, Kilia, Constantinople, to Stevenson, 25 January 1923.
177 Ibid., Ali Riza, 8131, to CSC, 28 January 1923.
178 Ibid., Ramis Mehmet, 3205, to CSC, 13 February 1923.
179 Ibid., Georgios Panayotopoulos, nos 3101 and 8969, to CSC, undated.
180 Ibid., Andreas Haralambou, no. 4341, to Stevenson, 7 April 1923.
181 Ibid., Nicholas Zachariades, no. 8649, to CSC, 11 June 1923; ibid., Zachariades to CSC, 22 October 1923; Zachariades to WO, 26 March 1924; ibid., undated. Zachariades also asked for the British Victory Medal.
182 SA1/978/1916/1, Christodoulos G. Theodoriades, Alexandria, to HCC, 28 Feb 1925.
183 SA1/1453/1920/2, George Ellinas, 12255, Constantinos Christoforou Katekos, nos 768 and Foreman O.P., and Georgios Economides, nos 8647 and 13647, to CSC, 7 September 1926.
184 SA1/1453/1920/3, Michael Ioannou Annas to Palmer, 11 January 1935.
185 See Nicolas Manitakis and Michalis N. Michael, 'Cypriot Emigration to the United States of America (1910 to 1930)', Chronos, 30, 2014, 99–143.
186 See Robin Oakley, 'Cypriot Migration to Britain prior to World War II', Journal of Ethnic and Migration Studies, 15/3, July 1989, 509–25; John Solomos and Stephen Woodhams, 'The Politics of Cypriot Migration to Britain', Immigrants and Minorities, 14(3), 1995, 231–56; Rolandos Katsiaounis, 'Η Κυπριακή Παροικία του Λονδίνου και το Αρχιεπισκοπικό Ζήτημα της Κύπρου, 1928–1936' (The Cypriot Community of London and the Archiepiscopal Question of Cyprus, 1928–1936), Annual of the Centre for Scientific Research, 22, 1996, 521–56; Rolandos Katsiaounis, 'Τα Πρώτα Βήματα της Επιτροπής Κυπριακής Αυτονομίας' (The First Steps of the Committee for Cypriot Autonomy), Annual of the Centre for Scientific Research, 26, 2000, 263–87. Remarkably there were no requests for medals from the UK as these probably went to the WO or the local British Legion branch.
187 SA1/1453/1920/2, M.R. Flynn, Danville, VA, USA, to Stevenson, 4 December 1922. Nicola had no. 2153.
188 SA1/978/1916/3, British Vice Consul, Minneapolis, to Stevenson, 12 January 1923. Konzou had 3871 and 10243.
189 See SA1/978/1916/1, Sophoklis Telonis, New York, to Stevenson, 5 October 1926. Also 5660 Nicolas Haji Achillea; 9368 Anastassis Constandi; 8126 Constantine Michalopoullos; 5536 George Kaniklides; 6729 Yiankos Louka; 8223 Kyriakos N.K. Strati; 9115 Kyriakos Ambiza; 9306 Arghyros Loizou Serghis; 9623 Vartholomeos

VETERANS AND THEIR FAMILIES AFTER SERVICE

Kleanthis; 10315 Yianis Vassili; 10558 Nicolas Michael; 11514 Ioannis Savva; 12858 Haralambos Nicola; 10892 Haralambos Kyprianou; 8437 Philippos Messes.
190 This includes: 8366 Christoforos Loizou; 9754 Kyriakos Haji Demetri; 4702 Dimokrito Haralambo; 9130 Avgustis Georgi; 9579 Alexandros Marneros; 10605 Nearchos Constandinou.
191 This includes: 6386 Christoforos Ioannou and 7172 Pavlos Zacharia.
192 This includes: 8770 Georgis Haji Pandeli, 10396 Stavrinos Christofi, 10445 Constandis Nicholaou.
193 SA1/1453/1920/3, DCFa to CSC, 25 June 1938.
194 SA1/978/1916/1, Costas Adamou, no. 13770, Melbourne, Australia, to CSC, 13 July 1926.
195 Ibid., CSC to Costas Adamou, 17 July 1926; J.N. Euthymiades and Son, on behalf of Costa Adamou, to CSC, 20 July 1926; CSC to J.N. Euthymiades and Son, 22 July 1926.
196 SA1/1453/1920/2, George Ioannou Florides, no. 9512, Sydney, to CSC, 23 April 1930.
197 Ibid., CSC to Florides, 9 May 1930.
198 Ibid., Nicholas Yiasemi, Orbost, Victoria to Storrs, received 1 April 1932.
199 Ibid., CSC to Yiasemi, 1 April 1932.
200 SA1/978/1916/2, H.V. Harris, Wheeler and Williams, Solicitors and Notaries, Newcastle, NSW, to the Military Commandant, Nicosia, 17 July 1937. Christofi had served with nos 6055 and 10787.
201 Ibid., Liassis Nicola, no. 6597, 227 Bulwer St, Perth, Western Australia, to Governor of Cyprus, 28 March 1940.
202 Ibid., CSC, to Liassis Nicola, 4 April 1940.
203 SA1/1453/1920/2, A.E. Ledgevarous to CSC, 14 Feb 1926. With no. 11727.
204 SA1/1453/1920/3, Messrs Baker, McEwin, Ligertwood and Millhouse, Morialta Chambers, Victoria Square West, Adelaide, to CSC, 21 August 1944.
205 Ibid., CSC to Messrs. Baker, McEwin, Ligertwood and Millhouse, 30 January 1945.

CHAPTER NINE

Remembering and forgetting the Cypriot Mule Corps

Growing up in Australia I could not avoid the Anzac legend and the Australian pride in the contribution of their ancestors to both World Wars. These contributions, especially at Gallipoli, play an important role in Australian national identity in new and evolving ways.[1] As an Australian of Cypriot heritage the place of the Great War in the Australian national script piqued my curiosity for the Great War, yet made me feel excluded because there was little information on the Cypriot contribution. The two World Wars predated my father's arrival to Australia in 1952 and although he was too young to have served in the Cypriot Regiment he experienced the limited impact of the Second World War, even being one of the first to the scene of a downed enemy airplane. The Cypriot contribution in the Second World War is obvious because of the Cypriot Regiment, even if there has been little scholarly work on it.[2] But for the Great War there is nothing. In 2002, as a PhD candidate, I found a reference in the *Chronology of Cyprus* by Governor Storrs to Cypriots serving as muleteers in the Great War.[3] I asked my father what he knew about it. To my surprise he revealed that his grandfather and namesake, Varnavas Michael Varnava, had 'gone to the war with the mules'.

I feel great pride that my great-grandfather served in the Great War and contributed to the coalition that defeated the Central Powers. Yet I did not then nor now feel any more included in the Australian commemorations as an ancestor of someone who had served in the Great War. My desire to feel included in the story of the Allied victory in the Great War and to understand the Cypriot story is not felt by Cypriots back in 'my old country' since there is a lack of awareness of and interest in the Cypriot contribution. Upon the revelation that my great-grandfather had served I immediately realised that since I had never heard anything of the Cypriot contribution in the Great War from Cypriots in Australia or from Cypriots when I had visited in 2000–1 and 2002, and lived there between September 2006 and January 2009, that it had been excluded from Cypriot national consciousness.

This chapter attempts to understand the individual and collective memory of the Cypriot Mule Corps from the 1920s until today. This necessitates exploring the post-war attitudes of the men who served towards their service and how it is remembered more broadly in the Cypriot national consciousness. This is no easy task given the limited sources. To adequately do so it is important to explore how attitudes and interpretations of the service changed as veterans and their broader community reflected, or not, on the war experience and how this sat with the growing anti-colonialism from both the right and the left, represented by nationalist and communist politics that emerged by the late 1920s.

Much has been written (see Chapter 1) about how societies involved remember and commemorate the Great War. Such studies have centred on memorialisation, commemoration and how remembrance has been transformed by various factors since the conflict ended. The focus of such studies has been on the English-speaking world, especially the UK and the USA, and the dominions, such as Australia, Canada and New Zealand. More recently some work has been done on India and how politicians there have attempted to forget the contribution it made.[4] Cyprus has a similar story.

The memory of the Mule Corps is complicated by the fact that there is no Cypriot national script, with a common Cypriot history. Remembering it was an undesirable point on the script of the 'Greek' or 'Turkish' nations in Cyprus. It would have been hard to explain it with the struggles for *enosis* (union) and *taksim* (partition) and the violence that gripped the island in the 1950s, 1960s and 1970s. Cypriots endured a violent war to unite the island to Greece (1955–9), followed by a civil war (1963–4) that collapsed the Republic created in 1960, and finally the coup orchestrated by the Greek Junta to force *enosis* and the Turkish military intervention in 1974 to prevent it, which partitioned the island between a 'Greek south' (the internationally recognised Republic of Cyprus) and a 'Turkish north' (the internationally unrecognised Turkish Republic of Northern Cyprus). The Christian and Muslim Cypriot peasant and labouring classes, which formed the bulk of the Corps, lacked the political voice and organisation to express their problems during the interwar years. They perhaps recalled their role and experiences in the Corps to family, but there was no possibility of using their involvement for their political, social or economic advantage. Thus there was no public discourse or consciousness on its existence. This is self-evident given the little interest in the Mule Corps of Cypriot elites during and after the Great War, which corresponded also with their lack of interest in the social and economic problems of the peasantry and labouring classes.

On the other hand, there are commemorations and a memorial for the Cypriot Regiment. Consisting of about 12,000 Cypriots, it was founded on 12 April 1940, served in the battle of France, Greece, Crete, North Africa (Operation Compass), the Middle East, Italy and in France again after the Normandy landings. It included infantry, mechanical and transport, but pack transport companies were the most important, and indeed Cypriot muleteers were the first colonial forces sent to the Western Front.[5] The memorial in Nicosia to the Cypriot Regiment sits on a busy intersection in front of buildings and not in a prominent spot. There are two fundamental reasons why the Cypriot Regiment is commemorated and remembered, although it was also an example of Christian and Muslim integration: (1) the nationalist elites and bourgeoisie, and after Nazi Germany's attack on the Soviet Union, the Cypriot Communists (represented by AKEL), actively supported enlistment for their own respective political ends; and (2) after the war, the peasant and labouring classes became integrated into the evolving political and ideological structures – they made political choices, which were limited to supporting the nationalists, who wanted *'enosis and only enosis'*, the communists, who now also supported *enosis*, or for Turkish Cypriot leaders who cultivated Turkish nationalism, opposition to *enosis* and preference for the status quo and later for *taksim*. The few voices from both communities that supported the British were marginalised and in many cases compelled to emigrate.[6] The co-option of the peasantry and labouring classes into the limited political structures meant the sidelining of the social issues that they had and that these problems would only be solved, in the minds of the 'Greek' Cypriot leaders, in life after *enosis*. It also meant that the discourse on the motivations to enlist in the Cypriot Regiment revolved around *enosis*, claiming that the Cypriots fought for the British expecting to be rewarded with *enosis*.[7]

The lack of a Cypriot public consciousness and official commemoration of the Cypriot Mule Corps was also reflected in the British failure to acknowledge the Cypriot contribution and to include the Cypriots in the commemorative events and memorials in the UK. There are no memorials in Britain to commemorate the service of Cypriots in the British armed forces in either of the World Wars. In Cyprus the British were confident of support from the peasantry and labouring classes, failing to grasp the changing social, economic and political landscape and the link between the increasing population, unemployment and anti-colonial ideologies.

This neglect on the part of both the British and the Cypriots is arguably best reflected in the significant discrepancy in the number of Cypriot Mule Corps deaths recorded by the Commonwealth War Graves Commission (CWGC) and the number found in this study, mostly arrived at through the official honour roll. The CWGC only has a portion of the dead in their cemeteries and many were buried at the front and graves were lost, destroyed or forgotten. According to the CWGC only about 40 Cypriot muleteers died in the Great War,[8] but the honour roll and other documents showed 177. The discrepancy indicates the failure of the CWGC to properly investigate the number of Cypriot muleteer deaths and therefore reflects their lack of interest, as well as that of Cypriots, at least until this study.

British Colonialists and Cypriot elites: the politics of the Cypriot Mule Corps

One reason for the Cypriots 'forgetting' the Mule Corps was the failure of the colonial government and local political elites, unlike Indian, Jamaican and Egyptian political elites,[9] to exploit it during and after the Great War for their own political ends. The government did not want to draw attention to it so it would not have to consider welfare or a benefits scheme for veterans and believed that the peasant and labouring classes were pro-British. Greek Cypriot politicians or the right and left could have used the contribution to show their loyalty to the British and that they deserved *enosis* or other political concessions, but loyalty to the British Empire contradicted their anti-colonialism. Meanwhile, Turkish Cypriot elites could also have used it to show their loyalty and support for the status quo, but this was couched in response to *enosis* and not examples of integration.

Instead of highlighting that the peasant and labouring classes were loyal to the British and thus deserving of *enosis*, they played no part in recruitment efforts. The local Greek language newspapers, controlled mostly by Greek Cypriot nationalists, mentioned basic information on shipping and numbers of muleteers, with the exception of the call by Savvides, but nothing on the momentous nature of the enlistment. There are many reasons to explain why Greek Cypriot nationalist elites acted the way they did. One reason was that after the failed British offer to cede Cyprus to Greece in October 1915 they expected it to be repeated after the war so their loyalty and support for the British war effort was unnecessary.[10] Also significant was that most of the Greek Cypriot elites supported King Constantine over Venizelos in the 'great schism' and thus held pro-German sympathies. Although not necessarily working for the enemy, they did not help the British either, unless it lined their own pockets.[11] The fact that the Mule

Corps would not have, except those few who bred mules, must also have been a turn-off, since fewer peasants would have borrowed from these usurers. It is a similar story for the Muslim Cypriot elites during the war. The majority preferred the status quo and feared *enosis*, yet believed that the British would handle their interests appropriately, despite the offer of 1915.[12] For this reason there was no need to constantly refer to their loyalty and when they did, reference to the Mule Corps was not considered necessary; most Muslims had remained loyal during the Great War despite the Ottoman Empire being on the side of the Central Powers. The British claimed that they were totally loyal; an exaggeration given what was discussed in previous chapters.[13]

During the interwar years much had changed, but not as regards using the significant wartime service of Cypriots to social, economic and political advantage. Although the economy and prospects for society in general were mostly bleak, especially when the Great Depression hit by 1930, there was no reference to the loyalty and service of the muleteers. This differs from Jamaica and India, where the political elites constantly advocated for a better deal for those who had served. Soon after the war ended the Jamaican government paid small sums to each veteran, gave them access to credit of up to £25 from the Agricultural Bank to buy land, stock or seed. In 1924 it introduced a scheme that gave five acres to veterans for farming if they had £10 in savings. Then in 1933, with the onset of the Great Depression, the government introduced a land settlement scheme to stem the flow of peasants and unskilled labourers to urban areas. Meanwhile, veterans groups were active.[14] The interwar experiences of the Jamaican peasantry and unskilled labourers were comparable to that of the Cypriots, except that the Cypriot government did not respond in the same way, there were no significant veteran groups active and the government referred Cypriots to the British Legion for welfare.

Cypriot elites from both communities continued to ignore the opportunity to exploit the Cypriot contribution. Muslim elites fought a rearguard defence against *enosis* agitation, steadfastly supporting the status quo,[15] although several also called for the 'return' of the island to Turkey, which succeeded the Ottoman Empire.[16] Several Cypriot Muslims led in trying to prevent conflict between the two communities.[17] The Orthodox Cypriot political elites, thoroughly obsessed with *enosis*, had only increased their demands for it after the war. Deputations to London in 1919 and 1920, led by Archbishop Kyrrillos III and members of the Legislative Council, including the firebrand Greek national Dr Zannettos, demanded *enosis*.[18] Opposition to it from other educated elites, especially merchants and civil servants, was damned, for example by the Bishop of Kyrenia, Makarios, in a sermon on 29 February 1920, and therefore silenced.[19] When Whitehall rejected *enosis*, the 'professional politicians and leading clerics', as Stevenson characterised them, protested by organising petitions in various towns and villages, mostly signed by the local teacher and cleric but by very few civil servants, merchants, peasants and labourers.[20] Stevenson claimed, not without foundation, that

> Your Lordship's announcement [rejecting *enosis*], which has caused much satisfaction to the Moslem Community has been received with apathy by the mass of the Greek Christian Community which evinces little interest in the activities of its political leaders regarding the union of Cyprus with Greece. The meetings, which were of a most orderly character, were poorly attended and little or no enthusiasm was displayed regarding union with Greece except on the part of the professional orators whose speeches were of the usual bombastic nature.[21]

Of these petitions only two protested at their denial of 'liberty' by claiming that they deserved it because they had contributed to the victorious British coalition. These petitions were from, Lapithos and Karavas in Kyrenia, which were major contributors to the Mule Corps.[22]

The orderly meetings may not have initially appeared threatening to Stevenson, but they soon took a nasty turn when the Greek Cypriot members of the Legislative Council resigned.[23] Initially Stevenson believed that 'the mischievous activities of the political leaders have led to no disorder whatever and do not appear to be likely to do so',[24] yet he recommended, as a precaution, that martial law continue until the Provisional Powers Law (1919) and the Provisional Powers (Amendment) Law (1920) came into force upon peace with the Ottoman Empire.[25] Indeed, initially the Greek Cypriot agitators, led by Kyrillos III, complained, asking that the new Colonial Secretary, Winston Churchill (who had visited the island as colonial undersecretary in 1907),[26] visit to ascertain the people's wishes.[27] But when this was rejected, the Greek Cypriot agitators became increasingly desperate, especially when a moderate faction emerged that accepted cooperation with the British.[28]

On 6 and 7 April 1921, during the 100-year anniversary of the Greek War of Independence, a rare celebration in Cyprus before 1900,[29] disturbances occurred in Nicosia. The police put them down, but Stevenson warned of intercommunal clashes and so he re-enlisted 90 ex-policemen and asked Egypt to send two platoons of troops.[30] The troops from Egypt could not be sent, despite Stevenson's pleas and those of the Colonial Office. Fiddes explained to the War Office, 'you will appreciate the importance just now of preventing anything like a serious shindy in the island'.³¹ Despite this setback the Cypriot government successfully cracked down on the most extremist agitators, exiling several Greek-born nationals.³² This further split the nationalists, caused Muslim ill-feeling and preparedness to defend and avenge their co-religionists, and showed how divorced these so-called representatives of the people were from the peasant and labouring classes. As Stevenson revealed to Churchill,

> There are also signs from the villages that the people are chafing at the agitation for Union with Greece. Several instances have just been reported to me in which the Village Councils have refused to sign resolutions for the Union of Cyprus with Greece which they had been directed by the agitators to pass.³³

These communities, who had husbands, sons and brothers serve in the Cypriot Mule Corps, were not interested in *enosis*, but for a better today and tomorrow for themselves and their families. Yet even when the threat of violence subsided, the Greek Cypriot members of the Legislative Council continued to ignore the real problems facing society. They refused to return to their seats; instead forming the so-called 'Political Organisation' which led a Greek Cypriot nationalist boycott of the upcoming elections, which the Colonial Office believed was modelled on the successful Maltese strategy.³⁴ But after summer 1922 the Cypriot government believed that the Political Organisation was 'moribund', that there was widespread dissatisfaction with it and by the end of the year Archbishop Kyrillos III had started lobbying the government for self-government rather than *enosis*.³⁵ Stevenson smashed the idea on its head in his letter to the Duke of Devonshire, the Unionist Colonial Secretary, in the new Conservative government:

> While I would naturally be disposed to consider in a liberal spirit the just desires of a subject people for greater responsibility, I fear that I cannot from my knowledge of the Cypriot or of his history honestly advocate under present conditions, the grant to the inhabitants of the Island of self-government or of any extended constitutional powers incapable of being balanced by precisely equivalent safeguards. The villager is ignorant, casual, credulous, and improvident; the townsman is half-educated, cunning, conceited, and selfish. The former is content to be ruled; the latter is happy to be protected at the expense, danger, and responsibility of anyone but himself. The average standard of intelligence and education of the Cypriot is low, while those who possess these advantaged in any degree turn them almost invariably to unworthy uses. While possessed of many good qualities, not the least of which is an attractive childlike simplicity of thought and expression, he is at heart Oriental. The Island is in truth immature even yet for the advanced constitutional system which was grafted on the country shortly after the British

Occupation in 1878, and any question of granting it a further measure of political liberty is one which, in my opinion, must be approached with the greatest care and deliberation.[36]

The elites of both communities, especially the Greek Cypriot, continued to focus on obtaining power in the island and determining its political status, failing to understand the possible political capital in referring to the Cypriot Mule Corps and the issues facing veterans. Meanwhile, the British also missed an opportunity to memorialise the Mule Corps and understand the needs of the veterans and broader peasant and rural labouring classes. The battle to win the hearts and minds of the Cypriot peasantry and labouring classes had not yet begun and in the process of ignoring them, the Mule Corps had been silenced.

During and after the 1931 events, which resulted in the burning of Government House in Nicosia and the subsequent British repression that impacted on all communities and classes,[37] nothing was said about the Cypriot contribution in the Great War to show prior loyalty. The Cypriot Mule Corps had all but been erased from memory, yet as the decade progressed there were signs of mass politicisation across the island that brought together classes and different religious groups, not behind the banner of *enosis*, but behind constitutional reform.[38]

Earlier, smaller, more ideologically based movements had united some peasants, labourers, and the more socially and politically conscious educated people, but these also failed to refer to the Cypriot Mule Corps. The British took peasant support for granted. In the 1925 legislature elections there was a massive defeat for the nationalists and for the first time more than 10% of the Greek Cypriot population voted.[39] The Communist Party of Cyprus (CPC), formed in 1926, had direct links to the Mule Corps yet failed to use this politically. In the spirit of the 'United Front' for workers and peasants and recognising the Christian-Muslim particulars in the island, it wanted to unite all Christians and Muslims against British rule and therefore advocated Cypriot independence and strongly criticised *enosis*. Its unofficial leader during the repressive early to mid-1930s, Christos Savvides, had served in the Mule Corps,[40] and yet he did not draw attention to it. Service in the Corps indicated a loyalty to a regime for which he was agitating against. Interestingly, he did not attempt to use the Corps in a negative way either given the British failure to look after veterans. Additionally in the 1920s there formed the Agrarian Party, which had much greater success than the CPC in forging Christian and Muslim membership, but did not survive after the events of 1931.[41] It too failed to use the Mule Corps and support veteran issues, although many of its members would have served. The movement that developed from the mid-1930s and climaxed in the unsuccessful delegation visiting London in 1937 to ask for constitutional reforms was far more numerous in support and broader ideologically. As Rappas argued, the movement failed not because it lacked legitimacy, but because it had legitimacy, as the first mass movement and one which included people from all socio-economic and ethno-religious groups, with the exception of the nationalists who had been sidelined. That the British succeeded through their harsh measures to create this movement and yet failed to embrace it was the tragedy.[42] That the Cypriots behind it continued to ignore the contribution of the Mule Corp in the Great War and the issues that the veterans faced was a political failure that can only be attributed to immaturity and the silencing of the Mule Corps.

Ultimately, their hearts and minds were still to be won and if the Cypriot government had focused on commemorating the Cypriot Mule Corps they may have shown that the 'Greek'-Christian and 'Turkish'-Muslim divide in Cyprus was a nationalist manifestation and that the peasants, as the British repeatedly argued during the interwar years, were in fact loyal. The British failed to win peasant and labourer 'hearts and minds' and after the Second World War pushed them into the anti-colonial movements that developed during the 1930s.

Australia remembers

It was not until the Second World War that the Cypriot Mule Corps was remembered, and it took an Englishman in Australia, Michael Terry.

> Set in the most historic corner of Europe, possibly of the world, Cyprus possessed 285,000 people when the last war started. Orthodox Greek Christians and Turkish Mohammedans were and still are in the proportion of five to one. There are also a few Latin Catholics, Maronites and Armenians. Many of them volunteered to assist the Allied cause, and were shipped in 1916 to Salonica as part of the Army Service Corps attached to various Allied Commands, wearing ordinary British uniforms, they rendered valuable service as muleteers and pack drivers.[43]

By any account Michael Terry was an extraordinary man. Born in England, he lived much of his life in Australia. During the Great War he served with the Royal Naval Air Service, Armoured Car Section and while serving in Russia in 1917 was captured by the Bolsheviks, and subsequently repatriated. Advised by medical staff to seek a warmer climate because of his damaged lungs, he set sail soon after November 1918 for Australia, where from 1923 to 1935 he led 14 expeditions into central Australia, publishing numerous articles, books and delivering lectures, including to the Royal Geographical Society in London, about his experiences. Despite being an explorer, he was deemed medically unfit for service in the Second World War and became informally associated with British counter-intelligence, writing propaganda for the war effort in Britain, Australia and Canada.[44] This included the above article on Cyprus in *The Sydney Morning Herald*. There is nothing to suggest that he had any connection with Cyprus and yet he knew a great deal about its role in the Great War and the Mule Corps.[45]

How did Terry know so much? In the absence of a thorough autobiography and/or biography it is not possible to know whether he had visited Cyprus, especially during the years of the two World Wars. There is a gap in his life during 1918, while he may have visited the Australian troops in the island during the Second World War.[46] It may be that he met or befriended a Cypriot in Australia who had served in the Cypriot Mule Corps. But his knowledge of other aspects of the role of Cyprus during the Great War suggests that he accessed the information from the Blue Books and *The Handbook of Cyprus*.[47]

On 22 May 1941, nine days before Terry's article appeared, across in Melbourne, *The Argus* published an interesting article (probably by Terry) on the role of Cyprus in the Second World War, which also referred to the Cypriot muleteers in the Great War.

> Cyprus, where Anzacs are reported to have landed, is strategically important because it lies in a direct line linking the Axis-occupied islands of the Dodecanese and the mainland of Syria ... Many former 'Diggers' will remember [from the Great War] the famous Cypriot muleteers, who, according to reports, are serving again.[48]

The world's attention was turned on the Eastern Mediterranean on 20 May 1941 when Nazi Germany began its airborne invasion of Crete. The two articles from leading Australian newspapers were published in the 11-day period in which the invasion lasted, ending with the German victory on 1 June. The above quote, in agreeing with Terry that the Cypriot muleteers served with distinction in the Great War, also claimed that many Australian 'diggers' would remember them because they were back again in the Cypriot Regiment. Interestingly, the Australians, who did not serve in Salonica or Constantinople, but may have met Cypriot muleteers in Egypt and in the Black Sea, were claimed as having a memory of the Cypriot Mule Corps, when their service was, at least at a public level, forgotten by the Cypriots and the British.

It was extraordinary to discover that the Australian newspapers were aware that the Cypriot contribution to the Second World War followed that of the First World War, while the British newspapers were not. On 10 January 1940, *The Times* reported that the Cypriots were the first colonial forces to serve in France in the Second World War, which was correct,[49] but then got it wrong when stating that this was 'the first time that natives of Cyprus have taken part in a European war on the side of the British Empire'.[50] This statement was corrected three days later when *The Times* published a letter from Mabel Laffan (formerly Lady Stevenson), the wife of Sir Malcom Stevenson, who had died in November 1927, while Governor of the Seychelles, stating that Cypriots had served as mule drivers in the Great War and that she and her husband had presided over the distribution of their medals in 1920.[51] Someone still had a memory.

The Argus also got it right when it stated that the Cypriot muleteers were 'serving again', because there were some who served in both World Wars. The only corroborating evidence comes from the Europeana project, which reveals that four men served in both wars.[52]

The Cyprus conflict, 1955-74

The Cyprus conflict does not begin in 1955 nor does it end in 1974, but during these 20 years mass political violence was used, on and off, resulting in the militarisation of both communities against each other. After the Second World War the British failed to build upon a second loyal contribution from both Christian and Muslim Cypriots. Instead they allowed the Greek Cypriot nationalist elites to use the Second World War contribution for political leverage on *enosis* and reignited the fire by returning to the island some of the most extreme nationalists interested in '*enosis* and only *enosis*'.[53] For this reason the British initiative to reintroduce a constitution (1946-8) with a legislative council was doomed.[54] The rejection of a constitution by Cypriot elites, explained by the failure of the British to properly introduce political modernity to the island, alongside the island's increasingly important role for British defence policy in the Middle East, helps explain the start of EOKA violence in April 1955.[55]

As part of these preparations for the use of violence the Greek Cypriot nationalist elites needed to convert the peasantry and labouring classes into *enosis* faithful and the youth into active, even violent, tools against the British and anyone opposed to EOKA.[56] After a long planning stage, starting in 1951,[57] civil disobedience and violence were adopted in April 1955. This civil disobedience did not resemble that in India, since it was not against damaging and exploitative British policies,[58] but took a cultural and symbolic form, such as when school children were ordered to break the commemorative mugs given to them to mark the coronation of Queen Elizabeth II.[59] Some veteran muleteers were also ordered to destroy their medals, but many did not, highlighting the more general opposition to EOKA methods and that the medals served to protect them and their families from British searches.[60]

Cypriotism, yet still no Cypriot Mule Corps

Independence in 1960, hastened by the out-of-control violence which resembled a civil war in the island between its two communities and the British ruler in the middle, did not forge a common history. Neither side wanted a common national history of shared memories. This was also enshrined in the constitution, which allowed for separate Communal Chambers that gave the Greek and Turkish communities separate powers to deal with the cultural needs independently of the 'other'. This was reflected in the 'research' of 'national historians', such as Constantine Spyridakis, the Minister of Education in the first decade of the Republic of Cyprus, the opponents of a university in Cyprus (so they could send their children to Greece and Turkey) and Makarios's new policy of independence (the policy of the 'feasible', i.e. independence, rather than the 'desirable', i.e. *enosis*) after 1967 because both would alienate Cyprus from its 'Greek motherland'.[61] The Greek Cypriot position was that they were the majority and so they should determine the status of the island, namely *enosis*. The Turkish Cypriot view was that both groups had lived peacefully under Ottoman and most of British rule, but that since *enosis* had become violent the two sides could not co-exist, and partition was desirable.[62]

After the 1974 war that partitioned the island both sides altered their official propaganda. The Greek Cypriot political establishment now argued that relations before 1974 were peaceful and neighbourly. This has been referred to in Cypriot historiography as 'peaceful coexistence' and 'Cypriotism', although there was no serious attempt to develop a Cypriot national consciousness.[63] Rather the aim was to downplay or blame foreign powers for the violence of the 1950s, 1960s and 1970s by showing that Greeks and Turks in Cyprus had lived peacefully before. One of the chief architects of this politically motivated revisionist history was Costas Kyrris, the director of the Cyprus Research Centre in the Ministry of Education and Culture. In his *Peaceful Coexistence in Cyprus* he offered various examples throughout the centuries of Greek and Turkish 'peaceful coexistence' in the island.[64] Kyrris, a thorough researcher, still failed to mention the Cypriot Mule Corps. On the other hand, the Turkish Cypriot official writers continued with the opposite extreme, focusing on what had divided rather than what had united Cypriots.[65]

It was left to a British officer serving in Cyprus in the 1970s to take an interest in the Cypriot Mule Corps. Major J.P.B. Condon, Royal Irish Rangers (formed 1968), while on service as part of the United Nations Force in Cyprus, produced a short report on the Cypriot Mule Corps, which is contained in various UK archives.[66] He readily admitted it was incomplete and would one day return to it, but he did not.

Europeana 1914–1918

Europeana 1914–1918, discussed in the introduction, was the first attempt since Condon to record the stories of Cypriot Mule Corp members, even if these were from second-hand accounts and there were several problems. In addition to those outlined in the Introduction, the most common error was the statement that the men served in the Greek army, which serves to show the Greek nationalist orientation of those relaying the stories, as they assumed their relatives had served in the Greek and not the British army, and those conducting and transcribing the interviews who did not correct this.[67]

Many of the accounts also focus on how some of the men followed their service in the British armed forces with service in the Greek army. This is celebrated in much greater tones in the accounts. But this must be questioned in light of the archival evidence. Few Cypriots served in the Greek army and the Greek authorities used coercion and even kidnapping to compel Cypriots to serve against their will, including former members of the Cypriot Mule Corps. In 1920 the Greek government, informed by the nationalist Greek Cypriot elites, claimed that there were 4,000 Cypriots in Cyprus willing to enlist in the Greek army and that they would be willing to send warships to collect them. The British government was utterly bemused since there were no Cypriots thronging to enlist and rejected the idea as a breach of British neutrality, which it was since Cypriots held British Cypriot nationality.[68] If it were not enough that the Greek government and their own political elites were trying to volunteer the peasant and labouring classes into the Greek army, Greek consular representatives in Egypt and Greek military personnel in Greece started kidnapping, even providing false identification papers, to British Cypriot nationals. This included at least four men who had served as muleteers.[69]

Conclusion

Despite the monumental contribution of Cypriot men in the Mule Corps, various issues and developments came together to result in its silencing. From nationalists creating separate scripts of the 'Greek' and 'Turkish' nations in Cyprus, excluding any common Christian-Muslim past, to simply not wanting to associate with the imperialists' war, the memory of the service of the men in the Cypriot Mule Corps was reduced to a personalised family affair at best, and at worst it was not discussed at all. The British failure to commemorate the service of the Cypriots, possibly linked to their unwillingness to compensate widows and incapacitated muleteers, contributed to its silencing.

Notes

1. See Michael J.K. Walsh and Andrekos Varnava, *Australia and the Great War*, Melbourne University Press, 2016.
2. See Jan Asmussen, '"Dark Skinned Cypriots will not be Accepted!" Cypriots in the British Army, 1939–1945', in Hubert Faustmann and Nicos Peristianis (eds), *Britain in Cyprus: Colonialism and Post-Colonialism 1878–2006*, Bibliopolis, Mannheim, 20065, 167–85; Yiangou's effort, *Cyprus in World War II*, is unsatisfying: see my review in *The Cyprus Review*, 24(2), 2012, 147–50. Marios Shamas is tackling this subject for his PhD at King's College.
3. Storrs, *A Chronology of Cyprus*, 35.
4. David A. Johnson, 'The Great War's Impact on Imperial Delhi: Commemorating Wartime Sacrifice in the Colonial Built Environment', in Michael J.K. Walsh and Andrekos Varnava (eds), *The British Empire and the Great War*, Routledge, London, forthcoming.
5. HS3/120 'Cyprus and the War', 14 September 1945.
6. This had started as far back as 1934 when Antonios Triantafyllides, a leading lawyer and member of the Advisory Council, was assassinated. See CO67/251/7, CO67/253/10, CO67/253/11, CO67/254/3, CO67/255/12 and FCO141/2497. In the early 1950s, people who preferred British to Greek rule left, including the Aristovoulos family, who migrated to Australia. Interview with Mr and Mrs Aristovoulos, December 2010.
7. Asmussen, 'Dark Skinned Cypriots'; Yiangou, *Cyprus in World War II*.
8. See *The War Dead of the British Commonwealth and Empire: The Register of the Names of Those Who Fell in the 1939–1945 War and Are Buried in Cemeteries in Syria, Turkey and Cyprus*, Commonwealth War Graves Commission, Maidenhead, 1959.
9. David Lockwood, *The Indian Bourgeoisie*, I.B. Tauris, London, 2012, 30–51; Smith, *Jamaican Volunteers in the First World War*; M.W. Daly and Carl F. Petry, *The Cambridge History of Egypt*, Cambridge University Press, 1998, 246.
10. Georghallides, *A Political and Administrative History of Cyprus*.
11. See Varnava, 'British Military Intelligence in Cyprus'.
12. Nevzat, *Nationalism amongst the Turks of Cyprus*, 218–55.
13. See Varnava, 'British Military Intelligence in Cyprus'; for the stolen vessel see SA1/806/1917.
14. Smith, *Jamaican Volunteers in the First World War*, 156–7.
15. CO67/198/40907, Stevenson to Milner, 6 August 1920, including letter by Musa Irfan Bey, member of Executive and Legislative Councils, 4 August 1920; CO67/199/63298, confidential, Stevenson to Milner, 12 December 1920, including message from Chief Cadi of Cyprus, 10 December 1920.
16. CO67/208/1092, confidential, Stevenson to Devonshire, 24 December 1922, including enclosures.
17. CO67/202/22445, confidential, Stevenson to Churchill, 25 April 1921.

18 CO67/197/21724, Stevenson to Milner, 15 April 1920. See also the pamphlet published by the Cyprus Deputation in CO67/201/30005, 'The Cyprus Cause: Official Correspondence'. No mention of the Cypriot contribution in the war is made. See also correspondence and other documents in this file.
19 CO67/197/21724, Stevenson to Milner, 15 April 1920.
20 CO67/199/56234, confidential, Stevenson to Milner, 6 November 1920.
21 Ibid.
22 CO67/199/59863, confidential, Stevenson to Milner, 25 November 1920, with relevant enclosures.
23 CO67/199/63192, 386, Stevenson to Milner, 14 December 1920; CO67/199/63301, confidential, Stevenson to Milner, 14 December 1920.
24 CO67/199/63301, confidential, Stevenson to Milner, 14 December 1920.
25 CO67/199/63302, secret, Stevenson to Milner, 14 December 1920. Martial Law was eventually lifted on 1 September 1921, despite the disturbances that had occurred. See CO67/204/46764.
26 Varnava, *British Imperialism in Cyprus*, 183–6.
27 See CO67/202/15566.
28 See CO67/202/15567 and CO67/203/24636.
29 Varnava, *British Imperialism in Cyprus*, 167.
30 See CO67/202/17380 and CO67/202/20543.
31 CO67/202/20073; on 4 May 1921 the battleship *Ajax* visited Famagusta, in response to Stevenson's pleas for assistance, but in something out of a comic-tragedy, nobody expected it. See CO67/205/31214, includes report from commanding officer of the *Ajax*. See also CO67/205/27114, CO67/205/22860, CO67/205/21978 and CO67/205/24117.
32 For the deportation of Nikolaos Katalanos see CO67/202/22444, CO67/203/32629 and CO67/203/30260; for Philios Zannetos see CO67/208/48068, secret, Fenn to Churchill, 16 September 1922, enclosures and minutes.
33 CO67/202/22445, confidential, Stevenson to Churchill, 25 April 1921. The British also questioned the petitions sent in June, which came from some villages with a Greek Cypriot majority, and only had the signatures of leading individuals, the priest, teacher, school councils and sometimes the mayor. The British had evidence that duress was used and that most of the population was unaware that they were sent in their name. See CO67/203/33691.
34 CO67/204/55086, confidential, Stevenson to Churchill, 25 October 1921, and see also minutes from this file. Also see, CO67/204/62275 and CO67/204/978. For more on the 'political organisation' see CO67/207/16623, confidential, Stevenson to Churchill, 23 March 1922, including articles of the political organisation.
35 See CO67/208/54911 and CO67/208/1091.
36 CO67/208/1091, confidential, Stevenson to Devonshire, 24 December 1922, also see enclosures.
37 George Georghallides, *Cyprus and the Governorship of Sir Ronald Storrs: The Causes of the 1931 Crisis*, Cyprus Research Centre, Nicosia, 1985; Rappas, *Cyprus in the Thirties*.
38 Rappas, *Cyprus in the Thirties*, 88–122.
39 Yiannos Katsourides, *The History of the Communist Party in Cyprus: Colonialism, Class and the Cypriot Left*, I.B. Tauris, London, 2014, 54–6.
40 Ibid., 138–9. He was probably not the only Cypriot communist to have served in the Cypriot Mule Corps.
41 Ibid, 75–82.
42 Rappas, *Cyprus in the Thirties*; and Andrekos Varnava, review of *Cyprus in the 1930s* by Alexis Rappas, *European History Quarterly*, 45(4), 2015, 787–9.
43 Michael Terry, 'Britain's Romantic Colony Faces a Crisis: Cyprus in the War', *The Sydney Morning Herald*, 31 May 1941, 9.
44 Mickey Dewar, 'Terry, Michael (1899–1981)', *Australian Dictionary of Biography*, National Centre of Biography, Australian National University, http://adb.anu.edu.

au/biography/terry-michael-15670/text26866, published first in hard copy 2012, accessed online 26 February 2015.
45 Perhaps even more astonishing than his knowledge of the Cypriot Mule Corps was his awareness of the French-trained Legion d'Orient in the island.
46 Robert S. Merrillees, 'Australia and Cyprus in the Second World War', *Defence Force Journal*, 43, 1983, 47–50.
47 Terry gave the population of Cyprus at the start of the Great War as 285,000, which was remarkably close to the estimated population given in the Blue Book of 1913–1914 as of 31 March 1914. *Annual Report for Cyprus 1913–14*, 4. On the other hand, the Blue Books do not mention the Legion d'Orient / Armenian Legion, but do mention the Cypriot Mule Corps. *Annual Report for Cyprus, 1916–17*, cd. 8434, HMSO, London, 1917, 17; *Annual Report for Cyprus, 1917–18*, cmd. 1–9, HMSO, London, 1919, 15; see Luke and Jardine, *The Handbook of Cyprus*, 293–4.
48 'Cyprus, Key Island of Mediterranean', *The Argus*, 22 May 1941, 4.
49 HS3/120 'Cyprus and the War', 14 September 1945.
50 'First Colonials in France: Cypriot Transport', *The Times*, 10 January 1940, 5.
51 'Cypriots in the Army', *The Times*, 13 January 1940, 7.
52 Europeana web-page entries for Costis Ttikkou, Lithrodontas, Nicosia, Jacob (Ioakim) Georgiou, Trahoni, Limassol, Christodoulos Georgallis, Palaikythro, Nicosia, and Haralambos Stavrou Xiarva, Ordidkia, Larnaca. This would be an interesting avenue to pursue for those researching the Cypriot Regiment, as would the extent to which sons of muleteers from the Great War enlisted in the Second World War, because the Europeana project shows there was at least one. Europeana web-page entry for Kyriakos Triantafyllis, Palaiohori, Nicosia.
53 Bishop of Kyrenia, Makarios, was one example, becoming Archbishop in 1946. See Yiangou, *Cyprus in World War II*, 147–51.
54 Rolandos Katsiaounis, *Η Διασκεπτική, 1946–1948: Με Ανασκόπηση της Περιόδου, 1878–1945* (The consultative assembly, 1946–48: with a survey of the period, 1878–1945), Cyprus Research Centre, Nicosia, 2000.
55 Varnava and Yakinthou, 'Cyprus: Political Modernity and the Structures of Democracy in a Divided Island'.
56 For a primary source see, George Grivas, *The Memoirs of General Grivas* (ed.), Charles Foley, Longmans, London 1964; for secondary sources see Nancy Crawshaw, *The Cyprus Revolt*, George Allen and Unwin, London, 1978, and David French, *Fighting EOKA: The British Counter-Insurgency Campaign on Cyprus, 1955–1959*, Oxford University Press, 2015.
57 Grivas, *Memoirs*, 13–32.
58 Lockwood, *The Indian Bourgeoisie*, 133–42 and 165–7.
59 I have been told this by many Cypriots growing up at the time. Also, see Chris Sutton, 'Gauge, Battleground, Weapon: Celebrations in Cold War Cyprus, 1945–1955', *ex plus ultra*, 3, April 2012.
60 Europeana, entries/web pages for Panay Polycarpou and Michael Michaelides, both from Palaiohori, and Demetris Christodoulou, Lapathos, Famagusta.
61 Constantine Spyridakis, *A Brief History of Cyprus*, Publications Dept. Greek Communal Chamber, Nicosia, 1963 (2nd edition, 1964); see Kyriacos C. Markides, *The Rise and Fall of the Cyprus Republic*, Yale University Press, London, 1977, 98–9.
62 See Rauf Denktash, *The Cyprus Triangle*, Allen Unwin, London, 1982.
63 Papadakis, Peristianis and Welz (eds), *Divided Cyprus*.
64 Costas Kyrris, 'Symbiotic Elements in the History of the Two Communities of Cyprus', *Kypriakos Logos*, 8, 1976, 243–82; Kyrris, *Peaceful Co-existence in Cyprus*.
65 See A.C. Gazioglu, *The Turks of Cyprus: A Province of the Ottoman Empire 1571–1878*, Rustem, London, 1990; A.C. Gazioglu and M.A. Demirer, *Cyprus: The Island of Sustained Crisis*, CYREP, Nicosia 1998.
66 Aside from at the National Archives, UK, it is also at the Imperial War Museum and the Shropshire Archives.

67 Europeana web-page entries for Apostolos Argyrou, Damianos Ioannis and Costis tis Haritous, all from Palaihori, and Demetris Christodoulou, Lapathos.
68 See CO67/198/32080, telegram, Stevenson to Milner, 29 June 1920; CO67/198/32699, telegram, Stevenson to Milner, 4 July 1920; CO67/200/33415, FO to CO, 7 July 1920; CO67/200/33991, FO to CO, 10 July 1920, including cable, very urgent, Granville to FO, 7 July 1920 (received 9 July 1920); CO67/200/33991, minute, undated; CO to FO, 14 July 1920; CO67/200/34783, cable, Granville to FO, 10 July 1920 (received 11 July 1920); CO67/201/35475, Cyprus Deputation to Colonial Secretary, 17 July 1920; CO67/201/35475, CO to Cyprus Deputation, 27 July 1920.
69 Victor Vernardakis, 4650, Limassol, S.G. Hatzakos, 8273, Pano Akourdalia, Paphos, Triphonas Irakli, Kilani, Limassol and Nearchos Christodoulides. See the relevant files in CO67/205/43709, CO67/204/62276, CO67/205/45201, CO67/205/47192, CO67/205/52622, CO67/205/57437, CO67/205/57871 and CO67/205/59599. There are two men on the honour roll with the name Nearchos Christodoulou, 9963, Evrihou, Nicosia and 12728, Kritou Marottou, Paphos.

CONCLUSION

Of Mules and Men
In the darkness of the freezing night,
They drove their mules with no light,
To the sounds of bombs and gunfire,
All in the service of this, our old Empire.
– Andrekos Varnava, 2015[1]

The power of history over the historian can often be all-consuming. The stanza from my poem above reflects how this project has dominated my thoughts and the poem goes on to show how day and night I would be transported to scenes from the stories of the Cypriot Mule Corps.

The power of history over the historian differs from the power of the British Empire, yet both have the ability to control lives. The British Empire had the ability to control the lives of its subjects and simultaneously it could command their loyalty not at the point of a gun, but through the power of its modernising ways. Modernisation had seen life expectancy rates rise and infant mortality rates drop, resulting in a dramatic increase in the Cypriot population, which led to a surplus of people searching for work by 1914. Undeterred by the indifference and in some cases opposition of their local political elites, the peasant and rural and urban labouring classes came forward to enlist in their droves because of poverty and lack of work opportunities in Cyprus. The British prevented them from migrating to places with work, thus making the Cypriot Mule Corps a golden opportunity. The service of Cypriots in the British armed forces during the Great War was truly enormous proportional to the population of the island. Not only did about 25% of the male population aged 18–35 serve at one time or another in the Cypriot Mule Corps, Cypriots also served in other capacities.[2] This, arguably, places Cyprus at the top of the list of colonial societies to contribute.[3] The British knew how to pull the Cypriots into the Mule Corps, and they certainly knew how to limit their own responsibilities towards these men too. This was British imperial power and control working at its optimum.

This power was on show during the service of the Mule Corps, even if there were moments when in the 'liminal space' the Cypriot muleteers could negotiate with the British. The British not only herded the Cypriots into the Corps, they shepherded them during their service into signing contracts that reduced their responsibilities to them and added more conditions onto the men. The contracts represented a small step up from indentured labour, although the Army Council had initially advised that the Cypriots be treated as much as possible as soldiers, with rights to a pension and compensation for invalids and widows. But the Cypriots had one thing going for them – they were in demand. This was not because they were skilled or especially effective, but because they were the only ones the British could get (aside from Indians, who were rejected on grounds of race) to relieve British personnel to do other tasks. It was the demand for Cypriots and the threat that enlistment would decrease or the entire enterprise flounder which saw some negotiation in the 'liminal space'. Yet the British controlled this space too. The Cypriots referred to their rights to be repatriated after a year and to a functioning allotment scheme for their dependents. The Cypriot government, having enlisted them under these conditions and having failed to initially establish the allotment scheme, supported the men, resolved the crisis with allotments and urged the military authorities to give in on the one-year contracts. The power of the military authorities proved flexible, yet they still flexed their muscles, imprisoning difficult muleteers and forcing others to keep working until repatriation could be arranged – effectively extending the 12-month contract indefinitely. To prevent a backlash they offered bonus pay to those wanting to sign up for another 12 months (and later to those serving until they could be repatriated instead of going to a concentration camp) and a free furlough back to Cyprus. Money was power and the British knew how to control the Cypriots. This power was extended to public health when venereal disease threatened the Corps. The British revised the contracts to dismiss muleteers with venereal disease and to charge them for their repatriation and treatment. In Cyprus the government blamed infected prostitutes, banishing them to rural areas and thus spreading the disease. British control was complete.

British imperial power was on full show after the men returned, since as veterans they practically had no rights. The military authorities gripped tightly to the contracts that stipulated that there would be no compensation in cases of injury or death, exercising their power to provide an 'ex gratia' payment in those few cases they pitied. Pensions were never entertained. The Cypriot government merely played pass the parcel, in the early years approaching the military authorities, and in later years pushing the problem onto charitable organisations. The Cypriot case is unique for the failure to provide welfare and other benefits, such as a land-settlement scheme, given the policies pursued in the metropole and in other colonial cases. In the UK (and indeed

CONCLUSION

the former settler colonies of Australia, NZ and Canada) welfare for men injured during the war and for the families of those who died was a standard. Other benefits were also offered. Several other colonial examples, namely Jamaica, also had well-considered schemes to help veterans and their families. In the Cyprus case the colonial government did not consider any welfare or benefits schemes, even though they had the power to do so. In forming the Mule Corps the political results that Clauson flagged on 26 June 1916 to the Colonial Secretary seemed to either fall by the wayside after the war or were considered automatic when it came to what the British perceived as the loyal peasant and rural labouring classes. Here the British did the unthinkable: they relinquished the ground to the nascent anti-colonial forces from both the nationalist right and the communist left, believing too much in the power of the British Empire and failing to understand that that the peasant and labouring classes had needs that required addressing. British imperialism needed to win over hearts and minds and the opportunity to win over veterans of such numbers was a missed opportunity.

British power did not merely apply to the men serving, but also to the mules. This study has gone a far way to address the history of mules in the Great War, especially in Salonica where they were pivotal. Without the Cypriot mules those behind the allied campaign in Salonica would have struggled to find enough mules, which were so pivotal for army transport logistics there. British imperial power was reflected in the passing of laws to procure mules more or less forcibly. In Salonica they were worked very hard. Yet it was soon realised that mules, no less than men, needed to be rested to reduce sickness and casualties, and extract more effective work out of them. This meant that there was a need to properly train and supervise the mule drivers.

Given the almost total, if not always effective, control that the British colonial and military authorities exerted over this entire enterprise, one can only wonder who were the real war asses. The title of this book says much about the story of the Cypriot Mule Corps. Serving the Empire is what the Cypriots did, loyalty is exactly what they showed, yet their service was reduced to a fading memory. This story has now been resurrected from the archival fragments available. Hopefully it will lead to memorials in Cyprus, England and Salonica to commemorate their service. Also one can only hope that their story will be prominent in an inclusive and holistic history of a reunified Cyprus as a historical example of Cypriot communities sharing life experiences, in this case during the first total war of the twentieth century.

Notes

1. Andrekos Varnava can be heard reciting the full poem on the Manchester University Press webpage (www.manchesteruniversitypress.co.uk/serving-the-empire-in-the-great-war-appendix/).
2. Several Cypriots served in the regular British army; see SA1/558/1919. Also about 100 served in the merchant marine; see Board of Trade (BT), NAUK, BT 351/1 files for individual entries of those in merchant marine.
3. The other comparable group were the Welsh in Patagonia, but Argentina had no jurisdictional links to the British Empire, the engagement here being informal. See Harris, 'British Informal Empire during the Great War', 103–17.

SELECT BIBLIOGRAPHY

This is an attempt at a comprehensive bibliography, but in any event all sources are listed in full the first time they are referenced in the endnotes of each chapter.

Primary sources

Official unpublished documents
Başbakanlık Osmanlı Arşivleri (Office of the Grand Vezir's Ottoman Archives)
DH.EUM.AYS
HR.MKT
I.HR

British Library
India Office (IO)
D'Abernon Papers, British Library, 48928, 113–14

Cypriot State Archives (SA1), Secretariat Archive (SA1), State Archives, Nicosia
SA1: 763/1915; 1267/1915; 1272/1915; 722/1916; 722/1916/1; 730/1916; 853/1916; 978/1916; 978/1916/2; 978/1916/3; 979/1916; 980/1916; 984/1916; 1024/1916; 1068/1916; 1083/1916/1; 1176/1916; 572/1917; 607/1917; 607/1917/A; 607/1917/B; 607/1917/C; 719/1917; 767/1917; 806/1917; 1010/1917; 1085/1917; 1143/1917; 591/1918; 625/1918; 680/1918; 777/1918/C; 902/1918; 909/1918; 1116/1918; 1183/1918; 558/1919; 863/1919; 910/1919; 957/1919; 1350/1919; 486/1920; 778/1920; 865/1920; 1058/1920; 1453/1920/1; 1453/1920/2; 1453/1920/3; 637/1921; 1223/1921; 1380/1921; 837/1923; 1558/1939

National Archives, Kew Gardens, London
Board of Trade (BT); Cabinet (CAB); Colonial Office (CO); Foreign and Commonwealth Office (FCO); Foreign Office (FO); War Office (WO); Special Operations Executive (HS)
Grey, Edward, Viscount Grey of Falloden; correspondence and papers, Reference: FO800/35–113, NRA 23627 Foreign Office (FO 800/106 folio 526)
Kitchener, Lord, correspondence and papers, Reference: PRO 30/57/77, PRO 30/57/1

Official published documents
Parliamentary papers
Annual Report for Cyprus, 1913–14, Cd. 7643, HMSO, London, October 1914.
Annual Report for Cyprus, 1914–15, Cd. 7662-56, HMSO, London, 1915.

SELECT BIBLIOGRAPHY

Annual Report for Cyprus, 1915–16, Cd. 8172-29, HMSO, London, 1916.
Annual Report for Cyprus, 1916–17, Cd. 8434-28, HMSO, London, 1917.
Annual Report for Cyprus, 1917–18, Cmd. 1–9, HMSO, London, 1919.
Annual Report for Cyprus, 1918–19, Cmd. 508–9, HMSO, London, 1919.
Annual Report for Cyprus, 1919–20, Cmd. 508–29, HMSO, London, 1920.
Bellamy, C.V., *The Main Roads of Cyprus*, Government Printing Office, Nicosia, 1903.
Cundall, Frank, *Jamaica's Part in the Great War, 1915–1918*, West India Commission, for the Institute of Jamaica, London, 1925.
Cyprus Gazette. British Colonial Government, Nicosia, Cyprus.
Cyprus: Horse, Mule and Donkey Breeding, 1901 and 1917, HMSO, London, 1917.
Cyprus: Report of the Commission Appointed to Enquire into the Extent, Causes and Effects of Indebtedness in the Island, Government Printing Office, Nicosia, 1918.
The Cyprus Law Reports: Cases Determined by the Supreme Court of Cyprus on Appeal from the Daavi Courts and District Courts, Nicosia, Cyprus, 1960.
Cyprus Census: Report on the Census of Cyprus 1881, by Frederick W. Barry, Superintendent of the Census, C.-4264, HMSO, London, 1884.
Cyprus Census: Report on the Census of Cyprus Taken 6th April 1891, by F.G. Glossop, Superintendent of the Census, Colonial Office, Mediterranean No. 39, HMSO, London, 1893.
Cyprus Census: Report and General Abstracts of the Census of 1901 Taken on the 1st April 1901, prepared by Alexander Mavrogordato, Superintendent of the Census, Government Printing Office, Nicosia, 1901.
Cyprus Census: Report and General Abstracts of the Census of 1911 Taken on the 2nd April 1911, prepared by, Superintendent of the Census, London, 1912.
Cyprus Census: Report and General Abstracts of the Census of 1921 Taken on the 24th April 1921, prepared by C.H. Hart-Davis, Superintendent of the Census, London, 1922.
Drought in Cyprus, Cmd. 1434, London, 1903.
FO, Historical Section, Cyprus, Handbook No. 65, London, HMSO, 1920.
General Staff, WO, *Military Report and General Information Concerning the Island of Cyprus*, London, 1907.
General Staff, WO, *Military Report and General Information Concerning the Island of Cyprus*, London, 1913.
General Staff, WO, *Military Report and General Information Concerning the Island of Cyprus*, London, 1936.
Hansard, House of Commons.
Heidenstam, F.C., *Leprosy in Cyprus*, C.-5980, HMSO, London, 1890.
Hopton, Reginald E., *The Campaign against Venereal Disease in Cyprus: Review of the First Year's Work*, Government Printing Office, Nicosia, 1929.
India's Contribution to the Great War, Government of India, Calcutta, 1923.
Kareklas, M.C., *The Criminal Activities of the Hassanpoulia*, Government Printing Office, Nicosia, 1938.

SELECT BIBLIOGRAPHY

Lukach, Harry Charles, and Douglas James Jardine, *The Handbook of Cyprus*, Edward Stanford, London, 1913.
Luke, Harry Charles, and Douglas James Jardine, *The Handbook of Cyprus*, Macmillan, London, 1920.
Report on the Census of Cyprus, 1881, C. 4264, London, 1884.
Storrs, Sir Ronald, *A Chronology of Cyprus*, Government Printing Office, Nicosia, 1930.
Surridge, B.J., *A Survey of Rural Life in Cyprus*, Government Printing Office, Nicosia, 1930.
Tyser, Sir Charles R., *Cyprus: Extract from the Annual Report of the Chief Justice Sir Charles Tyser for the Year 1913–14*, Government Printing Office, Nicosia, 1914.
The War Dead of the British Commonwealth and Empire: The Register of the Names of Those Who Fell in the 1939–1945 War and Are Buried in Cemeteries in Syria, Turkey and Cyprus, Commonwealth War Graves Commission, Maidenhead, 1959.

Unofficial published primary sources

Newspapers
Eleutheria, Nicosia
The Argus, Melbourne
The Sydney Morning Herald, Sydney
The Times, London
Illustrated London News
Various other Cypriot newspapers were sifted through for references.

Books

Alexander, Maj. H.M., *On Two Fronts*, New York: E.P. Dutton, 1917.
Baker, Sir Samuel W., *Cyprus as I Saw it in 1879*, Macmillan, London 1879 (repr. IndyPublish, Virginia, 2001).
Beadon, Colonel R.H., *The Royal Army Service Corps: A History of Transport and Supply in the British Army*, II, Cambridge University Press, 1931.
Burr, Malcolm, *Slouch Hat*, George Allen & Unwin, London, 1935.
Dawnay, G.C., *Campaigns: Zulu 1879, Egypt 1882, Suakim 1885: Being the Private Journal of Guy C. Dawnay*, Ken Trotman, Cambridge, 1989.
Falls, C., *Military Operations – Macedonia*, I, HMSO, London, 1933.
Fisher, Stanley, *The Statute Laws of Cyprus, 1878–1923*, I–II, Waterlow & Sons, London, 1923.
Galtrey, Captain Sidney, *The Horse and the War*, Country Life, London, 1918.
Grivas, George, *The Memoirs of General Grivas*, ed. Charles Foley, Longmans, London 1964.
Haggard, Rider D., *A Winter Pilgrimage in Palestine, Italy and Cyprus*, Longman, London 1901.
Lake, Harold, *In Salonica with Our Army*, Andrew Melrose, London, 1917.
Lanitis, Nicholas Constantine, *Rural Indebtedness and Agricultural Co-operation in Cyprus*, Limassol 1945 (revised, Proodos, Limassol 1992).

SELECT BIBLIOGRAPHY

Lucas, Sir Charles, *The Empire at War*, V, Royal Colonial Institute, Oxford University Press, 1926.
Mann, A.J., *The Salonica Front*, A.&C. Black, London, 1920.
Merewether, J.W.B., and Frederick Smith, *The Indian Corps in France*, William Clowes & Sons, London, 1917.
Owen, H. Collinson, *Salonica and After: The Sideshow that Ended the War*, Hodder and Stoughton, London, 1919.
Price, G. Ward, *The Story of the Salonica Army*, Hodder and Stoughton, London, 1918.
Royle, Charles, *The Egyptian Campaigns 1882 to 1885*, London, 1900.
Seligman, V.J., *Macedonian Musings*, George Allen & Unwin, London, 1918.
Seligman, V.J., *The Salonica Side-Show*, George Allen & Unwin, London, 1919.
Sinclair, Hugh, *Camp and Society*, London, 1926.
Studholme, John, *New Zealand Expeditionary Force*, W.A.G. Skinner, Wellington, 1928.
Villari, Luigi, *The Macedonian Campaign*, T. Fisher Unwin, London, 1922.
Vogt, Lieut.-Colonel Hermann, *The Egyptian War of 1882*, Kegan Paul, London, 1883.
Weldon, Captain L.B., *'Hard Lying': Eastern Mediterranean, 1914–1919*, Herbert Jenkins, London, 1925.

Articles and book chapters

Abraham, Phineas S., 'Remarks on Leprosy in the British Empire', *The British Medical Journal*, 13 November 1897, 1409–14.
Biddulph, Robert, 'Cyprus', *Proceedings of the Royal Geographical Society and Monthly Record of Geography*, 11, 1889, 707–19.
Gordon-Cumming, C.F., 'The Locust War in Cyprus', *Nineteenth Century*, 14, 1883, 306, 309–16.
Hake, G.G., 'Cyprus since the British Occupation', *Journal of the Society of Arts*, 1886, 788–97.
Michell, Roland L.N., 'A Muslim-Christian Sect in Cyprus', *The Nineteenth Century and After*, 63, May 1908, 751–62.
Murray, Sir Archibald, 'Egyptian Labour Corps, January 1916–June 1917', appendix F in *Sir Archibald Murrays Despatches*, J.M. Dent, London, 1920, 206–16.

Secondary sources

Monographs and edited volumes

Abington, Anthony, *For the Sake of Example Capital Courts-Martial, 1914–1920*, St Martin's Press, New York, 1983.
Baker, Richard St Barbe, *Horse Sense: Horses in War and Peace*, St Paul, London, 1962.
Ballhatchet, Kenneth, *Race, Sex and Class under the Raj: Imperial Attitudes and Policies and their Critics, 1793–1905*, Weidenfeld and Nicolson, London, 1980.

SELECT BIBLIOGRAPHY

Banerjee, Sukanya, *Becoming Imperial Citizens: Indians in the Late-Victorian Empire*, Duke University Press, Durham, NC, 2010.
Bhabha, Homi, *The Location of Culture*, Routledge, London, 2008.
Bourke, Joanna, *Dismembering the Male: Men's Bodies, Britain, and the Great War*, University of Chicago Press, 1996.
Brown, Antony, *Red for Remembrance: The British Legion, 1921–1971*, Heinemann, London, 1971.
Brugger, Suzanne, *Australians and Egypt, 1914–1919*, Melbourne University Press, 1980.
Bryant, Rebecca, *Imagining the Modern: The Cultures of Nationalism in Cyprus*, I.B. Taurus, London, 2004.
Butler, Simon, *The War Horses: The Tragic Fate of a Million Horses Sacrificed in the First World War*, Halsgrove, Wellington, 2011.
Chakrabarty, Dipesh, *Habitations of Modernity: Essays in the Wake of Subaltern Studies*, University of Chicago Press, 2002.
Chamberlin, J. Edward, *Horse: How the Horse Has Shaped Civilizations*, A.A. Knopf, Toronto, 2006.
Codrington, Geoffrey R., *The Territorial Army*, Sifton Praed, London, 1938.
Corns, Cathryn, and John Hughes-Wilson, *Blindfold and Alone: British Military Executions in the Great War*, Cassell Military, London, 2001.
Corrigan, Gordon, *Sepoys in the Trenches*, Spellmont, Stroud, 2006.
Crawshaw, Nancy, *The Cyprus Revolt*, George Allen & Unwin, London, 1978.
Criss, Nur Bilge, *Istanbul under Allied Occupation, 1918–1923*, Brill, Leiden, 1999.
Daly, M.W., and Carl F. Petry, *The Cambridge History of Egypt*, Cambridge University Press, New York, 1998.
Damousi, Joy, *The Labour of Loss*, Cambridge University Press, 1999, 65–102.
Denktash, Rauf, *The Cyprus Triangle*, Allen Unwin, London, 1982.
Dennis, Peter, *The Territorial Army, 1906–1940*, Royal Historical Society, Woodbridge, Suffolk, 1987.
Doumanis, Nicolas, *Before the Nation*, Oxford University Press, 2013.
Durflinger, Serge, *Veterans with a Vision: Canada's War Blinded in Peace and War*, University of British Columbia Press, Vancouver, 2010.
Echenberg, Myron J., *Colonial Conscripts: The Tirailleurs Sénégalais in French West Africa, 1857–1960*, J. Curry, London, 1991.
Eliophotou, Christos, *Ο Πρώτος Παγκόσμιος Πόλεμος και η Προσφορά της Κύπρου* (The First World War and the participation of Cyprus), Nicosia, 1987.
Emsley, Clive, *Soldier, Sailor, Beggarman, Thief: Crime and the British Armed Services since 1914*, Oxford University Press, 2013.
French, David, *Fighting EOKA: The British Counter-Insurgency Campaign on Cyprus, 1955–1959*, Oxford University Press, 2015.
Fussell, Paul, *The Great War and Modern Memory*, Oxford University Press, London, 1975.
Gaffney, Angela, *Aftermath: Remembering the Great War in Wales*, University of Wales Press, Cardiff, 2000.

SELECT BIBLIOGRAPHY

Gazioglu, A.C., *The Turks of Cyprus: A Province of the Ottoman Empire 1571–1878*, Rustem, London, 1990.

Gazioglu, A.C., and M.A. Demirer, *Cyprus: The Island of Sustained Crisis*, CYREP, Nicosia, 1998.

Georghallides, George, *A Political and Administrative History of Cyprus*, Cyprus Research Centre, Nicosia, 1979.

Georghallides, George, *Cyprus and the Governorship of Sir Ronald Storrs: The Causes of the 1931 Crisis*, Cyprus Research Centre, Nicosia, 1985.

Gerber, David (ed.), *Disabled Veterans in History*, University of Michigan Press, Ann Arbor, 2012.

Gerolymatos, André, *The Balkan Wars: Conquest, Revolution, and Retribution from the Ottoman Era to the Twentieth Century and Beyond*, Basic Books, New York, 2002.

Gorman, Daniel, *Imperial Citizenship: Empire and the Question of Belonging*, Manchester University Press, 2006.

Hall, Richard C., *The Balkan Wars 1912–1913: Prelude to the First World War*, Routledge, London, 2000.

Harding, Brian, *Keeping Faith: The Royal British Legion*, Leo Cooper, London, 2001.

Hill, George, *A History of Cyprus*, IV, ed. Sir Harry Luke, Cambridge University Press, 1952.

Jenness, Diamond, *The Economics of Cyprus: A Survey to 1914*, McGill University Press, Montreal, 1962,

Jennings, R.C., *Christians and Muslims in Ottoman Cyprus and the Mediterranean World, 1571–1640*, New York University Press, 1992.

Johnson, David, *Executed at Dawn: British Firing Squads on the Western Front 1914–1918*, Gloucestershire Spellmount, Stroud, 2015.

Johnson, Paul Louis, *Horses of the German Army in World War II*, Schiffer Military History, Atglen, PA, 2006.

Kappae, Demetrios, *Τα Μοναστήρια της Κύπρου* (The monasteries of Cyprus), 3rd edition, author, Limassol, 1998.

Katsiaounis, Rolandos, *Labour, Society and Politics in Cyprus during the Second Half of the Nineteenth Century*, Cyprus Research Centre, Nicosia, 1996.

Katsiaounis, Rolandos, *Η Διασκεπτική, 1946–1948: Με Ανασκόπηση της Περιόδου, 1878–1945* (The consultative assembley, 1946–48: with a survey of the period, 1878–1945), Cyprus Research Centre, Nicosia, 2000.

Katsourides, Yiannos, *The History of the Communist Party in Cyprus: Colonialism, Class and the Cypriot Left*, I.B. Tauris, London, 2014.

Kaushik, Roy (ed.), *The Indian Army in the Two World Wars*, Brill, Leiden 2012.

Keser, Ulvi, *Kıbrıs 1914–1923: Fransız Ermeni kampları İngiliz esir kampları ve Atatürkçü Kıbrıs Türkü* (Cyprus 1914–1923: French Armenian Camps, British prisoner camps and Kemalist Cypriot Turks), Akdeniz Haber Ajansı Yayınları, Istanbul, 2001.

Keshishian, Kevork K., *Famagusta Town and District Cyprus*, Limassol 1985.

SELECT BIBLIOGRAPHY

The Co-operative Movement in Cyprus, Public Information Office, 2004.

Koudounaris, Aristedis, *Βιογραφικόν Λεξικόν Κυπρίων, 1800–1920* (Biographical lexicon of Cypriots, 1800–1920), Nicosia, 2001.

Kyrris, Costas, *Peaceful Co-existence in Cyprus under British Rule (1878–1959) and after Independence*, PIO, Nicosia, 1977.

Larsson, Marina, *Shattered ANZACS: Living with the Scars of War*, University of New South Wales Press, Sydney, 2009.

Leese, Peter, *Shell Shock: Traumatic Neurosis and the British Soldiers of the First World War*, Palgrave, New York, 2002.

Leon, George B., *Greece and the Great Powers, 1914–1917*, Institute for Balkan Studies, Thessaloniki, 1974.

Levine, Philippa, *Prostitution, Race, and Politics: Policing Venereal Disease in the British Empire*, Routledge, London, 2003.

Liava'a, Christine, *Qaravi na'i tavi* (They did their duty), Polygraphia, Auckland, 2009.

Lockwood, David, *The Indian Bourgeoisie*, I.B. Tauris, London, 2012.

Mansfield, Nicholas, *English Farmworkers and Local Patriotism, 1900–1930*, Ashgate, Aldershot, 2001.

Markides, Kyriacos C., *The Rise and Fall of the Cyprus Republic*, Yale University Press, London, 1977.

Mather, Jill, *War Horses: Hoof Prints in Time: Amazing True Stories of Heroic Australian Walers and New Zealand Horses 1914–1918*, Jill Mather, 2012.

Mayhew, Emily, *Wounded: From Battlefield to Blighty, 1914–1918*, Thorpe, Leicester, 2014.

McCartney, Helen, *Citizen Soldiers: The Liverpool Territorials in the First World War*, Cambridge University Press, 2005.

Meyer, Jessica, *Men of War: Masculinity and the First World War in Britain*, Palgrave Macmillan, London, 2009.

Michael, Michalis N., *Η Εκκλησία της Κύπρου κατά την οθωμανική περίοδο (1571–1878): Η σταδιακή συγκρότηση της σε θεσμό πολιτικής εξουσίας* (The Church of Cyprus during the Ottoman period (1571–1878): the gradual establishment of an institution of political power), Cyprus Research Centre, Nicosia, 2005.

Miles, Simon, *Anzac Memorial, Adelaide, South Australia: Remembering the Sacrifice of Those Who Fought in the Great War, 1914–1918*, Workskil Inc., Adelaide, 1995.

Moore, William, *The Thin Yellow Line*, Cooper, London, 1970.

Morgan, Tabitha, *Sweet and Bitter Island: A History of the British in Cyprus*, I.B. Tauris, London, 2010.

Morton-Jack, George, *The Indian Army on the Western Front*, Cambridge University Press, 2014.

Nevzat, Altay, *Nationalism amongst the Turks of Cyprus*, Oulu University Press, 2005.

Omissi, David, *Indian Voices of the Great War*, Macmillan, London, 1999.

Osborne, John Moreton, *The Voluntary Recruiting Movement in Britain, 1914–1916*, Garland, New York, 1982.

Palmer, Alan, *The Gardeners of Salonika*, Andre Deutshe, London, 1965.

SELECT BIBLIOGRAPHY

Papadakis, Yiannis, *Echoes From the Dead Zone: Across the Cyprus Divide*, I.B. Taurus, London, 2005.

Papadakis, Yiannis, Nicos Peristianis and Gisela Welz (eds), *Divided Cyprus: Modernity, History, and an Island in Conflict*, University of Indiana, Bloomington, 2006.

Papadopoullos, Theodore, *Δημώδη Κυπριακά Άσματα εξ Ανεκδότων Συλλογών του ΙΘ' Αιώνος* (Cypriot folk songs on unpublished collections of the nineteenth century), Nicosia, 1975.

Papapolyviou, Petros, *Η Κύπρος και οι Βαλκανικοί πόλεμοι: Συμβολή στην ιστορία του κυπριακού εθελοντισμού* (Cyprus and the Balkan Wars: contribution to the history of Cypriot volunteerism), Nicosia, 1997.

Papapolyviou, Petros (ed.), *Εμμανουήλ Μ. Εμμανουήλ, Ημερολόγιον ή Πολεμικαί Σελίδες: Το ημερολόγιο ενός Κύπριου εθελοντή του ελληνοβουλγαρικού πολέμου του 1913* (Emmanuel M. Emmanuel, diary or war pages: the diary of a Cypriot volunteer in the Greek–Bulgarian War of 1913), Germanos, Salonica, 1996.

Papapolyviou, Petros, (ed.), *Πολεμικά Ημερολόγια, επιστολές και ανταποκρίσεις Κυπρίων εθελοντών από την Ήπειρο και τη Μακεδονία του 1912–1913* (War diaries, letters and responses of Cypriot volunteers from Epirus and Macedonia 1912–1913), Nicosia, 1999.

Patrick, Richard A., *Political Geography and the Cyprus Conflict: 1963–1971*, University of Waterloo, 1976.

Pennell, Catriona, *A Kingdom United: Popular Responses to the Outbreak of the First World War in Britain and Ireland*, Oxford University Press, 2012.

Pointer, Margaret, *Tagi tote e loto haaku* (My heart is crying a little), University of the South Pacific, Suva, 2000.

Pugsley, Christopher, *On the Fringe of Hell: New Zealanders and Military Discipline in the First World War*, Hodder & Stoughton, Auckland, 1991.

Rappas, Alexis, *Cyprus in the Thirties: British Colonial Rule and the Roots of the Cyprus Conflict*, I.B. Tauris, London, 2014.

Reid, Fiona, *Broken Men: Shell Shock, Treatment and Recovery in Britain, 1914–1930*, Continuum, London, 2010.

Reznick, Jeffery S., *John Galsworthy and Disabled Soldiers of the Great War: With an Illustrated Selection of his Writings*, Manchester University Press, 2009.

Robb, George, *British Culture and the First World War*, Palgrave, London, 2002.

Robinson, Gavin, *Horses, People and Parliament in the English Civil War: Extracting Resources and Constructing Allegiance*, Ashgate, Farnham, 2012.

Smith, Richard, *Jamaican Volunteers in the First World War*, Manchester University Press, 2004.

Spyridakis, Constantine, *A Brief History of Cyprus*, Publications Dept. Greek Communal Chamber, Nicosia, 1963 (2nd edition, 1964).

Stanley, Peter, *Bad Characters: Sex, Crime, Mutiny, Murder and the Australian Imperial Force*, Sydney Pier, 2010.

SELECT BIBLIOGRAPHY

Stirling, John, and Ivor Lee, *No Labour, No Battle: Military Labour during the First World War*, Spellmount, Gloucestershire, 2009.
Summerskill, Michael, *China on the Western Front*, Michael Summerskill, London, 1982.
Thirgood, J.V., *Cyprus: A Chronicle of its Forests, Land, and People*, University of British Columbia Press, Vancouver, 1987.
Thomson, Alistair, *Anzac Memories: Living with the Legend*, Oxford University Press, 1994 (revised 2013).
Tinker, Hugh, *A New System of Slavery: The Export of Indian Labour Overseas 1820–1920*, Oxford University Press, London, 1974.
Todorova, Maria, *Imagining the Balkans*, Oxford University Press, 1997.
Varnava, Andrekos, *British Imperialism in Cyprus, 1878–1915: The Inconsequential Possession*, Manchester University Press, 2009.
Varnava, Andrekos (ed.), *Imperial Expectations and Realities: El Dorados, Utopias and Dystopias*, Manchester University Press, 2015.
Varnava, Andrekos, Nicholas Coureas and Marina Elia (eds), *The Minorities of Cyprus: Development Patterns and the Identity of the Internal-Exclusion*, Cambridge Scholars, Newcastle upon Tyne, 2009.
Varnava, Andrekos, and Hubert Faustmann (eds), *Reunifying Cyprus: The Annan Plan and Beyond*, I.B. Tauris, London, 2009.
Varnava, Andrekos, and Michalis N. Michael (eds), *The Archbishops of Cyprus in the Modern Age: The Changing Role of the Archbishop-Ethnarch, their Identities and Politics*, Cambridge Scholars, Newcastle upon Tyne, 2013.
Wakefield, Alan, and Simon Moody, *Under the Devil's Eye: The British Military Experience in Macedonia 1915–18*, Pen & Sword Military, Barnsley, 2011 (orig. 2004).
Walsh, Michael, and Andrekos Varnava (eds), *Australia and the Great War*, Melbourne University Press, 2016.
Watson, J.S.K., *Fighting Different Wars: Experience, Memory, and the First World War in Britain*, Cambridge University Press, 2004.
Watts, Martin, *The Jewish Legion and the First World War*, Palgrave Macmillan, New York, 2004.
Weber, Eugen, *Peasants into Frenchman: The Mobilization of Rural France, 1879–1914*, Stanford University Press, 1976.
Westlake, Ray, *Remembering the Great War in Gloucestershire & Hertfordshire*, Brewin Books, Studley, Warwickshire, 2002.
Winter, Jay, *Sites of Memory, Sites of Mourning: The Great War in European Cultural History*, Cambridge University Press, 1995.
Winter, Jay, *Remembering War: The Great War between Memory and History in the Twentieth Century*, Yale University Press, 2006.
Wootton, George, *The Official History of the British Legion*, Macdonald & Evans, London, 1956.
Ziino, Bart, *A Distant Grief: Australians, War Graves and the Great War*, University of Western Australia Press, Perth, 2007.

SELECT BIBLIOGRAPHY

Journal articles

Aimilianides, Achilles, 'Η Εξέλιξει του Δίκαιου των Μικτών Γάμων εν Κύπρω' ('The development of the Law of Mixed Marriages in Cyprus'), *Kypriakai Spoudai*, 2, 1938, 197–236.

Anderson, Julie, '"Jumpy Stump": Amputation and Trauma in the First World War', *First World War Studies*, 6(1), 2015, 9–19.

Asmussen, Jan, '"Dark Skinned Cypriots will not be Accepted!" Cypriots in the British Army, 1939–1945', in Hubert Faustmann and Nicos Peristianis (eds), *Britain in Cyprus: Colonialism and Post-Colonialism 1878–2006*, Bibliopolis, Mannheim, 20065, 167–85.

Bakic-Hayden, Milica, 'Nesting Orientalisms: The Case of Former Yugoslavia', *Slavic Review*, 54(4), 1995, 917–31.

Barr, Monika, 'Prosthesis for the Body and for the Soul: The Origins of Guide Dog Provision for Blind Veterans in Interwar Germany', *First World War Studies*, 6(1), 2015, 81–98.

Brumby, Alice, '"A painful and disagreeable position": Rediscovering Patient Narratives and Evaluating the difference between Policy and Experience for Institutionalised Veterans with Mental Disabilities, 1924–1931', *First World War Studies*, 6(1), 2015, 37–55.

Cassia, Paul Sant, 'Religion, Politics and Ethnicity in Cyprus during the Turkocratia (1571–1878)', *European Studies of Sociology*, 1986, 3–28.

Cicek, Kemal, 'Living Together: Muslim–Christian Relations in Eighteenth-Century Cyprus as Reflected by the Sharia Court Records', *Islam and Christian–Muslim Relations*, 4(1), 1993, 36–64.

Constantinou, Costas M., 'Aporias of Identity: Bicommunalism, Hybridity and the "Cyprus Problem"', *Cooperation and Conflict*, 42(3), 2007, 247–70.

Coureas, Nicholas, 'The Cypriot Reaction to the Establishment of the Latin Church: Resistance and Collaboration', *Sources Travaux Historiques*, 43–4, 1995, 75–84.

Dawkins, R.M., 'The Crypto-Christians of Turkey', *Byzantion*, 1933, 247–75.

Dunbar, G.S., 'The Forests of Cyprus under British Rule', *Scottish Geographical Magazine*, 1983, 111–20.

Durey, Michael, 'South London's "Age-Fudgers": Kitchener's Under-Age Volunteers', *The London Journal*, 40(2), 2015, 147–70.

Elkins, W.F., 'A Source of Black Nationalism in the Caribbean: The Revolt of the British West Indies Regiment at Taranto, Italy', *Science and Society*, 33(2), 1970, 99–103.

Evans, David, 'Tackling the "Hideous Scourge": The Creation of the Venereal Disease Treatment Centres in Early Twentieth-Century Britain', *Social History of Medicine*, 5(3), 413–33.

Fawcett, Brian C., 'The Chinese Labour Corps in France, 1917–1921', *Journal of the Hong Kong Branch of the Royal Asiatic Society*, 40, 2000, 33–111.

Gagen, Wendy Jane, 'Remastering the Body, Renegotiating Gender: Physical Disability and Masculinity during the First World War: the Case of J.B. Middlebrook', *European Review of History*, 14(4), 2007, 525–41.

SELECT BIBLIOGRAPHY

Giagoullis, K., 'Ο Χριστοφής τζε η Εμινέ' ('Christophis and Emine'), *Laographiki Kypros*, 23, 1972, 15–21.

Goldman, Danny, 'Famagusta's Historical Detention and Refugee Camps', *Journal of Cypriot Studies*, 11, 2005, 29–53.

Griffin, Nicholas J., 'Britain's Chinese Labor Corps in World War I', *Military Affairs*, 40(3), 1976, 102–8.

Harris, Trevor, 'British Informal Empire during the Great War: Welsh Identity and Loyalty in Argentina', *Itinerario*, 38(3), 2014, 103–17.

Heraclidou, Antigone, 'Cyprus's Non-military Contribution to the Allied War Effort during World War I', *The Round Table*, 103(2), 2014.

Jennings, Ronald C., 'The Locust Problem in Cyprus', *Bulletin of the School of Oriental and African Studies*, 1988, 281–313.

Joseph, C.L., 'The British West Indies Regiment, 1914–18', *Journal of Caribbean History*, 2, 1971, 94–124.

Kakridis, John, 'The Ancient Greeks and the Greeks of the War of Independence', *Balkan Studies*, 4(2), 1963, 251–64.

Katsiaounis, Rolandos, 'Η Κυπριακή Παροικία του Λονδίνου και το Αρχιεπισκοπικό Ζήτημα της Κύπρου, 1928–1936' (The Cypriot community of London and the Archiepiscopal question of Cyprus, 1928–1936), *Annual of the Centre for Scientific Research* (Nicosia), 22, 1996, 521–56.

Katsiaounis, Rolandos, 'Τα Πρώτα Βήματα της Επιτροπής Κυπριακής Αυτονομίας' (The first steps of the Committee for Cypriot Autonomy), *Annual of the Centre for Scientific Research* (Nicosia), 26, 2000, 263–87.

Khalidi, Omar, 'Ethnic Group Recruitment in the Indian Army: The Contrasting Cases of Sikhs, Muslims, Gurkhas and Others', *Pacific Affairs*, 74(4), 2001–2, 529–52.

Koller, Christian, 'The Recruitment of Colonial Troops in Africa and Asia and their Deployment in Europe during the First World War', *Immigrants and Minorities*, 26(1/2), 2008, 111–33.

Kowalsky, Meaghan, '"This Honourable Obligation": The King's National Roll Scheme for Disabled Ex-Servicemen 1915–1944', *European Review of History*, 14(4), 2007, 567–84.

Kubicek, Robert, 'Joseph Chamberlain, the Treasury and Imperial Development, 1895–1903', *The Canadian Historical Association*, 1965, 105–16.

Kyrris, Costas, 'The Role of Greeks in the Ottoman Administration of Cyprus', *Proceedings of the First International Conference on Cypriot Studies*, 3(A), 1973, 149–79.

Kyrris, Costas, 'Symbiotic Elements in the History of the Two Communities of Cyprus', *Kypriakos Logos*, 8, 1976, 243–82.

Lal, V., 'Review: Subaltern Studies and its Critics: Debates Over Indian History', *History and Theory*, 40(1), 2001, 135–48.

Manitakis, Nicolas, and Michalis N. Michael, 'Cypriot Emigration to the United States of America (1910 to 1930)', *Chronos*, 30, 2014, 99–143.

Mikhail, Alan, 'Unleashing the Beast: Animals, Energy, and the Economy of Labour in Ottoman Egypt', *The American Historical Review*, 118(2), 2013, 317–48.

SELECT BIBLIOGRAPHY

Morton-Jack, George, 'The Indian Army on the Western Front, 1914–1915: A Portrait of Collaboration', *War in History*, 13(3), 2006, 329–62.

Oakley, Robin, 'Cypriot Migration to Britain prior to World War II', *Journal of Ethnic and Migration Studies*, 15(3), 1989, 509–25.

Papadakis, Yiannis, 'The Politics of Memory and of Forgetting in Cyprus', *Journal of Mediterranean Studies*, 1993, 139–54.

Papadakis, Yiannis, 'Greek Cypriot Narratives of History and Collective Identity: Nationalism as a Contested Process', *American Ethnologist*, 25(3), 1998, 149–65.

Papadakis, Yiannis, 'Nation, Narrative and Commemoration: Political Ritual in Divided Cyprus', *History and Anthropology*, 14(3), 2003, 253–70.

Papadopoullos, Theodore, 'Εθναρχικός Ρόλος της Ορθοδόξου Ιεραρχίας' (Ethnarchic role of the Orthodox hierarchy), *Kypriakai Spoudai*, 35, 1971, 95–141.

Phillips, Gervase, 'Writing Horses into American Civil War History', *War in History*, 20(2), 2013, 160–81.

Phylaktis, Kate, 'Banking in a British Colony: Cyprus 1878–1959', *Business History*, 1987–8, 416–31.

Richards, Eric, 'How Did Poor People Emigrate from the British Isles to Australia in the Nineteenth Century?' *Journal of British Studies*, 32, July 1993, 250–79.

Roudometof, Victor, 'From Rum Millet to Greek Nation: Enlightenment, Secularisation, and National Identity in Ottoman Balkan Society, 1453–1821', *Journal of Modern Greek Studies*, 16(1), 1998, 11–48.

Salih, Karmal O., 'British Colonial Military Recruitment Police in the Southern Kordofan Region of Sudan, 1900–1945', *Middle Eastern Studies*, 41(2), 2005, 169–92.

Salvante, Martina, '"Thanks to the Great War the blind gets the recognition of his ability to act": The Rehabilitation of Blinded Servicemen in Florence', *First World War Studies*, 6(1), 2015, 21–35.

Savage, Donald C., and J. Forbes Munro, 'Carrier Corps Recruitment in the British East Africa Protectorate, 1914–1918', *Journal of African History*, 7(2), 1966, 313–42.

Singh, H., 'Caste, Class and Peasant Agency in Subaltern Studies Discourse: Revisionist Historiography, Elite Ideology', *Journal of Peasant Studies*, 30(1), 2002, 91–134.

Singha, Radhika, 'Finding Labor from India for the War in Iraq: The Jail Porter and Labor Corps, 1916–1920', *Comparative Studies in Society and History*, 39(2), 2007, 412–45.

Singleton, John, 'Britain's Military Use of Horses, 1914–1918', *Past & Present*, 139, May 1993, 178–203.

Solomos, John, and Stephen Woodhams, 'The Politics of Cypriot Migration to Britain', *Immigrants & Minorities*, 14(3), 1995, 231–56.

Sutton, Chris, 'Gauge, Battleground, Weapon: Celebrations in Cold War Cyprus, 1945–1955', *ex plus ultra*, 3, April 2012.

Towers, Bridget A., 'Health Education Policy 1916–1926: Venereal Disease and the Prophylaxis Dilemma', *Medical History*, 24, 1980, 70–87;

SELECT BIBLIOGRAPHY

Varnava, Andrekos, 'Punch and the British Occupation of Cyprus in 1878', *Byzantine and Modern Greek Studies*, 29(2), 2005, 167–86.
Varnava, Andrekos, 'Recreating Rural Britain and Maintaining Britishness in the Mediterranean: The Troodos Hill Station in Early British Cyprus', *The Cyprus Review*, 17(2), 2005, 47–80.
Varnava, Andrekos, '"Martial Races" in the Isle of Aphrodite', *Journal of Military History*, 74(4), 2010, 1047–67.
Varnava, Andrekos, 'Reinterpreting Macmillan's Cyprus Policy, 1957–1960', *The Cyprus Review*, 22(1), 2010, 79–106.
Varnava, Andrekos, 'The State of Cypriot Minorities: Cultural Diversity, Internal-Exclusion and the Cyprus "Problem"', *The Cyprus Review*, 22(2), 2010, 205–18.
Varnava, Andrekos, 'British Military Intelligence in Cyprus during the Great War', *War in History*, 19(3), 2012, 353–78.
Varnava, Andrekos, 'French and British Post-War Imperial Agendas and Forging an Armenian Homeland after the Genocide: The Formation of the *Légion d'Orient* in October 1916', *The Historical Journal*, 57(4), 2014, 997–1025.
Varnava, Andrekos, 'Imperialism First, the War Second: The British, an Armenian Legion, and Deliberations on Where to Attack the Ottoman Empire, November 1914–April 1915', *Historical Research*, 87(237), 2014, 533–55.
Varnava, Andrekos, 'Recruitment and Volunteerism for the Cypriot Mule Corps, 1916–1919', *Itinerario*, 38(3), 2014, 79–101.
Varnava, Andrekos, 'The Politics and Imperialism of Colonial and Foreign Volunteer Legions during the Great War: Comparing Proposals for Cypriot, Armenian and Jewish Legions', *War in History*, 22(3), 2015, 344–63.
Varnava, Andrekos, 'The Vagaries and Value of the Army Transport Mule in the British Army during the Great War', *Historical Research*, forthcoming.
Varnava, Andrekos, and Peter Clarke, 'Accounting in Cyprus during Late Ottoman and Early British Rule, 1840–1918', *The Cyprus Review*, 26(2), 2014, 33–55.

Book chapters in edited volumes

An, Ahmet, 'The Cypriot Armenian Minority and their Cultural Relationship with the Turkish Cypriots', in Andrekos Varnava, Nicholas Coureas and Marina Elia (eds), *The Minorities of Cyprus: Development Patterns and the Identity of the Internal-Exclusion*, Cambridge Scholars, Newcastle-upon-Tyne, 2009, 268–82.
Bailey, Paul J., 'From Shandong to Somme: Chinese Indentured Labour in France during World War I', in A.J. Kershen (ed.), *Language, Labour, and Migration*, Ashgate, Farnham, 2001, 79–96.
Bailey, Paul J., 'Semi-Colonialism and Cultural Interaction: Chinese Indentured Labor in World War One France and the Sino–French Connection', in Friederike Assandri and Dora Martins (eds), *From Early Tang Court Debates to China's Peaceful Rise*, Amsterdam University Press, 2009, 111–20.

SELECT BIBLIOGRAPHY

Bailey, Paul J. '"An Army of Workers": Chinese Indentured Labour in First World War France', in S. Das (ed.), *Race, Empire and First World War Writing*, Cambridge University Press, 2011, 35–52.

Hagen, Gwynnie, 'The Chinese Labour Corps', in Dominiek Dendooven and Piet Chielens (eds), *World War I*, Lanoo, Tielt, 2008, 136–44.

Kazamias, Georgios, 'Military Recruitment and Selection in a British Colony: The Cyprus Regiment 1939–1944', in E. Close, M. Tsianikas and G. Couvalis (eds), *Greek Research in Australia: Proceedings of the Sixth International Conference of Greek Studies*, Flinders University, June 2005, Flinders University Department of Languages, Adelaide, 333–42.

Kitromilides, Paschalis, 'From Coexistence to Confrontation: The Dynamics of Ethnic Conflict in Cyprus', in Michalis Attalides (ed.), *Cyprus Reviewed*, Nicosia, 1977, 35–70.

Kizilyurek, Niyazi, 'The Turkish Cypriot Upper Class and Question of Identity', in idem, *Turkish Cypriot Identity in Literature*, Fatal Press, London, 1990.

MacKillop, Andrew, 'For King and Country? The Highland Soldiers' Motivation and Identity', in S. Murdoch and A. MacKillop (eds), *Fighting for Identity: Scottish Military Experiences, 1550–1900*, Brill, Leiden, 2002, 185–212.

Michael, Michalis N., 'The Unchanging "Turkish Rule", the "Fair Ottoman Administration" and the Ottoman Period in the History of Cyprus', in Michalis Michael, Matthias Kappler and Eftihios Gavriel (eds), *Ottoman Cyprus: A Collection of Studies on History and Culture*, Harrassowitz Verlag, Wiesbaden, 2009, 9–24.

Peristiany, J.G., 'Honour and Shame in a Cypriot Highland Village', in J.G. Peristiany (ed.), *Honour and Shame: The Values of Mediterranean Society*, University of Chicago Press, 1966 (repr. Midway, 1974).

Papapolyviou, Petros, 'Ο κυπριακός εθελοντισμός στους πολέμους της Ελλάδας, 1866–1945' (Cypriot volunteerism in the wars of Greece, 1866–1945), in Andreas I. Voskos (ed.), *Κύπρος: Αγώνες ελευθερίας στην ελληνική ιστορία* (Cyprus: struggles for freedom in Greek history), Athens, 2010, 204–29.

Spivak, G.C., 'Can the Subaltern Speak?', in C. Nelson and L. Grossberg (eds), *Marxism and the Interpretation of Culture*, Macmillan, Basingstoke, 1988.

Varnava, Andrekos, '"Cyprus is of no use to anybody": The Pawn, 1878–1915', in Hubert Faustmann and Nicos Peristianis (eds), *Britain in Cyprus: Colonialism and Post-Colonialism 1878–2004*, Bibliopolis, Mannheim, 2006, 35–60.

Varnava, Andrekos, 'British and Greek Liberalism and Imperialism in the Long Nineteenth Century', in Matthew Fitzpatrick (ed.), *Liberal Imperialism in Europe in the Long Nineteenth Century*, Palgrave Macmillan, London, 2012, 219–40.

Varnava, Andrekos, 'Chrysostomos I, 1977–2006: Makarios III was "a Difficult Act to Follow"', in Andrekos Varnava and Michalis Michael (eds), *The Archbishops of Cyprus in the Modern Age: The Changing Role of the Archbishop-Ethnarch, their Identities and Politics*, Cambridge Scholars, Newcastle upon Tyne, 2013, 293–310.

SELECT BIBLIOGRAPHY

Varnava, Andrekos, 'Sophronios III, 1865–1900: The Last of the "Old" and the First of the "New" Archbishop-*Ethnarchs*?' in Andrekos Varnava and Michalis Michael (eds), *The Archbishops of Cyprus in the Modern Age: The Changing Role of the Archbishop-Ethnarch, their Identities and Politics*, Cambridge Scholars, Newcastle upon Tyne, 2013, 106–47.

Varnava, Andrekos, 'Cypriots Transforming their Identity during the Early British Period: From a Class, Religious and Regional Identity to a Hellenic Ethno-Nationalist Identity', in Michalis N. Michael, Tassos Anastassiades and Chantal Verdeil (eds), *Religious Communities and Modern Statehood: The Ottoman and Post-Ottoman World at the Age of Nationalism and Colonialism*, Klaus Schwarz Verlag, Berlin, 2015, 148–72.

Varnava, Andrekos, 'El Dorados, Utopias and Dystopias in Imperialism and Colonial Settlement', in Andrekos Varnava (ed.), *Imperial Expectations and Realities: El Dorados, Utopias and Dystopias*, Manchester University Press, 2015, 1–25.

Varnava, Andrekos, 'Famagusta during the Great War: From Backwater to Bustling', in Michael Walsh (ed.), *Famagusta: City of Empires, 1571–1960*, Cambridge Scholars, Newcastle upon Tyne, 2015, 91–111.

Varnava, Andrekos, and Michalis N. Michael, 'Archbishop-*Ethnarchs* since 1767', in Andrekos Varnava and Michalis Michael (eds), *The Archbishops of Cyprus in the Modern Age: The Changing Role of the Archbishop-Ethnarch, their Identities and Politics*, Cambridge Scholars, Newcastle upon Tyne, 2013, 1–16.

Varnava, Andrekos, and Irene Pophaides, 'Kyrillos II, 1909–16: The First Greek Nationalist and *Enosist*', in Andrekos Varnava and Michalis Michael (eds), *The Archbishops of Cyprus in the Modern Age: The Changing Role of the Archbishop-Ethnarch, their Identities and Politics*, Cambridge Scholars, Newcastle upon Tyne, 2013, 148–76.

Varnava, Andrekos, and Christalla Yakinthou, 'Cyprus: Political Modernity and Structures of Democracy in a Divided Island', in John Loughlin, Frank Hendriks and Anders Lidström (eds), *The Oxford Handbook of Local and Regional Democracy in Europe*, Oxford University Press, 2011, 455–77.

INDEX

Abdul Hamid II 34
Abyssinian Campaign 131
Admiralty 44
Africa/Africans 9, 13, 14, 18, 24, 68, 170, 212
Agia Marina, Nicosia 85
Agia Phyla, Limassol 170, 173
Agia Varvara, Nicosia 174
Agii Omologites, Nicosia 125, 201
Agios Amvrosios, Kyrenia 166
Agios Andronicos, Karpas 196
Agios Athanasios, Limassol 196
Agios Elias, Karpas 149
Agios Georgios, Famagusta 172
Agios Loukas, Famagusta 126
Agios Photi, Paphos 184
Agios Theodoros, Karpas 77
Agios Theodoros, Larnaca 126, 171, 196
Aglanja, Nicosia 201
Agrarian Party 217
Akanthou, Famagusta 39, 145
Akapnou, Limassol 202
AKEL (Progressive Party of Working People) 212
Akrotiri, Limassol 34
Albania 58
Alektora, Limassol 81
Alexandria (place and Patriarchate) 3, 32, 148, 186, 188, 200-1
Altham, E.A. 152
American Civil War 18
Anadiou, Paphos 195
Anatolia 45
Anavargos, Paphos 183
Anglo-Boer War 65, 68, 71
Anglo-Turkish (or Cyprus) Convention 35
Antalya 46, 50
anti-colonialism 7, 15, 211, 213
Antioch 32
Anzacs 13, 24, 219
Aphania, Famagusta 197

Arabs/Arabic 91
Argaka, Nicosia 196
Argentina 131
Argostoli 44
Armenia 4, 46, 90, 91, 153, 168, 218
Arminou, Paphos 185
Armistice at Mudros (1918) 3
Arnadi, Famagusta 125
Asgata, Limassol 184
Asia Minor *see* Anatolia
Asomatos, Kyrenia 85
Aspri, Costis 80
Asquith, Herbert Henry 44
Astromeritis, Nicosia 195
Athens 33, 44, 50, 59, 60, 64, 90, 148, 165, 193, 194, 200
Athienou, Larnaca 40, 195-6
Atlee, Clement 194
Australia 11, 15-16, 24, 37, 180-1, 199, 201-2, 210-11, 218-9, 229
Australian Imperial Force 15, 202
Austria/Austria-Hungary 43

Balkan Wars 130, 137
Balkanisation 23
Bank of Cyprus 42
Battershill, William 197
Baxendale, Francis 118-19, 121, 123, 124, 140, 148-53
Bayly, George Croker 144-9
Beaconsfield, Lord (Benjamin Disraeli) 34-5
Beadon, R.H. 11-12
Bearne, Lewis Collingwood 61-2
Bermuda 13, 38
Berri (South Australia) 202
Bevan, J.A. 197-8
Biddulph, Sir Robert 65
Black Sea 5, 138, 187, 190, 199, 219
Black Sea Force 190
Bolton, Wilfred Nash 80, 107, 123, 152

INDEX

Bonar Law, Andrew 61, 63, 79–80, 109
Bosnia and Herzegovina 66
Bostancı 3, 138, 171, 175, 200
Bovill, A.K. 82
Boulter, E.C. 164
Bowring, Walter Andrew 118–24, 175–6
British Empire 2, 7–8, 11, 18, 20–1 23–4, 37–8, 43, 49, 58, 77, 103, 176, 213, 220, 227, 229
British Legion 7, 16, 180, 191, 197–9, 214
British Social Hygiene Council 144
British Victory Medal 180, 199, 202
British War Medal 83, 180, 199
British War Memorials Committee 1
British West Indies Regiment 9, 13
Bulgaria 44, 58, 99, 137, 186
Burr, Malcolm 12

Cade, C. S. 82, 120
Cairo 152, 164
camels 135
Canada 15, 131, 211, 219, 229
Catholic Church 32
Central Powers 42, 44, 210, 214
Cephalonia 44
Chamberlain, Joseph 38
China/Chinese 13–14, 18, 131
Churchill, Winston 43–4, 176, 190, 215–16
Cilicia 45–6
Clarke, Travers 61, 92, 94, 97
Clauson, John 44–7, 60–4, 71, 79–80, 94–5, 98–9, 109, 113–7, 119, 122, 124–6, 137, 144–6, 151–3, 162–4, 168–9, 173, 175, 185, 195, 229
Colonial Office 35, 49, 61–4, 66–8, 94, 110, 120, 193, 199, 215–16
Committee of Union and Progress/ Young Turks 42, 50
Commonwealth War Graves Commission 213
communism/Bolsheviks 8, 136, 211, 212, 217–18, 229
Communist Party of Cyprus (CPC) 217

Condon, J.P.B. 222
Constantine I, King of Greece 44, 49, 58, 61, 213, 221
Constantinides, C. 80
Constantinople/Istanbul xi, 1–3, 5–6, 9–10, 17, 32, 66, 68, 72, 96, 133, 136, 138, 161–2, 165–6, 169–75, 184–5, 187–8, 200, 202, 219
Contagious Diseases Act (1864) 151, 153
Cooperative Credit Societies Law (1914) 42
Corfu 44
Costa, Loizo 161, 173
Crete 43, 98, 212, 219
Crimean War/Crimean War Loan 35, 65, 131
Cypriot Mule Corps v, xii, 3–7, 9–13, 17, 19, 21, 24–5, 31, 34, 39–40, 42, 50–2, 58–9, 61, 63, 71, 73, 78, 103, 107, 110, 117, 130, 150, 161–3, 175, 176, 180–1, 186, 193, 197, 200, 203, 211–13, 216–19, 221–3, 227, 229
  allotment Scheme 2–3, 73, 101, 107, 118, 121, 123–6, 176, 228
  crime 7, 15, 151, 161, 166–8, 170–4, 176
  death 3–4, 16
  desertion 7, 161–2, 164–8, 170
  disability/invalids 3, 16, 110, 182, 186, 189, 194, 198, 202, 228
  foremen 4, 89–91, 98–9, 101, 109–10, 118, 140
  grieving 181
  interpreters 1, 3–4, 89–92, 95, 98–9
  meningitis 125–6
  muleteers xii, 1, 3–7, 11–13, 16, 18, 20, 22, 24, 47, 51–2, 58–65, 69–73, 77–9, 81, 83–4, 89, 91–2, 94–9, 101–3, 107, 109–26, 130–1, 133, 135–40, 144–51, 153–5, 161–2, 164, 166–7, 169–76, 182, 184, 189, 191–2, 197–8, 210, 212–4, 218–23, 227–8
  venereal disease 3, 7, 15, 73, 97, 116, 130, 138–40, 144–55, 173, 228

[247]

INDEX

Cypriot Mule Corps (*cont.*)
  veterans 2–3, 5–10, 14–16, 19, 65, 110, 173, 180–1, 186, 194–6, 198–203, 211, 213–14, 217–18, 228–9
Cypriot Orthodox Church 32, 51
Cypriot Regiment (Second World War) 10, 198, 210, 212, 219
Cypriots
  Armenians 46, 85–7, 90–1, 168, 218
  Eastern Orthodox Christians 23, 32–5, 50–1, 61, 71, 85–91, 141, 154, 165, 168, 190, 214, 218
  Latins 90–1, 165, 218
  Maronites 85–7, 90, 141, 154, 186, 218
  Muslims 5, 7, 11, 20, 32, 36, 46, 49–51, 65, 71, 85–7, 90–2, 153, 165, 211–4, 217–8

De Robeck, John 131
Demetriou, Ioannis 80
Denikin, Anton 136
Devonshire, Duke 216
Dicomo, Kyrenia 89
Dodecanese 219
Doiran 59
donkeys 59, 64, 66, 70, 80–1, 98, 135

Eassie, F. 132–6
East Africa Protectorate 18
Eastern Mediterranean Special Intelligence Bureau 45
Economides, Ioannis 41–2
Ecumenical Patriarchate 32–3
Egypt/Egyptians 3, 12–13, 17–18, 20, 35, 38, 43, 45, 47, 49, 60–2, 64–5, 68, 70, 80, 83, 98, 119–21, 125–6, 131–2, 136, 139, 151–2, 181, 199–200, 213, 215, 219, 222
Egyptforce 61–2, 81, 96
Egyptian Campaigns (1882–85) 65, 131
El Dorado 35
Elizabeth II, Queen 220
Elliot, Sir Francis 60
English Civil Wars 18

Enosis (union) 7, 36, 44, 50, 71, 131, 211–17, 220–1
EOKA (National Organisation of Cypriot Fighters) 180, 220, 221
Europeana (website) 5, 137, 220, 222
Ezard, C.N. 193

Fallias, Paphos 150
Famagusta (Old Town, Varosha, District and Harbour) 35–40, 46, 123–6, 186
Fenn, William 175
Fiji/Fijians 14
Fini, Limassol 83
First World War 5, 241
Fleury, Arthur Marlay 183, 186
Foreign Office 131, 194
France/French 3, 17, 21, 24, 43–7, 58, 60, 65, 98, 138–9, 150–1, 199, 212, 220
French, John 43
French West Africa 24

Gallipoli 17, 44–5, 58, 200, 210
Galtrey, Sidney 18
Gastria, Karpas 125
George, King of Greece 65
Georges-Picot, Francois 45
Georgiades, C.M. 80
Georgiou, Stavros 9, 199
Germany/German 13, 31, 44, 58, 212–13, 219
Gibraltar 38
Goodchild, T.P. 80, 82–3
Goold-Adams, Hamilton 45
Gorlie, H.V. 124
Goudi, Paphos 172
Gouri, Nicosia 171
Government Savings Bank Law (1900) 41
Great Depression 8, 194, 214
Great War *see* First World War
Greco–Serbian Treaty (1912) 44
Greece/Greek 6–7, 10–14, 20–1, 23, 33–7, 41–3, 49, 50–1, 58, 60–1, 63, 65, 87, 91–2, 101, 133, 138, 145, 147, 188, 193, 199–200, 211–18, 220–3
Greek Labour Corps 188

[248]

INDEX

Greenwood, Thomas James 183
Grey, Sir Edward 43–4
Gunnis, Rupert 197
Gypsou, Famagusta 198, 201

Hader Pasha 5
Haji Christodoulou, Agathocles 16, 186, 189–92
Haji Georji, Ioannis 133
Haji Philipou, Georgos 117
Harris, P.J. 135
Hart-Davis, Charles Henry 185
Haynes Smith, William 66–8
Heilbron, I. M. 92
Hirokitia, Larnaca 125

Imperial Ottoman Bank 148
India/British India 13, 35, 65–8, 82–3, 131, 133, 211, 214, 220
Indiana 201
Ionian Islands 34, 44
Ireland/Irish 3, 19, 59, 131–2, 222
Italy/Italians 3, 12–13, 17, 22, 41, 37, 43, 47, 67–8, 91, 138, 193, 212
Islam 23

Jamaica/Jamaicans 9, 14–15, 25, 78–9, 180–1, 213–14, 229
Jerusalem (place and Patriarchate) 32, 152
Jerusalem Theological School 33
Jesus Christ 1
Jones, Arthur Creech 193

Kadıköy 3, 138
Kadythada, Nicosia 195
Kaimakli, Nicosia 39–40
Kalavassos, Larnaca 149
Kalo Horio, Nicosia 196
Kalopanayiotis, Nicosia 117
Kambili, Kyrenia 87
Kaminarka, Limssol 198
Karasouli Cemetery 182
Karavas, Kyrenia 40, 89, 185, 193, 215
Kareklas, M.C. 80
Karmi, Kyrenia 170
Karpas Peninsula/Karpasia 36, 39–40, 77, 125, 182, 196

Karpasha, Kyrenia 85, 185
Kathikas, Paphos 137
Kato Drys, Larnaca 34
Kilinia, Paphos 200
Kimberley, Lord 65
King's National Roll Scheme 15
Kitchener, Lord 67
Knapp, Captain 68, 82
Kochino-chorka (red villages) 36
Kojambashi, Stavros Petrou 186, 192–3
Komi Kebir, Karpas 163, 200
Komodromou, Nicholas v, xii, 137
Kormakitis, Kyrenia 85
Kuchuk, Dr Fazil 83
Kyrenia (place & Harbour) 34, 37, 40, 71, 80, 85, 87, 89, 123, 173, 185, 202, 214–15
Kyrillos (Papadopoulos), Bishop and Archbishop of Cyprus 34
Kyrillos (Vasiliou), Bishop and Archbishop of Cyprus 71, 187, 215–16
Kythrea, Nicosia 70

labouring classes 7, 14, 21, 24, 33, 34, 49–50, 71, 98, 101, 103, 181, 211–13, 216–17, 220, 222, 227, 229
Lacadamia 80, 166
Lania, Limassol 147
Lanitis, N. K. 36
Lansdowne, Lord 67
Lapithos, Kyrenia 36, 40, 80, 89, 215
Larnaca (place and roadstead) 34, 37, 40, 46, 50, 65, 66–7, 70, 80, 117, 123–6, 133, 144–50, 162, 166, 171–3, 195–6, 200
Larnaca tis Lapithou, Kyrenia 173
Latin America 14, 22
Lawson, H.B. 97, 115
Lefka, Nicosia 36, 102, 183
Lefkoniko, Famagusta 39, 42, 83
Legion d'Orient/Armenian Legion 4, 45–6, 153
Legislative Council (Cyprus) 35, 191, 214–16, 220
Leonariso, Karpas 125, 195
Lethbridge, J.G.B. 119–23, 139

INDEX

Limassol (place and roadstead) 34, 36–7, 40, 45, 65, 80, 83, 89, 101, 107, 123–5, 139, 147, 152, 170, 172–4, 183–5, 188–9, 193, 196–8, 202
Linou, Nicosia 125
Lithrangomi, Karpas 170
Lithrodonta, Nicosia 137
Livadia, Larnaca 133
Liverpool/Liverpudlians 4, 13, 19, 21, 25
Lloyd George, David 43–4, 131
Locusts 32, 36–7, 47
Long, Arthur 47, 60, 62–3, 90, 92, 94–8, 99, 101–3, 111–13, 117–18, 122, 139–40
Long, Walter 94
Lourougina, Larnaca 40
Lucas, Charles Prestwood 49, 50
Lukach, Harry (Sir Harry Luke) 125

Macedonia/Macedonians 1, 3–4, 6, 12–13, 16–17, 44, 47, 58, 60–1, 63, 70, 78, 85, 89–91, 96–7, 99, 112, 130, 132, 135–6, 161, 164, 199
Macedonian Campaign 10, 16–17
McLaughlan, H. 80
Mahon, Bryan 59
Makarios II, Bishop of Kyrenia 71, 214,
malaria/malarial fever 37, 59, 136, 139
Malounda, Nicosia 185
Malta/Maltese 11, 13, 38, 43, 45, 91, 216
Maltepe 171, 174–5
Maltezos, Yannakos 80
Mann, A.J. 11
Marathovouno, Famagusta 39
Maroni, Larnaca 126
Melbourne 201, 219
Mesaoria 36, 38
Mesopotamia 45, 60
Metaxakis, Bishop of Kitium 50
Michaelides, Michael John 124
Middle East 45–6, 212, 220
Millia, Famagusta 126
Miliou, Paphos 170

Milne, George 60–1, 78, 92, 94, 113–17, 124, 132, 135, 137, 139, 146, 168–9, 173, 175
Milner, Lord 52, 81, 181
Minneapolis 201
Monastir 58
Montis, Theodoulos 124
Morphou, Nicosia 36, 83, 102, 125
Morpurgo, Michael 17
Mosfiloti, Larnaca 34
Mudros 3, 17
mules 1–3, 6–7, 10, 12, 17–18, 47, 58–70, 73, 78–83, 97–8, 130–38, 154, 164, 183, 210, 214, 227, 229
Muleteer Recruiting and Supply Purchasing Staff 71, 78, 79, 131
Myrtou, Kyrenia 34

nationalism 2, 7–8, 13–14, 20–2, 24, 34–6, 41, 50–1, 87, 189, 211–13, 216–18, 220, 222–3, 229
New Zealand 15, 24, 211
Newcastle (New South Wales) 202
Newfoundland 38
Newman, Canon 164
New York 201
Nicosia xi-xii, 4, 37–42, 65, 69, 70–1, 80, 82–5, 90, 102, 117, 119–20, 122–3, 125, 137, 139, 164, 170–2, 174, 185, 188–92, 195–6, 198, 200–1, 212, 215, 217

O'Brian, B.J. 197
Ohio 201
Omodos, Limassol 83
Omorphita, Nicosia 200
Operation Compass (Second World War) 212
Orfi Effendi, M. 123
Orientalism 23, 103
Orr, Charles William 43, 107, 118–23, 125, 145, 175
Ottoman Empire 35, 43–4, 50, 52, 65, 87, 200, 214–15

Palaeometocho, Nicosia 192–3
Paleokythro, Nicosia 163
Palaiochorio, Nicosia 40
Palestine 37, 45–6

INDEX

Pals battalions 19
Pan-Hellenic identity 2
Pan-Islamic identity 2
Panaou, Haris 3, 186, 188
Panayi, Yiannis 186–9
Papadopoulos, Nicolakis 80
Papapetrou, George C. 123–4
Paphos 9, 36–7, 40, 66, 80, 89, 101, 120, 123, 125, 137, 139, 150, 170, 172, 182–5, 188–9, 191, 195–6, 200
Paralimni, Famagusta 163
Parry, J.E. 122–3
Pavlou, Kyriacos 133, 195
Pearson, Sir Arthur 189
peasants/peasantry 2, 4, 6–8, 12–14, 16, 19, 21–2, 24, 33–4, 36, 42, 49–52, 71, 77–80, 88, 92, 98, 101–3, 126, 168, 181, 194–5, 211–18, 220, 222, 227, 229
Pennsylvania 201
Peristeronopigi, Famagusta 125
Pervolia, Larnaca 125
Platres, Limassol 80, 83, 197
Poitou 66
Polis, Kyrenia 139
Polistipos, Nicosia 189
Polymedia 40, 45, 65
Port Said 45
Prastio, Famagusta 197
Provisional Powers Law (1919) 215
Provisional Powers Amendment Law (1920)
Pyrgo, Tyllirias 102, 139
Pyrgos, N.K. 80

Queripel, A.E. 65–7

Ramadan 138
Red Cross 138, 182, 186–7
Ripon, Lord 37
Rizokarpaso 3, 39, 130, 163, 186–7
Royal Geographical Society 219
Ruad Island 46
Russia 35, 68, 218
Russo-Ottoman War (1877–78) 35
Rycroft, William Henry 78, 94–6, 101, 112, 135, 139

St Dunstans 186, 189
St Minas Monastery 34
St Nicholas of the Cats Monastery 34
St Panteleimonas Monastery 34
St Thekla Monastery 34
Salaminou, Paphos 163
Salamis, Famagusta 126
Salisbury, Lord 34
Salonica 1–3, 6, 9, 11–12, 15–18, 47–8, 59–64, 70–2, 78, 80, 81, 83, 94–9, 101, 103, 107, 110–2, 116–20, 121–6, 130–3, 136–7, 139–40, 144, 146–9, 150–1, 155, 161–2, 164–5, 169–171, 173, 176, 184, 188–9, 192–3, 195, 199, 200, 202, 218–19, 229
Sandham Memorial Chapel 1
Sarrail, Maurice 58
Savvides, Christos 217
Savvides, Evagoras 102, 213
Scottish Highlanders 20
Second World War 2, 198, 210
Seligman, V.J. 11
Sendall, Walter 37, 38
Serbia 12–13, 44, 58–9, 60–1, 81
Seychelles 13, 38, 220
Shevket Effendi, Hassan 123
Sims-Marshall, G. 187
Sinasian, Philip A. 124
Sinclair, Hugh 65
Sisman, L. 12, 47, 62–3, 94–6, 98–9, 101–3, 112, 117–19, 120–2, 124–5, 140, 147, 163–4, 183, 186–7, 189
Smol 1
Smyrna/Izmir 33
Sophronios III, Archbishop of Cyprus 33
Sotira, Limassol 174
South Africa 13, 68
South Australia 202
Spathariko, Famagusta 125
Spencer, Sir Stanley 1, 8
Spielberg, Steven 17
Spyridakis, Constantine 221
Stampalia (Astropalia) 35
Stavros tis Psokas Forest Station 191
Stevenson, Malcolm 81, 175
Stevenson, Mabel Laffan 220

INDEX

Storrs, Sir Ronald 10, 189, 191, 210
Strovolos, Nicosia 171
Struma River 12, 58, 201
subaltern/subaltern studies 3, 6, 10, 19, 22, 24, 79, 103, 126
Sudan/Sudanese 14, 65, 67, 70
Surridge, Brewster Joseph 144, 153, 189
Sutherland, Charles Leslie 66
Sydney 201, 219
Sykes, Mark 45
Sykes-Picot Agreement (1916) 45
Syria 45–6, 66, 68, 70, 151, 219

Taksim (partition) 211–12
Tala, Paphos 9, 185
Territorial Army 19
Terry, Michael 218–19
Thomas, J.H. 191
Thompson, F.B. 152–3, 190
Tompkins, Arthur Charles 184
Toufexis, Savas 137–8
Treaty of Lausanne (1923) 17
Treaty of Sèvres 17
Trikomo, Famagusta 39
Tripimeni, Famagusta 137, 202
Tris Elies, Limassol 183
Troodos (including Hill Station) 36, 45, 65, 71, 80, 83
Turkey 11, 49, 191, 199–200, 214, 221

Uganda 68
United States of America (USA) 46, 98, 131, 181, 199, 201, 211

Usury (Farmers) Law (1919) 36

Varnavas, Varnavas M. 12, 180, 210
Vassiliades, S.J. 188
Vatili, Famagusta 39, 83, 173, 200
Venizelos, Eleftherios 44, 50, 58, 60, 98, 164, 213
Victoria (Australia) 201
Villari, Luigi 12
Virginia 201
Vogolia, Karpas 125

War Office 5, 60–2, 64, 67–8, 70–1, 83–4, 94–5, 97, 120–1, 131–2, 184, 188, 190–1, 193, 201–2, 215
Ward Price, H. 11
West Indies 9, 13, 24, 203
Williamson, G.A. 151–3
Wilson, Alfred 80, 145, 147–8
Wolseley, Sir Garnet (later Lord Wolseley) 71
Wood, Evelyn 65
World War I *see* First World War
World War II *see* Second World War

Yenagra, Famagusta 197
Yeroskipou, Paphos 125, 182
Yialousa, Famagusta 39, 137, 166, 170, 182, 196, 201
Yusuf Islam (Cat Stevens) 9, 199

Zaimis, Alexander 44
Zannettos, Dr Philios 50, 214

EU authorised representative for GPSR:
Easy Access System Europe, Mustamäe tee 50,
10621 Tallinn, Estonia
gpsr.requests@easproject.com

www.ingramcontent.com/pod-product-compliance
Lightning Source LLC
Chambersburg PA
CBHW030120240426
43673CB00041B/1341